THE
BHILSA TOPES
OR
BUDDHIST MONUMENTS OF CENTRAL INDIA

THE
BHILSA TOPES

OR

BUDDHIST MONUMENTS OF CENTRAL INDIA:

COMPRISING

A BRIEF HISTORICAL SKETCH

OF THE

RISE, PROGRESS, AND DECLINE OF BUDDHISM;

WITH AN ACCOUNT OF THE

OPENING AND EXAMINATION OF THE VARIOUS GROUPS OF TOPES AROUND BHILSA

BY

BREV. MAJOR ALEXANDER CUNNINGHAM,

BENGAL ENGINEERS.

"You fabric huge,
Whose dust the solemn antiquarian turns,
And thence in broken sculptures, cast, abroad
Like Sibyl's leaves, collects the builder's name,
Rejoiced." Dyer–Ruins of Rome.

Illustrated with Thirty-three Plates

GYAN

Published by

Gyan Publishing House
5, Ansari Road
Daryaganj, New Delhi-110002
Phone: 011-47034999, 9811692060
E-mail: books@gyanbooks.com

Distribution Network
gyanbooks.com
India, USA, Canada, UK, Australia, France

ISBN : 978-81-212-2862-6 (HB)
First Published, 1854

2nd Impression 2021

Printed at: Gyan Press, Delhi.

The Bhilsa Topes
Author: Brev. Major Alexander Cunningham

THE

BHILSA TOPES;

OR,

BUDDHIST MONUMENTS OF CENTRAL INDIA:

COMPRISING

A BRIEF HISTORICAL SKETCH

OF THE

RISE, PROGRESS, AND DECLINE OF BUDDHISM;

WITH AN ACCOUNT OF THE

OPENING AND EXAMINATION OF THE VARIOUS GROUPS OF TOPES AROUND BHILSA.

BY

BREV.-MAJOR ALEXANDER CUNNINGHAM,

BENGAL ENGINEERS.

"Yon fabric huge,
Whose dust the solemn antiquarian turns,
And thence in broken sculptures, cast abroad
Like Sibyl's leaves, collects the builder's name,
Rejoiced." DYER.—*Ruins of Rome.*

Illustrated with Thirty-three Plates.

LONDON:

SMITH, ELDER AND CO., 65, CORNHILL.

BOMBAY: SMITH, TAYLOR AND CO.

1854.

Plate I

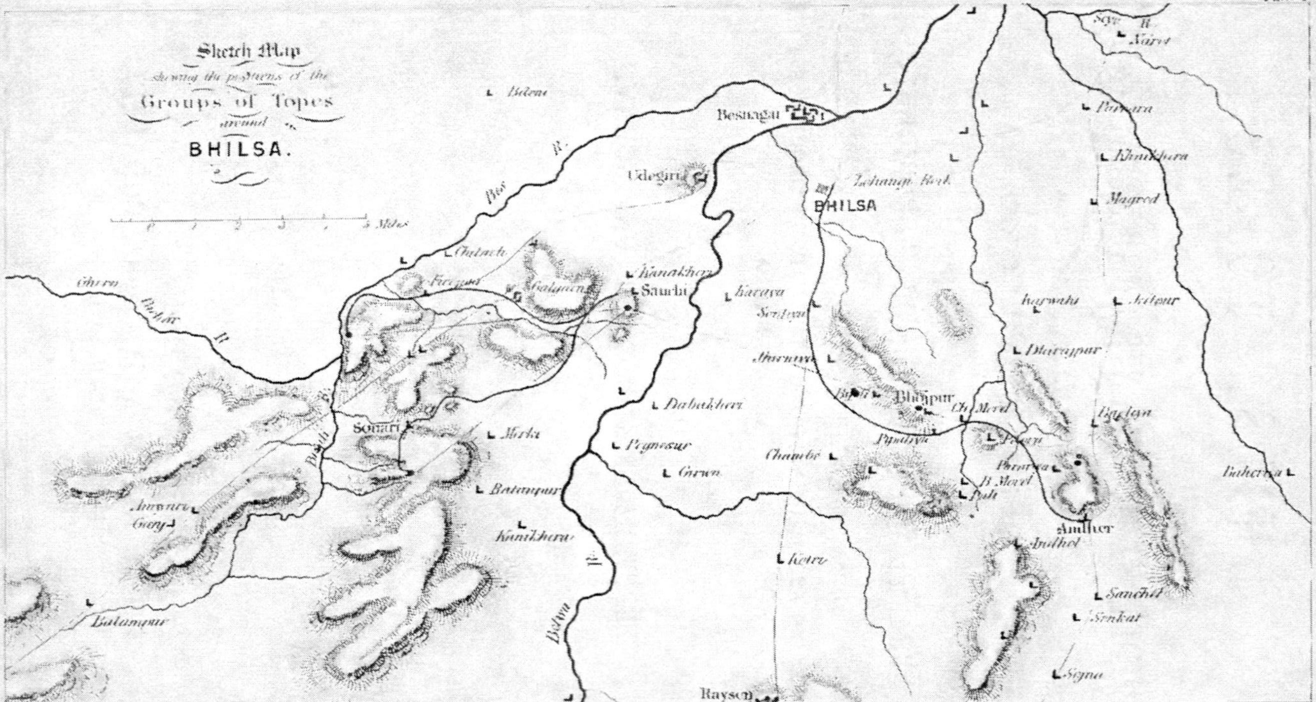

Published by Smith, Elder & Co. London

PREFACE.

1. The discoveries made by Lieutenant Maisey and myself, amongst the numerous Buddhist monuments that still exist around Bhilsa, in Central India, are described—imperfectly, I fear—by myself in the present work. To the Indian antiquary and historian, these discoveries will be, I am willing to think, of very high importance; while to the mere English reader they may not be uninteresting, as the massive mounds are surrounded by mysterious circles of stone pillars, recalling attention at every turn to the early earthworks, or barrows, and the Druidical colonnades of Britain.

In the Buddhistical worship of trees displayed in the Sánchi bas-reliefs, others, I hope, will see (as well as myself) the counterpart of the Druidical and adopted English reverence for the Oak. In the horse-shoe temples of Ajanta and Sánchi many will recognise the form of the inner colonnade at Stonehenge.* More, I suspect, will learn that there are Cromlechs in India as well as in Britain;† that the Brahmans, Buddhists, and Druids all believed in the transmigration of the soul; that the Celtic language

* Plate II. figs. 1, 2, and 3. † Plate II. figs. 4 and 5.

was undoubtedly derived from the Sanscrit;* and that *Buddha* (or Wisdom), the Supreme Being worshipped by the Buddhists, is probably (*most* probably) the same as the great god *Buddwás*, considered by the Welsh as the dispenser of good. These coincidences are too numerous and too striking to be accidental. Indeed, the Eastern origin of the Druids was suspected by the younger Pliny,† who says, "Even to this day Britain celebrates the magic rites with so many similar ceremonies, that one might suppose they had been taken from the Persians." The same coincidence is even more distinctly stated by Dionysius Periegesis, who says that the women of the British Amnitæ celebrated the rites of Dionysos, v. 375 :—

> As the Bistonians on Apsinthus banks
> Shout to the clamorous Eiraphiātes,
> Or, as the Indians on dark-rolling Ganges
> Hold revels to Dionysos the noisy
> So do the British women shout Evoë!

2. I have confined my observations chiefly to the religious belief taught by Sákya Muni, the last mortal Buddha, who died 543 B.C. There was, however, a more ancient Buddhism, which prevailed not only in India, but in all the countries

* The name of Druid may be taken as an example: Greek, δρῦς; Sanskrit, द्रु, *dru*; Welsh, *derw*; Erse, *dair*: a tree, or oak tree.

† Pliny, Nat. Hist. xxx. 1,—"Britannia hodie eam (magiam) attonite celebrat tantis ceremoniis, ut eam Persis dedisse videri possit."

populated by the Arian race. The belief in *Krakuchanda*, *Kanaka*, and *Kásyapa*, the three mortal Buddhas who preceded *Sákya Muni*, was in India contemporaneous with the worship of the elements inculcated in the Védas. The difference between Vedantism and primitive Buddhism, was not very great; and the gradual evolution of the worship of concrete Nature (called *Pradhán* by the Brahmans, and *Dharma* or *Prajná* by the Buddhists), from the more ancient adoration of the simple elements, was but the natural consequence of the growth and progressive development of the human mind. In Europe the traces of this older Buddhism are found in the *Caduceus*, or wand of Hermes, which is only the symbol of *Dharma*, or deified nature, and in the Welsh *Buddwás*, and the Saxon *Woden*;—but slightly altered forms of Buddha. The fourth day of the week, Wednesday, or *Woden's-day*, was named *Dies Mercurii* by the Romans, and is still called *Buddhwár* by the Hindus. *Maia* was the mother of the Greek Hermeias or Hermes; and *Maya* was the mother of the Indian Buddha. The connection between Hermes, Buddwás, Woden, and Buddha is evident; although it may be difficult, and perhaps nearly impossible, to make it apparent to the general reader.

Hermeias and his "golden wand," χρυσόῤῥαπις, are mentioned by Homer; but Hesiod* is the first who

* Theog. 938.

speaks of his mother "Maia, the Atlantis who bore to Zeus the illustrious Hermes, the herald of the immortals." In the Homeric poems, also, there is no trace of serpents entwining the wand in the manner represented in works of art. Even in the late Homeridian hymn the wand (which was Apollo's sheep-staff) is described as "a golden three-leaved innocuous rod." The epithet of three-leaved is peculiarly applicable to the three-pointed symbol of Dharma, so conspicuous an ornament on the Sánchi gateways of this volume.

In illustration of the ancient history of India, the bas-reliefs and inscriptions of the Bhilsa Topes are almost equal in importance to the more splendid discoveries made by the enterprising and energetic Layard in the mounds of the Euphrates. In the inscriptions found in the Sánchi and Sonári Topes we have the most complete and convincing proof of the authenticity of the history of Asoka, as related in the Maháwánso. In the Pali Annals of Ceylon, it is stated, that after the meeting of the Third Buddhist Synod, 241 B.C., Kásyapa was despatched to the *Hemawanta* country to convert the people to Buddhism. In the Sánchi and Sonári Topes were discovered two portions of the relics of Kásyapa, whom the inscriptions call the "Missionary to the whole *Hemawanta.*"

The Sánchi bas-reliefs, which date in the early part of the first century of our era, are more original in design and more varied in subject than any other examples of Eastern sculpture which I have seen in India. The subjects represented are religious processions, the worship of Topes and trees, and the adoration of the peculiar symbols of the Buddhist Triad. Besides these there are some spirited sieges of fortified cities, several stories from the life of Sákya Muni, and some little domestic scenes which I would rather attribute to the fancy of the artist than to their particular significance in Buddhistical story.

The plans and sections which accompany this work are all drawn from careful measurements on the same scale (of 40 feet to an inch), to preserve the relative proportions of the different Topes. The top of each drawing is the north, by which the relative positions of staircases, gateways, and other parts, may be determined at a glance. The plans of the different hills on which the several groups of Topes are situated, are all taken from my own surveys on the same scale of 400 feet to an inch. The eye can thus compare the disposition of one group with another. Lastly, the drawings of all the principal relic-boxes and caskets are one half the original size, sufficient (I have reason to think) for the correct delineation of the different shapes and various mouldings.

I am indebted to the kind liberality of Major H. M. Durand, of the Engineers, for the view of the Sánchi Tope, and for the drawings of the Sánchi bas-reliefs, containing the boat scene, or "Sákya's departure from this world," the "Religious Festival, with adoration of a Tope," and a scene in the royal palace, with a relic-casket.

The Topes were opened by Lieut. Maisey and myself in the end of January and beginning of February, 1851; and I attribute the success of our discoveries in great part to the vigilance of our personal superintendence. I had become aware of the importance of this strict watchfulness (after I had opened the great Sárnáth Tope, near Benares, in 1835), by the purchase of five beautiful gold coins of Kadphises, which were brought from Affghanistan at the very time that Mr. Masson was engaged in opening the Topes of the Kabul valley. I now learn from Major Kittoe that he has found a broken steatite vase amongst the rubbish at the foot of the great Sárnáth Tope. It is, I fear, more than probable that this vase was the relic-casket of the Sárnáth Tope, which must have been destroyed during my unavoidable absence on engineer duty at Mirzapore.

As the opening of the Bhilsa Topes has produced such valuable results, it is much to be hoped that the Court of Directors will, with their usual liberality, authorise the employment of a competent officer to open the numerous Topes which still exist in North and South Bahar, and to draw up a report on all the Buddhist remains of Kapila and Kusinagara, of

Vaisáli and Rájagriha, which were the principal scenes of Sákya's labours. A work of this kind would be of more real value for the ancient history of India (the territory of the Great Company) than the most critical and elaborate edition of the eighteen Puránas.

I would also venture to recommend that the two fallen gateways of the Sánchi Tope should be removed to the British Museum, where they would form the most striking objects in a Hall of Indian Antiquities. The value of these sculptured gateways will, I feel confident, be highly appreciated after the perusal of the brief account of them contained in this work; while their removal to England would ensure their preservation. For a most admirable view of one of these gateways I refer the reader to the frontispiece of Mr. Fergusson's beautiful and artistic illustrations of ancient Indian architecture.

Before parting, may I beg to draw the particular attention of the reader to my identification of the different classes of *Pramnæ* and *Germanæ*, as recorded by Kleitarchos and Megasthenes, with the different orders of Buddhist *Srámanas*. I do so because some of our most eminent scholars have doubted the prevalence and extension of the Buddhist religion before the beginning of the Christian era. Now the *Pramnæ* of Kleitarchos, and the *Germanæ* of Megasthenes, are both stated to have been the opponents of the Brahmans. Were this the case they can only be the *Srámanas*, which was a title common to all the orders of the Bauddha community; even Sákya himself being styled *Maha Srámana*, or the "Great Devotee." The identity of the *Germanæ* of Megasthenes is placed beyond all doubt by his mention that "women were allowed to join them on taking vows of chastity,"* for the Buddhists alone had nuns.

It will not, I trust, be out of place in a Preface to observe that the several orders of *Pramnæ*, mentioned by Kleitarchos, are,—

1. Ορεινοι, or "mountaineers," a Greek corruption of *Arhan* (or *Aran*, as it is sometimes spelt), which was a common title of the *Bodhisatwas*, or second class of the Bauddha community, who usually dwelt on hills.

2. Γυμνηται, the "naked," or rather the "half-clad,"—a descriptive title of the Bodhisatwas, who, during their devotions, wore only the *Sanghâti*, or kilt. Γυμνης, or Γυμνητης, was applied to a light-armed soldier,—not to an unarmed one; and, therefore, also, to a lightly-clad person.

3. Πολιτικοι, the "townsmen," I only take to be a corrupted transcript of the Sanscrit *Pratyeka*, the third class of the Bauddha community, whose duty it was to mingle with the people, and frequent the towns.

* Megasthenes in Strabo, v.—*Συμφιλοσοφεῖν δ'ἐνίοις καὶ γυναῖκας ἀπεχομένας καὶ αυτὰς ἀφροδισίων.*

4. Προσχωριοι, the "rural," which I take to be an alteration by some copyist, for the sake of the antithesis of "town and country," with the last. The original term used by Kleitarchos was, I see reason to believe, Προσεχωριοι, the "listeners," a literal translation of the Sanscrit *Srávaka*, the fourth class of the Bauddha community.

It is my belief that I have identified both the Ορεινοι and the Γυμνηται with the Bodhisatwa of the Buddhists. For, though there were four classes of Buddhists, yet, the superior grade being those who had attained the rank of Buddha, they had, of course, no representatives on earth. Kleitarchos, therefore, who had heard that there were four orders, has created one out of the Γυμνηται. Megasthenes, who resided for some years in India, states more correctly that there were only three classes of Γερμαναι; viz.,

1. Υλοβιοι, from the Sanscrit *alobhiya*, "without desire;" that is, the Bodhisatwa, who had suppressed all human passions.

2. Ιατρικοι, the "physicians," which I take to be a slight corruption of Πρατικοι, for *Pratyeka*, the third class of Buddhists, who, as they mixed much with the people, would no doubt have generally acted as physicians, as the Christian monks have done in later days.

3. Επαιται, or "beggars," equivalent to the *Bhikshu*, or mendicant monk of the Buddhists.

Now Kleitarchos was one of the companions of Alexander; and, as he did not advance into India beyond the *Hyphasis,* or Byâs River, his distinct mention of the different classes of the Bauddha community seems to me (at least) conclusive, that the religion of Sákya had not only become prevalent in Gangetic India, but that it had reached the Punjaub at the period of the Macedonian invasion, B.C. 330.

Let me add that a still earlier mention of the Buddhists may, I think, be found in Herodotus, who, writing about B.C. 420, shortly after the assembly of the second Synod says, — "There are other Indians, who, differing in manners from those before mentioned, put no animal to death, sow no grain, have no fixed habitations, and live solely upon vegetables." The name of this class of Indians is not given by Herodotus; but it is preserved by Nicolaus Damascenus, who calls them *Aritonii,* the same, I believe, as the Sanskrit *Arhanta.* Now *Arhanta* is a title of the Bodhisatwa, one of the classes of the Bauddha community, which observed all the peculiarities attributed by Herodotus to the Aritonii. They were prohibited from taking life; they sowed no grain, but begged their daily bread; they had no fixed habitations, and lived wholly upon vegetables.

ALEXANDER CUNNINGHAM.

Simla, 1853.

CONTENTS.

CHAPTER I.

INTRODUCTION.

		PAGE
§1.	Limits of Buddhism	1
2.	Decay of Buddhism	2
3.	Buddhist Remains	3
4.	Ditto	4
5.	Cave Temples	4
6.	Vihárs	5
7.	Inscriptions on Rocks and Pillars	5
8.	Topes	6
9.	Bhilsa Topes	6
10.	Ditto	7
11.	Description of Topes	7
12.	Origin of Topes	9
13.	Existing before Sákya's advent	10
14.	Ditto	11
15.	Various Buddhist Topes	11
16.	Ditto	12
17.	Dedicatory Topes	12
18.	Memorial Topes	12
19.	Funeral Topes	13
20.	Ditto	13
21.	Ditto	13
22.	Intimately connected with Buddhist religion	14

CHAPTER II.

LIFE OF SÁKYA.

		PAGE
§ 1.	Early Indian worship—Elements	15
2.	Conflicting opinions at Sákya's advent	16
3.	Doctrine of transmigration	16
4.	The Swástikas	17
5.	Their doctrine of eternal annihilation	19
6.	Swástikas, Bráhmans, and Buddhists, compared	19
7.	Ditto Ditto	20
8.	Birth and early life of Sákya	20
9.	The four predictive signs	21
10.	Ditto	21
11.	Ditto	21
12.	Ditto	21
13.	Probability of the story of his conversion	22
14.	Embraces a religious life	22
15.	His asceticism	23
16.	Ditto	24
17.	Braves the terrors of *Maro* or death	24
18.	His teaching	25
19.	Ditto	25
20.	Sákya's death	26
21.	Grief of his followers	26
22.	Burning of his corpse	28
23.	Division of his relics	28
24.	They are collected by Ajatasatra	30
25.	And again distributed by Asoka	30

CHAPTER III.

FAITH OF SÁKYA.

§ 1.	Early observations of mankind	31
2.	Discrimination of the elements	31
3.	Early worship of Greece and India	32

PAGE

§ 4. Philosophical systems of ditto . . . 32
5. The Pythagoreans 33
6. Sákya's faith; Buddha, Dharma, Sangha . . . 34
7. The Samádhikas (Contemplatists) and the Prádhánikas (Materialists) 35
8. Buddhists deny the Creator's providence . . . 36
9. Doctrine of Nirvritti and Pravritti, or rest and action . . 37
10. The five Dhyáni Buddhas, or personifications of the elements . 38
11. Similarity of the early Brahmanical and Bauddha schools . 38
12. The Sánkhy a doctrine of the eternity of matter . . 39
13. Buddhist belief of creation of matter 39
14. Doctrine of the Sánkhya teacher, Kapila . . . 39
15. Doctrine of the Sánkhya teacher, Patanjali . . . 40
16. The Brahmanical Nireswara similar to the Bauddha Swábhávika doctrine of supreme nature 40
17. Mystic roots of the elements 40
18. The Brahmanical Seswaras and the Aiswárika Buddhists . 41
19. All the schools agree that there is a compound of mind and matter 41
20. The three classes of Sakya's doctrine:—1. Vinaya; 2. Sutra; 3. Abhidharma 41
21. Called Tripitaka and Triyanika 42
22. Their compilation in B. C. 543 43
23. Káchháyana's Pali grammar 44
24. Ditto 45
25. Language of the Buddhist books 45
26. Ditto 46
27. Ditto 47
28. Identification of Káchhayana and Kátyáyana . . . 49
29. Ditto 50
30. Ditto 50
31. Sákya a social reformer 51
32. Ditto 52
33. Buddhism and Mahomedanism 53

CHAPTER IV.

FIRST SYNOD.

§ 1. The Bauddha community 55
2. First Synod of five hundred monks 56

PAGE

§ 3. First Synod of five hundred monks . . 57
4. Ditto . . . 57
5. Rehearsal of Vinaya 58
6. Rehearsal of Dharma 58
7. Buddha's Hymn of Joy 59
8. His last injunctions 59
9. Conclusion of the Synod 59
10. Admission of women 60
11. Dress of the ascetics 61
12. Ditto 62
13. Sarmanes, or Srámanas 63
14. Hylobii, or Arhats 63
15. Iatriki, or Pratyekas 64
16. The four classes of Kleitarchos 64
17. Types of the Buddhist classes 66
18. Difference between Buddhist and Christian ideas of immortality 67
19. The Grand Lama of Tibet a Bodhisatwa, and not a Buddha . 67
20. Rules for the Bhikshu 68
21. His dress and equipments 69

CHAPTER V.

CHRONOLOGY.

§ 1. Succession of teachers 71
2. Ditto 72
3. Chronological list of teachers 72
4. Date of Sákya's death—543 B.C. 73
5. Chandra Gupta's accession 74
6. Possible origin of the error in Buddhist chronology . . 75

CHAPTER VI.

SECOND SYNOD.

§ 1. Ten indulgences claimed by the Vaisáli fraternity 77
2. Assembly of Second Synod 78

PAGE

§ 3. Discussion on the indulgences 79
4. Sentence of degradation confirmed 80
5. Similarity of proceedings to those of English trial by jury . 80

CHAPTER VII.

BUDDHIST SCHISMS.

§ 1. The degraded monks originate the Maha Sanghika heresy . 81
2. Various sects 82
3. Ditto 82
4. The Vaibháshikas 83
5. The Sautrantikas 84
6. Names of eighteen schisms 84
7 Extent of Buddhism in 443 B.C. 85

CHAPTER VIII.

PROGRESS OF BUDDHISM.

§ 1. The Maurya dynasty: accession of Chandra Gupta . 87
2. He expels the Greeks from the Panjáb . . . 88
3. He conquers India 90
4. Palibothra, or Pátaliputra 90
5. Indian expedition of Seleukos Nikator . . . 91
6. Ditto ditto 91
7. Accession of Bindusára 92
8. Embassy of Dionysios 93
9. Asoka deputed to Taxila 93
10. Appointed Governor of Ujain 95
11. Death of Bindusára 96

CHAPTER IX.

REIGN OF ASOKA.

§ 1. Accession and conquests of Asoka 97
2. His conversion to Buddhism 98

PAGE

§3. He erects numerous Vihárs and Chaityas 99
4. Promulgates numerous edicts 100
5. Title of Priyadarsi doubted by Prof. H. H. Wilson . . 100
6. True meaning of Dharma 102
7. Ditto 103
8. Ditto 104
9. Ditto 105
10. *Buddha*, *Dharma*, and *Sangha*, mentioned in the Bhabra inscription 105
11. Antiquity of the Páli Scriptures vindicated . . . 106
12. Ditto Ditto 107
13. Ditto Ditto 107
14. Name of Asoka not mentioned in his own inscriptions . 108
15. Identity of Priyadarsi and Asoka 109
16. Chronological difficulties removed 110
17. Doubtful name in edicts, perhaps Ariobarzanes . . 111
18. Asoka's knowledge of the Greeks 111
19. No mention of the kings of Kabul and Parthia in his edicts . 112
20. Dates of the Rock edicts 113
21. Date of the Pillar edicts 113
22. Sincerity of Asoka's faith 114

CHAPTER X.

THIRD SYNOD.

§1. Heretics assume the dress of the Buddhists and enter their monasteries 115
2. Expulsion of the heretics 116
3. Rehearsal of Vináya and Dharma 116
4. Missions to foreign countries 116
5. Relics of the missionaries found in the Bhilsa Topes . . 119
6. Relics of Kásapa 120
7. Ditto, and of Majhima 120
8. Relics of Gotiputra 121
9. Explanation of the term *dáyáda* 121
10. *Gotiputra*, the missionary to Dardábhisára . . . 122
11. Other relics 123

PAGE
§ 12. The zeal of Asoka anticipated Christianity in religious missions 123
13. Kunála, son of Asoka—Asoka's death 123

CHAPTER XI.

RISE AND FALL OF THE INDO-SCYTHIANS.

§ 1. Division of Asoka's empire—Fall of the Mauryas . . 125
2. Conquests of Menander in India 126
3. The Scythian Manas expels the Greeks . . . 127
4. He is succeeded by Azas 127
5. Rise of the Yuchi or Tochari under Kadphises . . 128
6. Kanishka, a zealous Buddhist 128
7. Milindu, Raja of Sakala 130
8. Nágárjuna: Buddhism extended into Tibet . . . 131
9. Mention of Buddhists by Apollonius of Tyana . . 131
10. By Klemens of Alexandria 132
11. By Porphyrius 133
12. By Palladius and Scholastikos 135
13. In the Hindu dramas 136

CHAPTER XII.

THE GUPTA DYNASTY.—DECLINE AND FALL OF BUDDHISM.

§ 1. Rise of the Gupta dynasty—Gupta era . . . 138
2. Gupta era dates from establishment of dynasty . . 139
3. Gupta kings mentioned by the Chinese . . . 140
4. Chronological table of the Guptas 141
5. Data for chronology 141
6 & 7. Mr. Thomas's chronology 145
8. He dates the rise of the Guptas from 78 A.D. . . . 145
9. Reasons for adopting a later date 146
9.* Silver currency of Gujrat copied from the drachmas of Apollodotus 149
10. Inscription of Chandra Gupta at Udayagiri . . . 150
11. Sanakánika, name of the kingdom of Bhilsa . . . 151
12. Vaishnava faith of the princes of Sanakánika . . . 152

		PAGE
§ 13.	Inscription of Chandra Gupta at Sánchi	152
14.	Illustrations of the meaning of Prajna	153
15.	Prajna is nature deified	154
16.	Chandra Gupta's gift to Sánchi Tope	154
17.	Chandra Gupta, lord of Ujain	154
18.	Ditto not an orthodox Buddhist	155
19.	Buddhism prevalent in Pátaliputra	155
20.	Ditto paramount in the Panjáb and Northern India	156
21.	Religious belief of the earlier Guptas	156
22.	Tantrika belief of Skanda Gupta	158
23.	Extravagance of the Tantrists	160
24.	Their charms and incantations	160
25.	Spread of Tantrika doctrines	160
26.	Lokáditya	161
27.	Budha Gupta	162
28.	Toramána—inscriptions at Eran and Gwalior	163
29.	Conquests of Siladitya	164
30.	Decline of Buddhism	165
31.	Fall of Buddhism	166
32.	Causes of the decline and fall of Buddhism	167

CHAPTER XIII.

BUILDING AND DEDICATION OF TOPES.

§ 1.	Account of the building of a Tope from the Mahawanso	169
2.	Memorial pillar recording the builder's intentions	169
3.	Topes usually built by forced labour	170
4.	Foundations	170
5.	Laying the foundation stone	170
6.	Ceremonies attending it	171
7.	Form of the *chaitya*	172
8.	Construction of the relic-chamber	172
9.	Procession of the relic-casket	173
10.	Ceremonies on closing the relic-casket	173
11.	Ceremonies on placing it in the relic-chamber	174
12.	Completion of the Tope	174
13.	Cornices or copings added to it	175

PAGE
§ 14. Other additions by subsequent kings 175
15. The same description applies to the Great Sánchi Tope . 176
16. Different positions of the relic-chamber . . . 176
17. Consecration of the ground 176
18,19. Various shapes of Topes 177
20. Their age ascertained approximately from shape . . 178

CHAPTER XIV.

SÁNCHI TOPE.—NO. 1.

§ 1. Position of Sánchi Hill . . . 179
2. Description of ditto 179
3. Group of Topes at Sánchi 180
4. Sánchi, the same as Shá-chi of Fa Hian . . . 180
5. Name of Sánchi 181
6. Story of the holy nettle at Shá-chi 182
7. Village of Sánchi 182
8. Situation of the Great Tope No. 1 183
9. Other ruined Topes 183
10. Shape of the dome 184
11. Upper enclosure 184
12. Pinnacle, *chatta* 185
13. Height of the Tope 186
14. Colonnade or Buddhist railing 186
15. Pillars of colonnade 187
16. Rails of ditto 187
17. Architraves 187
18. Prevalence of Buddhist railings 187
19. Four gateways 188
20. Pillars of gateways—different capitals . . . 189
21. Architraves of gateways 189
22. Symbols of Buddha and Dharma 190
23. Variety of bas-reliefs 191
24. Figures of the four Buddhas 191
25. Hariswámini inscription 192
26. Lion pillar, with inscription 193
27. Capital of pillar 194
28. Height of ditto 194

PAGE
§29. Style of sculpture in the lions 195
30. Statue pillar 196
31. Capital of pillar 197
32. Description of statue 197
33. Height of pillar 197
34. Shafts of pillars cut into pieces for sugar-mills . . 198
35. Eastern pillar 199
36. Broken pillar of Hariswámini Gosha . . . 199
37. Flight of steps, and statues at entrance . . 199

CHAPTER XV.

DESCRIPTION OF THE SÁNCHI BAS-RELIEFS.

EASTERN GATEWAY.

Right Pillar—Front Face.

I. Palace Scene—Audience Hall 201
II. Palace Scene—Women dancing before the King . . 202

Right Pillar—Inner Face.

I. Adoration of Tree 202
II. Dream of Maya 202

Left Pillar—Front Face.

I. Adoration of Symbol of Dharma 203
II. Boat Scene—Sákya's Nirvána 204
III. Prince in Chariot leaving Kapila 205

Left Pillar—Inner Face.

I. Kitchen Scene 205
II. Worship of Buddha—as flame 207
III. Tope dedicated to the Supreme Buddha . . . 210

Architraves—Front.

PAGE
I. Worship of Topes 211
II. Procession of Buddha's feet 211
III. Worship of Tree 211

Architrave—Rear.

I. Worship of Trees 211
II. Worship of Trees by Animals 211
III. Worship of Tope by Elephants 212

SOUTH GATEWAY.

Right Pillar—Front Face.

I. Triple Symbol of Dharma 213
II. Scene in Palace 213
III. Casket Scene in Palace 213

Architraves—Front.

I. Worship of Topes 214
II. Worship of Tope 214
III. A Siege, and Relic-procession . . . 215

WEST GATEWAY.

Right Pillar—Front Face.

I. Trial of the Bow 218
II. Worship of Tree 222
III. Ditto 222
IV. Lions 223

Right Pillar—Inner Face.

I. Gateway—Worship of Tree 223
II. Worship of Tree surmounted by Chatta . . . 223

Left Pillar—Front Face.

PAGE
I. Social Scene 223
II. Love Scene 224

Left Pillar—Inner Face.

I. Ascetic Life—Archers . . . 224
II. Festival of the Tree 225
III. State Barge 226

Architraves—Front Faces.

I. Procession escorting a Relic-casket . . . 227
II. Worship of Symbol of Buddha . . . 229
III. Worship of Tree by Elephants . . . 229

Architraves—Rear Faces.

I. Worship of Topes 229
II. Triumphal Procession 229
III. Temple Worship 229

NORTH GATEWAY.

Right Pillar—Front Face.

I. Tree, with Staircase 230

Right Pillar—Inner Face.

I. Worship of Tree 230
II. Ditto 231
III. Ditto 231

Left Pillar—Front Face.

PAGE
I. Worship of Tree 231
II. Reverence paid to a Boy 232
III. Simple Adoration 232
IV. Procession 232
V. Domestic Scenes at Fountain 232

Left Pillar—Inner Face.

I. Cave Temple 233
II. Procession 233
III. Worship of Tree 233

CHAPTER XVI.

INSCRIPTIONS.—NO. 1 TOPE.—SÁNCHI.

Nos. 1 to 176. On colonnade—old 235-259
No. 177. On southern pillar 259
Nos. 178 to 196. Later inscriptions from gateways . 262-267

CHAPTER XVII.

OPENING OF SÁNCHI TOPE—NO. 1.

§ 1. Manner of opening the Tope—Brick Tope . . . 269
2. No discovery made 270
3. Probable age of the Tope—500 B.C. 270
4,5. Probable date of the colonnade—250 B.C. . . . 271
6. Date of the gateways—19 to 37 A.D. 272
7. Gateway inscriptions in a more recent character . . 272
8. Old inscription hidden by pillar of gateway . . . 273
9. Tope probably dedicated to the Supreme Buddha . 273

CHAPTER XVIII.

NO. 2 TOPE.—SÁNCHI.

		PAGE
§ 1.	Position of Tope	275
2.	Dimensions of dome	275
3.	Pinnacle	276
4.	Colonnade, or Buddhist railing	276
5.	Ornaments of pillars	277
6.	Bas-reliefs of entrance pillars	277
7.	Bas-reliefs of Tope and wheel pillar	278
8.	Wheel pillar	278
9.	*Sangha*, or the united symbols of *Buddha* and *Dharma*	278
10.	Probable age, about 220 B. C.	278

CHAPTER XIX.

INSCRIPTIONS FROM NO. 2 TOPE.—SÁNCHI.

Nos. 1 to 43. On colonnade 280

CHAPTER XX.

OPENING OF NO. 2 TOPE.—SÁNCHI.

§ 1.	Present appearance of the Tope	285
2.	Position of the relic-chamber	285
3.	Relic-box with inscription	286
4.	Remarks on inscription	286
5.	Inscriptions on the steatite boxes	287
6.	Remarks on the enshrined relics	289
7.	Relics of ten Buddhist teachers in 240 B. C.	291
8.	Tope originally intended for relics of two only	291
9.	Intimate connection between the principal Buddhist leaders	292
10.	Value of genealogies derivable from other Topes	293

CHAPTER XXI.

NO. 3 TOPE.—SÁNCHI.

	PAGE.
§ 1. Present appearance, and former size	295
2. Buddhist railing	295
3. Pillars of ditto	296
4. Square enclosure	296
5. Relic-chamber with two relic-boxes	297
6. Relic-box of Sáriputra	297
7. Seven precious things in relic-casket	297
8, 9. Series of seven precious things according to the Chinese	298
10. The seven precious things in this Tope	298
11. Relic-casket of Maha Mogalána	299
12. Initial letters of names written in ink	299
13. Relative position of relics to right and left	299
14, 15. Sáriputra's career	300
16, 17. Sákya's account of Sáriputra	301
18. His death and cremation	305
19. Origin of Mogalána	305
20. Relics of both found at Satdhára	306
21. Date of Tope uncertain—between 550 and 250 B. C.	306
22. Date of Tope, perhaps 500 B. C.—of railing, 250 B. C.	307
23. Other Topes at Sánchi	308

CHAPTER XXII.

SONÁRI TOPES.—NO. 1 TOPE.

§ 1. Position of Sonári—meaning of name	309
2. Wheel pillar at Srávasti	310
3. Situation of Topes	311
4. No. 1 Tope—Sonári	311
5. Dimensions of Tope	312

PAGE
§ 6. Surrounded by a Buddhist railing 312
7. Probable date, 250—200 B.C. 313
8. Opening of Tope—stone boxes . . . 313

CHAPTER XXIII.

NO. 2 TOPE.—SONÁRI.

§ 1. Position of No. 2 Tope 315
2. Dimensions of Tope 315
3. Opening of Tope 316
4. Large steatite relic-vase 316
5. Flat crystal relic-casket of *Gotiputra* . . . 316
6. Steatite relic-casket of *Majhima* 317
7. Ditto *Kásapa Gota* . . . 317
8. Ditto *Kosiki-putra* . . . 318
9. Ditto *Alabagira* 318
10. Date of Tope about 220 B.C. 318
11. Other Topes at Sonári 319

CHAPTER XXIV.

TOPES AT SATDHÁRA.

§ 1. Position of Satdhára 320
2. Tope, No. 1, of brick 321
3. Buddhist railing 321
4. Opening of Tope 322
5. Massive foundations of Temples 322
6. No. 2 Tope 323
7. Steatite Relic-caskets of Sáriputra and Mogalána . . 324
8. No. 7 Tope, Satdhára 325
9. Relics of No. 7 Tope 325
10. Other Topes at Satdhára 325

CHAPTER XXV.

TOPES AT BHOJPUR.

PAGE

1. Ruins of Bhojpur 327
2. Position of ditto 327
3. Situation of Topes 328
4. No. 1 Tope, A 329
5. No. 2 Tope, B 330
6. Opening of ditto 331
7. Relic-casket, a crystal Tope 331
8. No. 3 Tope, C 332
9. No. 4 Tope, D 333
10. Remains of other Topes, upper stage . . . 333
11. No. 7 Tope, a ; second stage 334
12. Opening of ditto 334
13. Relic-jar of *Patito*, the "degraded" 335
14. Relic-jar of Upahitaka 336
15. Probable date, 250—200 B. C. 336
16. No. 8, Tope, b 337
17. No. 9 „ c 337
18. No. 10 „ d 338
19. No. 11 „ e 339
20. Other Topes on the second stage 339
21. Third stage of Topes 340
22. Fourth stage of Topes 341
23. Bhojpur Topes, mostly opened before . . . 341

CHAPTER XXVI.

ANDHER TOPES.

1. Position of the Topes 342

	PAGE
§2. No. 1 Tope	342
3. Buddhist railing	343
4. Opening of No. 1	344
5. No. 2 Tope	345
6. Opening of ditto	346
7. Flat earthenware relic-box	346
8. Tall steatite relic-casket	347
9. Large steatite relic-vase	347
10. Probable date, 200 B. C.	347
11. No. 3 Tope	348
12. Opening of ditto—Relics of Háritíputra	348
13. Relics presented by Aswa Deva—Ink writing	349

CHAPTER XXVII.

SYMBOLS OF BUDDHA, DHARMA, AND SANGHA.

§ 1. Symbols on Sánchi gateways and caves	351
2. Triad of Buddha, Dharma, and Sangha	351
3. The wheel, a symbol of universal dominion	352
4. Crowns the summits of the Sánchi gateways	353
5. Various forms of wheel	353
6. Quadruple symbol of Buddha	355
7. Symbol of Dharma	355
8. Symbol of Sangha	358
9. Different spellings of Sangha	358
10. Triple symbol of Dharma	358
11, 12. Symbol of Dharma the same as Jagannáth	359
13. Probable Buddhist origin of Vithoba	360
14. Fair at Besnagar	361
15. Origin of the fair	362
16. Another account	362
17. Rukmángada, the same as Lohángada	362
18. Besnagar probably included in Vidarbha	363
19. Foundation of Besnagar	363
20. Foundation of Bhilsa	364

	PAGE
§ 21. Position of the various groups of Topes	364
22. Appearance of the Tope hills in ancient times	365

APPENDIX.

Description of ancient arms, &c. 369

LIST OF PLATES.

I. Sketch map of the country around Bhilsa.
II. Comparison of Druidical and Buddhist monuments.
III. Various specimens of Topes.
IV. Group of Topes—Sànchi.
V. Groups of Topes—Sonári, Satdhára, and Andher
VI. Group of Topes—Bhojpur.
VII. View of the great Sánchi Tope, No.-1
VIII. Plan and elevation of ditto.
IX. Elevation and section of colonnade.
X. Sánchi pillars.
XI. Boat scene—eastern gateway.
XII. Relic scene—southern gateway.
XIII. Tope scene—northern gateway.
XIV. Female dancer—west gate.
XV. Kitchen scene—leaf-roofed house and gateway
XVI. Inscriptions from No. 1 Tope.
XVII. Ditto ditto.
XVIII. Ditto ditto.
XIX. Ditto ditto.
XX. Plan and elevation of No. 2 Tope, Sánchi.
XXI. Inscriptions from No. 2 Tope.
XXII. Plan and elevation of No. 3 Tope, Sánchi.
XXIII. Ditto ditto No. 1 ditto, Sonári.
XXIV. Ditto ditto No. 2 ditto, Sonári.
XXV. Topes of Satdhára.

XXVI. Nos. 1, 2, and 4 Topes at Bhojpur.
XXVII. Nos. 8, 9, and 10 ditto.
XXVIII. Plan and elevation of No. 1 Tope, Andher.
XXIX. Ditto ditto No. 2 ditto.
XXX. Ditto ditto No. 3 ditto.
XXXI. Symbols of Buddha.
XXXII. Symbols of Dharma and Sangha.
XXXIII. Ancient arms and instruments.

THE

BHILSA TOPES.

CHAPTER I.

INTRODUCTION.

1. The Buddhist religion has long been extinct in India, but it still flourishes in Nepál and Tibet, in Ava, Ceylon, and China, and amongst the Indo-Chinese nations of Anam, Siam, and Japan. Its votaries far outnumber those of all other creeds, except the Christian, and they form one-fourth of the whole human race.* The valley of the Ganges was the cradle of Buddhism; which, from its rise in the sixth century before Christ, gradually spread over the whole of India. It was extended by Asoka to Kashmir and Kâbul shortly after Alexander's invasion; and it was introduced into China about

* The Christians number about 270 millions; the Buddhists about 222 millions, who are distributed as follows:—China, 170 millions; Japan, 25; Anam, 14; Siam, 3; Ava, 8; Nepál, 1; and Ceylon, 1: total, 222 millions.

the beginning of our era by five hundred Kashmirian missionaries. In A. D. 400, when Fa Hian visited India, Buddhism was still the dominant religion; but the *Vaishnavas* were already rising into consequence. In the middle of the seventh century, although the pilgrim Hwán Thsang found numerous temples of the *Saivas*, whose doctrines had been embraced by Skanda Gupta and the later princes of *Pátaliputra*, yet Buddhism was still the prevailing religion of the people. But the progress of religion is like the existence of a tree; which, after the first symptoms of decay, can neither be strengthened nor renewed. The faith of Sákya was evidently on the decline; and though it still lingered about the holy cities of Benares and Gaya for two or three centuries later, it was no longer the honoured religion of kings and princes, protected by the strong arm of power, but the persecuted heresy of a weaker party, who were forced to hide their images under ground, and were ultimately expelled from their monasteries by fire.*

2. Buddhism had in fact become an old and worn-out creed, whose mendicant monks no longer begged their bread, but were supported by lands

* In 1835 I excavated numerous Buddhist images at Sárnáth, near Benares, all of which had evidently been purposely hidden underground. I found quantities of ashes also; and there could be no doubt that the buildings had been destroyed by fire. Major Kittoe, who has made further excavations during the present year, is of the same opinion.

long since appropriated to the monasteries. The *Srámanas* and *Bhikshus* were not like those of ancient days, the learned and the wise, whose bodily abstinence and contemplative devotion, combined with practical exhortations and holy example, excited the pious wonder of the people. The modern Buddhists had relapsed into an indolent and corrupt body, who were content to spend a passive existence in the monotonous routine of monastic life. There was still the daily chanting of an appointed number of hymns; still the same observance of forms and ceremonies; there were still the same outward signs of religion; but there was no fervent enthusiasm in the lifeless performance of such monotonous routine; and the ardent zeal which once burned in the heart of every Buddhist monk for the propagation of his religion, had long since become extinct. The only virtue now consisted in abstinence from evil, which was accounted equal to the performance of good. Indolent listlessness and passive indifference took the place of devout contemplation and pious abstraction; and thus the corrupt practices of modern Buddhists would seem to countenance the idea, that the more useless they became in this life, the more fitted did they consider themselves for the next.

3. But though the religion of the Buddhists has long been extinct, and though the monks' "call to refection" has been silent for ages, yet their monasteries and temples still remain; their paintings and

sculptures still exist; their historical writings still live, to attest the wonderful sway which a single enthusiastic individual may succeed in establishing over the minds of a whole people.* The sculptures illustrate the history; and in both we may read of kings bowing reverentially before Topes and Trees; of princes bearing caskets of relics on their heads, to be shrined in the Topes; and of the universal reverence paid to the monks.

4. The Buddhist remains now existing may be divided into four distinct classes.

1st. *Cave* Temples, containing Topes, Sculptures, Paintings, and numerous inscriptions.

2nd. *Viháras,* or Monasteries.

3rd. *Inscriptions* on Rocks and Pillars.

4th. *Topes,* or Religious Edifices.

5. The Cave Temples have been made known by the beautiful pictorial illustrations of Fergusson; but the curious paintings which adorn the interior must be copied, and the numerous inscriptions must be deciphered, before the historical value of these remarkable monuments of the Buddhists will be fully appreciated. Captain Gill, of the Madras

* The principal paintings are in the Cave Temples at Ajanta and Ellora; the sculptures at Sánchi, on the gateways of the Great Tope. The identity of the head-dresses of the paintings with those of the sculptures, and more particularly the recent forms of the alphabetical characters in the Cave Temples, show that the caves cannot date earlier than the beginning of the Christian era. My own opinion is, that they are not earlier than A.D. 200.

Army, is now employed at Ajanta in copying the paintings; but the volumes of inscriptions in the Caves of *Nasik*, *Junir*, *Kanari*, and *Karli*, still remain to be copied.*

6. The *Viháras*, or Monasteries, are of two kinds:—1st, *Cave Viháras*, of which several magnificent specimens have been published by Mr. Fergusson; and 2nd, *Structural Viháras*; of which some specimens still remain at Sánchi, but in a very ruinous condition.

7. The Inscriptions on the Pillars at *Delhi* and *Allahabad*, and on the Tirhut Pillars at *Mathiya* and *Rádhiya* have long ago been deciphered and translated by the remarkable ingenuity of James Prinsep. The Inscriptions on the Rocks at *Junagiri* in Gujrat, and at *Dhauli* in Kuttack, were also interpreted by him. A third version of the rock inscriptions (but in the Ariano Pali character), which was found at Kapur-digiri, near Peshawur, has been carefully collated with the others by

* In Bird's learned "Historical Researches on the Origin and Principles of the Bauddha and Jaina Religions," there are several plates of inscriptions from the Caves of Kanari, Karli, Ajanta, Ellora, Nasik, &c. Of some of these, Dr. Bird has offered translations; but as he has an evident leaning towards identifying Buddhism with the ancient Sun-worship, the translations are not so accurate as could be wished. For instance, wherever the proper name of *Mitra* (a friend) occurs, he has translated it as if it was the Persian *Mithra*, the sun. His third inscription, p. 51, which gives the name of *Budha Mitra* (the friend of Buddha), should have taught him the true value of *Mitra*.

Professor Wilson. Many short inscriptions from Gaya, Sánchi, and Birât, as well as from the Cave Temples of Southern India, have also been published at different times; but, with the single exception of the edicts in the Rock Inscriptions, which contain the names of Antiochus, Ptolemy, Antigonus, and Magas, the inscriptions in the present volume are of greater interest, and of much higher importance, than all that have yet been published.

8. The numerous Topes which still exist in India are chiefly confined to a few localities. The Topes of Kâbul and Jelalabad were opened by Messrs. Honigberger and Masson in 1835, and those between the Indus and the Jhelam by Generals Ventura and Court in 1833 and 1834. The Topes near Benares were opened by myself in 1835, and those at Sánchi and other places around Bhilsa, were opened by Lieut. Maisey and myself in January and February of the present year. The Topes of Tirhut and Bahar still remain to be examined.

9. Of the Bhilsa Topes none have yet been described excepting the largest of the Sánchi group near Bhilsa. An accurate plan and section of this building, with a short account of the various subjects represented in the sculptured bas-reliefs of the gateways, was published by my brother Captain J. D. Cunningham, in the Journal of the Asiatic Society of Bengal. On his solicitation* and earnest repre-

* See Vol. xvi., p. 745. Just eighteen days before his death, my brother thus wrote to a friend regarding these discoveries,

sentation of the great value of these bas-reliefs, the Court of Directors were induced to employ Lieut. Maisey to make drawings of the building, and of its sculptured gateways. In January last I joined Lieut. Maisey at Sánchi, and I am therefore able to speak positively of the value of his drawings, which cannot be surpassed for strict fidelity of outline and minute accuracy of detail. The bas-reliefs of the great Tope at Sánchi will now be illustrated in a manner worthy of their value and importance.

10. In the present work it is my intention to describe the *Topes*, or Buddhist monuments, which still exist in the neighbourhood of Bhilsa, in Central India. These Topes consist of five distinct groups, all situated on low sandstone hills, more or less inaccessible. (*See Map.*)

1st, Sánchi, 5½ miles to S. W. from Bhilsa.

2nd, Sonâri, 6 miles to S. W. from Sánchi.

3rd, Satdhâra, 6½ miles W. from Sánchi.

4th, Bhojpur, 7 miles E. S. E. from Sánchi, and 6 miles S. S. E. from Bhilsa.

5th, Andher, 4 miles E. S. E. from Bhojpur, and 9 miles E. S. E. from Bhilsa.

—The extreme distance from west to east, or from Satdhâra to Andher, is 17 miles.

11 A Tope is properly a religious edifice de-

which had been early communicated to him. "It is no small pleasure to me to reflect that my residence in Bhopál brought about the delineation of this monument and that of others, and so led the way to many important antiquarian results."

dicated emphatically to Buddha; that is, either to the celestial *Adi Buddha*, the great First Cause of all things, or to one of his emanations, the *Mánúshi*, or "Mortal" Buddhas, of whom the most celebrated, and the only historical one, is Sákya Muni, who died in B. C. 543. In the Topes dedicated to the celestial *Buddha*, the invisible Being who pervaded all space, no deposit was made; but the Divine Spirit, who is "Light," was supposed to occupy the interior, and was typified on the outside by a pair of eyes, placed on each of the four sides either of the base, or of the crown of the edifice.* Such is the great *Chaitya* or *Tope* near Kathmandu, in Nepál, dedicated to *Swayambhunáth* (the "Self Existent"), in which the eyes are placed on the upper portion of the building. A specimen of the regular Chaitya is represented in the 3rd compartment (inner face) of the left-hand pillar of the eastern gate at Sánchi, in which the two eyes are placed one above the other. Such also are the numerous *Chhod-tens* in Tibet, which are dedicated to the celestial Buddha, in contradistinction to the

* The legend of *Kunála*, the son of Asoka, proves the antiquity of this practice. In a former birth, Kunála is said to have plucked the eyes from a Chaitya, for which he was punished by the loss of his own in the next birth; and because he then presented a pair of golden eyes to a Chaitya, he was afterwards born as the son of Asoka, with eyes beautiful as those of the Kunála bird,—from which circumstance he obtained his name. See Hodgson, p. 117; and Burnouf Buddhisme Indien, pp. 409-413. See also Plate III. of this volume.

Dung-tens, which are built in honour of the *mortal Buddhas*, and which ought to contain some portion of their relics either real or supposed. The first, *Chhod-ten*, means simply an "offering" to the Deity; the latter, *Dung-ten*, is emphatically a "BONE," or relic-receptacle. The same distinction is preserved in the Sanskrit terms, *Chaitya* and *Dhâtugarbha* or *Dhagoba*. The former is properly a religious edifice, dedicated to *Adi-Buddha*, while the latter is only a "relic-shrine," or repository of ashes. The word *Chaitya*, however, means any sacred object—as a tree, an altar, a temple—as well as any monument raised on the site of a funeral pile, as a mound or a pillar: *Chaitya* may therefore, perhaps, be only a general term for both kinds of mound; while *Dhâtugarbha* or *Dhágoba* is particularly restricted to the "relic" shrine.

12. The word TOPE is derived from Afghanistan, where it is used to designate all the solid mounds of masonry which were opened by Messrs. Honigberger and Masson. The same term also is applied to the massive tower of Manikyâla in the Panjáb, as well as to all the smaller towers in its neighbourhood. There can be no doubt therefore that the name of Tope is the same as the Páli *Thupo*, and the Sanskrit *Stupa*, a "mound" or "tumulus," both of which terms are of constant use in the Buddhist books. *Stupa*, or *Tope*, is therefore a name common to each kind of tumulus; whether it be the solid temple dedicated to the Supreme Being, or the massive

mound erected over the relics of Sákya, or of one of his more eminent followers.

13. From several passages in the Páli Buddhistical annals, it would appear that Topes were in existence prior to Sákya's advent; and that they were objects of much reverence to the people. Sákya himself especially inculcated the maintenance of these ancient *Chaityas*,* and the continuance of the accustomed offerings and worship. But this was, doubtless, only a politic accommodation of his own doctrines to the existing belief of the people, adopted for the purpose of ensuring a more ready assent to his own views. Like as Mahomed recognised the prophetic missions of Moses and Elias, and the divinity of our Saviour Christ, so did Sákya Muni acknowledge the holy *Munis Kakutsanda*,† *Kanaka*, and *Kásyapa*, as his immediate predecessors. They were, probably, heroes or saints, who had obtained the respect of their fellow-countrymen during life, and their reverence after death. *Stupas* had been erected over their relics in the neighbourhood of Kapila and of Benares, and their worship was too firmly established to be attacked with any chance of success.‡ Sákya therefore artfully engrafted them

* See his seven imperishable precepts, given to the people of Vaisáli. The sixth of these is, "to maintain, respect, reverence, and make offerings to the *Chaityas*; and to keep up the ancient offerings without diminution."

† Or Krakuchanda.

‡ *Fo-kwe-ki*, chap. 20,—"His body remained entire." And

on his own system as the *Buddhas of a former age.* In like manner, the farmer, who cannot check the mountain stream, turns its course into numerous rivulets for the irrigation of his lands.

14. It appears also that *Stupas* had been erected over Supreme Monarchs prior to Sákya's advent, for Sákya particularly informs his disciple* Ananda that, over the remains of a *Chakravarti Raja,* " they build the *thupo* at a spot where *four principal roads meet.*" It is clear, therefore, that the *Tope,* or " tumulus," was the common form of tombs at that period. In fact, the Tope, as its name implies, is nothing more than a *regularly-built* cairn or pile of stones, which was undoubtedly the oldest form of funereal memento.

15. In his last injunctions to Ananda,† Bhagawá likewise " dwelt on the merits to be acquired by building *thupá* over relics of *Tathágatá, Paché-Buddhá,* and *Sáwaká,*" or Buddhas, Pratyekas, and Sráwakas; and he more particularly pointed out that they who prayed at the shrines that *would be* raised to him would be born in heaven.‡ But, although the original object of a Tope was to cover the remains of the great, or to enshrine the relics of the holy, yet, in a short time, other Topes, or

Turnour quotes the same from the Pali Annals,—" The joints were not separated."—See Prinsep's Journal, vii. 797.

* See Turnour, in Prinsep's Journal, vii. 1006.

† Turnour, in Prinsep's Journal, vii. 1006.

‡ Turnour, in Prinsep's Journal, vii. 1005.

memorial monuments, were erected on spots rendered famous by the leading events of Sákya's *life.* These holy places rapidly increased in number, until there was scarcely a large city in India, from Kâbul to Orissa, and from Nepál to Ceylon, which did not possess a monument illustrative of some act of the Great Teacher. For this end, the doctrine of transmigration was highly accommodating; for although the mortal pilgrimage of Sákya was limited to the central provinces of the Ganges, yet there was no part of India which he might not have visited in some former existence; and in this way, indeed, he is said to have been in Ceylon.

16. The Topes were, therefore, of three distinct kinds: 1st, The *Dedicatory,* which were consecrated to the Supreme Buddha; 2nd, The strictly *Funereal,* which contained the ashes of the dead; and 3rd, the *Memorial,* which were built upon celebrated spots.

17. Of the *Dedicatory Topes* I have already spoken; but I may here observe, that, as it is improbable that any deposit would have been placed in them, we may plausibly conclude that the largest Topes, such as those of *Sánchi,* Satdhâra, and Bhojpur, were consecrated to the Supreme Invisible *Adi-Buddha.*

18. Of the *Memorial Topes,* little is at present known. It seems nearly certain, however, that the great Manikyála Tope was of this kind; for the inscription extracted from it, which begins with *Gomangasa,* " of the abandoned body," undoubtedly

refers to Sákya's abandonment of his body to a hungry lion. This Tope, therefore, dates earlier than the period of Fa Hian's Indian pilgrimage in A.D. 400.

19. The *Funereal Topes* were of course the most numerous, as they were built of all sizes, and of all kinds of material, according to the rank of the deceased and the means of his fraternity. At Bhojpur, the Topes occupy four distinct stages or platforms of the hill. The largest Topes, six in number, occupy the *uppermost* stage, and were, I believe, dedicated to Buddha; that is, either to the celestial Buddha, *Adináth*, or to the relics of the mortal Buddha, *Sákya*. This view is borne out by the facts that the largest Tope contained no deposit; and that the second and third sized Topes yielded crystal boxes, one of which, shaped like a Tope, contained only a minute portion of human bone smaller than a pea!

20. The second-rate Topes, sixteen in number, stand on the second stage. According to my view, these Topes contain the ashes of those who had reached the rank of Bodhisatwa. We discovered relics in five of these Topes, but there were no inscriptions of any historical value.

21. The third stage of the hill is occupied by seven small Topes, all of which I suppose to have been built over the remains of the third grade of Pratyeka Buddhas. Of the eight Topes which stand on the lowest stage of the hill, one is much larger than any of those on the third stage. These Topes

were, I believe, built over the ashes of the lowest grade of the Bauddha community, the Sráwaka Buddhas.

22. The few remarks which I have suggested above, will be sufficient to show the valuable light which the Topes are likely to afford in illustration of the religion of Buddha. But, before proceeding to the examination of the Topes and their contents, I propose to give a slight historical sketch of the progress of that combined system of practical morality and philosophical speculation which, under the name of Buddhism, was the dominant faith of India for nearly fifteen centuries.

CHAPTER II.

LIFE OF SÁKYA.

1. In the earliest times of which we have any authentic record, the Arian race,* both in Persia and India, was attached to the worship of the Sun. In Persia, the fiery element was looked upon as the earthly type of *Mithra*, or the heavenly orb; and the sacred flame was kept continually burning by the Magian priesthood. But the worship of the elements was not unknown to the Persians; for Herodotus expressly states that "they sacrificed to the Sun and Moon, to the Earth, to Fire and Water, and to the Winds."† In India, the worship of the

* I use the term *Arian* in its widest acceptation to signify the race of *Aryya*, whose emigrations are recorded in the Zendavesta. Starting from *Ericene-Veejo*, the Aryas gradually spread to the south-east, over *Aryya-vartta* or *Aryya-desa*, the northern plains of INDIA; and to the south-west, over IRAN, or PERSIA. The Medes are called Αρειοι by Herodotus.

† *Herodotus*, i. 131,—Θύουσι δὲ ἡλίῳ τε καὶ σελήνῃ καὶ γῇ καὶ πυρὶ καὶ ὕδατι καὶ ἀνέμοισι. So also Diogenes Laertius, quoted by Barker,—"They teach the nature and origin of the Gods, whom they think Fire, Earth, and Water."—*Barker's Lempriere*, in v. Magi. Strabo and others say the same.

material elements was intimately blended with that of the Sun; and VARUNA and INDRA (with his attendant MÁRUTS), or Water and Air, shared with AGNI, or Fire, in the daily reverence of the people. The religious rites consisted of sacrifices, and of the recitation or chanting of the ancient hymns of praise and thanksgiving, which are still preserved in the Vedas. The officiating priests were most probably Bráhmans; for, although there is no positive authority for such a belief, yet we know that, at the rise of the Buddhist religion, in the 6th century before our era, they formed an hereditary priesthood, and were the recognised teachers of the Vedas.*

2. At this particular period of Indian history, the minds of men were perplexed with conflicting systems of religious belief, and with various philosophical speculations on the origin of the world, and on the mystical union of mind and matter, or of soul and body. The most popular system was that of the *Bráhmans* and their followers, who believed in the immortality of the soul after transmigration; while their opponents, the *Swástikas*, affirmed that its existence was finite, and was limited to its connection with the body.

3. The doctrine of the transmigration of souls was one of the earliest religious beliefs of the ancient world. In Egypt its acceptance was universal; and

* Turnour, in Journal of Asiatic Society, Bengal, vii. pp. 805, 809.

in India* it was denied only by the atheistical *Swástikas*; for the *Bráhmans*, notwithstanding the differences of their metaphysical schools, agreed in believing that mankind were destined, by means of successive regenerations, to a prolonged existence in this world. By the attainment of true knowledge, through abstract meditation, and more especially by the endurance of painful mortifications of the flesh, it was held possible to alleviate the misery of each successive existence by regeneration in a higher and a happier sphere of life. But it was not enough that the general tenor of a man's life was virtuous, for even a single sin was sufficient to draw down the punishment of a lower state of existence in the next birth. The sole aim, the one motive impulse of man, in each successive existence, was to win for himself a still happier state of life at each birth, and a still higher stage of perfection at each death. It was, therefore, only with the greatest difficulty that the most virtuous could wring from the reluctant gods his final exemption from the trammels of this "mortal coil" by the emancipation of soul from body, and by the re-absorption of the liberated spirit into the divine essence or Godhead, which was its original source.

4. The *Swástikas* received their name from their

* The migration of souls was the fundamental belief of all classes, both Buddhist and Brahmanical. The principal difference between the two creeds lay in the means for attaining final exemption from migration.

peculiar symbol the *Swástika*, or mystic cross, which was typical of their belief in *Swasti*. This term is a compound of *Su*, "well," and *asti*, "it is;" meaning "it is well," or, as Wilson expresses it, "so be it;" and implying complete resignation under all circumstances. But it was the stupefying submission of the Fatalist, not the meek resignation of the Christian, which bows to the chastening of the Almighty, and acknowledges that "whatever is, is right," *because* it is the will of God. According to the Chinese* the *Swástikas* were Rationalists, who held that contentment and peace of mind were the only objects worthy of attainment in this life. Whatever advanced those ends was to be sought; whatever hindered them was to be shunned. All impulses and desires were to be subdued; all hopes and fears were to be suppressed;

> "All thoughts, all passions, all delights,
> Whatever stirs this mortal frame,"

were accounted violators of the peace; and all the common cares of life were considered as so many different forms and degrees of pain. In the anxious quest for quietude, even the memory of the past was to be forgotten; and, what was a more rational

* They are the *Tao-sse* of the Chinese; and the founder of their doctrine is said to have flourished between 604 and 523 B.C. The *Swasti* of Sanskrit is the *Suti* of Pali; and the mystic cross, or *Swástika*, is only a monogrammatic symbol formed by the combination of the two syllables, *su* + *ti* = *suti*.

object, although perhaps not a more attainable one, there was to be no vain solicitude for the future.

5. The fatalist doctrine of eternal annihilation, and consequent escape from future punishment, will always be popular amongst people of weak minds and strong passions; and as these have ever been the prevailing characteristics of mankind in the East, the Atheistical principles of the *Swástikas* were received by the bulk of the people with very great favour. They assumed the name of *Tirthakaras*,* or "pure-doers;" but by the Buddhists of Tibet they are said to have been indecent in their dress, and grossly Atheistical in their principles. Their Tibetan name *Mustegs*, or "Finitimists," is significant of their doctrine of finite existence; but they are more generally known as the PON, or PON-PO. This sect, which prevailed throughout Tibet until the seventh century, is now confined to the furthest parts of the most eastern province of Tibet. The name of PON is evidently only the Sanskrit पुण्य, *punya*, "pure,"—a synonyme of *Tirthakara*.

6. Between the *Swástikas*, who promised nothing after this life, and the Bráhmans, who offered an almost endless series of mortal existences, people of strong minds and deep thoughts must have been sadly perplexed. Few men of vigorous intellect could have believed that their never-sleeping souls

* See *Fo-kwe-ki*, 22, 23, and Csoma's Tibetan Grammar, pp. 181, 192. The old name of *Tirthakara*, तीर्थकर, is still preserved amongst the Mogals as TER.

were subject to decay and dissolution; and yet how few of them, by the most zealous asceticism, could reasonably expect the final attainment of incorporation with the Divinity. For the mass of mankind there could have been no hope whatever; for few would attempt the attainment of that which was so difficult as to be almost impossible.

7. During the prevalence of such beliefs, the success of any more rational system was certain; and the triumphant career of *Sákya Muni*, and the rapid propagation of his religion, may be attributed as much to the defects of former systems as to the practical character of his own precepts, which inculcated morality, charity, abstinence, and the more speedy attainment of Buddhahood, with the abolition of caste, and of the hereditary priesthood.

8. SÁKYA SINHA, or SÁKYA MUNI, the great mortal teacher of the Buddhist religion, was the son of *Máyá*, by *Suddhodana*, Raja of Kapila, a petty principality near the present Gorakhpur. He was born in the year 623 B. C., and was, by his father's side, a descendant of *Ikshwáku*, of the *Suryavansa*, or solar race.* His original name was *Suddhatto*, or *Siddhartha*. He was reared in the palace of his father in all the accomplishments of a young prince of that period; and at sixteen years of age he was married to the Princess *Yasodará*, or *Subhaddakachháná*. From that time until his twenty-ninth year, he was

* Turnour's *Mahawanso*, p. 9. See also Turnour's Extracts from the *Atthakattha*, published in Prinsep's Journal, vol. vii. p. 927.

wholly wrapped up in the pursuit of human pleasures, when a succession of incidents awakened in him a train of deep thought, which gradually led to a complete change in his own life, and which eventually affected the religious belief of one-half of the human race.*

9. Mounted in his chariot, drawn by four white steeds, the prince was proceeding as usual to his pleasure-garden, when he was startled by the sudden appearance of an old, decrepid, toothless, gray-haired man, tottering feebly along with a staff. The sight roused him to reflection, and he returned to his palace full of the sad belief that man, in whatever state he may be born, is still "subject to decay."

10. Four months later, on a second excursion towards the pleasure-garden, he met a poor wretch, squalid with disease; and he returned to his palace sadder than before, with the reflection that man is subject to disease as well as to decay.

11. Four months later on a third occasion, he met a corpse; and he returned to his palace still sadder than the last time, with the reflection that man, however high his station, is subject to decay, disease, and death.

12. Four months later, he noticed a healthy, well-clad person, wearing the peculiar robe of those de-

* In the time of Trajan, when the Roman Empire had attained its greatest extent, *Buddhism* was the prevailing belief of China and India, which must then have contained more than one-half of the population of the globe.

dicated to religion. This caused another reflection on the propriety of that mode of life which could produce both cheerfulness of mind and healthiness of body; and the prince determined at once to join the religionists. These four incidents are called the "four *predictive signs*," which are shown at intervals to the persons destined to become *Buddhas.**

13. The whole story of *Sákya's* early life, when stripped of the superhuman incidents fondly added by his followers, seems both natural and true: for nothing can be more probable than the religious retirement of a young prince, who for twelve years had abandoned himself to every variety of pleasure until he was cloyed with enjoyment, and the cup of desire was brimful to satiety. Even the miraculous incidents narrated by devout Buddhists, are not more wonderful than those which are recorded and believed of the Virgin Mary, and scores of Roman Catholic saints, as well as of the Arabian Mohammed.

14. *Sákya Sinha* was twenty-nine years of age when he left his wife *Yasodará* and her infant son *Ráhula*, and quitted his native city of Kapila to assume the garb of the ascetics. When near his journey's end, on the bank of the *Anoma* river, he cut off his long

* Turnour's Extracts from the *Atthakattha*, in Prinsep's Journal, vol. vii. p. 805. These four predictive signs are generally believed to have been witnessed at intervals of four months. The *Dighabhánaka* fraternity, however, assert that Sákya witnessed all the four predictive signs on the same day.

hair with the tiara still attached to it,* and donned the three religious garments, with the begging pot, razor, sewing needle, waistband, and bathing cloth, peculiar to the *Bhikshu*, or mendicant ascetic. Thus clad, the prince entered the city of Rájagriha (fourteen miles from Gaya), and begged for alms and food, which having collected, he retired from the city, and seating himself with his face to the East, ate without loathing his first mendicant meal of the broken scraps of bread which had been thrown into his begging pot.

15. Thence pursuing his alms-pilgrimage, *Sákya* acquired from certain priests the knowledge of *Samápatti*;† but "finding that *Samápatti* was not the road that led to Buddhahood," he gave it up, and devoted himself to *Pradhán*.‡ For six years he dedicated himself to the study of *Mahá pradhán*, and subjected himself to the utmost extremes of penance and starvation, until he was reduced to a "perfect skeleton;" but finding that the mortification of the flesh was attended with prostration of the mind, he gave up this system also, as not being the right road to Buddhahood. *Sákya* then resumed his begging pilgrimages, and with proper food he

* The *Sánchi* bas-reliefs, and *Ajanta* frescoes, both represent the hair intertwined with the head-dress in a manner now only practised by the people of Burmah.

† *Samádhi*, समाधि, silent abstraction, and contemplation of the Supreme Being.

‡ *Pradhán*, प्रधान, Nature, or concrete matter.

regained his bodily strength and mental vigour; but was abandoned by the five disciples who had followed him for six years.*

16. After this he passed four weeks under the *Bodhi* tree, then one week under the *Nigrodho* tree (*Ficus Indica*), then another week under the *Machalindo* tree (*Stravadia*), then another week under the *Rajayatana* tree (*Buchanania latifolia*).† For seven whole weeks he thus continued absorbed in deep meditation until he had obtained *Bodhi-jnyán*,‡ and was prepared to make known unto mankind the wonderful efficacy of *Dharmma* (both faith and works), and the desirableness of *Nirvána*.

17. During his fit of abstract meditation under the *Bodhi* tree, Sákya was assailed by the terrors of death § (MARO, or Death personified) and his army of horrors; but, to one whose belief taught him that the dissolution of the body was the liberation of the soul from its earthly trammels, the approach of death was received with calm joy, instead of cowardly apprehension. This event, which is supposed to have ended Sákya's trials in this mortal body, took place in the month of *Asárh*, or

* Turnour's Extracts in Prinsep's Journal, p. 811.

† I have purposely retained the mention of these trees, because the *Sánchi* bas-reliefs, which exhibit the adoration of trees, may be best explained by the knowledge that certain trees, under which Sákya had sat, were held sacred.

‡ Supreme wisdom.

§ *Namuchi-Mara*, the Demon of Death.

June, 588 B. C. A few days afterwards, on the full moon of *Asárh*, or 1st July, 588 B. C., Sákya, clad in his ascetic dress, and with his begging pot in his hand, proceeded to the *Isipatana Vihâra* at Benâres. On his approach, he was recognised by the five *Bhikshus* who had formerly deserted him, and who were still resolute not to pay him reverence, but under the influence of his benign spirit they bowed down to him with every mark of adoration. *Sákya* then explained to them that he had attained Buddhahood, and preached to them on the supremacy of *Dharmma*.

18. From this time *Sákya* travelled over the greater part of North-West India, continually inculcating the efficacy of *Dharmma*, and the vast reward of *Nirvâna* (or final emancipation). In the first year of his ministry he is said to have assembled a synod of no less than twelve hundred and fifty sanctified disciples; of whom the chief were *Sáriputra* and *Mangalyána*, and the three *Kásyapas*.

19. The various acts of *Sákya*, during his long ministry of forty-five years, are too numerous to detail, and are too much mixed up with the fond exaggerations of his followers to admit of any satisfactory selection from them. But they may be taken generally as so many illustrations of the peculiar tenets which Sákya inculcated—amongst which are charity, abstinence, and the prohibition against taking life of any kind.

20. The death of this mortal Buddha took place at *Kusinára*, in January 543 B. C., when he was eighty years of age. On his death-bed he thus addressed his followers: " *Bhikshus!* should there be anything doubtful or incomprehensible regarding *Buddho, Dhammo, Sangho, Maggo*, or *Pati-padá*,* inquire (now)." Three times did *Bhagawá* [the Supreme, *i. e.* Sákya] address them in the same words; but they were all silent. Among the five hundred *Bhikshus* present, there was not one who doubted, or who did not understand. *Bhagawá* again spoke: " *Bhikshus!* I now exhort you for the last time: transitory things are perishable; without delay qualify yourselves (for *Nirvâna*)." These were the last words of *Tathágata*.†

21. The lower orders of Bhikshus, and all the *Mallians* of Kusinára, lamented aloud with dishevelled hair and uplifted arms, saying, " Too soon has *Bhagawá* died! too soon has *Sugato* died! too soon has the EYE (*chakku*) closed on the world!" But those *Bhikshus*, who had attained the state of *Arahat*, comforted themselves with the last words of the sage, that all " transitory things are perish-

* Turnour's Extracts in Prinsep's Jour. vol. vii. p. 1007. *Buddha, Dharma*, and *Sangha*, are the persons of the Buddhist Triad. *Maggo*, the Sanskrit *Márga*, मार्ग, " road," " way," was one of the lower stages of initiation in the *way* of Buddhism. *Patipadá*, the Sanskrit *Pratipada*, was the first or lowest stage of Buddhism.

† Turnour's Extracts in Prinsep's Journal, vol. vii. p. 1008.

able." This very scene is, I believe, represented in one of the compartments of the eastern gateway at *Sánchi.* Three figures are seated in a boat—one rower, one steersman, and one passenger—all in the dress of the religious class. On the shore are four figures, also in religious garb; one with dishevelled hair and uplifted arms, and the others, who wear caps, with hands clasped together in attitudes of devotion. The passenger is, I think, *Sákya Muni*, who is represented after *Nirvâna* on his passage over the waters which are said to surround this transitory world.* The figures on the shore are a *Bhikshu* of the lower grade bewailing the departure of *Sákya* with dishevelled hair and uplifted arms, which, from the description given above, would seem to have been the customary manner of expressing grief.† The others are *Bhikshus* who had attained the higher grade of *Arahat*, and who comforted themselves with the reflection that "all transitory things are perishable." The difference of rank is known by the bare head of the mourner and the capped heads of the others—a distinction which still prevails in Tibet, where the lower grades of *Ge-thsul* and *Chhos-pa* invariably go bare-headed; whilst all the *Lámas* (or higher grades), includ-

* Hodgson's Literature and Religion of the Buddhists, p. 151. "The world is surrounded by water,"—"Le tourbillon d'eau qui embrasse les mondes."

† See Turnour, in Prinsep's Journal, vol. vii. pp. 1009, 1011, for these instances. See also Plate XI. of this volume.

ing the Grand Láma himself, have their heads covered.

22. The corpse of the Great Teacher was escorted by the Mallians of *Kusinára* with music, singing, and dancing, to the east side of the city. It was first wrapped in a new cloth, then wound about with floss cotton, and again wrapped in numerous other cloths. Thus prepared, the corpse was laid in a metal oil vessel, covered by another, and placed upon a funeral pile of sandal wood. At this moment the venerable *Mahá Kássapo*, having arrived from *Páwá*, approached the funeral pile. With one shoulder bare (the right), and, with clasped hands, having performed the *padakhinán* (perambulation) three times; and, after opening the pile at the end, he reverentially bowed down at the feet of *Bhagawá*.* The five hundred Bhikshus did the same; and the pile was lighted. When the body was consumed, the metal vessel was escorted back to the town; where, with music, song, and dance, and with garlands of sweet flowers, the people for seven days showed their reverence and devotion to *Bhagawá's* mortal remains.

23. After this, the burnt bones were divided into eight portions by the Bráhman Dono (Drona), and

* Turnour's Extracts in Prinsep's Journal, vol. vii. p. 1012. This act of Kásyapa I believe to have been the origin of the worship of Buddha's feet. The reverence shown to the feet is undoubtedly old, as the feet are represented on the central architrave of the Eastern Gateway at Sánchi, in a procession.

distributed amongst those who applied for them. Eight Stupas or Topes were erected over the relics at the following places:—*

1st. At RAJAGRIHA, in Magadha, by *Ajáta-satta.*

2nd. At VISÁLI, by the *Lichawi* family.

3rd. At KAPILAVASTU, by the *Sákyas.*

4th. At ALLAKAPPO, by the *Balayas.*

5th. At RÁMAGRÁMA, by the *Kausalas.*

6th. At WETTHÁDIPO, by the *Bráhmans.*

7th. At PÁWÁ, by the *Malliyans.*

8th. At KUSINÁRA, by the *Malliyans.*

The *Moriyans* of PIPPHALIWANO having applied too late for a share of the relics, received some charcoal from the funeral pile, over which they built Stupa the

9th. At PIPPHALIWANO;

* Turnour's Extracts in Prinsep's Journal, vol. vii. p. 1013. The whole of these places, including *Allakappo,* although it has not been identified, were situated in Tirhut and Bahar.—1. RAJAGRIHA was the ancient capital of *Magadha,* or Bahar Proper. 2. The ruins of VISÁLI still exist at *Bassahr,* to the north of Patna. 3. KAPILAVASTU was somewhere between *Ayodhya* and Gorakhpur. 5. RÁMAGRÁMA was in the neighbourhood of Gorakhpur: it was most likely the *Selampura* of Ptolemy, or *Sri-Rámpura.* 6. WETTHADIPO was most probably *Bettiya.* 7. PÁWÁ was to the west of Visáli, on the high road to *Kusinára.* 8. KUSINÁRA was about equi-distant between Benares and Visáli, or in the position of *Kusia* on the Little Gandak. 9. PIPPHALIWANO, or the place of the Charcoal Tope, was between Kapilavastu and Kusinára. The people of Visáli are called *Passalæ* by Ptolemy.

and lastly the Bráhman Dono, over the vessel (*kumbha*) in which he had measured the relics, built the

10th *Stupa*.

24. The relics which remained uninjured by the fire were the four canine teeth, two collar bones, and one frontal bone with a hair attached to it, which was therefore called the *renhísa*, or hair relic. One of the teeth was ultimately enshrined in Gandhára, the country on the lower Kâbul river around Pesháwur; a second in Kalinga, at Dántapura, or "tooth-town;" and the others are said to have been worshipped by the Devas and Nágas.

25. But within twenty years after the death of *Sákya*, his relics were all brought together, excepting the portion at *Rajagráma*, by Ajatasatta, King of *Magadha*, through the influence of *Maha Kásyapa*, the patriarch or head of the Buddhist religion, and a great Stupa was erected over them to the south-east of Rajagriha.*

26. In the reign of Priyadarsi or Dharmmásoka, King of Magadha, about 250 B. C., these relics were again distributed over the whole of India.

* Turnour's Extracts in Prinsep's Journal, vol. vii. p. 1014. See also the *Mahawanso*, p. 185. In one of the Topes opened at *Bhojpur*, we found, amongst numerous fragments of bone, four *teeth*, all in good order.

CHAPTER III.

FAITH OF SÁKYA.

1. In the infancy of the world, when Man was left to his own unaided reason to solve the mysteries of nature, and the destiny of his race, the most casual observer must have seen that nothing of this earth is lasting; that the loftiest tree, the loveliest flower, the strongest animal, the hardest rock, are all subject to decay; nay, that man himself is nought but dust, and that to dust does he return. Closer observers would have been struck with the perpetual recurrence of seasons; the ever-changing yet unchanged moon; the continued production of plants; and, above all, with the never-failing stream of human life.

2. Such observations would naturally lead to the discrimination of the various elements—earth, water, fire, and air; to a belief in the eternity of matter, and to the doctrine of the transmigration of souls. And thus the material elements, or Nature, with her supposed inherent power of combination and reproduction, became the Deity of this world. But even the most thoughtless man must at times have felt

conscious that he possessed within himself an unseen power which controlled the actions of his body. Hence arose a belief in the existence of Spirit, which was at first made only an inherent power of Nature, but was afterwards preferred before her; and was eventually raised to the position of the Great First Cause and Creator of all things.

3. Such is the course which the human mind most probably went through both in India and in Greece. In process of time the more commanding spirits, who ruled the passions of their fellow-men by the ascendancy of genius, and by unbending firmness of will, were held to be mortal emanations or *avatárs* of the Supreme Being; and, after death, were exalted to the rank of demigods. Thus, in both countries, hero-worship had prevailed from remote antiquity; and the tombs of the mighty had become objects of reverence. In India, the Topes or Tumuli of Krakuchanda, Kanaka, and Kasyapa, existed before the preaching of Sákya; and the ancient elemental deities of the Vedas preceded the worship of Dharma, or concrete Nature.

4. The religious systems of India are all deeply imbued with metaphysical speculations; and the close agreement between these and the philosophical systems of Greece would be an interesting subject to the classical scholar. A strict analysis and comparison of the systems of both countries would most probably tend to mutual elucidation. The Indians have the advantage in point of time; and I feel

satisfied that the Greeks borrowed much of their philosophy from the East. The most perfect system of the Ionics, as developed by Anaxagoras,* is the same as the Sánkhya school of India; and the famous doctrines of Pythagoras are intensely Buddhistical. The transmigration of souls is Egyptian as well as Indian: but the prohibition against eating animal food is altogether Buddhist. Women were admitted as members both by Sákya and by Pythagoras; and there were grades in the brotherhood of Pythagoreans, as in the San'gha, or Community of Buddhists. These coincidences between the two systems seem too strong to be accidental.

5. Pythagoras is said to have visited India; and there are some curious verbal coincidences which really seem to countenance the story. Pythagoras married *Theano* (Sanskrit, *Dhyána*, "devout contemplation"); and by her had a daughter whom he named *Damo* (Sanskrit, *Dharmma*, "virtue, or practical morality"), and who became a most learned Pythagorean. He was the first who assumed the title of φιλοσοφος (Sanskrit, Buddha Mitra), the lover of wisdom, or Budha. His own name is perhaps only a compound of πυθας, or Buddha, and αγορευω,

* Anaxagoras held that Νους, Mind or Intellect, was not the creator of all things, but only the artist who gave form to preexistent matter. According to him, matter consisted of various particles, which were put in motion by the action of Mind; the homogeneous particles were blended together into an infinite variety of forms, and the heterogeneous were separated.

to expound or announce; and the names of two of his followers, Damon and Pythias (or Dharmma and Buddha), have become celebrated for their disinterested friendship. All these coincidences can scarcely be accidental; and though we may not be able to trace the actual progress of Buddhism from India to Greece, yet the evidence in favour of its transmission is much too strong to be doubted.

6. The system of faith taught by Sákya Muni has been tersely and truly characterized by Mr. Hodgson as "monastic asceticism in morals, and philosophical scepticism in religion." This is especially the case with the two more ancient philosophical systems, the *Swábhávika* and *Aiswárika*, which he has made known to us from the Sanskrit books of Nepál. The former, Mr. Hodgson thinks, was that of primitive Buddhism; but as the *Swábhávika* was essentially a doctrine of materialism, it must have been closely allied to the *Niriswara Sánkhya* school of Kápila. In this system* *Pradhan*, or *Mahá-Pradhán*, or "supreme nature," was held to be the *Mula-Prakriti*, or "plastic origin" of all things, from which *Budhi*, or "intelligence," was produced. Now this is the very system which Sákya had rejected, after six years' study at Rajagriha. The supremacy of Nature† taught by the *Swábhávikas* is also utterly at variance with the

* Colebrooke, Trans. Roy. As. Soc.

† Hodgson, pp. 33, 77. The Swábhávikas were simple materialists.

solemn address made by SÁKYA to his disciples from his death-bed under the *Sál* tree at *Kusinagara.** "*Bhikshus!*" said the dying teacher, "if any points seem doubtful or incomprehensible to you regarding *Buddho, Dhammo, Sangho,* &c., inquire now." In this address, which was three times repeated, *Buddha,* or "supreme intelligence," is placed before *Dharma,* or "material nature," as the first person of the Triad. The system of faith taught by SÁKYA must, therefore, have been that of the Theistical Triad of *Buddha,*† *Dharma,* and *Sangha.* This is placed beyond all doubt by the edict of Priyadersi, published after the meeting of the 3rd Buddhistical Synod in B. C. 247, at which the orthodox doctrines of Sákya were upheld.‡ In this edict, the names of the orthodox Buddhist Triad are distinctly mentioned as *Buddha, Dharma,* and *Sangha.* The existence of the Buddhist Triad at that particular period, is further proved by the occurrence of such names as *Budha-Pálita, Dharma Rakshita,* and *Sangha-Mitra,* among the colonnade inscriptions of No. 2 Tope at Sánchi.

7. When Sákya Muni began his religious career, he first tried the system of the *Sámádhikas,* who placed the attainment of everlasting bliss in the continued practice of *Samádhi,* or of deep and

* Turnour, in Prinsep's Journal, vol. vii. p. 1007.

† Buddha, Dharma, and Sangha, are the *Sanskrit* names; the others are *Páli.*

‡ See Jour. As. Soc. Bengal, vol. ix. p. 619, where the three names of *Buddha, Dharma,* and *Sangha,* are improperly translated "Buddhist faith."

devout abstraction.* Dissatisfied with this belief, he next tried that of the *Prádhánikas,* or worshippers of "universal nature" as the sole First Cause of all things. This atheistical doctrine he also abandoned; and, in its stead, either invented or adopted the theistical Triad of *Buddha, Dharma,* and *Sangha,* in which Triad Buddha, or "supreme intelligence," is the Creator of all things. "In the transcendental and philosophical sense, BUDDHA means MIND; DHARMMA, *Matter;* and SANGHA, the concretion of the two former in the sensible or phenomenal world. In a practical or religious sense, BUDDHA means the mortal author of this religion (*Sákya*); DHARMMA, his law; and SANGHA, the congregation of the faithful."†

8. But though the early Buddhists admitted the *existence* of a Supreme Being, they denied his *providence,* in the full belief that without his aid, and solely by their own efforts of *Tapas*‡ and *Dhyán,* or Abstinence and Abstraction, they could win for themselves the "everlasting bliss" (*Moksha*) of absorption into the Divine Spirit.§

* So complete was the power of abstraction held to be, that the author of the *Mahawanso* (p. 262) gravely relates the following story:—"This Raja (*Dhátusena*), at the time he was improving the *Kálawápi* tank, observed a certain priest absorbed in the *Samádhi* meditation; and, *not being able to rouse him from that abstraction,* had him *buried* under the embankment (of the tank) by heaping earth over him."

† Hodgson, p. 39.

‡ Hodgson, page 35. The *Tapas* of the Buddhists was not penance, or self-inflicted bodily pain, like that of the Bráhmans, but a perfect rejection of all outward things (*pravrittika*).

§ Hodgson, p. 37.

9. One belief common to Buddhism is the doctrine of *Nirvritti* and *Pravritti*, or Rest and Action.* The latter state is that of MAN, and the former that of the celestial, self-existent BEING, whether Buddha or Dharma. According to the Aiswárikas, the Supreme Being *Adi Buddha*, or *Iswara*, though formless as a cypher or mathematical point, and separate from all things (in *Nirvritti*), is infinite in form, pervading all, and one with all (in *Pravritti*).† His proper and lasting state is that of *Nirvritti*, but for the sake of creation, he spontaneously roused himself into activity (*Pravritti*), and by means of his five spiritual faculties (*Panchajnyána*), and by five exertions of mental reflection (*Panchadhyána*), he created the *Pancha-Dhyani-Buddha*, or "five celestial Buddhas," together with the "five elements," the "five senses," and the five "objects of sense," in the following order:‡

	Buddhas.	Elements.	Senses.	Objects of Sense.
1	VAIROCHANA.	Earth.	Light.	Colour.
2	AKSHOBYA.	Water.	Hearing.	Sound.
3	RATNA SAMBHAVA.	Fire.	Smell.	Odour.
4	AMITÁBHA.	Air.	Taste.	Savour.
5	AMOGHA SIDDHA.	Ether.	Touch.	Solidity.

* प्रवृत्ति and निर्वृत्ति.

† Hodgson, pp. 81, 40, 110. These terms were also applied to human beings, according as they passed secular or monastic lives. Thus *Sákya*, while Prince *Siddharta*, was exercising *Pravritti-Márga*; but when he adopted the religious garb, and the devotional abstraction of the ascetics, he was then in a state of *Nirvritti-Márga*.

‡ Hodgson, pp. 40, 83, 111.

10. These five celestial Buddhas appear to be simple personifications of the five elements, and their inherent properties; or, to use Mr. Hodgson's expression, "of the active and intellectual powers of nature." The five Bodhisatwas, as well as the five *Lokeswaras*, or inferior celestials, likewise possessed *Saktis*.

11. I omit the long train of *Bodhisatwas, Lokeswaras*, and *Buddhasáktis*, as I believe that they formed no part of original Buddhism, but were engrafted afterwards when the religion of Sákya had become firmly established, and when its votaries took more delight in the indolent enjoyment of metaphysical speculations than in the active exertions of propagandism. I believe also that, as Buddhism gradually obtained an ascendancy over men's minds, the whole of the Bráhmanical schools, by an easy change of phraseology, accommodated their own doctrines so as not to clash with those of the dominant party. At least it is only by a supposition of this kind that I can account for the great similarity which exists between the philosophical systems of Buddhism and those of the Bráhmanical Sánkhyas. This similarity, which has already been noticed by Colebrooke,* is, indeed, so great as to render it difficult to discriminate the doctrines of the one from those of the other. The phraseology varies, but the ideas are the same; so that there is a distinction, but without a difference.

* Colebrooke, Trans. Roy. As. Society, vol. i. p. 19—On the Philosophy of the Hindus.

12. There is, however, one doctrine of the *Sánkhyas*, which neatly and clearly distinguishes them from the Buddhists — a belief in the *eternity of matter*, as well as in the immortality of the soul. The Sánkhyas asserted that nothing can be produced which does not already exist; and that effects are educts and not products.* This is the old classical dogma of *ex nihilo nil fit*, "from nothing, nothing can come."† The stately tree sprang from a seed; the costly jar was formed from the potter's clay. There might be infinities of form and ever-varying combinations of substance; but the materials existed before, and the difference consisted only in the shape and mixture, and not in the matter.

13. The orthodox Buddhists, on the contrary, believed that every thing was the creation of the self-existent *Adi Buddha*, who willed it, and it was.

14. The *Sánkhya* teachers, whose doctrines correspond with those of the primitive Buddhists, are *Kapila* and *Patánjali*. The first held that all things owed their origin to *Mula-Prakriti*, or Radical Nature, in which *Purusha*, or Soul, was inherent, and from which *Budhi*, or Intelligence (in a female and inferior form), was brought forth. His system

* Colebrooke, Trans. Roy. As. Society, vol. i. p. 38—On the Philosophy of the Hindus.

† This is the doctrine of Lucretius, de Rerum Natura—Nil fieri ex nihilo, in nihilum nil posse reverti. "From nonentity nothing can be produced; and entity cannot be reduced to nothing."

was called *Niriswara Sánkhya*,* or "atheistical Sánkhya," because he denied the existence of an all-ruling Providence. Kápila also prohibited sacrifice, as its practice was attended with the taking away of life.

15. The followers of Patanjali were called *Seswara Sánkhyas*,† or "theistical Sánkhyas," because they recognised a Supreme Being who was the ruler of the world, infinite and eternal.

16. The Brahmanical *Niriswara* system agrees very nearly with that of the Buddhistical *Swabháva*, in which *Dharma* is made the first person of the Triad, as *Mahá-Prajna*,‡ or "supreme nature," which is *Swabhava* (or self-existent), the sole entity, from which all things proceeded in this order§:—

17. From the mystic root of the letter Y air
„ „ R fire
„ „ V water
„ „ L earth
„ „ S Mount Sumeru.

In the Swabhávaka Triad, *Dharma* is repre-

* *Nir*, without, and *Iswara*, God — that is, Godless or Atheistical.

† *Sa*, with; *Iswara*, God.

‡ Hodgson, p. 77.

§ Hodgson, p. 109. These are the Sanskrit radicals,—*ya, ra, va, la*, which signify air, fire, water, and earth. From Mount Sumeru proceeded all trees and vegetables, and from the earth proceeded the *Dhátwátmika*, or bases of all the metals.

sented as a female, with *Buddha* on the right hand, and *Sangha* on the left.

18. The *Seswará* school of the Bráhmans agrees very closely with that of the *Aiswárika* Buddhists. Both take their names from the recognition of a Supreme Being (*Iswara*), whom the Buddhist considers as the first Intellectual Essence, the *Adi-Buddha*, by whom all things were created. In the Aiswárika Triad, *Buddha* holds the first place, and *Dharma*, who is represented as a female, the second place on his right hand, while *Sangha* occupies the left hand.

19. All these schools, both Bráhmanical and Buddhistical, whether they deify intellectual spirit or material nature, agree in considering that man is the united production of both—a compound of mind and matter, or soul and body. According to the Aiswárikas, the human body, as well as the material universe, was compounded of the five elements: earth, water, fire, air, and ether.* The soul, which animates it, was an emanation from the self-existent God. Man was, therefore, emphatically the "Union" (*Sangha*) of "material essence" (*Dharma*) with a portion of the "divine intelligence" (*Buddha*).†

20. But these metaphysical speculations were imparted only to the initiated, or highest class of *Bhikshus*, who had attained the rank of *Arahat*, or *Bodhisatwa*. For Sákya had divided his doctrines

* Hodgson, p. 112.

† Hodgson, p. 127.

into three distinct classes, adapted to the capabilities of his hearers.* 1st, The *Vináya*, or "religious discipline," addressed to the *Sráwaka*, or "auditors," who were the lowest class of the Bauddha community; 2nd, The *Sutra*, "aphorisms," or Principles of Faith, addressed to the *Pratyekas* or "distinct intelligences," who formed the middle class of monks; and 3rd, the *Abhidharma*, or "supreme law," or Transcendental Principles of Faith, imparted only to the *Bodhisatwas*, or "true intelligences," who were the highest class of the Bauddha community.

21. These three classes of doctrine are collectively called the *Tri-Pitaka*, or "three repositories;" and the *Tri Yanika*,† or "three-means-of-progression;" and separately they are generally known as the LOWEST, the MIDDLE, and the HIGHEST means of ADVANCEMENT. These terms are of common occurrence in the Buddhist writings, and especially in the works of the Chinese travellers; from whom we learn that the pastoral nations of the Northern Hills, accustomed to active habits, were content with the LOWEST-MEANS-OF-ADVANCEMENT, while the more intellectual and contemplative people of India generally strove for the attainment of the superior degrees of *Madhyima-Yánika*, and *Mahá-*

* *Fo-kwe-ki*, c. 2, note. Csoma de Koros,—Analysis of the Tibetan Works, in Prinsep's Journal, vol. vii. p. 145.

† *Yána* means a vehicle of any kind, by which progress or advance is obtained.

Yánika, or "MIDDLE AND HIGHEST MEANS-OF-ADVANCEMENT."

22. The *Tri-Pitaka* were compiled immediately after Sákya's death, in B. C. 543, by three of his chief disciples, with the assistance of five hundred learned monks. The ABHIDHARMA was the work of *Kásyapa*, the head of the Bauddha fraternity; the SUTRA of *Anánda*, Sákya's favourite disciple; and the VINÁYA of *Upáli*.* The language in which these works was written, has been the subject of much dispute; but the account given by the Tibetans† is so probable, and at the same time so natural, that it ought, as James Prinsep has observed, to set the matter at rest. Their account is that the SUTRAS in general, that is, the Vináya, as well as the Sutrá proper, were first written in the SINDHU language; but that the whole of the *Sher-chin*,‡ that is, the *Prajná Páramitá*, or "transcendental wisdom," and the whole of the *Gyud*, that is, the *Tantras*, or "religious mysticism," were composed in SANSKRIT. This appears to be the only conclusion that anyone can come to who examines the subject attentively. For the *Vináya* and *Sutra*, which were addressed to the people at large, as well as to the *Sráwakas* and *Pratyekas*, must necessarily have been published in the vernacular language of the country; while

* Prinsep's Journal, vol. i. p. 2; and Transactions As. Soc. Bengal, vol. xx. p. 42.

† Csoma's Index to the *Kahgyur*, in Prinsep's Journal, vol. vi. p. 688.

‡ See Csoma, in Prinsep's Journal, vol. vi. p. 503.

the abstruse and metaphysical philosophy of the *Abhidharma*, which was addressed solely to the learned, that is, to the *Bráhmans* and *Bodhisatwas*, would, without doubt, have been enunciated in Sanskrit, for the simple reason that its refined elegance of ideas, and delicate shades of meaning, could not be adequately expressed in any of the vernacular languages. The *Tantras* are of much later date; but the same reasoning holds equally good for them; as the esoteric mysticism of their doctrines could only have been expressed in Sanskrit. In a few words the *speculative principles* of Buddhism were expounded and recorded in *Sanskrit*,* while the *practical system of belief*, deduced from those principles, was spread abroad and propagated by means of the vernacular Prakrit.

23. In the *Rúpasiddhi*, which is the oldest Páli grammar now extant, and which the author *Buddhapriya* compiled† from the ancient work of *Kachháyana*, a quotation from the latter is given, apparently in the original words. According to this account, Kachháyana was one of the principal disciples of Sákya, by whom he was selected for the important office of compiling the first Páli grammar, the rules of which are said to have been propounded by *Tathágata* himself. This statement seems highly probable; for the teacher must have soon found the

* See also Hodgson's opinion on this point. Prinsep's Journal, vol. vi. p. 683.

† Turnour's Introduction to the *Mahawanso*, p. 26.

difficulty of making himself clearly understood when each petty district had a provincial dialect of its own, unsettled both in its spelling and its pronunciation.

24. A difficulty of this kind could only be overcome by the publication of some established rules of speech, which should fix the wavering pronunciation and loose orthography of a common language. This was accomplished by the Páli Grammar of *Kachháyana*, compiled under Sákya's instructions; and the language, thus firmly established, was used throughout India by the Buddhist teachers, for the promulgation and extension of the practical doctrines of their faith.

25. In the Buddhist works of Ceylon, this language is expressly called *Mágadhi*, or the speech of *Magadha*; and as this district was the principal scene of Sákya's labours, as well as the native country of himself and of his principal disciples, the selection of *Mágadhi* for the publication of his doctrines was both natural and obvious. It is true, as Professor H. H. Wilson has remarked,* that there are several differences between the language of existing Buddhist inscriptions and the *Mágadhi* of Páli Grammars; but these differences are not such as to render them unintelligible to those whom PRIYADARSI addressed in his Pillar edicts in the middle of the third century before Christ. The Pro-

* Journal of the Royal Asiatic Society, vol. xii. p. 238.

fessor admits that the Páli was most likely selected for his edicts by Priyadarsi, "*that they might be intelligible to the people;*" but he is of opinion that the language of the inscriptions was rather the common tongue of the inhabitants of Upper India than a form of speech peculiar to a class of religionists; and he argues that the use of the Páli language in the inscription is not a conclusive proof of their Buddhistical origin.

26. The conclusion which I have come to is exactly the reverse; for it is a well known fact, that the Bráhmans have never used any language but *Sanskrit* for their religious writings, and have stigmatised the *Mágadhi* as the speech of men of low tribes.* In their dramas also the heroes and the Bráhmans *always* speak Sanskrit, while the use of Mágadhi is confined to the attendants of royalty. Professor Wilson has, however, identified the *Mágadhi* with *Prákrit,* the use of which, though more honourable, was still confined to the principal *female* characters; but the extensive employment, in the dramatic works of the Brahmans, of various dialects, all derived from one common stock, seems to me to prove that they were the vernacular language of the people. In this vernacular language, whatever it was, whether the high Prákrit of the *Saurasenas,* or the low Prákrit of the *Mágadhas,* we know certainly that the *Vináya* and *Sutra,* or the practical doctrines

* Colebrooke, in Trans. As. Soc. Bengal, vol. vii. p. 199. Wilson's Hindu Theatre, vol. i. p. lxiii. iv.

of Sákya, were compiled, and *therefore* also promulgated.*

27. In the opinion of Turnour, the celebrated scholar, the Páli is a "rich and poetical language, which had already attained its present refinement at the time of Gotama Buddha's advent" (B. C. 588). According to Sir William Jones,† it is "little more than the language of the Bráhmans, melted down by a delicate articulation to the softness of Italian." To me it seems to bear the same relation to Sanskrit that *Italian* does to *Latin*, and a much nearer one than modern English does to Anglo-Saxon. The nasal sounds are melted down; the compounds are softened to double and even single consonants; and the open vowels are more numerous. It is the opinion of all European scholars that the Páli language is derived almost entirely from the Sanskrit; and in this opinion I fully coincide. Messrs. Burnouf and Lassen, who jointly formed a Páli Grammar, state, as the result of their labours, that Páli is almost identical with Sanskrit;‡ and Pro-

* Csoma, in Prinsep's Journal, vol. vi. p. 503. I use the term *Prákrit* as comprehending all the written and cultivated dialects of Northern India. *Prákrit* means "common" or "natural," in contradistinction to the "artificial" or "refined" Sanskrit.

† Preface to *Sakuntala*.

‡ Essai sur le Pali; par E. Burnouf et Chr. Lassen, p. 187,—"Il en est résulté qu'elle etait *presque identique* à l'idiome sacré des Brahmanes."

fessor Lassen, at a later date,* when more conversant with the Páli books, states authoritatively, that the whole of the Prákrit language is derived from the Sanskrit. Turnour† also declares his conviction that all researches tend to prove the greater antiquity of Sanskrit. Professor Wilson‡ and James Prinsep§ are likewise of the same opinion. This conclusion seems to me self evident; for there is a tendency in all spoken languages to suppress dissimilar consonants, and to soften hard ones: as in the Latin *Camillus* for the Tuscan *Cadmilus*, and the English *farthing* for the Anglo-Saxon *feorthling*; or, as in the Páli *assa*, "a horse," for the Sanskrit *aswa*, and the Páli *majha*, "middle," for the Sanskrit *madhya*. There is also a natural inclination to clear away the semi-vowels and weaker consonants; as in the English *King*, for the Anglo-Saxon *Kyning*, or as in the Páli *Olakita*, "the seen" (*i. e.* Buddha), for the Sanskrit *Avalakita*; and in the Páli *Ujeniya*, a "man of Ujain," for the Sanskrit *Ujjayaniya*. It is always therefore easy to determine between any written languages, that resemble each other, which of the two is the original, and which the borrowed;

* Institutiones Linguæ Prakriticæ; Chr. Lassen, p. 6,—"Prakriticam linguam derivatam esse *totam* a Sanskriticâ."

† Turnour—*Mahawanso*, Introduction, p. xiii. The general results of all researches tend to prove the greater antiquity of the Sanskrit.

‡ Hindu Theatre, vol. i. p. lxiii.

§ Prinsep's Journal, vol. vi. p. 688.

because letters and syllables are never added, but, on the contrary, are always suppressed or curtailed in the process of time. The Páli is, therefore, without doubt, derived from the Sanskrit, and must, moreover, have been a spoken language for many centuries.

28. For the publication of his esoteric theories regarding the origin of the world, and the creation of mankind, Sákya made use of the Sanskrit language only. But the perfect language of our day, perhaps, owes much of its refinement to the care and sagacity of that Great Reformer; for it seems highly probable that KÁTYÁYANA, the inspired saint and lawgiver who corrected the inaccuracies of Pánini's *Sanskrit* grammar,* is the same as the KACHHÁYANO† who compiled the *Páli* grammar during the life-time of Sákya. *Kátyáyana's* annotations on Pánini, called *Vártikas*, restrict his vague rules, enlarge his limited ones, and mark numerous exceptions to others. "These amended rules of Sanskrit grammar were formed into memorial verses by *Bhartrihari*, whose metrical aphorisms, entitled *Káriká*, have almost equal authority with the precepts of Pánini, and emendations of *Kátyáyana*. According to popular tradition,‡ *Bhartrihari* was the brother of Vikramaditya, the author of the Hindu

* Colebrooke, Trans. As. Soc. Bengal, vii. 199.

† *Kachháyano* is only the Páli form of the Sanskrit *Kátyáyana;* the *tya* of the latter being invariably changed to *chha.*

‡ Colebrooke, Trans. As. Soc. Bengal, vii. 204.

Samvat, which dates from B. C. 57. The age of Kátyáyana is unknown; but as he flourished between the date of Pánini, in about 1100 B. C., and that of Bhartrihari, in 57 B. C., there is every probability in favour of the opinion that he was one of the disciples of Buddha.

29. But this identification of the two greatest grammarians of the Sanskrit and Páli languages rests upon other grounds besides those mentioned above. Colebrooke, Wilson, and Lassen, have all identified the commentator on *Pánini* with *Vararuchi*, the author of the "Prákrit Grammar," called *Prakrita-prakása*, or *Chandrika*. Of *Vararuchi* nothing more is known than that his work is the oldest Prákrit grammar extant, and that his body of rules includes all that had been laid down by *earlier* grammarians regarding the vernacular dialects.

30. This identification is still more strikingly confirmed by the fact that *Kachháyano* is not a name but only a patronymic,* which signifies the son of *Kachho*, and was first assumed by the grammarian himself. If, therefore, *Vararuchi Katyáyana* is not the *same person* as *Kachháyano*, he must be posterior to him and of the *same* family. We shall thus have

* Turnour's *Mahawanso*, Introduction, p. xxvi. where the original passage of the *Rupasiddhi* is given. See also Csoma de Koros, in Prinsep's Journal, vii. p. 144, where the fact is confirmed; as the Tibetans call the Grammarian *Kátyáhi-bu*—that is, the son of KÁTYA.

two Kátyáyanas of the same family living much about the same time, each of whom compiled a Páli or Prákrit grammar; a conclusion which is much more improbable than that the two were one and the same person.

31. I have been thus particular in stating all the evidences in favour of this supposition, as the probable identity of the two great grammarians seems to me to offer an additional reason for considering *Sákya Muni* as one of the chief benefactors of his country. For I believe that we must not look upon *Sákya Muni* simply as the founder of a new religious system, but as a great social reformer who dared to preach the perfect equality of all mankind, and the consequent abolition of caste, in spite of the menaces of the most powerful and arrogant priesthood in the world. We must regard him also as a patriot, who, in spite of tyrannical kings and princes, had the courage to incite his countrymen to resist the forcible abduction of their wives and daughters by great men.* To him the Indians were indebted for a code of pure and practical morality, which inculcated charity and chastity, performance of good works, and abstinence from evil, and general kindness to all living things. To him also I believe they owe the early refinement and systematic arrangement of their language in the selection of the learned

* See the fifth of the "Seven Imperishable Precepts, imparted by Sákya to the people of Vaisáli."—Turnour in Prinsep's Journal, vii. p. 991.

Kátyáyana as the compiler of the Sanskrit and Páli grammars.

32. As the champion of religious liberty and social equality, *Sákya Muni* attacked the Bráhmans in their weakest and most vulnerable points; in their impious assumption of all mediation between man and his Maker, and in their arrogant claims to hereditary priesthood. But his boldness was successful; and before the end of his long career he had seen his principles zealously and successfully promulgated by his *Bráhman* disciples Sáriputra, Mangalyána, Ananda, and Kásyapa, as well as by the *Vaisya* Kátyáyana and the *Sudra* Upáli. At his death, in B.C. 543, his doctrines had been firmly established; and the divinity of his mission was fully recognized by the eager claims preferred by kings and rulers for relics of their divine teacher. His ashes were distributed amongst eight cities; and the charcoal from the funeral pile was given to a ninth; but the spread of his influence is more clearly shown by the mention of the numerous cities where he lived and preached. Amongst these are *Champa* and *Rájagriha* on the east, *Srávasti* and *Kausambi* on the west. In the short space of forty-five years,*

* Sákya began his public career at thirty-five years of age, and died at eighty. Mahomed was born in 569 A. D.: he announced his mission in 609 at forty years of age, and died in 644, when he was seventy-five. In A. D. 640, or in thirty-one years from the announcement of his mission, the arms and the religion of Mahomed had spread over the ancient empires of Egypt, Syria, and Persia.

this wonderful man succeeded in establishing his own peculiar doctrines over the fairest districts of the Ganges; from the Delta to the neighbourhood of Agra and Cawnpore. This success was perhaps as much due to the early corrupt state of Bráhmanism, as to the greater purity and more practical wisdom of his own system. But, rapid as was the progress of Buddhism, the gentle but steady swell of its current shrinks into nothing before the sweeping flood of Mahomedanism, which, in a few years, had spread over one half of the civilized world, from the sands of the Nile to the swampy fens of the Oxus.

33. The two most successful religious impostures which the world has yet seen, are Buddhism and Mahomedanism. Each creed owed its origin to the enthusiasm of a single individual, and each was rapidly propagated by numbers of zealous followers. But here the parallel ends; for the *Korân* of Mahomed was addressed wholly to the "passions" of mankind, by the promised gratification of human desires both in this world and in the next; while the *Dharma* of *Sákya Muni* was addressed wholly to the "intellect," and sought to wean mankind from the pleasures and vanities of this life by pointing to the transitoriness of all human enjoyment. Mahomed achieved his success by the offer of material or bodily pleasures in the next life, while Sákya succeeded by the promise of eternal deliverance of the soul from the fetters of mortality. The former propagated his religion by the merciless edge of the sword; the latter

by the persuasive voice of the missionary. The sanguinary career of the Islamite was lighted by the lurid flames of burning cities; the peaceful progress of the Buddhist was illuminated by the cheerful faces of the sick in monastic hospitals,* and by the happy smiles of travellers reposing in *Dharmsâlas* by the road-side. The one was the personification of bodily activity and material enjoyment; the other was the genius of corporeal abstinence, and intellectual contemplation.†

* *Mahawanso,* p. 249. Upatisso, son of Buddha Dás, builds hospitals for cripples, for pregnant women, and for the blind and diseased. Dhatusena (p. 256) builds hospitals for cripples and sick. Buddha Dás himself (p. 245) ordained a physician for every ten villages on the high road, and built asylums for the crippled, deformed, and destitute.

† There is a curious coincidence also in the manner of death of the two teachers. According to the Buddhists, Máro, the Angel of Death, waited upon Sákya to learn *when it would be his pleasure to die.* The Musulmáns assert the same of Muhammad. Azraïl, the Angel of Death, entered the chamber of the sick man to announce that "he was enjoined *not to interfere with the soul of God's prophet,* without an entire acquiescence on his part."—See Price's Muhammadan History, vol. i. p. 16.

CHAPTER IV.

FIRST SYNOD.

1. The whole Bauddha community, or all who had taken the vows of asceticism, were known by the general name of *Sangha*, or the "congregation." The same term, with the addition of the local name, was used to distinguish any one of the numerous Buddhist fraternities; as *Magadhe-Sangham*, the fraternity of Magadha; *Santi Sangham*, the fraternity of *Sánti*, or *Sánchi*.* It was also employed to denote the general assemblies† of monks, which were held at stated periods; as well as the Grand Assemblies, which took place only on particular occasions. Three of these extraordinary assemblies, called respectively the First, Second, and Third Synods,‡ were held at different periods, for the

* See the Bhabra inscription, Jour. As. Soc. Bengal, for the first; the other is used in the Sánchi pillar inscription, published in this volume.

† Μεγαλην συνοδον is the expression of Megasthenes for the annual assembly held at Palibothra.

‡ *Prathamé, Dwitaye*, and *Tritaye Sangham*, or *Sangiti*.

suppression of heresy, and the solemn affirmation of orthodoxy.

2. The first of these assemblies was convoked after the death of Sákya, in the middle of the year 543 B. C., by the great *Kásyapa*, on hearing the insidious address of the aged *Subhadra*.* "Revered ones!" said the dotard, "mourn no more! We are happily released from the control of the great *Srámana* (Buddha): we shall no more be worried with 'this is allowable,' and 'that is not allowable;' we can now do what we wish, and can leave undone what we do not desire." Kásyapa reflected that the present was the most fitting time to summon a general assembly for the solemn rehearsal of *Dharma* and *Vináya*, according to the injunction of Sákya. "Ananda," said the dying sage, "let the *Dharma* and *Vináya*, which I have preached and explained to thee, stand in the place of a teacher after my death." Reflecting on this, and on the first of the imperishable precepts, "*to hold* frequent religious meetings," Kásyapa addressed the assembled Bhikshus.† "Beloved! let us hold a rehearsal both of the *Dharma* and of the *Vináya*." "Lord," replied they, "do thou select the *Stháviras* and *Bhikshus*." Kásyapa therefore selected five hundred holy mendicant monks who had mastered the *Tripitaka*, or Three Repositories. By them it was decided that the First Synod should be held at Rajagriha during the rainy

* Turnour, in Prinsep's Journal, vii. 512.

† Turnour, in Prinsep's Journal, vii. 513.

season, when the regular pilgrimages of the Buddhist monks were suspended.

3. At the full moon of the month of *Asarh* (1st July, 543 B. C.), the five hundred monks having assembled at Rajagriha, spent the whole of that month in the repairs of their *Vihars*, lest the heretics should taunt them,* saying, "the disciples of GOTAMA kept up their *Vihars* while their teacher was alive, but they have forsaken them since his death." With the assistance of *Ajátasatra*, Raja of Magadha, the Vihars were renewed; and a splendid hall was built for the assembly of the First Synod, at the mouth of the *Sattapanni* Cave, on the side of the *Webhára* Mountain. Five hundred carpets were spread around for the monks; one throne was prepared for the abbot on the south side, facing the north,† and another throne was erected in the middle, facing the east, "fit for the holy Buddha himself." Placing an ivory fan on this throne, the Raja sent a message to the assembly, saying, "Lords, my task is performed."

4. On the fifth of the increasing moon (first week of August), the monks, having made their meal, and having laid aside their refection dishes and extra

* Turnour, in Prinsep's Journal, vii. 516.

† *Sthavirásan*, the *ásan* or "seat" of the *Sthavira*. In the *Mahawanso*, p. 12, the position of this throne is exactly reversed. The pulpit, or *Dharmásan*, "throne of Dharma," was placed in the middle of the Assembly.—See Turnour, in Prinsep's Journal, vii. 517.

robes, assembled in the hall of the *Dharma Synod*, with their right shoulders bare. They ranged themselves according to their rank, each in his appropriate place; and the hall "glittered with the yellow robes" of the monks.

5. The Synod was opened with the rehearsal of the *Vináya*, superintended by Upáli, whom Buddha himself had pointed out as the most learned of all his followers in "religious discipline." Upáli mounted the *Dharmásan*, and with the ivory fan* in his hand, answered all the questions of Kásyapa regarding the Vináya, in which there was nothing to be added or omitted. During this examination, the whole of the assembled monks chanted the *Vináya*, passage by passage, beginning with "The holy Buddha in *Weranja* dwells." This ended, Upáli laid aside the ivory fan, and descended from the *Dharmásan*; and, with a reverential bow to the senior monks, resumed his own seat. Thus ended the rehearsal of *Vináya*.

6. For the rehearsal of *Dharma*, the assembled Bhikshus selected Ananda (the nephew and companion of Buddha)† who, with his right shoulder bare, and the ivory fan in his hand, took his seat on the pulpit

* The "jewelled fan," as a symbol of authority, is mentioned in the *Mahawanso*, p. 189; and it is *still used* by the chiefs of religious fraternities in Ceylon, on all state occasions.

† According to some, he was the son of Dotodana, the younger brother of Suddhodan, the father of Sákya.

of religion. He was then interrogated by Kásyapa on *Dharma*, beginning with the first words of *Sákya*, after his attainment to Buddhahood, under the Bodhi-tree at Bodhi-Gaya. These words are called—

7. Buddha's "Hymn of Joy:"*

> "Through a long course of almost endless beings
> Have I, in sorrow, sought the Great Creator.
> Now thou art found, O Great Artificer!
> Henceforth my soul shall quit this House of Sin,
> And from its ruins the glad Spirit shall spring,
> Free from the fetters of all mortal births,
> And over all desires victorious."

8. The examination ended with Buddha's last injunction to his disciples, given under the *Sál* tree at Kusinára.

> "Bhikshus! I now conjure you—earthly things
> Are transitory—seek eternal rest."

9. These rehearsals of *Vináya* and *Dharma* lasted for seven months, and were concluded at the beginning of March, 542 B. C., when it was announced that the religion of the "ten-power-gifted Deity" should endure for five thousand years.† This synod was known by different names; as the *Prathama-Sangham*, or First Synod, the *Pancha-Satika-San-*

* Turnour, in Prinsep's Journal, vi. 523. In this hymn the Supreme Being is twice called *Gahákáraka*, the "house-builder"—that is, the artificer or creator of the human house, or body.

† See Turnour, in Prinsep's Journal, vi. 527; and *Mahawanso*, p. 11. The "gifted with ten powers."

gham, or Synod of Five Hundred, and the *Stháviraka Sangham*, or Saints'-Synod, because all its members belonged to the higher grade of monks.*

10. From this time until the end of the long reign of Ajátasatra, 519 B. C., the creed of Buddha advanced slowly, but surely. This success was partly due to the politic admission of women, who, even in the East, have always possessed much secret, though not apparent, influence over mankind. To most of them the words of Buddha preached comfort in this life, and hope in the next. To the young widow, the neglected wife, and the cast-off mistress, the Buddhist teachers offered an honourable career as nuns. Instead of the daily indignities to which they were subjected by grasping relatives, treacherous husbands, and faithless lords, the most miserable of the sex could now share, although still in a humble way, with the general respect accorded to all who had taken the vows. The *Bhikshunis* were indebted to Ananda's intercession with Sákya for their admission into the ranks of the Baudha community; and they showed their gratitude by paying their devotions principally to his relics.†

* See *Fo-kwe-ki*, chap. xxv. note 11; and *Mahawanso*, chap. v. p. 20; and Turnour, in Prinsep's Journal, vi. 527. See also Csoma's Analysis of the Dulva, Trans. As. Soc. Bengal, vol. xx. p. 92.

† See Csoma's Analysis of the Dulva, Res. As. Soc. Bengal, vol. xx. p. 90; also *Fo-kwe-ki*, chap. xvi. p. 101. The *Pi-khicu-ni*, or Bhikshunis, at Mathura, paid their devotions chiefly

11. The dress of the Ascetics was the same both for males and females. It consisted of three garments, all of which were yellow; 1st, The *Sanghâti*, or kilt, fastened round the waist and reaching to the knees; 2nd, The *Uttara-Sanghâti*, a mantle, or cape, which was worn over the left shoulder, and under the right, so as to leave the right shoulder bare; 3rd, The *Antara-vâsaka*, an under vest or shirt for sleeping in.* The first and second garments are represented in many of the Sánchi bas-reliefs. They are

to the *Stupa* of *A-nan* (Ananda), because he had besought Buddha that he would grant to women the liberty of embracing ascetic life. The observances required from the nuns may be found in note 23, chap. xvi. of the *Fo-kwe-ki*. The female ascetic even of 100 years of age was bound to respect a monk even in the first year of his ordination.

* *Fo-kwe-ki*, chap. xiii. note 14. Csoma, Res. As. Soc. Bengal, p. 70, Analysis of the Dulva, states that these three pieces of clothing were of a *dark red* colour; but *yellow* is the colour everywhere mentioned in the Pâli annals. These two colours are still the outward distinctions of the Buddhists of Tibet; and therefore it is probable that the Buddhist dress may have been dark red in Sákya's time, and yellow during the reigns of Asoka and Milindu. According to the Chinese (*Fo-kwe-ki*, xiii. 10), the *Sanghâti* consisted of seven pieces; the *Uttara-Sanghâti*, of seven pieces; and the *Vâsaka* of five pieces: but the number of pieces is stated differently in another place (*Fo-kwe-ki*, c. viii. p. 5) as nine, seven, and five. The dress also is said to have been of divers colours; while in the Buddhist annals it is invariably mentioned as yellow. Ladies of wealth in Ladák have their petticoats formed of numerous perpendicular strips of cloth, of different colours, but generally red, blue, and yellow. See Plate XI. of this volume for these dresses.

all *barred* perpendicularly to represent their formation of separate pieces sewn together. In after times, the number of pieces denoted the particular school or sect to which the wearer belonged. The mantle or cape was scarcely deep enough to hide the right breasts of the nuns—at least it is so represented in the bas-reliefs; but as the same custom of baring the right arm and shoulder still prevails amongst the females of Middle Kanâwar, on the Sutlej, without any exposure of the breasts, I presume that their representation by the sculptor at Sánchi was only the result of his own clumsiness, as he could not otherwise show the difference of sex.

12. When engaged in common occupation, such as fetching water, felling wood, and carrying loads,* the monks are always represented without their mantles or capes. At religious meetings, as we have seen at the First Synod, and as they are represented throughout the Sánchi bas-reliefs, they wore all their robes. But during their contemplative abstraction in the woods, the devotees are represented naked to the waist, their upper garments being hung up inside their leaf-roofed houses. These devotees are, no doubt, the Γυμνηται of Kleitarchos; for Γυμνης or Γυμνητης does not mean a *naked* man, but only a

* All these acts are represented in the Sánchi bas-reliefs. The first is found on the left pillar of the eastern gateway, second compartment, inner face. The others are shown in the third compartment of the same pillar.

lightly-clad man; and with this signification it was applied to the *light-armed* soldier of Greece. These same devotees are, most probably, the Γυμνοσοφισται of other Greek writers; for the Buddhists were positively prohibited from appearing naked.*

13. All members of the Bauddha community, who led an ascetic life, were called *Srámana*, or *Srámanera*. They who begged their food from motives of humility were dignified with the title of *Bhikshu* and *Bhikshuni*, or male and female mendicants. The *Srámanas* are, beyond all doubt, the Γαρμάναι (or *Garmanes*) of Megasthenes, and the Πραμναι (or *Pramnæ*) of Kleitarchos;† while the *Bhikshus* are they who went about "begging both in villages and in towns."‡

14. Megasthenes divides the Garmanes or *Srámanas* into three classes, of which the most honourable were called *Hylobii*, Ὑλοβιοι. These are clearly the *Bodhisatwas* or *Arhatas*, the superior grade of monks, who, having repressed all human passions,

* See *Fo-kwe-ki*, chap. viii. n. 8; and chap. xvii. n. 21. See also Csoma's Analysis of the Dulva, Trans. As. Soc. Bengal, vol. xx. p. 70, where Sagama presents cotton cloths to the monks and nuns, because she had heard that they *bathed naked*.

† Strabo, xv. The Buddhist belief of the Γαρμάναι, Ὑλοβιοι, and Ιατρικοι, of Megasthenes, is proved by his mention of the fact that women were allowed to join some of them. Συμφιλοσοφεῖν δ'ενίοις καὶ γυναῖκας.

‡ Strabo, xv. Επαιτουντας καὶ κατὰ κώμας καὶ πόλεις.

were named *Alobhiya** or "without desires." They lived in the woods upon leaves and wild fruits. Several scenes of ascetic life in the woods are represented in the Sánchi bas-reliefs. On the lowermost architrave of the northern gateway (inside), there is a very lively scene of monks and nuns, who are occupied in various acts. Elephants and lions appear amongst the trees, and the king on horseback is approaching to pay them a visit.

15. The second class of Megasthenes are the Ιατρικοι, Iatriki, which is a pure Greek word, signifying physicians. But I have little doubt that this word is a corrupted transcript of *Pratyeka*, the name of the middle class of Buddhists. The Páli name is *Pachhé*, which seems fully as far removed from the original as the Greek term. The third class, or *Srávaka*, are represented by the mendicants before described.

16. According to Kleitarchos,† there were four classes of *Pramnæ:* the Ορεινοι, or Mountaineers; the Γυμνηται, or *Naked;* the Πολιτικοι, or *Townsmen;* and the Προσχωριοι, or *Rural.* All these are pure Greek names: but it is not unlikely that *Oreinos* is only a transcript of the Páli *Aran*‡ (Sanskrit *Ar-*

* Sanskrit, अलोभिय, from *a*, without, and *lobh*, desire. Compare the old latin *lubedo*, and the name of Queen *Lab*, of the Arabian nights.

† Strabo, lib. xv.

‡ On the stone box, extracted from No. 2 Tope at Sánchi, this title is twice written 𑀅𑀭𑀁, *Aran;* but in the inscriptions generally

hanta), which was a title of the *Bodhisatwas*, or first class of monks. As the Arhans, however, dwelt chiefly in caves cut out of the living rock, the name of "hill-men" is, perhaps, a marked one. *Gumnetes*, or "light-clad," was, as I have already shown, only another name for the *Arhan*, or hermit, who, during his fits of musing, wore nothing but the kilt, reaching from his waist to his knees. The name given to the next class, *Politikos*, seems only a copy, and a very near one, of the Sanskrit title *Pratyeka*, or "single understanding." But the Greek term may, perhaps, be descriptive of the duty of the Pratyeka; who, while he sought deliverance for himself, was not to be heedless of that of others.* As this duty would lead him to mingle with the people, and chiefly with those of the towns, the appellation of "townsman" seems intended to distinguish the *Pratyeka* from the "hill-monk" or *Arhan* of the rock-cut caves. The name of the last class of Kleitarchos has, I think, been slightly changed; and I would prefer reading Προσεχωρίους, the "listeners," instead of Προσχωριους, the "rural;" as the former is the literal

it is written either *Araha* or *Arahata*. The Sanskrit word is अर्हन्त, *Arhanta*. In Turnour's Annals (Prinsep's Journal, vi. 513), the *Sthåviras* who held the First Synod are called *Arahantá*. It is possible that the Greek name of Ορειvοι may be derived from the Sanskrit *Aranyaka*, a desert place, because the Bhikshus were directed to dwell in such a place. See *Fo-kwe-ki*, chap. viii. note 5, where the Chinese term *A-lan-yo* is used for *Aranyaka*.

* See *Fo-kwe-ki*, c. ii. n. 4.

translation of the Sanskrit *Sráwaka*, a "hearer," which was the designation of the lowest class of Buddhist monks. These identifications of the different classes of *Pramnæ* with those of the *Srámanas* are of the highest importance to the history of the Buddhist religion. For Kleitarchos was one of the companions of Alexander; and his distinct mention of these four classes of the Bauddha community proves that the religion of *Sákya Muni* had already been established in the Panjab at the period of Alexander's invasion. The worship of the Bodhi tree is also mentioned by Curtius, who says: "Deos putant, quidquid colere cœperunt; *arbores* maxime, quas violare capital est." —"They hold as gods whatever they have been accustomed to worship; but principally *trees*, which it is death to injure." *

17. The old Buddhists neatly distinguished the different grades of monks by the types of sheep, deer, and oxen.† The Sheep, when in flight, never looks back, and, like the *Sráwaka*, cares only for self-preservation. The Deer turns to look back on the following herd, and, like the *Pratyeka*, is mindful of others while he seeketh his own deliverance. The Ox, which beareth whatever burden is put upon him, is typical of the *Bodhisatwa*, who, regardless of himself, careth only for the salvation of others. But the last type is less happy than that of the sheep and deer; for the *Bodhisatwa*, who is supposed to have

* Curtius, viii. 9.

† *Fo-kwe-ki*, c. ii. n. 4.

earned his own deliverance,* could not possibly have any anxiety for himself,—whereas the most patient of laden oxen must yearn for his own freedom.

18. The Bodhisatwa is the highest grade of mortal being; for on his attaining Buddhahood he can no more be regenerated. He has then become absorbed into the Divine Spirit, and has altogether lost his individuality or separate existence. The Christian believes in the distinct immortality of each sentient being; and that each soul will for ever retain its personality in the world to come. But the Buddhist, while he admits the immortality of the soul, yet believes that its individuality will have an end; and that, after it has been linked to a mortal body for an unknown but finite number of existences, it will at last be absorbed into the Divine Essence from which it sprang; like as waters wafted from the ocean in clouds, return to it again in streams; or as the particles of sand, borne away from the mountains to the bottom of the sea, are again imbedded together and consolidated into rock.

19. There has been some misapprehension regarding the Buddhas and Bodhisatwas; the regeneration of the Grand Lama being considered as an exceptional case of a Buddha returning amongst mankind.† But

* Therefore in Tibet called བྱང་ཆུབ་, *Byang-chhub* or *Changchhub*, "the perfect."

† Mr. Hodgson, pp. 137, 138, truly calls the "divine Lamas" of Tibet, *Arhantas*; but he believes "that a very gross superstition has wrested the just notion of the character to its own use," and so created the "immortal mortals, or present palpable divinities of Tibet."

the explanation which I received in Ladák, which is the same as that obtained by Fra Orazio* in Lhasa, is simple and convincing. The Grand Lama is only a regenerated Bodhisatwa, who refrains from accepting Buddhahood, that he may continue to be born again and again for the benefit of mankind. For a Buddha cannot possibly be regenerated; and hence the famous epithets of TATHÁGATA, "thus gone," and SUGATA, "well gone," completely gone, or gone for ever.

20. The monk who aspired to the rank of *Bhikshu*, or Mendicant, was obliged to beg his daily food; which, when obtained, was to be divided into three portions—one for the hungry, the second for the birds and beasts, and the third for himself; and even this portion he was not allowed to eat after noon.† He was forbidden to ask for gold and silver; he was to prefer old and tattered raiment; and to eschew ornaments of all kinds. He was to dwell in the wilderness (*áranyaka*), or amongst the tombs (*smásánika*), where the daily sight of birds of prey, and of funeral pyres, would show him the instability of all earthly things, and the utter nothingness of the human body,

* Nouv. Jour. Asiat. t. xiv. p. 408. "Il Lama sempre sarà coll' istessa anima del medesimo *Ciang-c'iub*, oppure in altri corpi." Remusat was not aware of this fact when he stated "Les Lamas du Tibet se considèrent eux mêmes comme autant de divinités (Bouddhas) incarnées pour le salut des hommes." Journal des Savantes, Mai, 1831, p. 263.

† See the twelve observances, in the *Fo-kwe-ki*, c. viii. n. 5.

which endures but for a little time, and then passeth away into the five elements of which it is composed.

21. The equipments or indispensable necessaries of a *Bhikshu*, or Mendicant, consisted of (1) an "alms-dish" (*pátra*), or vessel for collecting the food which he begged; (2) an ewer, or "water-vessel" (*uda pátra*); (3) a stick or staff (*pinda*); (4) a razor; (5) a sewing needle; and (6) a waistband. The alms-dish was of common material, such as earthenware or iron. According to the Chinese it was a shallow vessel,* narrow at top and broader at bottom; but the vessel which was shown to me in Ladák as the exact copy of *Shakya-Thubba's* alms-dish was just the reverse, being broad at top and narrow at bottom; of a parabolic form, and of red earthenware coloured black. The shape was exactly the same as that of the *large* steatite vases from the Sonári and Andher Topes.† The colour was most probably black, because Fa Hian‡ states that the kingdom of KIE-CHHA (that is *Kha chan-pa*, "Snow-land," or Ladák §) possessed a stone bowl of the same colour as the alms-dish of Buddha. The thin earthenware bowls which have been found in the Topes of Bhojpur and Andher, are also black; those of the latter being of a glossy metallic lustre. The shapes of these vessels would, of

* See *Fo-kwe-ki*, c. xii. n. 8.

† See Plate XXIV. Fig. 3—and Plate XXIX. Fig. 8, of this volume.

‡ See *Fo-kwe-ki*, chap. v.

§ Ladák is still called *Kha-chan-pa*, or "Snow-land."

course, vary; but I have little doubt that the Bhojpur dishes, Nos. 4, 5, Pl. XXVII.,* and the Andher dish, No. 7, Pl. XXVIII., are the actual alms-dishes, or *pátras*, of the monks whose relics were deposited there. And I am the more inclined to this belief because the bowls which were inside these dishes seem to answer exactly as water vessels or ewers. A monk with his staff is represented on the leaden coin (Fig. 11, Pl. XXXII.) which was found in the Ganges at Patna, the ancient *Pátaliputra* or Palibothra.

* See also Plate XXVI. for the black earthenware vessels, extracted from No. 4 Tope, D., Bhojpur.

CHAPTER V.

CHRONOLOGY.

1. During the first century after Sákya's death, the Buddhist religion was perpetuated, if not extended, by a succession of learned monks. Of these great *Arhans* but little is related, and even that little is contradictory. During this period the great preceptors of the Buddhist Faith are so variously named, that it is clear the recorded succession cannot be continuous. Even Buddhaghoso gives two different successions* down to the third convocation.

I.	II.
1. Upáli.	1. Sáriputto.
2. Dásako.	2. Bhaddaji.
3. Sonako.	3. Kosyaputto.
4. Siggawo.	4. Siggawo.
5. Moggaliputto.	5. Moggaliputto.
	6. Sudatto.
	7. Dhammiko.
	8. Dásako.
	9. Sonako.
	10. Rewato.

* See Turnour's Páli Annals, in Prinsep's Journal, vi. 728, and vii. 791.

2. Mahánámo, the author of the Mahawanso, gives the succession agreeably to the first, and makes each *achárya* the disciple of his predecessor.* In the second list the places of the names have been completely changed, for we know that *Mogaliputra* should be the last, as he conducted the proceedings of the Third Synod. We know also that *Rewato* was the leader of the Second Synod. The other list is called by Buddhaghoso, the "unbroken succession of *Stháviras*," or elders of the faith. It seems likely, therefore, that it contains the names of *all* the teachers; while the first list gives only those of the most famous. By a new arrangement of the names of the longer list, the succession becomes complete and satisfactory.

3. But there is still one difficulty to be accounted for, in the assertion that all the leaders of the second synod had *seen* Buddha. This assertion, however, carries its own denial with it; for both *Buddhaghoso* and *Mahánámo* agree in stating that six of these leaders were the disciples of *Ananda*.† Now the companion of Buddha did not qualify himself as an *Arahat*, or holy teacher, until after the death of his patron. None of his disciples could, therefore, have seen Buddha. In the following amended list it must be remembered that *Sáriputra* died a few years before Buddha himself; and that *Upáli*, the com-

* *Mahawanso*, pp. 28, 29.

† *Mahawanso*, p. 19; and Turnour's Annals, in Prinsep's Journal, vi. 730.

piler of the *Vináya*, was one of the disciples of Buddha.

	SÁRIPUTRA.	B.C. 435.	KOSYAPUTRA.
B.C. 543.	UPÁLI and KÁSYAPA.	395.	SIGGAWO.
523.	BHADRAJI or ANANDA.*	355.	SUDATTA.
493.	DÁSAKA.	315.	DHARMIKA.
473.	SONAKA.	275.	MOGALIPUTRA.
453.	REWATA.	233.	MOGALIPUTRA'S DEATH.

4. This arranged list has the advantage of placing *Rewato* at the period of the Second Synod, instead of that of the Third Synod, which we know was conducted by *Mogaliputra*. If we could be positively certain of the accuracy of the date given for *Sákya's* death, in 543 B.C., the chronology might perhaps be arranged in a satisfactory manner. But, even in early times, there would seem to have been a difference of opinion as to the period of *Sákya's* death; for *Hwan-Thsang*, who travelled in India about 632-640 A.D., says that accounts differ† as to the year of the *Nirvâna* of Buddha. "Some make it 1,200 years ago, others more than 1,300; others again more than 1,500. There are some, too, that assure us that this event occurred about 900 years ago, and that 1,000 years are not yet fulfilled." The same uncertainty would seem to have prevailed even at an earlier date; for *Buddhaghoso*, speaking about the succession of teachers from the death of Buddha to

* *Bhadra* is a synonyme of *Ananda*.

† See *Fo-kwe-ki*, c. xxiv. n. 4.

the period of the Third Synod, says that the religion was perpetuated from Upáli to Mogaliputra, "*whatever the interval might be.*"* This expression clearly shows that there was a difference of opinion even in his day (A. D. 420) regarding the exact date of the death of Buddha. But as *Buddhaghoso* was a *Magadha* Bráhman, he must have known the Indian date of Sákya's *nirvâna*, and as this date coincides with that of the Burmese and Ceylonese chronicles, I do not well see how it can be set aside. It is a curious fact also that the *mean* of the dates, obtained by *Hwan-Thsang*, agrees within one year of the Burmese and Ceylonese dates. Thus the *average* interval which elapsed from Sákya's death to Hwan-Thsang's visit, is 1,180 years, from which, deducting 636, the mean period of Hwan-Thsang's travels, we obtain B. C. 544 for the death of Buddha. The coincidence is remarkable.

5. In this work I have made use of the generally received date of B. C. 543, as it appears to me to be sufficiently well established. In adopting this date, I am aware that a correction will be necessary for the Buddhistical date of Asoka's succession in the 218th year after the *Nirvâna*. But as the exact amount of this correction can be obtained from a source independent of the Buddhist annals, I think that every reliance may be placed upon its accuracy. Both Buddhaghoso and Mahánámo agree in making the accession of Nanda, King of Magadha, in the

* Turnour's Annals, in Prinsep's Journal, vi. 727.

118th year after the *Nirvâna*, or in B. C. 425; and they assign to him, and to his successors, the nine Nandas, a joint period of only forty-four years. Now all the Bráhmanical Purânas, in their accounts of the kings of Magadha, agree in stating that the Nandas reigned one hundred years. By using this amount as the correct one, we obtain *Anno Buddhæ* 218, or B. C. 325, as the date of Chandra Gupta's accession; thus making him a contemporary of Alexander the Great and Seleukos Nikator; a fact which has long since been proved by several passages from the Greek historians. The happy identification of Chandra Gupta with the Sandrocottos, or Sandrokuptos* of the Greeks was first made by Sir William Jones, and its accuracy has since been generally admitted: for the identification depends fully as much upon the similarity of their personal histories as upon the positive identity of their names.

6. It would be difficult, and, perhaps, impossible, to ascertain the real origin of this error of sixty-six years in the Buddhist annals; but I may hazard a guess that the pious and enthusiastic Buddhists of Asoka's age may in the first instance have adopted the date of his conversion as that of the true foundation of the Mauryan Dynasty, by omitting the Bráhmanical reigns of his father and grandfather, as well as the first four years of his own reign before his acknowledgment of Buddhism. Under this supposition, his inauguration would have been antedated

* Σανδροκυπτος is the spelling of Athenæus.

by sixty-six years, which is the exact amount of difference between the Buddhist and Bráhmanical lengths of reigns, as well as the precise amount of correction required to make the Buddhist chronology harmonise with that of the Greeks. In after times, when Buddhaghoso composed his commentaries on the Singhalese Annals, I suppose that the date of Asoka's inauguration was assumed to be correct, and that the duration of his father's and grandfather's reigns, and the first four years of his own reign, were deducted from the one hundred years of the Nandas. This supposition is rendered more probable by the valuable opinion of Mr. Turnour,* the learned translator of the Mahawanso, who points to the difference between the Bráhmanical and Buddhistical authorities, and more particularly to "some confusion in the durations assigned to the reigns of the ten Nandas," as the most likely causes of error. He was unable to account for the error himself; but he did "not despair of seeing the discrepancy accounted for in due course of time." He adopted the same fixed points, as I have done; namely, the Buddhist era of Sákya's death, in B. C. 543; and the Greek age of Sandrocottos, about 325 B. C.; but he was inclined to believe that the anachronism was the result of design and not of accident.

* See Prinsep's Journal, vi. 725.

CHAPTER VI.

SECOND SYNOD.

1. Having thus adjusted the chronology, I can proceed with confidence to the historical account of the progress of Buddhism. I have already given the proceedings of the First Synod, and some brief details of the manner of life and strict observances of the different grades of the Bauddha community. But these observances, which the early Buddhists practised with enthusiastic zeal, were found irksome by many of their successors. At the end of the first century after Sákya's death, a numerous fraternity of monks at *Vaisáli* asserted the lawfulness of the following indulgences*:—

1st. "*The preservation of salt in horn* for any period is lawful," instead of the seven days allowed by Sákya.

2nd. "*The allowance of two inches* in length of the shadow of the declining sun, to partake of food," which Sákya had prohibited after midday.

* See *Mahawanso*, p. 15; and Turnour's Páli Annals, in Prinsep's Journal, vi. 728, 729.

3rd. "*In villages it is allowable* to partake of indulgences" forbidden in the monasteries.

4th. "*Ceremonies in their own houses* may be performed by the monks," instead of in the public hall.

5th. "*Obtaining subsequent consent is allowable* for the performance of any act;" whereas, consent should always precede it.

6th. "*Conformity to example is allowable,*" that is, they might act as their superiors did; whereas no example was admitted as an excuse if the act was forbidden.

7th. "*The drinking of whey is allowable* after midday," which whey, as a component part of milk, had hitherto been forbidden.

8th. "*The drinking of toddy is allowable* because it looks like water:" whereas all fermented beverages were forbidden.

9th. "*Cloth-covered seats are allowable.*"

10th. "*Gold and silver may be accepted* in alms:" whereas the very use of the precious metals was prohibited; and more especially the begging for money.

2. When the tidings of this formidable heresy reached the revered Yasa, son of Kákandaka, he repaired to Vaisáli; and, in the midst of the assembled monks, he denounced the asking for money as unlawful. On this he was subjected to various indignities by the schismatic monks, from whose vengeance he escaped with difficulty to

*Kausambi.** Thence, despatching messengers to *Patheya* and *Ujain*, he collected a small body of orthodox monks, who with him waited upon the *Soreyan* teacher *Rewato*, the most famous in his day for depth of knowledge and holiness of character. The schismatics tried to influence Rewato with presents, but failing in this, they petitioned the king, who was at first inclined to favour them. But the king's intentions were changed by a dream, and he proceeded to Vaisáli in person, where, having heard both parties, he decided in favour of the orthodox, and directed them to take steps for the due maintenance of religion; after which he departed for his capital.

3. A stormy discussion then arose between the assembled monks, which was only quieted by the proclamation of the *Ubbáhika* rules for preserving order at religious assemblies. Eight of the most learned teachers, four from the eastern fraternities and four from the western, were selected by Rewato to examine into the lawfulness of the indulgences now claimed. These monks retired to a quiet spot to consider the matter; and, after much questioning amongst themselves, they decided upon rejecting the heresy. They accordingly returned to the assembly, and denounced the ten indulgences as unlawful; on which the penalty of "degradation" was awarded to the schismatic monks.†

* See *Mahawanso*, p. 16.

† The sentence of degradation was Sákya's punishment for all who caused dissensions amongst the Bauddha community. See

4. This sentence was afterwards confirmed by the Second Synod, which was composed of seven hundred monks selected by the learned *Revato*. The synod was held at the Bálukaráma Vihára at Vaisáli, under the protection of Kalasoka, King of Magadha. The proceedings, which were conducted by question and answer in the same manner as at the First Synod, occupied eight months. The *Vináya* and *Dharma* were again rehearsed; and the suppression of the ten indulgences was pronounced. This meeting was called the *Dwitiye Sangiti* or Second Synod, and the *Saptasatika*, or Synod of Seven Hundred.[1]

5. The English reader will be struck with the resemblance which this synod bears to that of a trial by jury, in which we have the hearing of both parties; the retirement of the jury to consider their verdict; and the last sentence of the judge.

[1] Csoma's Analysis of the Dulva, Researches As. Soc. Bengal, xx. 80. See Plate XXVII. Fig. 4, for a memorial of a degraded monk. The inscription is simply *patito* (Sanskrit *patitah*), the "degraded."

CHAPTER VII.

BUDDHIST SCHISMS.

1. The sentence of degradation which could be carried out against an individual, was powerless when pronounced against a multitude. The body of schismatic monks who had been degraded amounted to ten thousand: they were refractory, and would not submit; and their secession originated the *Mahásanghika* heresy, or schism of the "Great Union."* In the Tibetan books, the origin of this sect is referred to Kásyapa,† one of the disciples of Buddha; but the account of the Máhawanso is too circumstantial, and the orthodoxy of the great Kásyapa is too well established, for the admission of such an origin. There is indeed an heretical Kásyapa, whom the Chinese call *Fu-lan-na-Kia-she* (Purána Kásyapa?), "who repudiated all law—who recognised neither prince nor subject, neither father nor son—and who considered *void space*

* *Mahawanso*, c. xx.

† Csoma de Koros, in Prinsep's Journal, vii. 143. It is probable that his followers may have been the originators of the *Mahá-Sánghika* heresy.

as the Supreme Being."* But, as it would appear that this *Kásyapa* was a follower of the Bráhmanical Sánkhya philosopher Kapila, it is scarcely possible that he could have been the leader of the *Maha-Sanghika* Buddhists.

2. According to the Tibetans, the earliest systems of Buddhism were the *Vaibháshika* and the *Sautrantika*, both of which were dogmatical.† The followers of the former believed in everything written in the Scriptures, and would not dispute; those of the latter "proved everything on the authority of Scripture, and by argument."

3. The *Vaibháshikas* were divided into four principal classes, which bore the names of four of Sákya's disciples: *Ráhula*, *Kásyapa*, *Kátyáyana*, and *Upáli*. But it seems scarcely possible that these celebrated Buddhist leaders, the companions of Sákya, would have originated any schisms themselves. The more probable conclusion is, that they established schools, each instructing his own individual disciples, but all teaching one common doctrine. That these schools, though all professing the same belief at first, should, after the lapse of time, differ from each other, is but a natural result common to all human beliefs. In this view there seems nothing extraordinary in the

* *Fo-kwe-ki*, c. xvii. n. 21.

† Csoma, as quoted above. The Vaibháshikas were named from वि, *vi*, certainty, and भाषा, *bháshá*, speech; *i. e.* the dogmatics. The *Sautrantikas* adhered strictly to the *Sutras*, or Scriptures, from which they obtained their name.

principal sects of Buddhism being named after four of Sákya's chief disciples.

4. The four schools of the Vaibháshikas were—

1st. *Ráhula*, son of Sákya, a *Kshatriya*. The Ráhulakas were divided into four sects. They recited the Sutras in Sanskrit, and affirmed the existence of all things. Their religious garb was formed of from nine to twenty-nine narrow strips of cloth. Their distinctive mark was a "water-lily-jewel" (*utpala-padma*) and a tree-leaf, put together like a nosegay.*

2nd. *Kásyapa*, a Bráhman. His followers, who were divided into six sects, were called "the great community" (*Mahasanghika*). They recited the Sutras in a corrupt dialect; their religious garb was formed of from three to twenty-three strips of cloth; and they carried a shell as the distinctive mark of their school.

3rd. *Kátyáyána*, a Vaisya. His followers were divided into three sects; and they recited the *Sutras* in the vulgar dialect. Their religious garb was formed of from five to twenty-one strips of cloth; and they wore the figure of a wheel as a distinctive mark of their school. They were styled "the class that have a fixed habitation" (query *Sthápitaka*).

4th. *Upáli*, a Sudra. His followers were divided into three sects, and they recited the *Sutra* in the *Pisáchika* language. Their religious garb was formed of from five to twenty-one strips of cloth;

* See Csoma de Köros in Prinsep's Journal, vii. 143.

and bore a *sortsika* flower as a mark of their school. They were styled "the class honoured by many" (query the *Sabbattha* schismatics of the Mahawanso;* perhaps from *sambhram*, reverence, respect, and *atishay*, much.)

5. The *Sautrantikas* were divided into two sects, the names of which are not given.

6. Altogether, according to the Tibetans, there were eighteen sects of Buddhists; a number which agrees exactly with that of the Máháwanso. But this agreement extends farther than the mere coincidence of numbers; for two out of three names are the same as those of the Máháwanso.

The 1st schism of the Máháwanso is that which followed the silly speech of *Subhadra* to the assembled Bhikshus, shortly after the death of Buddha. It was immediately suppressed by Maha-Kásyapa at the First Synod; but, as it was listened to by the *Sthaviras*, it is named the *Sthavira*, or *Thera* schism.

The 2nd schism is that of the *Mahasanghika*, which it was the object of the Second Synod to suppress.

The 3rd schism was that of the *Gokulika*, and the 4th was the *Ekabbyohárika*.

The *Gokulika* schismatics gave rise to the (5th)

* *Mahawanso*, p. 21. The derivation of the term *Sabbattha* is uncertain; but the most probable etymology of *Sabba* is the Sanskrit *Sarvva*, "all." The name is of some importance, as it was most probably the original appellation of the Samarkand River, which the Greeks translated by Πολυτιμητος "the much-honoured."

Pannatti; the (6th) *Báhulika*; and the (7th) *Chetiya* heresies. The last no doubt originated at the great monastic establishment of *Chetiyagiri*, or *Sánchi*, near Bhilsa.

From these again proceeded the (8th) *Sabbattha* and the (9th) *Dhammaguttika* schisms (which arose simultaneously); and from the *Sabbattha* proceeded the (10th) *Kassapiya* schism. Lastly the (11th) *Sankantika* priesthood gave rise to the *Sutta* schism.

Six other schisms arose in India during the second century after the death of Buddha; namely the (13th) *Hemáwanta*; the (14th) *Rajagiriya*; the (15th) *Siddhatiki*; the (16th) Eastern and the (17th) Western *Seliya*; and lastly the (18th) *Wádariyá* schism.

"Thus there were eighteen inveterate schisms" (including the *Théra* schism, which was suppressed at the First Synod), of which seventeen arose in the second century after Buddha, or between B. C. 443 and 343. I have been thus particular in enumerating these different secessions from the Buddhist faith, because the very names are of value in pointing out the geographical extension of the religion to the *Hemáwanta*, or Himálayan region, and to *Chetiya*, or the present district of Bhilsa.

7. The gradual spread of the Buddhist faith is thus clearly and naturally developed. At Sákya's death in 543 B. C., the influence of his religion was confined to the central provinces of the Ganges, from the neighbourhood of Cawnpore and Agra to the head of the Delta. One hundred years later, at the

period of the Second Synod, the Dharma of Buddha had been preached throughout Malwa, from Chetiya (or Bhilsa)* to *Avanti* (or Ujain), and to the undefined *Patheya*, or "Western" country. Of the farther progress of the Buddhist religion, nothing is certainly known until Alexander's invasion; at which time *Bráhmans* and *Srámanas* would appear to have been held in about equal honour by the princes of the land.

* This identification of Chetiya or Chetiyagiri with the modern Bhilsa is proved by parallel passages in Mahánámo and Buddhaghoso, in which the former gives *Chetiya* and *Chetiyagiri*, where the latter gives *Wessanagara*, which is no doubt the old ruined city of Besnagar, two miles to the northward of Bhilsa.

CHAPTER VIII.

PROGRESS OF BUDDHISM.

1. *Chandra Gupta*, the founder of the Mauryan dynasty of Magadha, was the illegitimate son of the last Nanda by the beautiful, but low caste, *Murá*, from whom he obtained the name of *Maurya*. In the Mudra Rakshasa, a Sanskrit drama detailing his elevation, Chandra Gupta is frequently named Vrishala, a term said to be equivalent to *Sudra*; and as Nanda himself was the son of a Sudra woman, there can be little doubt that the celebrated *Maurya* family were of Sudra extraction. In the early part of his career, Chandra Gupta led a wandering life in the Panjáb;* and was, most probably, engaged with his fellow-countrymen in opposing Alexander. His chief adviser, the Bráhman Chánakya, was a native of Takshasila, or Taxila, the capital of the Western Panjáb; and it was in that country that Chandra Gupta first established himself by the complete expulsion of the Greek troops left by Alexander.†

* See Turnour, Introduction to the *Mahawanso*, p. xli., quoting the Tika or Commentary.

† Justin. xv. 4.—"Auctor libertatis Sandrocottus fuerat."

2. It would appear that the Greek colonists in the Panjáb had first been placed under, Philip, while the civil administration of the country remained in the hands of its native princes, Taxiles and Porus. After wards, on the murder of Philip by the mercenary soldiers, Alexander* directed *Eudemos* and *Taxiles* to govern the country until he should send another deputy. It is probable, however, that they continued to retain the charge; for after Alexander's death in B. C. 323, *Eudemos* contrived to make himself master of the country by the treacherous assassination of king Porus.† Some few years later, in B. C. 317, he marched to the assistance of Eumenes, with 3,000 infantry and 5,000 cavalry, and no less than 120 elephants. With this force he performed good service at the battle of Gabiene. But his continued absence gave the Indians an opportunity not to be neglected; and their liberty was fully asserted by the expulsion of the Greek troops and the slaughter of their chiefs.‡ Chandra Gupta was the leader of this national movement, which ended in his own elevation to the sovereignty of the Panjáb. Justin attributes his success to the assistance of *banditti*;§ but in this I think he has been misled by a very natural mistake; for the *Arattas*, who were the

* Arrian, Anabasis, vi. 27. † Diodorus, xix. 5.

‡ Justin. xv. 4.—"Præfectos ejus occiderat;" again, "Molienti deinde bellum adversus præfectos Alexandri."

§ Justin. xv. 4.—"Contractis *latronibus* Indos ad novitatem regni solicitavit."

dominant people of the Eastern Panjáb, are never mentioned in the Mahábhárata without being called robbers.* They were the *republican* defenders of Sangala, or Sákala, a fact which points to their Sanskrit name of *Aráshtra*, or "kingless." But though their power was then confined to the Eastern Panjáb, the people themselves had once spread over the whole country.† They were known by the several names of *Báhika*, *Járttika*, and *Takka*; of which the last would appear to have been their true appellation; for their old capital of *Taxila*, or *Takka-sila*, was known to the Greeks of Alexander; and the people themselves still exist in considerable numbers in the Panjáb hills. The *ancient* extent of their power is proved by the *present* prevalence of their alphabetical characters, which, under the name of *Tákri*, or *Tákni*, are now used by all the Hindus of Kashmir and the northern mountains, from Simla and Subathu to Kábul and Bámiyan. On these grounds I venture to identify the banditti of Justin with the *Tákkas*, or original inhabitants of the Panjáb, and to assign to them the honour of delivering their native land from the thraldom of a foreign yoke.

* Lassen, Pentapot. Indica.—"Aratti profecto latrones," and "Bahici latrones." The Sanskrit name is *Arashtra*, the "kingless," which is preserved in the Adraistæ of Arrian, who places them on the Rávi.

† "Ubi fluvii illi quini * * * ibi sedes sunt Arattorum." —Lassen, Pentapot Indica, from the Mahábhárat.

3. This event occurred most probably about 316 B. C., or shortly after the march of Eudemos to the assistance of Eumenes. It was followed immediately by the conquest of Gangetic India;* and in 315 B. C., the rule of Chandra Gupta was acknowledged over the whole northern peninsula, from the Indus to the mouths of the Ganges. The authorities differ as to the length of Chandra Gupta's reign, which some make thirty-four years, and others only twenty-four.† This difference may, perhaps, have originated in two distinct reckonings of the date of his accession; the one party counting from the death of Nanda Mahapadma, in B. C. 325; and the other party from the conquest of India, in B. C. 315. Some assumption of this kind is clearly necessary to reconcile the different authorities; unless, indeed, we take the only alternative of adopting the one and of rejecting the other.

4. At this period the capital of India was *Pátaliputra* or *Palibothra*, which was situated on the *Ganges*, at the junction of the *Erranaboas* or *Aläos* River.‡ The former name has already been identified with the Sanskrit *Hiranyabáhu*, an epithet

* Justin. xv. 4.—"Indiam possidebat."

† The Mahawanso gives thirty-four years, the Dipawanso and the Vayu Purána give only twenty-four years.

‡ Arrian, Indica, x., gives the Erranaboas; and Strabo, xv., uses the following words,—*και του αλλου ποταμου*, for which I propose to read—*και τοῦ Αλᾶου ποταμου*. The change is very slight from Λ to Α. The Greek text has *τοῦ* and not *του*.

which has been applied both to the *Gandak* and to the *Son*. But the latter name can only refer to the *Hi-le-an* of the Chinese travellers, which was to the north of the Ganges, and was therefore undoubtedly the Gandak. Indeed, this river still joins the Ganges immediately opposite to *Patna*—that is, "the city," or metropolis, as its proper name (*patana*) implies, while the junction of the Son is some nine or ten miles above Patna. But as there is good reason for believing that the *Son* once joined the Ganges at Bákipur or Bankipur, immediately above Patna, it is quite possible that the *Erranaboas* may have been intended for the *Son*, and the *Aläos* for the Gandak. According to Megasthenes, Palibothra was eighty *stadia*, or nearly nine miles in length; and fifteen *stadia*, or one mile and two-thirds, in breadth. It was surrounded with a deep ditch; and was enclosed by lofty *wooden* walls, pierced with loop-holes for the discharge of arrows.*

5. Towards the close of the 4th century before our era, when Alexander's successors were at peace with each other, the great Seleukos, having consolidated his own dominions, turned his arms towards the East, with the intention of recovering the Indian provinces of Alexander.

6. But the plains of Northern India were no longer divided amongst a set of petty chiefs, whose

* Arrian, Indica, x., and Strabo, xv.; both quoting Megasthenes. Strabo has ξύλινον περίβολον.

gallant but useless resistance had scarcely checked the great Macedonian's advance. For the Mauryan prince, who now wielded the sceptre of the East, could bring into the field that vast army of six hundred thousand men,* whose very numbers had before daunted even the stout hearts of the soldiers of Alexander. The main object of this expedition was therefore impossible. Where a successful advance cannot be made, an honourable retreat becomes a decided advantage; and this Seleukos secured for himself, by yielding to Chandra Gupta the doubtful allegiance of the provinces to the west of the Indus for a valuable present of five hundred elephants.† These friendly relations were cemented at the time by a matrimonial alliance, and were afterwards continued by the embassy of Megasthenes to the Indian court at Palibothra.

7. Chandra Gupta died in 291 B.C., and was succeeded by his son *Vindusára* or *Bimbisára;* to whose court a second Greek embassy was sent either by Seleukos, or by his son Antiochus Soter. Nothing is known of the object or results of this embassy; but the ambassador, *Daimachos,* was considered by Strabo to be the most "lying" of all the Greek historians of India.‡ He calls the king *Allitrochades,* or *Amitrochates,* which Professor Lassen supposes to be the Sanskrit *Amitraghâta,*

* Plutarch, Life of Alexander.

† Strabo, xv.; and Plutarch.

‡ Strabo, xv., ψευδολογος.

or "foe-killer." The difference between the Greek name of Amitrochates and the native one of Bindusára, proves nothing more than that the Hindu princes delighted in a variety of names. For, though the Buddhist authorities agree with the Vishnu Purána in calling this king Bindusára, yet each of the other Puráns gives him a different name. Thus he is called *Bhadrasára* in the *Váyu*, *Várisára* in the Bhágavata, and apparently *Vrihadratha* in the Motsya Purána. If we might read *Varisăra*, the "foe-killing arrow," instead of *Várisára*, then the name of Amitraghàta, or "arrow to his enemies," might be considered as synonymous with that of the Váyu Purána.

8. But in spite of the difference of names, there can be no doubt of the identity of the persons; for Strabo particularly states that Amitrochates was the son of Sandrokottos. A third Greek embassy is mentioned by Pliny,* who states that the ambassador Dionysius was deputed by Ptolemy Philadelphus, and that he remained for some time at the Indian court; but as the name of the king is not given, and as Ptolemy's long reign extended from B. C. 285 to 246, we are left in doubt whether Dionysius paid his respects to Bindusára or to his son Asoka.

9. About the middle of his reign (B. C. 280), Bindusára deputed his son Asoka to quell a serious

* Pliny, Hist. Nat. vi. 17.—"Dionysius a Philadelpho missus."

revolt in the district of Taxila.* The people came forth to meet him with offerings, and to assure him that they were not displeased with the king, but with the minister who oppressed them; on which Asoka made his entry into the town with great pomp. He then conquered the kingdom of the *Swasas*, or *Khasas*, who were most probably the people of Kashmir.† For the Khasas were the early inhabitants of Persia and of Northern India before the Arian immigration, which drove them from the plains to the hills, where they still exist in great numbers, and now form a considerable part of the population of that vast chain of mountains which stretches from the banks of the Helmand to the Brahmaputra. In Manu's Hindu Code they are coupled with the *Daradas* or *Dards*; and in

* Burnouf, Introd. à l' Hist. du Buddhisme Indien, pp. 361, 362.

† The difference between the *Khasas* and *Kusas*, is about the same as that between the "men of Kent" and the "Kentish men." The *Kásmiri* pandits repudiate all connection with the *Khasas*, and even so might an English *Lander* deny his ancestor the *Lavandier*. The difference of spelling only shows the influence of Brahmanism, or rather of Hinduism, which changed the Khasas of *Kha-che* (the Tibetan name for Kashmir) into descendants from Kásyapa. The connection between the names is shown by the story which makes *Kásyapa* and *Khasá* the parents of the Imps and Goblins. As well might the *Oggs* and *Hogges* repudiate their real ancestors the swineherds, and claim descent from the King of Basan. But even this would be more probable, for King *Og* was an actual historical personage, whereas *Kásyapa* Muni (according to the Brahmans) was the father of *gods* and men.

the Mahábhárat they are classed with the *Gándháras*, *Arattas*, and *Sindhu-Sauviras*. Professor Lassen has doubted the accuracy of Professor H. H. Wilson's reading of Khasa in the Mahábhárat; but this reading is supported, as M. Burnouf observes, by the above mention of the Swasas or Khasas as neighbours of the Taxilans; and is fully confirmed by a copy of the Mahábhárat in the possession of a Brahman at Thánesar.

10. Shortly after the reduction of Taxila, the successful Asoka was appointed to the government of Ujain, the capital of Malwa. Asoka set forth to assume charge of his government in about 274 B. C. On his way he tarried some time at *Chaityagiri* or *Baisnagara*,* situated at the junction of the Besali River with the Betwa, two miles to the northward of Bhilsa. Here he gained the affections of Devi, the lovely daughter of the *Sreshti* or "chief man" of the place. A year afterwards she bore him a son named *Mahendra*, and one year later a daughter called *Sanghámitra*, both of whom became celebrated in after times as

* See Turnour's Pali Annals, Prinsep's Journal, vii. 930, where Buddhaghoso calls the city *Wessanagara*, which Mahánámo calls *Chetiya* and *Chetiyagiri* (Mahawanso, p. 76). The story is the same in both authors; and as the ruins of the old city of *Baisnagar*, or Besnagar, two miles to the north of Bhilsa, are situated on the high road between Pátaliputra and Ujain, there can be no doubt of the identification. *Wessanagara* was the city; *Chetiyagiri* was the hill of the great *Chaitya* at Sánchi, about four miles to the south of the city.

the introducers of the Buddhist religion into Ceylon.

11. Of Asoka's administration of Ujain little is known, save the establishment of a celebrated place of punishment, which was significantly named *Hell,** because criminals were therein subjected to the same tortures in this life, as have been generally accorded to the wicked in the next. During Asoka's government of Ujain, the people of Taxila again revolted against *Bindusára,* who deputed his eldest son *Susíma* to reduce them; but the prince was unsuccessful.† During his absence the king fell grievously sick, and directed his ministers to send Prince Asoka to Taxila, and to recall Prince Susíma to court, that he might establish him on the throne. But the ministers, who were friendly to Asoka, deceived the king by a false report of his illness, and at the same time informed the young prince that his father was on his death-bed. Asoka instantly hurried from Ujain to his father's palace at Pátaliputra; but the sudden appearance of his younger son showed the king that he had been deceived; and in the midst of a fit of passion, he burst a blood-vessel and died. This event happened in the year 263 B. C., when Bindusára had reigned twenty-eight years.

* *Fo-kwe-ki,* c. 32, for Fa Hian's mention, and p. 393, for Hwan Thsang's account of "Hell."

† Burnouf, Buddhisme Indien, p. 363.

CHAPTER IX.

REIGN OF ASOKA.

1. IMMEDIATELY on his father's death Asoka seized the government, and gave orders for the slaughter of all his brothers, save *Tishya*, who was born of the same mother. His eldest brother, Prince *Susíma*, who had marched against him from Taxila, was cut off by an artifice; and the Mauryan dynasty was thus reduced to the single family of Asoka; who, finding himself safe from the usual jealousies and intrigues of relatives, gave up his whole energies to the achievement of military glory. In the short space of four years he succeeded in reducing the whole of Northern India, from the mountains of Kashmir to the banks of the Narbadda, and from the mouth of the Indus to the Bay of Bengal;* and

* *Nepál* was probably included in the conquests of Asoka; for the kings of Tibet trace their origin to the *Lichhavis* of Vaisáli; and *Khri-tsanpo*, the first king, is said to have taken refuge in Tibet about 250 B. C.—that is, in the reign of Asoka. See Csoma's List of Tibetan Kings in Prinsep's Useful Tables, p. 131; and also *Fo-kwe-ki*, c. xxiii. n. 6.

India, perhaps for the first time, was brought under the control of one vigorous and consolidated government.

2. During the first three years of his reign, the mind of Asoka was fully occupied with views of worldly ambition and personal aggrandizement; but in the fourth year, when all India was at peace, his restless activity found a more pleasing occupation, and a more lasting employment, in the acquisition of the Buddhist faith. Like his father Bindusára, he had been brought up as a worshipper of Agni and Surya, of Indra and Váyu; and, like him, he showed his respect for the Brahmans by feeding sixty thousand of them daily.* But Asoka was of a passionate and impulsive temperament; and when he became a convert to the Buddhist faith, he embraced it with all the fervid zeal of his ardent nature; and though, like Alexander, he may once have wept that no more worlds were left for him to conquer, he now found that he had still himself to subdue. The task, though difficult, seemed not impossible; and the royal convert, who had before been called *Chand-Asoka*, or "Asoka the Furious," now submitted himself to the outward discipline of the Buddhist faith, and at last became so distinguished a follower of *Dharma*, that he acquired the more honourable title of *Dharm-Asoka*, or "Asoka the Virtuous."

* *Mahawanso*, c. 23; but *Buddhaghoso* has the more moderate number of eight thousand.—See Turnour's Páli Annals in Prinsep's Journal, vi. 731.

3. The first proof which Asoka gave of his conversion to Buddhism was the dismissal of the sixty thousand Brahmans, in whose stead an equal number of *Srámanas*, or Buddhist ascetics, were daily fed. His next act was the distribution of the relics of Sákya to all the chief cities of India. These relics had been collected by Ajátasatra, at the instance of Kásyapa, and were deposited together in one large *Stupa* at Rájagriha. But the king had now determined to manifest his zeal for the faith of Buddha, by the erection of eighty-four thousand *Vihárs*, or monasteries, in honour of the eighty-four thousand discourses of Buddha.* As this precise number has always been deemed a fortunate one both by Brahmans and Buddhists, it may be looked upon as the common expression for any very large number.† These Vihárs are said to have been erected in eighty-four thousand different cities. I would reject the thousands, and read simply eighty-four cities and eighty-four Vihárs. The building zeal of Asoka is fully confirmed by the Chinese pilgrim Hwan-Thsang, who travelled through India in the middle of the 7th century of our era. At different places on his route, from Anderáb, beyond the sources of the Kabul River, to Conjeveram, in the south of India, and from Pitoshilo, in the delta of the Indus, to Tamluk, at the mouth of the Ganges, this pilgrim saw upwards of

* *Mahawanso*, p. 26.

† See Sir H. M. Elliott's Supplementary Glossary of Indian Terms for a number of proofs.

fifty large Topes, besides numerous Vihárs, all of which were attributed to Asoka. This account agrees with the statements of the Maháwánso, which ascribe to Asoka the building of splendid Chaityas on all the spots rendered memorable by the acts of Buddha.* All these buildings were completed within three years.

4. This great king was not, however, content with the erection of stately buildings for the service of his religion, but, like a true Buddhist, while he sought the achievement of his own salvation, he wished for the eternal happiness of others. With this view he is said to have promulgated eighty-four thousand royal edicts† for the extension of *Dharma*. Numbers of these edicts, engraved on massive rocks, and on stone pillars, still remain in different parts of India to attest the general accuracy of the Buddhist annals. The oldest edicts are contained in the rock inscriptions, which have been found at Dhauli in Kuttack, at Girnar in Gujrat, and at Kapurdigiri near Peshâwar. As these three places were the most distant points in Asoka's dominions, they were no doubt specially selected as the fittest positions for the inscription of these important religious ordinances.

5. In all these edicts the promulgator names himself "PRIYADARSI, the beloved-of-the-Devas." This appellation, which is evidently only a title, has led

* *Mahawanso*, p. 34.

† Burnouf, Buddhisme Indien, p. 403, quoting the Asoka Avadána.

Professor H. H. Wilson to doubt the generally accepted identification of Asoka with the Priyadarsi who published the edicts.* The learned professor rests his scepticism on the following grounds, which it is necessary to examine in detail, out of respect for one who has rendered such distinguished services in every branch of Indian literature.

1st. " It is doubtful whether the edicts of Priyadarsi have any connection with Buddhism, the meaning of the inscriptions, to say the least, being equivocal." Again, " There is nothing in the injunctions promulgated that is decidedly and exclusively characteristic of Buddhism."†

2nd. The total omission of any allusion to Buddha himself by any of his appellations, *Sugata*, *Tathágata*, *Gautama*, or *Sákya*.‡

3rd. The identification (of Asoka with Priyadarsi) rests upon a passage in the Dipawanso, "a work of rather doubtful character," which is besides a composition of the fourth century of our era.‡

4th. "It seems very inexplicable, why in none of the inscriptions his own appellation Asoka, or Dharmasoka, should ever be mentioned."§

5th. Chronological difficulties of which it is not easy to dispose.‖

* Journal of the Royal Asiatic Society, xii. 236.

† Ibid. p. 288.

‡ Ibid. p. 241.

§ Ibid. p. 243.

‖ Ibid p.. 244.

6. The first objection appears to me to rest entirely upon the translation of a single word, *Dharma*, which, as James Prinsep truly observed, is the "keystone" of all the edicts. By translating *Dharma*, wherever it occurs, sometimes as "piety," or "religion," and sometimes as "morality," or "virtue," the whole scope and purport of the edicts of Priyadarsi are entirely lost sight of. These ordinances, on all the pillars, and on the rocks, both at Girnar and at Kapurdigiri, are styled by the king himself, *dhamalipi*, or "edicts-on-Dharma." James Prinsep translates this word as "religious edict;" and Professor Wilson omits all mention of *dharma*, and simply calls the inscription an "edict;" but to obtain the full force and meaning of the term, it should be rendered as I have given it above, "edict or ordinance on *Dharma*," that is on the "religious law" of BUDDHA. If the word *Dharma* had occurred but once or twice in these inscriptions, it might have been rendered by any one of the ordinary meanings given above; but in the rock inscriptions it occurs no less than thirty-seven times; and in combinations with other terms which prove it to be wholly and emphatically Buddhistical. Thus, in the 5th Tablet, we have *Dhamma-vádhiya*, which Prinsep translates "increase of religion," and Professor Wilson, "augmentation of virtue," but which ought to be rendered "advancement of Dharma"—that is, the propagation of the Religious Law of Buddha. This is still more clearly shown in the opening of the 11th Tablet, in

which Dharma has been translated by both as "virtue."*

> " *Devánampiyo* PIYADASI *rája evam áha :*
> *násti etárisam dánam yárisam Dhamma-dánam*
> *Dhammasanstavo va Dhammasam vibhago*
> *va Dhammasam bandho va.*"

"Thus saith King PRIYADARSI, the beloved of the Devas:—There is no gift like the gift of *Dharma*; whether it be knowledge of *Dharma*, or inheritance of *Dharma*, or close union with *Dharma*."

And towards the end of the same Tablet:—

> " *idam sádhu, idam katavyam sotathá*
> *karni—lokavasa árádha hoti*
> *parato vá anantam punam*
> *bhavati tena Dhammadánena.*"

"This is well: this should be done: (and for him) who doeth thus, there is happiness in this world; and everlasting holiness hereafter is obtained by this gift of *Dharma*."

7. Other passages of similar force and value might be quoted at length; but it will be sufficient to mention that the whole of *Priyadarsi's* edicts are dedicated to the attainment of one object, *Dharma-varddhana*, the "advancement of *Dharma*." For this purpose he directed that "men learned in *Dharma*" should be appointed to "establishments of *Dharma*," to preach "sermons on *Dharma*," to

* Journal of Royal Asiatic Society, xii. p. 213.

the "people united in *Dharma*."* These doctors of *Dharma* were also directed to penetrate amongst the unbelievers, to mix with high and low, rich and poor, hermits and worldly men, for the purpose of instructing them in the perfect observance of *Dharma*.†

8. Throughout all these edicts, both on the pillars and on the rocks, Priyadarsi announces his own adherence to *Dharma* (or the law of Buddha), and his belief that the love of Dharma (*Dhammakáma*) would continue to increase. He inculcates that Dharma consists in the strict observance of moral duties, in the performance of pious acts, and in the entire subjection of the passions;‡ and he declares that Dharma will be advanced by the prohibition (*ahinsa* or *avihinsa*) against taking life.§ Dharma is in fact the only key by which the meaning of these inscriptions can be unlocked; and its frequent and emphatic use, throughout these royal edicts, shows that their promulgator was a firm and zealous adherent of *Dharma*, or the law of Buddha. Asoka was the same; for which reason the people called him *Dharmasoka*.

* Prinsep's Journal, vi. 602. *Dhamma-mahámatá*, "learned men, or doctors of Dharma." *Dhamma-thabavi*, "establishments-for-Dharma." *Janam-Dhammayutum*, "people-joined-by-Dharma." *Dhamma-sávánáni*, "lectures-on-Dharma."

† *Dhammápadána*, perfect observance of Dharma; from *apadán* well-doing, or complete performance.

‡ Prinsep's Journal, vi. 582.

§ Prinsep's Journal, vi. 608.

9. I may observe here that Mr. Turnour, the translator of the Páli Annals of Ceylon, appears to have felt the full force and meaning of *Dharma*, which he *always* gives in its Páli form of *Dhammo*. Had he translated it simply as "religion," the true sense of many passages would have been utterly lost. But he was living in a Buddhist country, and in daily intercourse with Buddhist monks, and he therefore knew and appreciated the peculiar significance of the term; which stamps the follower of *Dharma* as an undoubted Buddhist, or observer of the "Religious Law" of Buddha.

10. Professor Wilson's second objection is the omission of any mention of Buddha himself, by any of his well-known appellations. But this is met by the frequent and emphatic use of *Dharma*, the name of the second person of the orthodox Buddhist Triad. *Bhagaván* is also twice mentioned in the 13th Tablet of the Kapurdigiri inscription; but this title, although very commonly used by the Buddhists, is only an epithet for the Supreme Being, and *might* therefore have been used by the Brahmans of those days as well as by the Buddhists. The common Brahmanical term, however, is *Bhagavat*, and I believe that the use of Bhagaván is almost peculiar to the Buddhists. But though the omission of Buddha's own name in these inscriptions cannot, perhaps, be now explained, yet the Buddhistical faith of Priyardarsi is placed beyond all doubt by his mention of *Buddha*, *Dharma*, and *Sangha*, the three

members of the orthodox Buddhist Triad, in the short rock inscription found at Bhabra, near Jaypur.*

11. Professor Wilson's third objection is the asserted identification of Asoka with Priyadarsi, which rests upon a passage in the Dipawanso, "a work of doubtful character and of comparatively modern date." Regarding the authenticity of the Dipawanso, I hold an opinion entirely different to Professor Wilson's. His doubts of its genuineness were, I presume, based on the statement of Mahánámo, which Mr. Turnour has brought prominently forward,† that "the *Páli Pittakattaya* and its *atthakathá* (or Commentaries), had been *orally* perpetuated" previous to B. C. 88-76. If this statement were true, it is clear that *all* events recorded previous to that date could only be regarded as so many traditions. It is quite possible that the monks may have made a mystery of their learning to increase the reverence of the people, by asserting that all the doctrines which they taught had been handed down orally; and this assertion might have gradually grown into a belief which in Mahánámo's time nobody disputed. But it is much more likely that the assertion is a mere error of the text; for it is most fully contradicted by another statement of Mahánámo,‡ which has every appearance of truth to recommend it to our implicit belief. According to

* Jour. As. Soc. Bengal, ix. 618.

† *Mahawanso*, c. 33, p. 207.

‡ *Mahawanso*, c. 37, p. 251.

this statement, the Singhalese *Atthakatha* were composed by *Mahendra* (the son of Asoka), who had *previously* consulted the discourses of Buddha, and the dissertations and arguments of *Sáriputra* and others. But, in addition to this counter statement, we have the testimony of Buddhaghoso,* who translated the Singhalese Atthakatha into Páli, between A. D. 410—432. He states distinctly, that for his own work he had availed himself of the Atthakatha, which had been in the first instance authenticated by the five hundred *Arahanta* at the First Synod, and subsequently at the succeeding synods; and which were afterwards brought to *Sihala* (or Ceylon) by the holy *Mahendra*, and "translated into the *Sihala* language for the benefit of the people."

12. This account is older by some seventy years than that of Mahánámo, the author of the Mahawanso; and as Buddhaghoso was a Magadha Brahman, he must have known that the Buddhist scriptures had been compiled by the disciples of Buddha, immediately after the meeting of the First Synod. A *Páli* version of the *Atthakatha*, or Commentaries, is mentioned as having been studied by *Tisso Mogaliputra*, while he was a Sámanera, in the early part of the third century before our era.†

13. There is, besides, the most convincing internal evidence in the Maháwánso of the correctness of the

* Turnour's Páli Annals, in Prinsep's Journal, vi. 510.

† Buddhaghoso, quoted by Turnour in Prinsep's Journal, vi. 731.

above statement of Buddhaghoso, in the fact, that no mention whatever is made of Indian affairs after the advent of Mahendra. This proves, in my opinion, that all the knowledge of Indian history which the Singhalese possessed had been derived from Mahendra: a conclusion which is supported by the direct testimony of Buddhagoso.

14. The fourth objection, urged by Professor Wilson against the identity of Asoka and Priyadarsi, is the non-occurrence of the name of Asoka or Dharmasoka in any of the inscriptions. The same objection might be offered to the identity of Prince Salim and Jahángir, and of Prince Kurram and Sháh-Jehán. In fact, it is a common practice in the East for a prince to assume a new name upon his accession to the throne; and such we know was the custom in Asoka's own family. His grandfather had three names,—1st, a birth name, which is not given, but which was perhaps *Vrishala*; 2nd, a local name, *Palibrothes*, or lord of *Pátaliputra*; and 3rd, a royal name, *Chandra Gupta*, which he assumed on his accession to the throne.* Asoka's brother, named *Vitásoka*, was also called *Tishya*; his son *Kunála* had a second name, *Dharma-Varddhana*;† and his daughter, *Sanghamitrá*, was also named *Sumitra*.‡ At that period it was therefore the common custom, for a prince at least, to have two

* Megasthenes in Strabo, xv.

† Burnouf's Buddhisme Indien.

‡ *Mahawanso*, p. 121.

names; and if Asoka, as the Dipawanso explicitly states, bore also the title of Priyadarsi, it is evident that the inscriptions which gave him this title would omit all mention of his original name of Asoka. In the edicts promulgated by himself, he is mentioned by the name which he had assumed; but in the annals written by others he is called by that name which he had always borne, and by which he was best known to the people. An almost similar case is that of the Roman Emperor Elagabalus, or Bassianus, who assumed the name of Antoninus, by which he is always mentioned on coins and inscriptions; while the historians and annalists invariably call him Elagabalus.

15. But the statement of the Dipawanso is most happily confirmed by the Bhabra edict, from which we learn that Priyadarsi, the worshipper of Buddha, Dharma, and Sangha, was the Raja of Magadha at the period of the Third Synod.* Now we know, from the Buddhist annals, that this synod took place in the reign of Asoka Maurya, the Buddhist King of Magadha. The statement is further confirmed by a fact mentioned by the Chinese pilgrim Fa-Hian;

* Jour. As. Soc. Bengal, ix. 618. The opening words are "*Piyadasi-rája Magadha-sangham abhiváde-mánam cha,*" or "Raja Priyadarsi, saluting the Synod of Magadha, declareth." This most valuable document should be translated critically; for the version already published renders the above passage as follows: —"Piadasa Raja, unto the *multitude* assembled in Magadha saluting him, speaks (thus).

who, writing in A.D. 400, attributes the erection of a Lion-pillar at Samkissa to Asoka.* "The king (Ayu or Asoka) felt sensible of a great increase of his faith and veneration. He caused therefore a chapel to be built. . . . . Behind the chapel was erected a pillar, 30 cubits high. . . . . Thereon was placed a Lion. . . . . The interior and the exterior were polished and resplendent as crystal." Now, it is remarkable that the pillars which bear Priyadarsi's inscriptions have all *polished* shafts, about 30 cubits in height, of which some are still surmounted by Lions. The chain of evidence is therefore complete; and there can no longer be any doubt of the identity of Asoka Maurya with the Priyadarsi of the inscriptions.

16. The minor difficulties of chronology, which form Professor Wilson's last objection, are easily disposed of; for they seem to me to have arisen solely from the erroneous assumption that Priyadarsi must have been a contemporary of Antiochus the Great. In the Girnar and Kapurdigiri rock inscriptions, King Priyadarsi mentions the names of five Greek princes who were contemporary with himself. Of these, four have been read with certainty—Antiochus, Ptolemy, Antigonus, and Magas; and the fifth has been conjectured to be Alexander. James Prinsep, who first read these names, assigned them to the following princes:—

* Fo-kwe-ki, c. xiii.

ANTIOCHUS II.	*Theos* of SYRIA.	B. C. 262, 247.
PTOLEMY II.	*Philadelphus* of EGYPT.	B. C. 285, 246.
ANTIGONUS.	*Gonatas* of MACEDON.	B. C. 276, 243.
MAGAS.	CYRENE.	B. C. 258.

and with these identifications the learned of Europe have generally agreed.

17. The fifth name has been read by Mr. Norris as Alexander; and if this reading is correct, we may identify this prince with Alexander II. of Epeiros, who reigned from B. C. 272-254. But the two copies of this name, published by Mr. Norris, from fac similes by Masson and Court, appear to me to read *Alibhasunari*,* which may be intended for Ariobarzanes III., King of Pontus, who reigned from B. C. 266-240. But in either case the date of Priyadarsi's inscription will be about B. C. 260-258, shortly preceding the death of Magas.

18. As the last-fitting pieces of a child's puzzle-map test the accuracy of the previous arrangements, so do these identifications prove the correctness of Sir William Jones's happy conjecture of the identity of Chandra Gupta and Sandrakottos. The *facts* are undeniable. *Asoka*, or *Priyadarsi*, the Indian King of Magadha, was the contemporary of five Greek princes, all of whom began to reign a little before the middle of the third century B. C. The nature of the relations which Asoka established with these princes, has been lost by the abrasion of the rock-inscription; but

* See Plate of Inscription in Journal Roy. As. Soc. xii.

we may conjecture that the chief point was the propagation of the Buddhist religion, and the toleration of Buddhist missionaries. To some it may seem difficult to understand how any relations should exist between the Indian Asoka and the Greek princes of Europe and Africa; but to me it appears natural and obvious. Asoka's kingdom on the west was bounded by that of Antiochus; his father, Bindusára, had received missions from Antiochus, Soter, and Ptolemy Philadelphus; and as Asoka was forty-five years of age when he was inaugurated, in B. C. 259, he might have conversed with both of the Greek ambassadors, *Daimachos* and *Dionysios*. He had been governor of Ujain for many years in the lifetime of his father, during which the Egyptian fleet had anchored annually at Barygaza, while the merchants proceeded to the viceroy's court at Ozene, with choice specimens of their valuables—wines, gold and silver plate, and female slaves. Asoka had known the Greeks before he became king; he had seen their ambassadors and their merchants; and he knew that his grandfather had given five hundred elephants to Seleukos Nikator in exchange for a barren and mountainous territory, and a Grecian wife.

19. But there is another fatal objection to Professor Wilson's identification of Antiochus the Great with the Antiochus of Priyadarsi's inscriptions, in the omission of any of the Greek princes of Kabul and of the native princes of Parthia; for we know that Artabanus I. and Euthydemus were the contempo-

raries of the Syrian prince, who, after an unsuccessful attempt to reduce them, was obliged to recognize them both as independent kings.

20. The ordinances of Asoka, or Priyadarsi, were issued at different periods of his reign. Those of the 10th and 12th years are found on the rocks of Kapurdigiri, Girnar, and Dhauli; while the pillar-edicts are all dated in the 27th year of his reign. Much has been written about the confused dates of the different pillar-edicts, in spite of the clear and decisive language of the ordinances themselves; which shows that they were all *published* in the 27th year. It is true that the Eastern tablet refers to an edict of the 12th year, but this, as Priyadarsi states, had been *abrogated,* and the Eastern tablet, which mentions the abolished ordinance, is *itself* dated in the 27th year.* The words of the inscription referring to the edict of the 12th year are *dhamma-lipi likhapita,* "*an* ordinance on *Dharma* was published;" whereas each of the edicts of the 27th year is described as *iyam dhamma-lipi,* "*this* ordinance on *Dharma.*" The rock-inscription at Bhabra, near Jaypur, is of uncertain date; but, as it mentions the Third Synod, it must be posterior to 241 B. C.

21. The pillar inscriptions, therefore, contain the latest edicts published by Asoka, as they date nine years posterior to the assembly of the Third Synod. The precepts inculcated in them are, however, generally

* Prinsep's Journal, vi. 596, 597.

the same as those of the 12th year; but a greater tenderness is expressed for animal life, and a more comprehensive view is taken of the moral duties of charity towards *all mankind*, and of the sacred duty of a king towards his subjects. This difference shows the advance made by Asoka in his acquirement of the Buddhist faith, which is essentially one of good will and toleration towards all men.

22. But the sincerity of Asoka's belief is further proved by the zealous earnestness with which he sought to propagate his new faith over all the distant provinces of his own empire, as well as in the neighbouring kingdoms of his allies. His own family had been early converted. His wife Asandhimitrá was a zealous Buddhist; his brother Tishya took the vows of an ascetic; his son Kunála became celebrated for his early misfortunes and after attachment to the faith; while his children Mahendra and Sanghamitrá, who were initiated at twenty years of age, immortalized themselves by converting the people of Ceylon. Their mission formed part of the great scheme for the propagation of Buddhism, which was arranged between Asoka and the principal Arhat Mogaliputra at the meeting of the Third Synod, in B. C. 241, in the 18th year after Asoka's inauguration.

CHAPTER X.

THIRD SYNOD.

1. The Third Synod was composed of one thousand holy *arhats*, selected by TISHYA, the son of the Brahman MUDGALA, from whom he received the patronymic of *Maudgalaputra* (Páli, *Mogaliputa*), by which he is generally known.* This Synod was assembled, at the express desire of Asoka, for the purpose of discovering and expelling the multitude of heretics,† who had insinuated themselves into the monasteries, by shaving their heads, and by assuming the yellow dress of the Buddhist ascetics. Each sect professed its own creed, saying, "This is *Dharma;*

* The assumption of patronymics became quite necessary, owing to a partial fondness for particular names. Thus, there were four other Tishyas, besides the leader of the Third Synod:—1st, Tishya, the brother of Asoka; 2nd, Tishya, the Arhata, who died of an ulcer in his foot; 3rd, Tishya, the King of Ceylon; 4th, the ambassador of the Ceylonese king. Of these, Asoka's brother alone is called Tishya: the others have additional names.

† *Tithaya;* that is, the *Tirthakas,* or *Tirthakaras.* See Turnour's Páli Annals, in Prinsep's Journal, vi. 732.

this is *Vinaya;*" and the Buddhist *Vihárs* were defiled by the presence of worshippers of Fire and adorers of the Sun.*

2. The Bhikshus and ascetics of all descriptions who attended the Third Synod, were assembled in the Asokaráma Vihár, at Pátaliputra, by the King in person, accompanied by the venerable Arhat Mogaliputra, then seventy-two years of age. The Bhikshus professing different faiths were separated according to their sects; and to each sect was put the question, "What faith did Buddha profess?" The *Sussata* said, "The *Sussata* faith;" and each answered according to its own belief. There were eight different sects, all of which Asoka readily distinguished by his own knowledge of the true doctrines. These heretics, sixty thousand in number, were then stripped of their yellow robes, supplied with white dresses, and expelled from the Assembly.†

3. After the expulsion of the heretics, the Synod were occupied for nine months in rehearsing the *Vinaya* and *Dharma*, in the same manner as had been done at the First and Second Synods by the Great *Kásyapa*, and *Yasa*. From the number of Arhats who composed it, this Assembly was called the *Sahasrika Sangiti*, or "Synod of one Thousand."

4. At the conclusion of this Synod in B. C. 241, several missions were despatched to foreign countries

* Turnour, in Prinsep's Journal, vi. 833.

† Turnour's Páli Annals, in Prinsep's Journal, vi. 736, 737.

for the propagation of the Buddhist religion.* The missionaries, who were selected by Mogaliputra, were the principal *Stháviras*, or leaders of Buddhism, men who had acquired the rank of *arhat*, and were respected for superior sanctity. The following list gives the names of the missionaries, and of the scenes of their labours.

1st. *Majjhantiko*, or *Madhyantika*, was deputed to KASMIRA and GANDHÁRA, or Kashmir and Pesháwar, where he is said to have ordained 100,000 persons, of whom 80,000 attained superior grades.† He was at first opposed by the Nága, King of the *Araválo* or *Wular* lake; but the Nága was finally converted, together with 84,000 of his subjects, and "the land glittered with the yellow robes" of the monks.

2nd. MAHÁDEVA was deputed to MAHISAMANDALA, where he converted 80,000 persons. This country is not known: it may be *Maheswara*, on the Narbada.

3rd. RAKKHITO or *Rakshita* was deputed to *Wanawási*, which is probably the country on the *Banás* River, or the modern Mewár and Bundi. 60,000 persons are said to have attained sanctification, and 37,000 to have been ordained monks in five hundred monasteries.

4th. *Yona, Dhammarakkhito, or* YAVANA DHARMA RAKSHITA (the Greek,—Preserver of *Dharma*) was deputed to *Aparantaka* (the western country), where 70,000 persons were converted. This country

* *Mahawanso*, p. 71. † *Mahawanso*, pp. 71, 73.

is probably the *Apanchha,* or Northern Sind of Hwan Thsang.

5th. MAHA DHARMA RAKSHITA was deputed to the Mahráratta country, where 97,000 persons were converted.

6th. MAHARAKSHITA was deputed to the YONA or *Yavana* country, that is, either to the Greek province of Kabul, or to Arachosia; for the name of the capital, *Alasadda** or Alexandria, was common to both countries. The former, however, seems the more probable—180,000 persons are said to have been converted, but only 10,000 ordained.

7th. *Majjhimo,* or *Madhyama,* was deputed to the HIMAWANTA, or country of the Himálayas; along with four other *Stháviras,* named *Kassapo* (or Kásyapa), *Mulikadevo, Dhandabinasso, Sahasadevo.* These five *Stháviras* are said to have converted 80 *kotis* of people in the five divisions of the Himalayas. Relics of Majjhima and of Kassapa were discovered in No. 2 Tope at Sánchi.

8th. SONO and UTTARO were deputed to *Súvarnabhumi,* or "golden land." As this country was on the sea-coast, it may be identified either with Ava, the *Aurea Regio,* or with Siam, the *Aurea Chersonesus.* Six millions of people are said to have been converted, of whom 25,000 men became monks, and 1,500 women became nuns.†

9th. Maha Mahendra the son of Asoka, with four other *Stháviras,* named *Ittiyo, Uttiyo, Sambalo,* and

* *Mahawanso,* p. 171. † *Mahawanso,* p. 74.

Bhaddasálo, were deputed to *Lanka*, or *Ceylon*, where they converted the king *Devánampriya-Tishya*, and the whole of his court.

5. The narrative of these missions is one of the most curious and interesting passages in the ancient history of India. It is preserved entire in both the sacred books of the Singalese, the *Dipawanso* and *Maháwanso*; and the mission of Mahendra to Ceylon is recorded in the sacred books of the Burmese. But the authenticity of the narrative has been most fully and satisfactorily established by the discovery of the relics of some of these missionaries, with the names of the countries to which they were deputed. According to the Maháwanso, the *Stháwira* KASSAPO, or KÀSYAPA accompanied the holy MAJJHIMA or MADHYAMA to the Himawanta or Himalayan region. Thus united in life, they were not separated after death, and their relics were found enshrined together in the same casket in No. 2 Tope at Sánchi. This casket bears three inscriptions, each mentioning a different name.* The legend on the top of the lid is—

Sapurisasa, KÁSAPA-GOTASA, *savahemavatáchariyasa*

"(Relics) of the emancipated KÁSAPA-GOTA, the spiritual teacher to the whole *Hémawanta*."

On the inside of the lid is this legend:—

Sapurisa (sa) MAJHIMASA

"(Relics) of the emancipated MAJHIMA."

---

* See Plate XX. for these inscriptions.

And on the bottom of the casket is this inscription:—

Sapurisasa HÁRITÍ-PUTASA.

"(Relics) of the emancipated HÁRITÍ-PUTRA."

6. In the first inscription KÁSAPA is distinctly styled the *achariya;* that is, the spiritual teacher or missionary to the *Hémawanta.* The perfect agreement between this inscription and the record of the Maháwánso, in the names both of the missionary and of the scene of his labours, is too remarkable to be the result of any combination of chances. But the identity of the two persons is rendered positively certain by the discovery of the relics of *Majhima,* the companion of *Kásapa,* in the same casket, and of the relics of the great *Mogaliputra* in another casket which was found in the same stone box.

7. In the text of the Maháwánso *Majjhimo* alone is mentioned, but the other names are given in the commentary; and Mr. Turnour has therefore inserted them in his translation. It is probable, therefore, that Majhima was the senior monk or head of the mission, and that *Kásapa* was the most successful missionary. I infer this from the significant manner in which he is styled "Missionary to the whole *Hemawanta;*" a marked distinction, which cannot be accidental, as it is repeated on a second casket containing his relics which was found in No. 2 Tope at Sonári.* This inscription is the same

* See Plate XXIV. Inscription on No. 3 Box.

as that of the Sánchi casket, but with the important addition of the name of the missionary's father.

Sapurisasa KOTI-PUTASA, KÁSAPA-GOTASA, *savahemavatá-chariyasa.*

"(Relics) of the emancipated son of *Koti*, KÁSAPA-GOTA, the spiritual teacher of the whole *Hemawanta.*"

From this inscription we learn that *Kásapa* was also known by the patronymic of KOTI-PUTRA.

8. But there was another missionary companion of Majhima and Kásapa whose labours in the Hemawanta region are recorded on a crystal casket which was found in No. 2 Tope at Sonári.* The legend is—

Sapurisasa GOTI-PUTASI *Hemavatasa Dadabhisarasa dáyádasa.*

"(Relics) of the emancipated GOTI-PUTRA, the relation [of the faith] amongst the *Dadabhisaras* of the *Hemawanta.*"

Dárdabhisára is the hilly country lying on both banks of the Indus, to the west of Kashmir. *Dardu* was on the right bank, and *Abhisára* (the present Hazára) on the left bank of the river. The meaning of *dáyáda* (literally son, offspring, relative) is best illustrated by the following anecdote from the Maháwanso.†

9. When Asoka had dedicated his son *Mahendra* and his daughter *Sanghamitrá* to the religion of

* See Plate XXIV. Inscription on No. 1 Box.

† *Mahawanso,* p. 36.

Buddha, he inquired from the *arhats*—" Lords! whose acts of pious bounty to the Buddhist religion have been the greatest?" The crafty Mogaliputra answered with ready wit, " Ruler of Men! a greater benefactor to the faith than thou art can only be called a benefactor, but he who dedicates a son or daughter to the ministry of our religion, that person is more than a 'benefactor' (*dáyako*), he is a 'relation (*dáyáda*) of the faith.'" GOTI-PUTRA had therefore earned the title of *dáyáda*, or " relation of the faith" by the ordination of one of his children to the Buddhist religion.

10. It seems strange that *Gotiputra*, who was so famous amongst his contemporaries for the success of his missionary labours, should not be mentioned in the Mahawanso. But I have a suspicion that both himself and the scene of his labours are mentioned in the Commentary. Mr. Turnour gives *Kassapo*, *Mulikadewo*, *Dhandhabinasso*, and *Sahassadewo*, as the name of the four *theros* or *stháviras* who accompanied *Majjhima* to the Hemawanta country. One of these, therefore, must be the missionary to Abhisára, unless the patronymic *Gotiputra* has been omitted as superfluous; for I propose to read the barbarous *Dhandhabinasso* as *Dardabhisára*, and to insert *Gotiputra* as the name of the missionary who was deputed to that country. I should be inclined to identify Gotiputra either with *Múlikádewo*, or with *Sahasadewo*, were it not that the text of the Maháwanso particularly mentions *four theros* (*chatuhi therehi*) as the com-

panions of Majjhimo. It is indeed possible to read *Dadabhisára* as the missionary's name; but as the name of the country, *Hemavata*, is placed between Gotiputra and Dardabhisara, it seems much more probable that the latter is intended for the name of the well-known country of Dardu and Abhisara.

11. The name of the other *Arhats*, whose relics have been found in company with those of Majjhima, Kasapa, and Gotiputra, will be found in the account of the discoveries made in the Topes at Sanchi and Sonári.*

12. The proselytizing zeal of Asoka is the more worthy of record, as it anticipated by nearly three centuries one of the most characteristic institutions of the early Christian Church. Though his notions of a Supreme Being were of a less lofty and of a more indistinct nature than those of the Christian, yet the Buddhist Prince was imbued with the same zealous wish for the propagation of his faith, and with the same good will and brotherly love towards all mankind. He was especially desirous that all men should be brought into the right way; but he was content to propagate his own faith by persuasion and by argument, and to pray for all those who differed from him in religion, with the hope that his example might perhaps induce some to labour for their own everlasting salvation.†

13. Like the great Constantine, the Indian King was doomed to learn the guilty passion of his Queen

* See Plates XX. and XXIV.

† Eastern inscription of Delhi Pillar.

for the most promising of his sons; but, more fortunate than the Roman Emperor, Asoka was saved from the pain of condemning his own child. The Queen, *Tishya Rakshitá*, was enraged by the beautiful-eyed *Kunála's* rejection of her overtures, and meditated revenge. An opportunity soon occurred by the deputation of Kunála to Taxila to quell another revolt. Through the Queen's influence (but unknown to the King), a royal order, sealed with the King's signet, was sent to the Taxilans to put out those beautiful eyes which had excited the Queen's love for *Kunála*. The people hesitated, but obeyed; and the unfortunate Kunála, guided by his faithful wife, Kánchanamálá, took his dreary way to the King's court at Pátaliputra. When Asoka saw his beloved son, his anger was inflamed against the Queen, and in spite of Kunála's entreaties for mercy, she was made over to the torturers to be burned to death. Such is the legend which the Buddhists relate of their king and his favourite son;* but as they add that Kunála was restored to sight on account of his piety, we may perhaps conclude that the Queen's evil intentions were not fulfilled. Asoka died in the year 222 B. C. after a long and prosperous reign of forty-one years, including the four years that elapsed between his accession and his inauguration. As he was forty-five years old when he was crowned in B. C. 259, he lived to the good old age of fourscore and two years.

* Burnouf's Buddhisme Indien, pp. 409-413.

CHAPTER XI.

RISE AND FALL OF THE INDO-SCYTHIANS.

1. AFTER the death of Asoka, the wide dominions of the Maruyas were divided amongst several of his descendants. The whole of Central India, with the royal metropolis of Pátaliputra, fell to his son Sujasas, or, according to others, to Sampadi, the son of Kunála.* Kashmir was seized by Jaloka, another son of Asoka, who reverted to the Brahmanical faith; Kunála established himself in the Panjâb; and a fourth son, whom the Burmese call *Rahanman*, became king of Ava.† But though India was thus politically dismembered, it was strongly united in the bands of one common faith. The large monastic establishments instituted by Asoka, possessed all the learning and much of the wealth of the land. Their influence was everywhere superior to the power of the king; and the people deposed and accepted their monarchs at the bidding of the monks.‡ The power

* Burnouf's Buddhisme Indien, p. 430.

† Prinsep's Useful Tables.

‡ See the *Mahawanso*, for several instances.

of the Mauryas was overthrown by Pushpamitra, who encountered the Greeks on the Indus during the reign of Menander. By the advice of a Brahman, whom he had chosen for his family priest, Pushpamitra persecuted the Buddhists throughout India.* At Pátaliputra on the Ganges, and at Sákala in the Panjáb, the monks were massacred, and their monasteries were overturned. But Buddhism was too strongly rooted in the soil to be thrown down by the passing whirlwind of a single king's persecution; and in little more than a century later we know that it grew more flourishing than before, under the fostering care of the holy *Nágárjuna* and *Milindu*, Rája of Sákala.

2. During this period the Greek sovereigns of Bactria extended their dominions to the south of the Indian Caucasus; and as they were gradually dispossed of their Turanian territories by the Scythian Tochári, they took from the weaker Indians the whole of the Kabul valley and western districts of the Panjáb. Menander even is said to have pushed his conquests as far as the Isamus or Isan, a small stream which flows between the Jumna and Ganges. The Buddhist faith of Menander's subjects is proved by the contention of eight different cities for portions of his relics, over which Tombs (or Topes) were erected.† This story is similar to that which has been already related regarding Buddha's remains,

* Burnouf, p. 431.

† Bayer, Historia Regni Græcorum Bactriani, p. 77.

which were divided amongst the claimants of eight different cities. It may also serve to illustrate the extent of Menander's rule, when we remember the injunction of Buddha that his own remains were to be treated exactly in the same manner as those of a *Chakravartti Raja.* Menander therefore must have been a Chakravartti, or supreme monarch; whose power was sufficient to render himself entirely independent of all his neighbours. In another work* I have shown from the monogrammatic names of cities, in which his coins were minted, that Menander's rule extended over the whole of the Kabul valley, the Panjáb and Sindh, including the capital city of Minnagara on the Lower Indus. His reign lasted from about 165 to 130 B. C.

3. Menander was succeeded in his northern dominions by the Greek Princes Strato and Hippostratus; and in Sindh by the Scythian *Mauas.* This chief expelled the Greeks from the Panjáb, and confined their power to the modern districts of Kábul and Jelálábád. About 126 B. C. Hermæus, the last Greek Prince of India, became a mere puppet in the hands of the Scythian Kadphises (or Kadaphes) of the *Khorán* tribe.

4. Mauas was succeeded in the Panjáb and in Sindh by the Scythian Azas, who extended his dominions beyond Jelálábád, while the Kabulian kingdom of the Scythian Kadphizes, was subverted by the

* Monograms on the Grecian coins of Ariana and India, published in the *Numismatic Chronicle* of London.

Parthian Princes Vonones, Spalygis, and Spalirisas; during the reign and perhaps with the assistance of the Arsacidan king, Mithridates the Great. But it was wrested from them by the Scythian Azilisas, the successor of Azas; and about 80 B. C., the whole of Khorasan, Afghanistan, Sindh, and the Panjáb, were united under the dominion of some nameless king of the Sakas, or Sacæ Scythians.*

5. A few years later the Sakas were dispossessed of their conquests in Afghanistan and the Western Panjáb by the *Yuchi* or *Tochári* Scythians, who, with their leader Kadphises, of the *Hieu-mi* tribe, were at once converted to Buddhism. The possessions of the Sakas on the Lower Indus were seized by the Ujain Prince, Vikramaditya, who after his conquest assumed the title of *Sákári*, or foe-of-the-Sákás. By these losses the Sakas were confined to the south-western parts of Khorasan; which, after them, was called Sákásthan (or Sacastene), a name which still exists in the modern Sistan.

6. The Hieumi Prince, Kadphises, was followed by Kanishka of the *Khorán*† tribe, who is celebrated

* All these details of the Greek princes of Kabul and the Panjáb have been derived principally from coins. They will be treated at full length in my forthcoming work of "Alexander's Successors in the East."

† The name of Khorasán is most probably due to the occupation of the country by the Khorán tribe: *Khorasán* or *Khorastán* would be the country of the Khor tribe, as *Sacassene* or *Sákastán* was that of the Sákás.

as one of the most eminent patrons of Buddhism. His coins, which are now discovered in very great numbers over the whole of Afghánistan and the Panjab, attest the wide spread of his dominions; and their common occurrence in Rajputána and the North Western Provinces of India perhaps shows the extent of his conquests. He subdued the valley of Kashmir, and there founded a town named after himself which is still called Kámpur or Kánikpur.* For the honour of his religion he erected numerous Topes, of which the most magnificent is still standing in the Khaibur Pass beyond Pesháwar.† Another of his Topes at Manikyála was opened by General Court; and its deposits form one of the most interesting discoveries that have yet been made in the archæology of India. At ten feet above the ground level, General Court obtained a stone box covered with a flat slab, which on its under surface bore an inscription of nine lines in the Ariano-Pali character.‡ The published copy is very corrupt; but through the kindness of Professor Lassen I possess a more correct transcript, from which I have been able to read with certainty the name of *Maharaja* KANISHKA of the *Gushang* tribe. The second line contains a figured date which I have not yet been able to read, but which looks like either 520 or 120. Inside the

* Raja Tarangini, i. 168.

† Hwan Thsang, in the Appendix to the *Fo-kwe-ki*.

‡ See the account of this discovery in Prinsep's Journal, vol. iii. p. 558.

stone box were found three cylindrical caskets of copper, silver, and gold, each containing a certain number of coins. The copper casket held eight copper coins; the silver casket held seven silver coins; and the gold casket held four gold coins. On the lid of the stone box also there were four copper coins. The gold coins and all the copper ones, excepting three, belong to Kanerki or Kanishka himself; two of the copper coins are of his predecessor *Kadphises Hieumi*, and the third is of *Kadphizes* or *Kadaphes Khóran*. The seven silver coins all belong to the last years of the Roman Republic, from B. C. 73 to 33,* and they serve to establish the period of Kanishka's reign in the latter end of the first century before the Christian era.

7. At this time the Eastern Panjáb was governed by Milindu, Raja of Sákala or Sangala, one of the most learned disputants in India. He had challenged the Buddhist Arhats of Sákala to argue with him, and had silenced them all.† The discomfited monks retired to *Rahkhita-talo* or Rakshita-Tál in the Hemawanta region; where after a lapse of twelve years they were joined by the youthful Nágásena or Nágárjuna, whom they persuaded to undertake the difficult task of coping with Raja Milindu in argu-

* Journal des Savans, Fevrier, 1836, p. 74. The battle of Actium was fought in B.C. 31.

† Turnour's Páli Annals, in Prinsep's Journal, v. 533; also Colonel Low. Jour. As. Soc. Bengal, xvii. 616.

ment. The challenge was accepted by Nágásena, and the whole body of monks returned to *Ságala* which once more "glittered with the yellow robes" of the Buddhist fraternities. The disputation, which was held in the king's palace in the presence of ten selected *Sthaviras*, ended in the immediate conversion of Milindu to Buddhism, and in his ultimate ordination as a monk.

8. The teaching of Nágárjuna extended through the reigns of Milindu of Sákala, and of Kanishka of Kashmir.* By his influence five hundred Kashmirian Arhans were deputed to Tibet for the propagation of Buddhism, and to the enthusiasm created by his example must be attributed the contemporary extension of the Buddhist religion to the island of Java at the beginning of the Christian era, when twenty thousand families arrived from India.† The conversion of the Javanese to the faith of Sákya is attested by the numerous Buddhist remains, which still exist on the island.

9. About twenty years later, when the sophist Apollonius visited India, the dominion of the Parthian Bardanes extended to the banks of the Indus.‡

* Csoma, Tibetan Grammar, p. 182, states that Nágárjuna was born in B.C. 93. The Raja Tarangini places him 500 years after the death of Buddha, and makes him a contemporary of the Indo-Scythian Kanishka.

† Klaproth, in Prinsep's Useful Tables, places this event between the years 24—57, A.D. Raffles, Java ii. 69, places it in A.D. 10. The difference is only a few years.

‡ Philostratus, ii. 18. Tacitus, Ann. xi. 10.

A petty chief named Phraortes reigned at Taxila; and a more powerful but nameless sovereign possessed all the country between the Hyphasis and the Ganges. The whole story of this sophist's travels is so full of fables that it is difficult to know what to believe and what to reject; but from the agreement of several passages, it may be inferred that both of the Indian kings were Buddhists. The Gangetic prince abstained from animal food,* and his Sages (that is wise men, or *Bauddhas*) let their hair grow long, wore white mitres on their heads, and had no clothing save short tunics. This is an exact description of the *Bodhisatwa*, or upper class of Buddhist monks, who throughout the Sánchi bas-reliefs are represented seated in abstract meditation with long hair, covered by a low conical cap or mitre, and with no clothing save the kilt or *sanghúti*.

10. For the next four centuries the history of India is almost a blank; and for this dark period we must be guided by the feeble glimmer of a few slight notices preserved by the Chinese. From them we learn that the Yuchi or *Scythian Tochári* retained their power in Northern India until the beginning of the third century of our era.† They abstained from wine and from animal food, and practised the law of Buddha. The prevalence of Buddhism at this period is also attested by several classical authors, of whom

* Philostratus, iii. 15-26.

† Until A. D. 222. See Chinese account of India, in Prinsep's Journal, vi. 63.

Klemens of Alexandria is the most precise. He flourished from 180 to 230 A.D., when the power of the Yuchi was already on the decline. The Brahmans are said to have been worshippers of Herakles and Pan; while the Σεμνοι (*Srámanas* or Monks) and the Σεμναι (*Srámanás* or Nuns) were distinguished by the worship of *certain pyramids* which they believed to contain the bones of some God.* This is a most accurate description of the Buddhist fraternities, with their adoration for Topes or Chaityas, which contained relics of Buddha, or of some of his more eminent disciples and followers.

11. About a century later (A. D. 270-303), the learned Porphyrius divided the Gymnosophists (or half-naked philosophers of India) into two classes, the *Brachmanes* and *Samanæi*: the former being a family or tribe, the latter a mixture of all classes.† The *Samanæi* or Srámanas shaved their heads, wore nothing but a stole or tunic, abandoned their families and property, and lived together in colleges outside the city walls. Their time was spent in holy conversation, and at the sound of a bell they assembled for prayers; for the monks no longer begged their daily bread, but each received his dish of rice from the

* Σεβουσι τινα πυραμιδα ὑφην οστεα τινος Θεου.

† Ε'ξ ἑνός γαρ πατρὸς καὶ μῖας μητρὸς παντες διάγουσι; that is, the Brahmans—but of the Sramanas, he says, Σαμαναιοι δέ οὐκ εἰσὶ τοῦ γένους αὐτῶν, ἀλλ' ἐκ παντὸς τοῦ τῶν 'Ινδῶν ἔθνους, ὥσ ἔφαμεν, συνειλεγμένοι.

king. Colonel Sykes* has already remarked the close agreement of this description with the account of the Chinese pilgrim Fa Hian, who travelled through India just one century after the death of Porphyrius. But the details given by Porphyrius become the more valuable, when we know that his own religion and philosophical principles were almost the same as those of the Indian Buddhists. He believed in one Supreme Being; and held that "Reason" or Intellect (*Buddha*) was superior to "Nature" (Dharma); for by reason we are uplifted towards the Deity, while we are only degraded by our natural appetites and material desires. Man's chief object therefore should be to free himself from all outward and sensual influences. With this view Porphyrius rejected animal food, and refrained from making material offerings to the Supreme Being, because all material objects are unclean. Like the Buddhist also Porphyrius recognized four degrees or classes of virtue, of which the lowest was *political virtue*, or the moral goodness acquired by temperance and moderation of the passions. The next grade was *purifying virtue*, in which man has entirely conquered all human affections. In the third grade man is wholly influenced by *Reason*, and more and more resembles the Deity, until at last he has acquired such perfection that he becomes "one with the one

* Notes on Ancient India, in Journal of the Royal Asiatic Society.

Supreme Being."* These principles have so much in common with the doctrines of Buddhism, that we can only account for the coincidence by supposing that Porphyrius must have possessed the most ample and correct details of the religious beliefs and philosophical speculations which then prevailed in India. We need therefore no longer wonder at the accuracy with which he has described the daily discipline and outward observances of the Buddhist monks. The learned Pagan was in fact a European Buddhist.

12. The travels of Palladius and of the Thebæan Scholastikos only preceded the pilgrimage of Fa Hian by a few years. The former, it is true, did not reach India; but he could have obtained much information regarding the Indians from the merchants of Egypt and of Persia; and he gives at some length the account of Scholastikos, who was detained for six years as a prisoner in the pepper districts of Malabar. The result of his information is given in some imaginary conversations between Alexander the Great and the Indian Sage Dandamis; in which the Indian declares that "God, the great king, causes injury to no man; but gives light, peace, and life, a human body and soul; and that God was his master and only Lord." This sage Dandimis was therefore a monotheistic Buddhist, as indeed might be inferred from his name which is evidently a compound of

* C. P. Mason: Article Porphyrius, in Dr. Smith's New Biographical Dictionary.

Dharma in the Páli form of *Dhama*; perhaps *Dhamadháni*, the "receptacle of Dharma."

13. The prevalence of Buddhism about this period is further proved by several passages in the Brahmanical Dramas and in the Institutes of Manu. The uncertain date of these compositions, however, somewhat lessens their value as precise authorities. The *Mrichhakati*, which is the oldest Hindu Drama now extant, exhibits "not only absolute toleration, but a kind of public recognition" * of the Bauddha faith, by the appointment of a Buddhist ascetic as chief of all the *Vihars* of *Ujain*. That virtuous city could not "*tolerate even the death of an animal.*" This play is of later date than the Hindu code, for the Judge in the 9th act quotes Manu †; and as Manu himself mentions NUNS, or "female anchorites of an heretical religion,"‡ it is certain that the Buddhist faith was still honoured and flourishing when these works were composed. There is internal evidence that the code of Manu is posterior to the Rámáyana and the Mahábhárata in the mention of "heroic poems,"§ which should be read at the celebration of obsequial rites in honour of ancestors; and in the allusions to image-worship,‖ which is not mentioned either in the Rá-

* Wilson's Hindu Theatre, vol. i. p. viii.

† The *Mrichhakati*, or "Toy-cart," act. viii. Wilson's Hindu Theatre, i. 140.

‡ Haughton's Laws of Manu, viii. 363.

§ Haughton's Laws of Manu, iii. 232.

‖ Wilson, Preface to Vishnu Puván, p. xiii.

máyana or Mahábhárata. Bentley assigned the Rámáyana to the fourth century of our era, and the Mahábhárata to the eighth century or even later. But the latter date is certainly too low; for the Great War is mentioned in a copper plate inscription of a date not later than the first half * of the sixth century, along with the names of Vyása, Parásara, and Yudhishtara. Bentley's method of compression is in fact too much like the Prokrustean bed of Damastes, into which the large were squeezed, and the small were stretched until they fitted. The composition of the Mahábhárata cannot therefore be dated *later* than the beginning of the fifth century, and it should no doubt be placed even earlier; perhaps about A. D. 200 to 300. The code of Manu is a mere compilation, filled with the most contradictory injunctions; but in its present state it is certainly later than the great epics, and may be dated about A. D. 400.

* This valuable inscription is the property of Captain Ellis The date is thus stated: *Likhitam samvatsara satadwaye chaturdasa*—"written in the year two hundred and fourteen." As the characters are similar to those of the Gupta inscriptions, the date is most probably of the Gupta era, or 319 + 214 = 533, A. D. If of the Sáka era, the date will be 78 + 214 = 292, A. D.; but the characters are not so old as those of the early Gupta inscriptions of A. D. 400.

CHAPTER XII.

THE GUPTA DYNASTY.—DECLINE AND FALL OF BUDDHISM.

1. At the period of Fa Hian's pilgrimage, the Gupta dynasty occupied the throne of Magadha. Their dominions extended from Népal to the Western Gháts,* and from the Indus to the mouths of the Ganges. The family was established by *Maharaja* Gupta, in 319 A. D., which became the first year of the Gupta era. This epoch is not mentioned in the Allahabad inscription of Samudra Gupta; but it is used in the Sánchi and Udayagiri inscriptions of Chandra Gupta; in the Kuhaon Pillar inscription of Skanda Gupta; and in the Eran Pillar inscription of Budha Gupta. It is besides especially mentioned by Abu Rihán,† who, in his account of Indian eras, identifies the Gupta-kàl, or Gupta era, with the Ballaba-kàl, or era of *Balabhi*, which commenced

* The Western Ghats are called *Sainhádri;* and the inscription on the Allahabad pillar records Samudra Gupta's influence over that country.

† M. Reinaud: Fragments Arabes et Persans inédits relatifs à l'Inde, pp. 138-143.

in A. D. 319. These eras are mentioned no less than three times by Abu Rihán; and each time he has identified them as starting from the same date. But it appears to me that the most important of these passages must either be corrupt or obscure, for the translation given by M. Reinaud makes the epoch of the Guptas commence from the date of their extermination! If this is a correct translation there can be little doubt that the text of Abu Rihán must be erroneous; for we know positively that the Guptas were reigning during the fifth and sixth centuries of our era. But I will venture to suggest a different translation of this important passage, by which the error is got rid of without any alteration of the text:—

فاما كوبت كال فكان كما قيل قوما الشرارا اقويا
فلما انقرضوا ارج بهم وكان بلب كال اخيرهم
اول تاريخهم ايضا متاخر عن شككال ٢٤١

"With regard to the *Gupta Kál* (or era of the Guptas), the name was that of a wicked and powerful family; *whose epoch became extinct with themselves*; and truly Ballaba was after them; for the beginning of their era is the the same as (that of) the the last; (namely) 241 of the SÁKA-KÁL."

2. The underlined passage in the original text is thus translated by M. Reinaud:* "Et l'ère qui porte leur nom est l'èpoque de leur extermination;" but

* Fragments, p. 143.

the literal translation appears to be, "and then became extinct along with their epoch," which agrees with the version that I have given above. The statement made in M. Reinaud's version is so extraordinary that, even without any direct proofs of its inaccuracy, I would have set it aside as erroneous. The era of the Seleukidæ *began* with the foundation of the Syrian empire by Seleukos; the Christian era is dated from the *establishment* of Christianity; and the era of the Guptas without doubt commenced with the *settlement* of their own dynasty. For the Guptas, as I have mentioned before, date their inscriptions in an era of their own; which, though not so named by them, was actually a *Gupta-kál*, and must, therefore, have been called such by the people.

3. The direct evidence of the period when the Guptas flourished is derived from the Chinese. In A. D. 428, the king of Kapila was named *Yuegai*, or "moon-beloved," which is a synonyme of *Chandra Gupta*, or "moon-cherished." In A. D. 502, the king of India was named *Keu-to*, that is *Gutto*, the Páli form of the Sanskrit *Gupta*. Lastly, Hwán-Thsáng* names five Princes of Magadha who flourished previous to the conquest of the country by Siladitya, in the following order:—

Lo-kia-lo-a-yi-to,	or	*Lagraditya.*
Fo-tho-kiu-to,	or	*Budha Gupta.*
Tha-ka-ta-kiu-to,	or	*Taktu Gupta.*
Pho-lo-a-yi-to,	or	*Baladitya.*
Fa-che-lo,	or	*Vajra.*

* *Fo-kwe-ki*, Appendix.

4. Now Siladitya died between 642 and 648 (say in 645), and as he reigned sixty years, his accession must have taken place in A. D. 585; and his conquest of Magadha may be dated about A. D. 600. The chronology of the Guptas as derived from all sources will then stand thus:—*

NAMES.	TITLES.	GUPTA ERA.	A.D.
I. GUPTA............	....	0	319
* II. GHATOT KACHA	....	21	340
* III. CHANDRA GUPTA 1ST	....	41	360
* IV. SAMUDRA GUPTA ..	*Parákrama*......	61	380
* V. CHANDRA GUPTA 2ND	*Vikramáditya*....	81	400
* VI. KUMÁRA GUPTA	*Mahendra*	111	430
* VII. SKANDA GUPTA	*Kramaditya*	121	440
VIII.	*Lagráditya* †	133	452
* IX. BUDHA GUPTA......	....	161	480
X. TAKTA GUPTA......	....	191	510
XI. NARA GUPTA	*Baladitya*	221	540
XII. VAJRA	....	251	570
Conquest of *Siladitya*............		281	600

5. The stars placed against the names in this

* The dates obtained from various sources are: For Chandra Gupta Vikramaditya, 82 (Udayagiri inscription), and 93 (Sanchi inscription), equivalent to A.D. 401 and 412, from Jain authorities A.D. 409; and from Chinese authorities A.D. 428—for Skanda Gupta—his death in 133, or A.D. 452, as stated on the Kuhaon pillar; for Budha Gupta 165, or A.D. 484, as given in the Eran pillar inscription.

† Or Lokaditya.

table denote that coins have been discovered of each of those princes; and it is from coins alone that I have ascertained that BALADITYA was named *Nara Gupta.* The chronological table has been framed upon the following data.

1st. The power of the Indo-Scythians did not begin to decline until the time of the later Hans in China, whose dynasty was only established in A. D. 222. During the latter half of the third century their power was on the decline, and may be supposed to have been finally overthrown by Gupta in A. D. 319. There are great numbers of gold coins of Indo-Scythian type with corrupt Greek and Indian legends which can only be attributed to this dynasty.

2nd. A short inscription of Chandra Gupta, at Udayagiri, is dated in the year 82; and a second of the same prince, at Sánchi, is dated in the year 93. These dates of the Gupta era are equivalent to A. D. 401 and 412, which agree with the Chinese date of A. D. 428* for Yue-gai. But Chandra Gupta on his coins takes the title of *Vikramaditya,* and in the Agni Purana,† it is said that *Vikrama,* the son of Gadharupa, should ascend the throne of Málawa seven hundred and fifty-three years after the expiation of Chánakya. This event I have already placed in B. C. 325, from which, deducting 753 years, we

* This is the date given in the Chinese account of India, in Prinsep's Journal, vi. 665; but Des Guignes, i. 45, says A.D. 408.

† Prinsep's Journal, iv. 688.

obtain A.D. 428 for the date of Vikrama of Malwa. Colonel Tod also quotes a Jain inscription of Chandra Gupta, dated either in A.D. 370 or 409,* in which he is styled *Avanti-náth*, or "lord of Ujain," which was the capital of Malwa. Here then we have a Vikrama and a Chandra Gupta both kings of Malwa at the same time: two statements which can only be reconciled by supposing them to be the same person under different names or titles. This supposition is confirmed by the coins of Chandra Gupta, on the reverses of which we find that he took the titles of Vikrama and Vikramaditya. A cave inscription at Udayagiri of the Samvat year 1093, or A.D. 1036, couples the name of Chandra Gupta with the kingdom of Vikramaditya (*Vikramaditya Rájyam*). In the Raja Tarangini also it is mentioned that Mátrigupta was placed on the throne of Kashmir by Vikramaditya, King of Ujain. According to my corrected chronology of the Raja Tarangini, this happened in A.D. 430. The Satrunjaya Mahatmya† also places the third Vikramaditya in Samvat 466, or A.D. 409. From this accumulation of evidence it seems to me certain that a Chandra Gupta, with the title of Vikramaditya, was the sovereign of Malwa in the early part of the fifth century of our era.

* See Transactions Roy. As. Soc., pp. 140-211, where Colonel Tod, by some inadvertence, gives both 427 and 466 Samvat as the date of this inscription.

† Wilford: Researches As. Soc. Bengal, ix. 156; and Wilson: Researches As. Soc. Bengal, xv. 39, note.

3rd. The date of Skanda Gupta's death, which is found upon the Kuhaon Pillar, is the year 133.* No era is stated; but it must of course be that era which was used by the "royal race of Guptas," of which he is said to have been born, and which could only have been the *Gupta-kál*, or Gupta era. His death, therefore, occured in 319+133=452 A. D., as given in my table.

4th. The date of Budha Gupta has been determined by the inscription at Eran,† which records the erection of a pillar in the year 165, or A. D. 484. An inspection of the table will show how well this date agrees with the period which must be assigned to Budha Gupta on the authority of Hwan Thsang; according to whom Fo-tho-kiu-to, or *Budha Gupta*, was the fourth prince prior to Siladitya's conquest of Magadha in A. D. 600. The coins of Budha Gupta may be seen in Plate II., figs. 55, 57, of Mr. Thomas's essay on the Sah kings of Surastra. I can confirm the reading of the legend which he gives with some hesitation as Budha Gupta. I procured five of these silver coins from a traveller at Benares, of which I have given away four; but I still possess sealing-wax impressions of them all, from which I have been able to recognize the engraved specimens.

5th. The coins of Nara Gupta *Báladitya* are scarce. Of two specimens in gold that have been in my own possession, I still have impressions; but

* Prinsep's Journal, vii. 37.

† Prinsep's Journal, vii. 634.

the type may be seen in Fig. 22, Plate xviii. of Wilson's "Ariana Antiqua." On the obverse, under the Raja's arm, is written *Nára*, and on the reverse, *Báladitya*. The small silver coin Fig. 19, Plate xv. of the same work, most probably also belongs to Nara. I read the legend:—

Paramadhi Raja Sri NARA-GUPTA. *Baladitya.*

6. As the correct determination of the epoch of the Gupta dynasty is of the first importance to the religious as well as to the political history of ancient India, it becomes necessary to examine the chronology which Mr. E. Thomas, with much critical skill and ingenuity, has proposed for the Sáh kings of Gujrat and the Gupta princes of Magadha.* We agree as to the facts, but differ in our deductions. The facts are these:—

1st. The beautiful silver coins of the Sáh kings are all dated in the fourth century of some unknown era.

2nd. The silver coins of Kumára Gupta and of Skanda Gupta are evident and undoubted copies of those of the Sáh kings, and therefore these two princes must have reigned at a *later* date than the last of the Sáh kings.

7. In making his deductions from these facts, Mr.

* See Journal of the Royal Asiatic Society, vol. xii., "On the Dynasty of the Sah Kings of Suráshtra;" by Edward Thomas, esq., Bengal Civil Service; a most valuable contribution to the ancient history of India.

Thomas has based all his calculations on M. Reinaud's translation of the passage in Abu Rihán, which gives the year 319 A.D., for the beginning of the Gupta era, and also for the *final extinction* of *the Gupta dynasty*. In adopting this version of Abu Rihán's statement, Mr. Thomas is obliged to search for some other epochs as the starting points from which to count the dates of the Surashtra and Gupta coins. The earlier era which he uses for this purpose is that of Sri Harsha,* which was entirely unknown until the publication of M. Reinaud's extracts from Abu Rihán. This era dates from B. C. 457, and the epoch of the Sáh kings of Surashtra is thus fixed between 157 and 57 B. C.†

8. Between the Sáh kings and the Guptas, Mr. Thomas interposes the Indo-Scythians, whose conquest he places in 26 B. C., and he proposes to count the date of Chandra Gupta's inscription at Sánchi‡ from 78 A. D., which is the well-known commencement of the Sáka era. This will place the reign of Chandra Gupta in 78 + 93 = 171 A. D., and the reign of Buddha Gupta in 78 + 165 = 243 A. D., after whom there is time for the reigns of a few more princes before the asserted extinction of the family in 319 A. D.

9. My reasons for assigning the Guptas to a later period have been given already; and I will

* See Mr. Thomas's Essay, p. 43.

† See Mr. Thomas's Essay, p. 45.

‡ See Mr. Thomas's Essay, p. 5.

now state as briefly as possible all my objections to Mr. Thomas's chronology.

1st. According to the Chinese historians, the power of the Indo-Scythians remained in full force *until* 222 A. D.; after which it began to decline. This statement is supported by Ptolemy the geographer, who between A. D. 140-160, assigns the whole valley of the Indus, *including Sirastrene*, or Surashtra, to the Indo-Scythians.

2nd. Samudra Gupta, according to the Allahabad and Bhitari inscriptions, was the fourth prince of the Gupta dynasty, and if we allow twenty years to each reign, Samudra will date from 60 to 80 of the Gupta era, or from 138 to 158 A. D. But in the Allahabad pillar inscription, Samudra mentions the *Sháhán-sháh* (that is, one of the Sassanian kings of Persia) as his contemporary, whose dynasty did not attain the throne until A. D. 223; and as in his account of the tributary and conquered provinces he omits Magadha, Suráshtra, and Ujjayani, it has been inferred by James Prinsep,* and is admitted by Mr. Thomas himself, that these provinces must have formed his own proper dominion. But as Sirastrene belonged to the Indo-Scythians at the very date that must be assigned to Samudra by Mr. Thomas's chronology, we must either reject his scheme altogether, or conclude, that both the Chinese historian and the Alexandrian geographer were in error.

* Journal vi. 975.

3rd. The independence of the native princes of Gujrat between 157 and 57 B. C. is completely at variance with the Greek accounts of Menander's conquest of *Sarioustos* or *Surashtra,* between 160 and 130 B. C., which is further authenticated by the long-protracted currency of his coins at Barygáza or Baroch.

4th. The alphabetical characters of the Surashtran coins * are so widely different from those of the Pillar and Rock inscriptions, and at the same time are so much similar to those of the Guptas, that it is impossible not to conclude that there must have been a long interval between Asoka and the independent Sáh kings, and an almost immediate succession of the Sáh kings by the Guptas. But Mr. Thomas's proposed chronology exactly reverses this conclusion, by making the interval between Asoka's death and the earliest date of the Surashtra coins not more than sixty-five years, while the interval between the last of the Sáh kings and the rise of the Guptas is one hundred and thirty-five years, or more than double the other.

* Another evidence in favour of the later date of the Sah kings of Gujrat is furnished by the gateway inscriptions at Sánchi. These date in the early part of the first century of our era (see No. 190); and though they show the nearest approach to the forms of the Sah alphabet, yet the latter is certainly posterior to the Sánchi inscriptions. This result agrees with the period which I have assigned to them, from A.D. 222 (the beginning of the Indo-Scythian decline) to A.D. 380, the accession of Samudra Gupta.

5th. The author of the Periplus of the Erythræan sea, who lived between 117 and 180 A. D., states that *ancient* drachmas of Apollodotus and of Menander were then current at Barygáza.* This prolonged currency of the Greek drachmas points directly to the period of the Indo-Scythian rule; for though we have some hundreds of their gold coins, and many thousands of their copper coins, yet only one solitary specimen of their silver coinage has yet been discovered. The Indo-Grecian silver probably continued current until after 222 A. D., when the Indo-Scythian power began to decline. From this period, about 250 A. D., I would date the independence of the Sáh kings, and the issue of their silver coinage, which was a direct copy in weight, and partly in type, from the Philopater drachmas of Apollodotus.

9.* We have thus a continued series of silver currency in Gujrat for upwards of six hundred years, from Menander's conquest, in B. C. 150-140, to Budha Gupta's death, in about 510 A. D. From this period thick silver pieces of the same type and of the same value, but one half more in weight, were issued by the Balabhi kings down to the Mahomedan conquest. In the more precious metal the coinage of the Indo Scythians was immediately succeeded by the golden dinars of the Guptas, whose earliest pieces are almost

* Hudson, Geogr. Min., i. 87—" Vixit, teste Suida, Hadriani, Marci et Antonini temporibus;" that is, between 117 and 180 A.D., or about 160 A.D.

exact copies of the well-known Ardokro coins of Kanishka and his successors.*

10. The importance of establishing the correct era of the Guptas becomes apparent when we learn that Chandra Gupta was most probably one of the last paramount sovereigns of India who professed the Buddhist faith. The inscriptions of his reign, which still exist at Sánchi and at Udayagiri, confirm the account of the contemporary traveller Fa-Hian; that Buddhism, though honoured and flourishing, was certainly on the decline, and that temples of the Brahmans were rising on all sides. The earliest inscription of Chandra Gupta is dated in 82 of the Gupta era, or A. D. 401. It consists of two lines carved on a rock tablet at the foot of the Udayagiri hill, which was intended for a longer inscription. There is room for five more lines; and, as no event is commemorated, it is evident that the record is incomplete. The tablet is placed to the right of the entrance of a cave-temple apparently dedicated to Surya, whose image is represented on each side of the doorway. Immediately to the left of the cave there is a large alto-relievo of the *Varáha* or Boar *Avatár*, ten feet and a half in height. The inscription is partially injured by the peeling of the rock on the right hand; but the

* See Prinsep, in Journal iv. 629, and Plates XXXVIII. and XXXIX., in which the imitation is clearly developed; but I was the first to point out to James Prinsep the seated *Ardokro* on the Indo-Scythian coins, which figure afterwards became the most common reverse of the early Gupta coins.

date is perfect, and the only part that is completely lost is the name of the Raja who excavated the cave. A fac-simile of the inscription will be found in Plate XXI., No. 200. The following is a transcript in Roman characters :—

Siddham samvatsare 82 *Sravana-mása suklekadasya parama-bhattáraku Mahárájadhi* CHANDRA-GUPTA *pádánadátasya Mahárája* CHAGALIGA *potrasya, Mahárája* VISHNU-DÁSA *putrasya Sanakánikasya Mahá* (*ràja* * * *

" Finished in the year 82, on the 11th of the bright half of the month of Srávana; [the cave] of him, bowing to the feet of the paramount, homage-receiving, Supreme Maharaja CHANDRA-GUPTA, the grandson of Maharaja CHAGALIGA, the son of Maharaja VISHNU-DÁSA, Maharaja (name obliterated) of *Sanakánika.*"

11. *Sanakánika* is included by Samudra Gupta amongst his tributary provinces,* but unfortunately the name of its Raja is not given. The position of Sanakánika is, however, now placed beyond all doubt; as it must have included Udayagiri, Bhilsa, and Sánchi. It is even possible that *Sanakánika* may have some connection with the names of Sánchi—Kánakhera.

12. The Vaishnava faith of this petty royal family

* Allahabad Pillar inscription, in Prinsep's Journal, vi. 973. The name of *Chagaliga* or *Chaglig* recalls those of Kutlugh, Toghlak, and others of undoubted Tartar origin, so strongly, that one can scarcely help assigning this petty family to the Indo-Scythian stock.

is shown by the name of Vishnu Dás, the "slave of Vishnu;" and by the Vaishnava subjects of all the rock sculptures at Udayagiri. The Boar Incarnation of Vishnu has already been mentioned. On the top of the hill there is a colossal figure of Vishnu himself, twelve feet in length, reposing on the folds of the serpent *Sesha* or *Ananta*, the emblem of eternity. The worship of Vishnu, which then prevailed at Udayagiri, has been supplanted by that of Siva; and the votaries of the *lingam* have occupied the cave-temples of Vishnu. In the principal temple, now dedicated to Mahadeo, there is a native inscription on a pillar dated in the Samvat year 1093, or A. D. 1036, in which the votary records his "adoration at the feet of Vishnu."*

13. The second inscription of Chandra Gupta is carved on one of the railings of the colonnade of the great Tope at Sánchi. It was translated and published by James Prinsep in 1837;† but its date was not properly ascertained. Since then, Mr. Thomas has satisfactorily shown that the Samvat date is 93; but he has failed to see that the day of the month is likewise represented in figures. I have given a facsimile of this date in Plate XXI., No. 197. It reads S. 93, *Bhádrapada* 14 = "the year 93, the 14th (of the month) Bhádrapada." This inscription records a grant of money by the paramount sovereign Chandra Gupta, through his local agent, to the Srámanas of the *Mahá-Vihára*, or Great Monastery at Sánchi.

* Vishnu-pádo-nityam. † Journal, vi. 455, 456.

Prinsep's translation gives the general sense of the text; but, in documents of this kind, it is always desirable to have as literal a version as possible. The opening lines especially have been much abridged; and, as they are thoroughly Buddhistical in their language, I will venture to give my own translation of them.

Ku (la Dhamma) si Mahávihâre sila-samádhi Prajnyáguna bhavitendrayáya paramapunya kri (ta sramántara) garbhya gatáya sramana-punggavvásatahâyáryya sanghâya. * * *

" To the followers of *Dharma* in the Great Monastery, who, by the practice of morality, and by deep meditation on the attributes of wisdom (*Prajná*), have subdued their passions, and become distinguished for virtue; to the Srámanas of the venerable fraternity, pre-eminent in private religious observances (Avasatha)," &c.

14. *Prajná* means " wisdom, understanding," or more literally, " foreknowledge." The author of the Ashta Sahasrika thus addresses Prajná:—

" Thou mighty object of my worship! Thou *Prajná!* art the sum of all good qualities; and Buddha is the *Guru* of the world. The wise make no distinction between thee and Buddha. He who devoutly serves thee serves the *Tathágata* also."*

The author of the *Pujá-kand* thus addresses Prajná:—" I make salutation to *Prajná-Devi*, who is the *Prajná Páramitá* (Transcendental Wisdom), the *Prajná-rupa* (multiform), the *Nir-rupa* (formless), and the universal mother."

* Hodgson, p. 123.

The author of the Sádhana-málá offers his "salutation to Prajná-Devi, from whom, in the form of desire, the production of the world was excellently obtained, who is beautiful as the full moon, the mother of Adi Buddha."* And again, "Salutation to Prajná Páramitá, the infinite, who, when all was void, was revealed by her own will."†

15. *Prajná* or *Prajná Devi* is deified Nature, or *Diva Natura*, and the same as Dharma. In the Sánchi inscription her supremacy is acknowledged by Chandra Gupta's belief in the attainment of purity and the subjection of the passions by meditation on the attributes of *Prajná*. The great king was therefore not an orthodox Buddhist, but a heterodox materialist, who held Dharma or material nature as the first person of the Triad.

16. If James Prinsep's restoration of the text be correct, and I believe that it is so, Chandra Gupta was a most munificent patron as well as a faithful follower of Buddhism. His gift to the Sánchi Tope for its regular illumination, and for the perpetual service of *Srámanas* or ascetics, was no less a sum than twenty-five thousand dinars, or 25,000*l.*, equal to two lakhs and a half of rupees.

17. But the religious belief of Chandra Gupta does not rest solely on the authority of this inscription; for, according to the sacred books of the Jains, the last Tirthankara MAHAVIRA is said to have ex-

* Hodgson, p. 125.

† Hodgson, p. 126.

pounded his twelve dreams to Chandra Gupta, the lord of Avanti or Ujain.*

18. The same story is related in the Buddha vilása,† but the dreams are said to have been fourteen, and to have been expounded to Chandra Gupta, the monarch of Ujain, by Bhadra Báhu Muni. From this it may be inferred that the Prince was certainly not a worshipper of the Brahmanical Pantheon; and as we have seen that he was not an orthodox Buddhist, we may conclude that his heterodoxy was not very dissimilar from *Jainism*, which is generally acknowledged to have been a sectarian offspring of Buddhism.

19. But, if my chronology of the Guptas be correct, we have the most clear proof of the Buddhist belief of Chandra Gupta in Fa Hian's travels. The Chinese pilgrim left his native land in A. D. 399, and returned to it again in A. D. 415. His visit to *Pa-lian-fu*, or Pátaliputra,‡ the capital of the kingdom of Mo-kie-thi, or Magadha, therefore took place in the early part of Chandra Gupta's reign. He describes the city as very large;§ the people as rich and fond of discussion; but just in all their dealings. They celebrated Sákya's birthday annually by a procession

* Transactions Royal Asiatic Society, i. 211—Colonel Tod.

† At p. 413 of the same volume, Major Delamaine states the same thing, on the authority of the *Buddha Vilâsa*, a Digambara Jain work.

‡ *Fu* is only the Chinese translation of the Sanskrit *putra*, a son.

§ *Fo-kwe-ki*, c. xxvii.

of four-wheeled cars, with little chapels at the four corners, each containing a seated *Buddha*, with Bodhisatwas standing by him. This festival still survives in the *Rath Játtrá*, or annual procession of *Jagannáth*, which the crafty Brahmans have adopted into their own creed, because it was too popular to be suppressed.*

20. At the time of Fa Hian's visit Buddhism was the prevailing religion of the Panjáb, and of Northern India from Mathura to the mouth of the Ganges. Between the Panjáb and Mathura, that is in Brahmavartta Proper, the law of Buddha was not held in honour.† But this was the original seat and stronghold of the Brahmans and their religion; and its exception by Fa Hian is one amongst the many proofs of the pilgrim's accuracy. Everywhere else Buddhism was honoured and flourishing; the kings were firmly attached to the law, and showed their reverence for the ascetics by taking off their tiaras before them. But at *Shâchi* and at *Shewei*, in Oudh, the heretical Brahmans had attempted to destroy a sacred nettle and some holy Topes. The very attempt shows the increasing power of the Brahmans, and their confident hope of ultimate success.

21. In the Bhitari Pillar inscription, no mention is made of the religious belief of the first Chandra

* See note 9 to chapter xxvii. of Mr. Laidlay's translation of the pilgrimage of Fa Hian; and the concluding chapter of this volume.

† *Fo-kwe-ki*, c. xv.

Gupta, but his son Samudra would appear to have been a strict observer of the Vedas, as he is represented offering vast sacrifices to the ancient elemental Deities, Indra, Varuna, and Yama.* In his own inscription on the Allahabad Pillar he is also compared to Dhanada, Varuna, Indra, and Antaka;† that is, to the Gods of the four elements, earth, water, fire, and air. His son, the second Chandra Gupta, and his grandson Kumára Gupta, are called worshippers of the *Supreme* BHAGAVAT,‡ whom Dr. Mill identifies with Krishna. But as the Vishnu Purana, which was most probably written in the tenth century,§ makes no mention of the *worship* of Krishna, although it gives a long account of his *history*, the Bhagavat who was worshipped by Chandra and Kumára, must be either Vishnu or Buddha. In his remarks on this inscription, however, Dr. Mill drops Krishna|| altogether, and makes Vishnu the object of Chandra's and Kumára's worship. But as Bhagavat is one of the commonest of the many titles of Buddha, the balance of evidence still remains very much in favour of Chandra Gupta's attachment to Buddhism. It is even possible that Chandra Gupta may have professed Buddhism in the

* Prinsep's Journal, vi. 5.

† Prinsep's Journal, vi. 980.

‡ Prinsep's Journal, vi. 5—parama Bhagavata.

§ Prinsep's Journal, i. 441—Professor H. H. Wilson says middle of the tenth century.

|| Prinsep's Journal, vi. 7.

early part of his reign,* and Vaishnavism in the latter part; for the difference between the two is more nominal than real. Indeed the mention of Vishnu himself would no more invalidate the Buddhism of Chandra Gupta than the Tantric pictures of Mahadeva and Káli can disprove the present Buddhism of the Tibetans and Népalese. The exoteric or outward worship of Chaityas, and of statues of Buddha, no doubt remained unchanged; but the esoteric or philosophical speculations of the learned were continually changing; and the comparatively pure theism and practical morality of Buddha were first encumbered with the mild quietism of the Vaishnavas, and at last deformed by the wild extravagances of the Tantrists.

22. Skanda Gupta, the grandson of Chandra Gupta, ascended the throne of Magadha about A. D. 440. He inherited the vast dominions of his family, including the whole of Northern India, from Gujrát to the mouth of the Ganges; and though his reign was disturbed by the rebellion of a minister, yet he left his kingdom undivided to his successor. Of his religious faith there is no doubt; for, in the Bhitari Pillar inscription,† he is stated to have possessed "a clear insight into the wisdom of the Tantras." The mysteries of the Tántrikas were secret and incommunicable. They taught formulas of incantation and

* His gift to the Sánchi Chaitya is dated *Anno Guptæ* 93, or A. D. 412; and we know that he was reigning so late as A. D. 428.

† Prinsep's Journal, vi. 6.

mystic charms for the attainment of superhuman power. They degraded the material worship of the reproductive powers of Nature by a sensual and obscene interpretation, in which Siva and Durga, or their emblems the *lingam* and *yoni*, played a conspicuous part. One of their orders, the *Kápálikas*, or "men-of-skulls," has been well represented in the Prabodha Chandrodaya,* a native metaphysical drama. The speakers are a *Buddhist* monk, a *Brahman* mendicant, and the Kápálika.

Buddhist: "This man professes the rule of a *Kápálika.* I will ask him what it is." (Going up to him.) "Ho! you with the bone and skull necklace, what are your notions of happiness and salvation?"

Kápálika: "Wretch of a Buddhist! Well, hear what is our religion:—

> "With flesh of men, with brain and fat well smeared,
> We make our grim burnt offering; break our fast
> From cups of holy Brahman's skull; and ever,
> With gurgling drops of blood, that plenteous stream,
> From hard throats quickly cut, by us is worshipped
> With human offerings meet, our God, dread Bhairava."

Brahman mendicant (stopping his ears): "Buddhist, Buddhist, what think you of this? Oh! horrible discipline!"

Buddhist: "Sacred Arhata! some awful sinner has surely deceived that man."

Kápálika (in a rage): "Aha! sinner that thou art

* Prinsep's Journal, vi. 14—translated by Dr. Mill.

—vilest of heretics, with thy shaven crown, drest like the lowest outcasts — uncombed one! away with thee!"

23. The extravagance of this class of Tántrikas is further displayed by the Kápálika's boast:—

> "I call at will the best of Gods, great *Hari*,
> And HARA's self, and Brahma: I restrain
> With my sole voice the course of stars that wander
> In heaven's bright vault; the earth with all its load
> Of mountains, fields, and cities, I at will
> Reduce once more to water; and, behold!
> *I drink it up!*"

24. From this specimen of the Tántrika faith, it may be inferred that the cabalistic charms and mystic incantations, added to the *free use of spirituous liquors*, induced an excited state of mind in the votaries that was highly favourable to a full belief in the attainment of superhuman power. No wonder that the Buddhist considered such extravagance as the effect of delusion.

25. But the Tántrika doctrines continued to spread in spite of their wildness; and they at length became so popular that they were even carried into Nepal and Tibet, and permanently engrafted on the Buddhism of those countries. Their success was, however, as much due to force as to persuasion, for zealots are always persecutors. To Skanda Gupta, therefore, I would attribute the persecution of the Buddhists mentioned by Hwan Thsang.* Writing in the first half of the

* *Fo-kwe-ki*, c. xxiv. note 12.

seventh century, the Chinese pilgrim says:—"Not long ago the king, *She-shang-kia*, who persecuted and sought to abolish the Law of Buddha, tried also to destroy the stone which bore the holy impressions of his feet." As *She-shang-kia* is not included by Hwan Thsang amongst the five kings who reigned over Magadha previous to Siladitya's conquest, he must be looked for amongst the predecessors of Budha Gupta. Of these, the only one whose name at all resembles *She-shang-kia* is *Skanda*; and as his Tántrika zeal would naturally have led him to persecute the Buddhists, there is every probability in favour of the proposed identification. It is also not unlikely that the rebellion of Skanda Gupta's minister may have been caused by his persecution of Buddhism. But the followers of Sákya recovered their influence; and the holy stone, which She-shang-kia had thrown into the Ganges, was restored to its original position, where it was seen by Hwán Thsang about A. D. 642.

26. The interval between the death of Skanda Gupta and the date of Budha Gupta's pillar at Eran is only thirty-two years;* and as Hwan Thsang places *Lo-kia-lo-a-yi-to* (perhaps *Lokáditya*) as the immediate predecessor of Budha Gupta, a reign of about twenty-five years might be assigned to him to connect the series of the earlier Guptas found in the Pillar inscriptions with the later series recorded by the Chinese pilgrim. In the Seoni copperplate grants there is mention of Deva Gupta, a paramount sove-

* From 133 to 165, Anno Guptæ.

reign * whose authority was acknowledged by the petty Rajas of the Narbada. He must therefore have been one of the Magadha dynasty; and he might either be placed between the two series of Guptas, or be identified with the first of Hwan Thsang's princes. As Lo-kia-lo-a-yi-to is evidently some title, such as Lokáditya, "Sun-of-the-world," similar to those which we know were assumed by other members of this dynasty, it seems quite probable that Deva Gupta and Lo-kia-lo-a-yi-to were one and the same person.

27. The name of *Budha Gupta*, "cherished by Budha," refers so distinctly to his own faith that there can be no hesitation in classing him amongst the royal followers of Sákya. His pillar inscription is dated in the Gupta year 165, or A. D. 484; and I suppose that he may have reigned from about 480 to 510 A. D. During this period, in A. D. 502, the Chinese record † an embassy sent by the "King of India," named *Keu-to* (that is, *Gutto* or *Gupta*), to the Emperor of China with presents of crystal vases, perfumes, precious talismans, and other articles. The "kingdom of India" is afterwards described to be the country watered by the Ganges and its affluents; that is, Magadha as it existed under the Guptas, which included Magadha proper, and all the tributary provinces between the Himálayan and Vindhyan mountains. This vast empire was possessed by four Gupta

* Prinsep's Journal, v. 730, "Maharajadhiraja;" that is, the King of Kings.

† Chinese account of India, in Prinsep's Journal, vi. 65.

princes, the predecessors of Budha Gupta; and there is sufficient evidence to prove that *his* sway was equally extensive. He is mentioned by Hwan Thsang* amongst the kings of *Magadha;* he is called, in the Eran pillar inscription, king of the "beautiful country situated between the *Kálindi* and the *Narmada*,"† or Jumna and Narbada; and his silver coins are of the *Gujrat* type of the Sáhs of Surashtra, which was used by his predecessors, Kumára and Skanda. Mr. Thomas doubts the accuracy of James Prinsep's reading of Kálindi; but I can vouch for its correctness, as I have examined the inscription carefully, and am now writing with a fac-simile before me. What Mr. Thomas calls the very legible *r* over the concluding compound letter is only the long vowel *i*. The name is perfectly distinct on the pillar.

28. According to Hwan Thsang, Budha Gupta was succeeded by *Tha-ka-ta-kiu-to*, or *Takta Gupta;* but his dominions must have been confined to Magadha proper, as we learn from the inscription on the colossal *Varáha Avatár*, at Eran, that the paramount sovereign *Toramána* possessed all the country about Bhupâl and southern Bundelkhand not many years after the elevation of Budha Gupta's pillar; for the pillar was erected by Vaidala Vishnu, at the expense of his cousin Dhanya Vishnu, while the colossal Boar was set up by Dhanya Vishnu himself. The death of Budha Gupta, and the accession of Toramána,

* *Fo-kwe-ki*, Appendice. † Prinsep's Journal, vi. 634.

therefore both took place during the life-time of Dhanya Vishnu. But there must have been an interval of some years between the two events, as Dhanya's elder brother, Mátri Vishnu, who is not even mentioned in the pillar inscription, had since assumed the title of Mahárajа, and was then dead. Dhanya himself then became regent, apparently to the young prince, Toramâna; for, in another inscription from the Fort of Gwalior, I find Toramána described as the son of Mátri Dása, and the grandson of Mátrikula, who is probably the same as Matri Vishnu. As the celebrated hill of Udayagiri is mentioned in the Gwalior inscription, there can be little doubt of the identity of the two Toramánas, and of the consequent extension of the principality of Eran to the banks of the Jumna. The reign of Toramána* probably extended from A. D. 520 to 550, contemporary with Takta Gupta of Magadha.

29. From this time until the conquests of Siladitya, King of Malwa, in the early part of the seventh century, nothing certain is known of the history of India. Takta Gupta was succeeded by Nara Gupta Baladitya, and he was succeeded by Vajra, who was reigning when Siladitya conquered Magadha. According to Hwan Thsang, this warlike prince "fought battles such as had never been seen before," and all the northern provinces submitted to him. Hwan Thsang

* Mr. Prinsep read this king's name as *Tárapáni*; but I have examined the inscription myself, and can state positively that the name is *Toramána*.

visited his court in A. D. 642; and from him* we learn that the king sent an embassy with a present of books to the Chinese Emperor. This present proves that Siladitya was a follower of Buddha, for none but Bauddha works would have been acceptable to the Buddhist Emperor of China.

30. At the time of Hwan Thsang's visit, Buddhism was rapidly declining, many of the monasteries were in ruins, and temples of the heretical Brahmans were rising on all sides. At Benares there were one hundred heretical temples, and ten thousand heretics who worshipped Iswara,† while the Bauddhas had only thirty monasteries, and some three thousand monks and their disciples. Beyond the city, however, at the great temple in the Deer Park, there were about fifteen hundred monks and disciples; but altogether in this once holy place, where Buddha preached the law, there were twice as many heretics as Buddhists. In Kalinga,‡ also, the faithful were few, and the heretics very numerous. But, notwithstanding this spread of heretical opinions, the rulers of the land were still attached to Buddhism. The King of Chi-chi-to, Jajávati (that is, modern Bundelkhand), was a firm believer in the three precious ones,§ Buddha, Dharma, and Sangha. The great Siláditya of Malwa and Magadha was a Buddhist, and these two coun-

* *Fo-kwe-ki*, Appendice.

† *Fo-kwe-ki*, c. xxxiv. note.

‡ *Fo-kwe-ki*, Appendice, p. 389.

§ *Fo-kwe-ki*, Appendice, p. 393.

tries were still the most eminent in India for the study of Buddhism.*

31. From the fifth to the seventh century, the decline of Buddhism was gradual and gentle; but the farther progress of decay was then stayed for a time, and the expiring religion, like a dying lamp, still burst forth with occasional brightness, and its sudden flashes of light threw a transient brilliance over the wide-spreading gloom. In the seventh century Buddhism was propagated over the whole of Tibet; the magnificent stupa of *Sárnáth*, upwards of two hundred feet in height, was erected near Benares; and a colossal copper image of Buddha was set up, and several chaityas and vihárs built by the great Lalitáditya in Kashmir.† But, from the eighth century, the fall of Buddhism was rapid and violent. New dynasties arose who knew not Sákya; and the Tuärs of Delhi, the Rahtors of Kanoj, and the Chándels of Mahoba, succeeded to the vast empire of Siláditya. The rise of all these families has been traced to the eighth century; and both coins and inscriptions remain to attest their Brahmanical belief. But Buddhism continued to linger in Benares, in Malwa, and in Gujrát; and was not finally extinguished until the eleventh or the twelfth century, when the last votaries of Buddha were expelled from the continent of India. Numbers of images, concealed by the departing monks, are found buried near *Sárnáth*, and heaps of ashes still

* *Fo-kwe-ki*, Appendice, p. 392.

† Raja Tarangini, iv. sl. 188-216.

lie scattered amidst the ruins to show that the monasteries were destroyed by fire.*

32. The fall of Buddhism was a natural consequence of closing all roads to salvation, save the difficult path which led from one grade to another of the monastic orders. No layman could hope to be saved; and even the most zealous votary must have felt that the standard of excellence was too lofty to be reached. Absolute faith, perfect virtue, and supreme knowledge, were indispensable; and, without these, no man could attain Buddhahood, and final freedom from transmigration. Continued celibacy, abstinence, and privation, were expected from all who had taken the vows; and a long course of prayer, penance, and devout abstraction, were requisite before the votary could gain the rank of Arhata or Bodhisatwa. But as this was the *only* path to salvation, people of all ranks flocked to the monasteries—men crossed by fortune or disappointed in ambition, wives neglected by their husbands, and widows by their children, the sated debauchee, and the zealous enthusiast, all took the vows of celibacy, abstinence, and poverty. In the early ages of Buddhism the votaries supported themselves by daily

* I wrote this passage from my own knowledge, as I made many excavations around Sárnáth in 1835-36. Major Kittoe has since (1851) most fully confirmed my opinion by his more extended excavations in the same neighbourhood. He writes to me: "All has been sacked and burned—priests, temples, idols, all together; for in some places, bones, iron, wood, and stone, are found in huge masses, and this has happened more than once."

begging; but the pious generosity of individuals had gradually alienated the finest lands in the country for the support of the monasteries; and the mass of the people looked with envy upon the possessions of an idle multitude of monks. The rich domains of the monasteries attracted the notice of kings, and the desire of possession was soon followed by its accomplishment. The people looked on unmoved, and would not defend what they had long ceased to respect; and the colossal figure of Buddhism, which had once bestridden the whole continent of India, vanished suddenly like a rainbow at sunset.

CHAPTER XIII.

BUILDING AND DEDICATION OF TOPES

1. The following description of the building and dedication of a Tope is taken from the Mahawanso; and chiefly from the account of Dutthagámini's erection and consecration of the *Máha-thupo,* or "Great Tope" in Ceylon. A short notice of this kind is necessary for the better understanding of the minute details of the opening of the Bhilsa Topes, and for the easier comprehension of various scenes pictured in the Sánchi bas-reliefs.

2. When any wealthy or powerful person undertook to build a Tope, he first raised a pillar on the spot inscribed with a record of his intentions; which pillar was afterwards removed when the building of the Tope was begun. The Raja Devánampriya, who began to reign in Ceylon in the year 240 B.C., wished to erect a Tope on a spot consecrated by the teachings of Buddha; but being warned by the holy Mahendra that this great work was reserved for Dutthagámini, he was content to raise a stone pillar,* with an inscription recording his wish.

* *Mahawanso,* p. 97.

Dutthagámini, who reigned over Ceylon between the years 161 and 137 B.C., removed this pillar before laying the foundations of the Maháthupo.*

3. It would seem that the Topes were usually built by forced labour,† for Dutthagámini evidently made an exception in the case of the Maháthupo, for which he did not think it right to exact compulsory or unpaid labour.

4. The foundations were formed of round stones (perhaps boulders), which were trodden down by elephants. Above these were placed courses of fine clay, bricks, cement, *kuruwinda* stones, iron plates, divine incense (brought by the *Srámaneras*, from the Hemawanta), *phalika* stones (steatite), common stone, plates of brass (imbedded in *Kapittho* gum which had been moistened with the milk of small red cocoa-nuts), and plates of silver (cemented with vermilion mixed in oil of sesamum).‡ I have preserved this extravagant account simply because I think it probable that most of these particulars may be partially true. The plates of silver and brass, and even of iron, were possibly only small discs; and the course of *phalika* stone only a single slab; each deposited in the centre of the building.

5. The laying of the foundation stone was attended with as much solemnity as now takes place at the same ceremony in England. "Revered ones!" said the Mahárája, "To-morrow, I will lay the festival-

* *Mahawanso*, p. 169. † *Mahawanso*, pp. 165 and 175.

‡ *Mahawanso*, p. 169.

brick of the Great Chaitya; let all the fraternities assemble there:" and further, he proclaimed, "Let all my people attend with offerings for Buddha, and with garlands." The road leading from the city to the site of the Tope was decorated; and on the appointed morning, the moon being full, the king, attended by his ministers, and accompanied by thousands of troops, with dancing and singing women, and bands of musicians, proceeded to the site of the *Maháthupo.** On reaching the place he made an offering of one thousand and eight suits of clothing; which were deposited in the middle, and at the four sides, of the intended site.

6. The ceremony was attended by numbers of Bhikshus from the principal monastic establishments in India; from Rájagriha and Vaisáli; from Benares, Srávasti, and Kosambi; from Ujain, and from the wilderness of Vindhya; from Kashmir, and from Alasadda (or Alexandria), the capital of Yona (or Greek country of Kabul).† The king, encircled by the multitude of Bhikshus, entered the holy space, and, bowing with reverence to them, presented an offering of garlands. Then walking thrice round the site, he stationed himself in the centre, and with a pair of highly polished silver compasses pointed with gold, described a circle for the lower course of bricks. He next placed in the centre eight gold and eight silver vases, and encircled them with eight

* *Mahawanso*, p. 170. † *Mahawanso*, p. 172.

gold and eight silver bricks.* Around each brick he deposited one hundred and eight pieces of cloth, and around the whole one hundred and eight new earthen vases. Then taking up the eastern brick the king deposited it again in a fragrant cement formed of the jessamine flowers which had been offered on the holy spot. In the same manner seven ministers of state deposited the other seven bricks. Then the king, bowing down to the assembled Bhikshus, again made offerings on the four sides of the site; and repairing to the north-east point, bowed with reverence to the great *Sthavira* PRIYADARSI, who at once began to chant the *jaya mangala*, "or hymn of joy," which was uttered by Sákya at the moment of his attaining Buddhahood.†

7. The bricklayers were assembled by beat of drum; and the Rajah inquired from the architect, "In what form dost thou propose to construct the chaitya?" The architect, taking some water in the palm of his hand, dashed it into a golden vessel full of water, and pointing to a hemispherical bubble of air which stood for a moment on the surface, he said, "I will build it in this form."‡

8. The relic-chamber was formed of six clouded slabs of stone (*méghawanna*). One was placed flat, four were arranged like the sides of a box, and the sixth (which was the lid) was placed to the eastward.§

* *Mahawanso*, p. 173.

† See chap. iv. 7, of this volume for Buddha's hymn.

‡ *Mahawanso*, p. 175. § *Mahawanso*, p. 179.

In the middle of this chamber was deposited a golden *bodhi*-tree, and round it were placed golden images of Buddha. Various acts in the life of Buddha were depicted on the sides of the chamber, which was illuminated with rows of lamps fed with scented oil.

9. On the evening of the day of full moon the king Dutthagámini, in a chariot drawn by four white horses, carried the golden relic-casket on his head, surmounted by the canopy of dominion, towards the Tope. The procession was headed by the state elephant *Kandulo*, fully caparisoned; and the chariot was surrounded by men and women bearing vases, baskets of flowers, torches, and flags. Elephants, horses, and chariots, followed in the procession; and the crash of all kinds of vocal and instrumental music was so loud that it seemed as if the earth was being rent asunder.*

10. On reaching the Tope the pious monarch received the relics from the chief *sthavira*, and deposited them in a golden casket. Then placing the casket on a throne he made his offerings to the relics; and bowing reverentially down, stood with uplifted hands joined in adoration. He now dedicated his canopy of dominion (that is, the royal chatta) to the relics, and exclaimed with joy, "Thrice over do I dedicate my kingdom to the redeemer of the world, the divine teacher, the bearer of the triple canopy, the canopy of the heavenly host, the canopy of mortals, and the canopy of eternal emancipation."

* *Mahawanso*, p. 186.

11. Then placing the relic-casket on his head, the monarch presented more offerings, and, encircled by the Bhikshus, thrice perambulated the Tope; and mounting the eastern side he descended into the relic-chamber. On all sides stood the *arhatas* with uplifted hands joined in adoration, while the king deposited the relic-casket on the golden altar. He next made an offering of all the royal ornaments on his person, and for seven days invested the relics with the sovereignty of *Lanka.** The ministers and all the people in attendance likewise made offerings of all the ornaments on their persons. Hymns were chanted throughout the night by the Bhikshus; the lid of the relic-chamber was closed by two *srámaneras;* and the enshrinement of the relic was completed.

12. After this "thousands of relics" were deposited by the people above the relic-chamber,† and the dome was closed, and crowned by a square capital.‡ At this time, when only the *chatta* (or canopy) and the plastering remained to be done, the Raja fell sick, and enjoined his younger brother *Tisso* to finish the Tope. As the Raja was at the point of death Tisso quickly covered the whole Tope with white cloth sewn together, and raised a cloth umbrella with a bambu

* Or Ceylon. *Mahawanso,* p. 190.

† *Mahawanso,* p. 192—"*Sahassa dhatunan,*" thousands of relics.

‡ See the relic-casket in the shape of a crystal Tope found in No. 2 Tope, at Bhojpur, Plate XXVI. See also the restoration of the great Sánchi Tope, Plate VIII.

handle on the summit; and then announced to the king that the Tope was finished. The dying monarch was carried to the holy spot, and laid upon a carpet opposite the southern entrance, where, after gazing with delight on the Tope, he breathed his last. The pinnacle and the plastering of the dome, and the enclosing parapet wall, were all completed by his brother *Saddhátisso* who succeeded him on the throne of Ceylon.

13. About one hundred and twenty years afterwards, between 19 and 9 B. C., the Raja *Bhátikábhayo* festooned the great Tope with garlands of jessamine flowers from top to bottom, and fixed flowers in the intervals by their stalks. He next covered the Chaitya with a paste of red lead, one finger thick, and studded the paste with flowers. He then buried the whole chaitya, from the steps at its enclosure to the top of its pinnacle, in a heap of flowers: and lastly he white-whashed it with oyster-shell lime, and studded it over with a net-work of *pánála* stones, and fixed golden flowers, of the size of chariot-wheels, in the interstices. He likewise added two cornices,* or copings, to the basement of the building.

14. Between the year 21 and 30 A. D., the Raja *Amandagámini* erected another *chatta*† on the pinnacle of the Great Tope, and added copings to the base and crown of the dome. Images of the four

* *Mahawano*, p. 211-215.

† *Mahawanso*, p. 221—*Chattadhichattan*, or "Chatta-above-chatta." See the Sanchi Chaitya No. 1.

Buddhas were presented to the Great Tope by Raja *Wasabho* who reigned from 66 to 110 A. D. And lastly, Raja Sirinágo, between the years 184 and 209 A. D., gilded * the *chatta* of the *Maháthupo*, and inserted gems in the centre of each of the " four emblems of the sun."†

15. This account agrees so closely with the present state of the great Sánchi *chaitya* that it might be taken as an actual description of that building. The hemispherical form, the square crown, the chatta above chatta, are all the same, and there are also the same statues of the four Buddhas, and the same " emblems of the sun" over the four gateways.

16. In the *Maháthupo*, the relic-chamber was placed low down in the building, for the king had to " descend" into it to deposit the casket. But in the *Thupárámo*, which was built by Devánampriya about 240 B. C., the chamber was excavated knee deep on the summit of the dome for the reception of the relics.‡ This agrees with the position of the chamber in the great Tope at Sonári.

17. Lastly, the ground was consecrated by the Bhikshus with the performance of *uposatho* and other rites, after the boundary had been marked out by the king in procession with a golden plough drawn by two state elephants.§ This ceremony was performed

* *Mahawanso*, p. 226.

† *Mahawanso*, p. 229—*chattunan suriyanan*, " four suns."

‡ *Mahwanso*, p. 104.

§ *Mahawanso*, p. 98.

with the same display which has already been described in the procession of the relic-casket.

18. But this account describes only the older kind of Tope, which was a simple hemisphere, such as the great Chaityas at Sánchi and at Satdhára, and which probably date as high as the middle of the sixth century before our era. The next in point of antiquity are the Topes around Bhilsa, which contain the relics of Asoka's missionaries, and of the venerable Mogaliputra, who conducted the proceedings of the Third Synod. In these, which were built in the end of the third century before Christ, the dome is raised a few feet above the basement by a cylindrical plinth. The third class of Topes are those represented in the Sánchi bas-reliefs, which date between 19 and 37 A. D. In these the hemisphere is placed on a plinth of equal height, so that the centre of the dome is the centre of the whole building. Six representations of this kind of Tope occur amongst the Sánchi bas-reliefs, of which one is on the southern gate of No. 2 Tope, and another on the southern gate of No. 3 Tope.*

19. The crystal Chaitya discovered in No. 2 Tope, at Bhojpur, is also of the same shape; and I am therefore inclined to attribute the erection of that Tope to the beginning of the Christian era. The Topes in Affghanistan are mostly of this shape. In the latest Topes, of which Sárnáth, near Benares, is a magnificent specimen, the plinth is equal in height to the diameter of the hemisphere. Two specimens of

* For two of these Topes see Plate III., figs. 1 and 2.

this kind are given in Plate III., from the small dedicatory Topes now lying in the enclosure of the Great Sanchi Chaitya.

20. From these remarks it is evident that the age of almost every Tope may be obtained approximately from its shape; the most ancient being a simple hemisphere, and the latest a tall round tower surmounted by a dome.

CHAPTER XIV.

SÁNCHI TOPES.

1. The small village of Sánchi is situated on the low ridge of a sandstone hill, on the left bank of the Betwa, about five miles and a half to the south-west of Bhilsa, and twenty miles to the north-east of Bhupál. The hill is flat-topped and isolated, with a steep cliff to the eastward; and to the westward an easy slope covered with jungul at the foot, and near the top broken into steps by horizontal ledges of rock.

2. The general direction of the hill is from north to south, and its whole summit is covered with ruins. But the principal buildings that now remain occupy only the middle part of the level top, and a narrow belt leading down the hill to the westward. The summit itself has a gentle slope in the same direction with the dip of the strata; and the level of the court of the great Tope is some twelve or fifteen feet below that of the ruined vihar and temple on the eastern edge of the precipice. The hill, which is about three hundred feet in height, is formed of a light red sandstone, hard and compact in texture, but subject to

split. This stone has been used for all the Topes and other buildings where mere hardness and durability were required; but for the colonnades and sculptured gateways a fine-grained white sandstone was brought from the Udayagiri hill, three miles and a half to the northward.

3. The group of Topes at Sánchi is represented in Plate IV. The Topes are numbered from 1 to 11, and the other objects are described in the plan. Of these the most remarkable is a large stone bowl, now lying on a small mound between the two principal Topes. The interior dimensions of the bowl are—diameter, 4½ feet; depth, 2½ feet. The thickness at top is 6 inches, at bottom 18 inches. The size of this bowl agrees so closely with that of the golden vessel,* in which Asoka despatched the "cutting" of the great Bo-tree to Ceylon, that it seems highly probable the Sánchi bowl must once have held a sacred tree. Indeed I feel inclined to go even farther, for I suspect that this bowl once held the holy nettle which Buddha himself had bitten off and planted. But this depends upon the identification of *Sánchi* with the *Shá-chi* of Fa Hian, a point which I will now examine.

4. On leaving *Ki-jao-i*, or Kanoj, Fa Hian proceeded about twenty miles to the opposite bank of the Ganges; and from thence, he says, "ten *yojans* to

* *Mahawanso*, pp. 111, 112. Asoka's vase was nine cubits in circumference, three cubits in diameter, five cubits in depth, and eight fingers (*atthangula*) in thickness.

the south-west you come to the great kingdom of *Sha-chi*;" and "thence, proceeding south to the distance of eight *yojans*, you arrive at the kingdom of *Kiu-sa-lo*, and the town of *She-wei*" (Ajudhya, or Audh). There is a difficulty in this part of the route which (I agree with Mr. Laidlay* in thinking) can only be explained away on the supposition of a misprint in the French edition, or an error in the original Chinese. Ajudhya is almost due *east* from Kanoj; and the direct distance is much more than eighteen *yojans*. Hwan Thsang is silent regarding Sháchi, although he travelled over this part of the country, and describes it in detail; besides which we know of no place of Buddhist celebrity between Kanoj and Ajudhya. On the other hand, we have the absolute identity of the names of Shá-chi, and Sánchi or Sáchi,† and the knowledge that Sánchi was a large Bauddha establishment, as well as the capital of a kingdom, at the time of Fa Hian's visit. The south-westerly direction is correct, but the distance should be about fifty *yojans* instead of ten.

5. The name of Sánchi, or Sáchi, is most probably only the spoken form of the Sanskrit *Sánti*: for I find the term *Sánti-sangham* (the Sánti community)

* *Fo-kwe-ki*, c. xix. note 2—Mr. Laidlay's translation. It is impossible to conceive that any "great" kingdom, as Fa Hian calls Sháchi, could have intervened between the kingdoms of Samkassa and Kosala, or the present Mainpuri and Oudh.

† See Journal As. Soc. Bengal, vol. xvii. p. 746. The name is always written *Sátchi* by my brother.

used in the inscription on the southern pillar of the Great Tope.* The Chinese also transcribed *sánti* by *sá-chi*; for they say that it signifies "silence, repose."† This proves the identity of the names; but until the original text of the Fo-kwe-ki has been re-examined, nothing more can be insisted upon than the probability of the identification.

6. The story of the nettle is thus told by Fa Hian. "On leaving the town of *Sha-chi* by the Southern Gate you find to the East of the road, the place where Fo bit a branch of nettle and planted it in the ground. This branch sprang up and grew to the height of seven feet, and afterwards neither increased nor diminished. The heretical Brahmans, fired with envy, cut and tore it to throw it away; but it always sprang up again in the same place."

7. The present village of Sánchi is situated on the low spur connecting the Tope-hill with the Kánakhera-hill. The village is now very small; but the numerous ruins scattered over the hill between Sánchi and Kánakhera prove that there has once been a large town on this site. At the time of Fa Hian's visit it was one of the principal places in the kingdom of Sanakánika. On leaving it by the South gate, the road led (as it does now) along the foot of the hill; and the great stone bowl was therefore to the eastward, as described by Fa Hian.

* See Plate XIX. No. 177, for this inscription.

† *Fo-kwe-ki*, c. xvii. note 17.

No. 1 Tope.—Sánchi.

8. The great Sánchi Tope is situated on the western edge of the hill. The ground has once been carefully levelled, by cutting away the surface rock on the east, and by building up a retaining wall on the west. The court (as it now exists) averages one hundred and fifty yards in length, and is exactly one hundred yards in breadth. In the midst stands the Great Chaitya, No. I.,* surrounded by a massive colonnade. The bald appearance of the solid dome is relieved by the lightness and elegance of the highly picturesque gateways. On all sides are ruined temples, fallen columns, and broken sculptures: and even the Tope itself, which had withstood the destructive rancour of the fiery Saivas and the bigoted Musalmáns, has been half-ruined by the blundering excavations of amateur antiquaries.

9. In the north-east, south-east, and south-west corners of the court there are small ruined Topes, marked Nos. 5, 6, 7 in the plan, Plate IV. In the south there is a small temple of middle age, and an old Chaitya temple with lofty square columns. The semicircular end of this temple was first traced by my brother,

* "There is a stern round tower of other days,
Firm as a fortress with its fence of stone;
Such as an army's baffled strength delays,
Standing with half its battlements alone,

Captain J. D. Cunningham,* and afterwards more leisurely by Lieut. Maisey, who made an excavation on the supposed site of the Chaitya, and was rewarded by the discovery of a small chamber containing a broken steatite vase.

10. The great Tope itself is a solid dome of stone and brick, 106 feet in diameter, and 42 feet in height, springing from a plinth of 14 feet, with a projection of 5½ feet from the base of the building, and a slope of 2½ feet. The plinth or basement formed a terrace for the perambulation of worshippers of the enshrined relic; for, on the right pillar of the North Gateway there is a representation of a Tope and of two worshippers walking round it,† with garlands in their hands. The terrace was reached by a double flight of steps to the south, connected by a landing ten feet square.‡

11. The apex of the dome was flattened into a terrace 34 feet in diameter, surrounded by a stone railing of that style so peculiar to Bauddha monuments, that I will venture to call it the "Buddhist Railing."

> And with two thousand years of ivy grown,
> The garland of eternity—where wave
> The green leaves, over all by Time o'erthrown,
> What was this tower of strength? Within its cave
> What treasure lay so locked, so hid? A *hermit's* grave."
>
> BYRON: *Childe Harold.*

* Journal As. Soc. Bengal, xvii. Plate XXVIII.

† See Plate XIII.

‡ See Plate VIII.

Many of the pillars of this colonnade are now lying at the base of the monument; and several portions of the coping or architrave prove that the enclosure was a circular one. The inscriptions Nos. 173, 174, 175, and 176, are taken from the fallen pillars of this colonnade. The pillars are 3 feet 4 inches high, 9 inches broad, and 7½ inches thick. They are of the same pattern as those of the lower enclosure, and in fact of all the enclosures of Buddhist Topes throughout India.* I counted nearly forty of these pillars, but several must be buried beneath the rubbish of the destructive excavation made by the amateur antiquaries in 1822.† As the spaces between the pillars were, as nearly as can now be ascertained, about one foot, this enclosure would have required exactly sixty-one pillars.

12. Within the upper enclosure there was a square altar or pedestal surrounded by pillars of the same description, but much taller, some of which are still lying on the top of the dome. In 1819, when Captain Fell visited Sánchi,‡ these pillars were all there; but one of the corner pillars is now lying at the base of the monument to the north-west. It is proved to have belonged to a *square* enclosure, by its having faces at right angles to each other with two rows of mortices for the reception of the ends of the stone

* See Plates VII., IX., XXIII., and XXVIII., for specimens of enclosures.

† Prinsep's Journal, iv. 712.

‡ Prinsep's Journal, iii. 490.

rails. The projecting cornice of this altar or pedestal is restored from the numerous representations of Topes amongst the bas-reliefs of the gateways. The cupola or umbrella-pinnacle is restored from existing fragments guided by the designs of Topes just mentioned.* One piece is now lying on the top of the dome, and another at the foot of the breach. This cupola was 5 feet 6 inches in diameter, and 2 feet high. It is hollowed out underneath; and above it has a mortice 8 inches deep for the reception of a staff of a second cupola, such as we see represented in the bas-reliefs.

13. The total height of the building including the cupolas must have been upwards of one hundred feet.

14. The base of the Tope is surrounded by a massive colonnade, 144½ feet in diameter from west to east, and 151½ feet in diameter from north to south. This enclosure is therefore elliptical; the greater diameter exceeding the lesser by 7 feet. By this arrangement a free passage is obtained round the southern staircases, and a greater breadth at the foot of the ascent. The breadth of the cloister on the north-west and north-east sides averages 9 feet 7 inches, the several measurements only differing by a few inches. From east to south the cloister increases rapidly in width; the breadth at the east being only 9 feet 11 inches, and at the foot of the staircase 13 feet 8 inches. The elliptical form is

* See two specimens in Plate III., figs. 1 and 2.

shown distinctly in my brother's plan,* although he does not mention it in his description.

15. The pillars of this colonnade are 9 feet 10½ inches in height, with an average thickness of 1 foot 10½ inches. The front and back of each pillar have three faces; a middle one, 9½ inches in breadth, and two side ones, slightly bevelled, each 6½ inches broad. The pillars are let into the ground from 15 to 18 inches. The interval or inter-columniation is 2 feet 1½ inch.

16. The rails are three in number with intervals of 4 inches. Each rail is 2 feet 1½ inch long, and the same broad. The section is formed of two intersecting circular segments, with a double versed sine of 9½ inches, which forms the thickness of the rail. The mortices in the pillars are of the same section as the rails, and are from 3 to 4 inches in depth.

17. The architrave or coping is formed of long solid blocks rounded at top, each 2 feet 3 inches in height, by 2 feet 1 inch in thickness. Each beam spans two intercolumniations, and has three mortices for receiving the tenons of the three pillars. Some of the beams are connected together by tenons and mortices, and others by stone joggles.

18. A view of this remarkable stone-railing is given in Plate IX., which shows the general disposition of the numerous inscriptions. The style is evidently characteristic and conventional, as it is

* Journal As. Soc. Bengal, xvii. Plate XXVIII.

found wherever the Bauddha religion prevails.* It is in fact so peculiar to Buddhism that I have ventured to name it "the Buddhist railing." This peculiar railing is still standing around the principal Topes at Sánchi and Andher; and some pillars and other fragments are still lying around the great Topes at Sonári and Satdhára. The same railing was placed around the holy Bodhi Trees,† and the pillars dedicated to Buddha.‡ The balconies of the City Gates,§ and of the King's Palace,|| were enclosed by it. It formed the bulwarks of the State Barge.¶ It was used as an ornament for the capitals of columns, as on the northern pillar at Sánchi;** and generally for every plain band of architectural moulding. At Sánchi it is found in many places as an ornament on the horizontal bars which separate the bas-reliefs from each other.

19. The Sánchi railing has one entrance at each of the four cardinal points; as represented in the plan in Plate IV. Each entrance is covered in

* No less than nine specimens of this kind of railing were found amongst the Bhilsa Topes, all of which are described in the following pages. In Plate IX. fig 3, I have added a specimen from the great Dipaldinna Mound at Amaravati, for the description of which see Prinsep's Journal, vol. vi. Plate X.

† See coins, in Plates XXXI. and XXXII.

‡ See Plate XXXI. fig. 1, and Plate XXXII. fig. 11.

§ Bas-relief at Sánchi, Eastern Gateway, Plate XV. fig. 3.

|| Bas-relief of Eastern Gateway—Fergusson's Illustrations.

¶ Bas-relief of Western Gateway, Left Pillar, Inner Face, No. III.

** See Plate X.

front, and to the left (as seen from the outside), by a short railing of the same style. In after times another short railing was added to the right of each, and the entrance was changed to the front through a lofty gateway.

20. These four gateways are the most picturesque and valuable objects at Sánchi, as they are entirely covered with bas-reliefs representing various domestic scenes and religious ceremonies. Each gateway is formed of two square pillars, 2 feet 3 inches thick, and 13 feet 8 inches in height. The capitals of these pillars vary. The pillars of the western gate have each four human dwarfs; those of the southern gate have four lions; and those of the other gateways have four elephants surmounted by their riders. The height of the capital is 4 feet 6 inches. The total height of the gateway is 18 feet 2 inches, and its breadth is 7 feet 1 inch.

21. The pillars are crowned by an architrave 19 feet 9 inches in length, with an arched rise of 4 inches in the middle, and a projection of 4 feet 5 inches on each side. These projecting ends are supported by brackets, each formed of the stem and foliage of a tree, beneath which is a *náchni*, or dancing woman. The style of hair and the peculiar bead-girdle of these female dancers, is so much like those of some of the Tibetan women of the present day, that one is naturally led to trace them to an Indo-Scythian origin; especially when we know that the Indo-Scythian power was paramount in India at

the very time that these gateways were erected.* A second architrave is placed above the other at a height of 2 feet 2½ inches, and is supported by five uprights, of which two are simple continuations of the pillars. This second architrave is 2 feet and ¾ inch in height; and its ends project only 4 feet 2 inches. Five uprights of the same height as this architrave, support a third architrave only 1 foot 9½ inches, in height, with diminished projections of 3 feet 11 inches. The ends of the architraves are formed into narrow threaded volutes surmounted by winged lions. The open spaces between the uprights contain small figures of elephant riders below, and of horsemen above; and on the outside of the pillars there are small figures of female dancers.

22. The summit is crowned in the middle by a wheel (half broken) upwards of three feet in diameter, supported by four elephants. On each side, immediately above the pillars, there is a peculiar emblem, which will be described hereafter. Between each of these emblems and the wheel there is a male attend-

* See Plate XIV. for one of these dancing figures. The features are quite Tibetan; and this peculiarity is so strong that it has struck others besides myself. Thus Captain Eyre writes to me: "A very remarkable feature in the sculptures is the peculiar Tartar-like physiognomies of the principal figures. How is this to be accounted for? The sculptors must have been familiar with that peculiar form of the 'human face divine,' or they would not so successfully have chiselled it. It seems to me probable, therefore, that the conquering race must have been of Tartar origin." For the complete figure, see the Frontispiece of Fergusson's Illustrations.

ant with a *chaori*, or Tibetan cow's tail. The wheel is the symbol of Buddha; and the peculiar monograph on each side is the emblem of Dharma.*

23. The whole of these gateways, excepting where they abut on the railings, are most elaborately carved. The faces of the pillars are divided into compartments, each containing a scene either religious or domestic. The faces of the architraves, both front and rear, represent—(1st) sieges; (2nd) triumphal processions either entering or leaving cities; (3rd) adoration of Topes, and of trees; (4th) processions escorting relic-caskets; and (5th) ascetic life in the woods. A short description of these valuable delineations of ancient Indian manners and customs will be given at the end of this account of the Great Sánchi Tope, along with the translations of all the inscriptions.

24. Within the enclosure, and immediately facing each entrance, there is a large figure. Each figure has once rested under a canopy supported in front on a couple of pillars; but these have long since been broken, and the figures themselves have been very much injured. The eastern statue is now lying on its face; but, by digging under it, Lieutenant Maisey discovered that it was a seated figure, which I believe to be that of KRAKUCHANDA, the first mortal Buddha.

* See Plate VII. for a view of the Great Tope, with its peculiar gateways. The wheel, or emblem of Buddha, will be found in Plate XXXI. fig. 2; and the other emblem, which is that of Dharma, in Plate XXXII. fig. 10.

The southern statue is a standing figure, with a halo round the head. To the right and left there are two attendant figures of half size, and a small elephant. This is most probably a statue of KANAKA, the second mortal Buddha. The western figure is much mutilated, and the head is entirely gone. It is seated, and probably represents KÁSYAPA, the third mortal Buddha. The northern statue is seated cross-legged, with both hands in the lap, the palms uppermost. The head is surrounded by an ornamental nimbus. A small figure, sceptre in hand, hovers above each shoulder; and a male attendant stands on each side, with his left hand resting in his girdle, and his right bearing a mace, or *chaori*. This is no doubt a statue of SÁKYA SINHA, the last mortal Buddha, seated in the very attitude in which he obtained Buddhahood.

25. These four statues are referred to in one of the longer railing inscriptions which has been translated by James Prinsep.* Amongst other things this inscription records a gift of money, the interest of which was to be expended in daily lamps, for the four shrines of *the four Buddhas.* The inscription is very rudely cut, and fully merits the description which James Prinsep gave it, of a "network of scratches." But as the four Buddhas and the four Buddhist shrines are twice mentioned, there is no doubt of the correctness of Prinsep's reading. The date of the

* Journal, vi. 459. This inscription is generally called the Hariswámini inscription, from the names of the recorder.

record is doubtful;* but it appears to me to be in the fourth century of the Vikramaditya Samvat. The figure for 300 is clear, and so is that for 1; but the middle figure, which is the same as the letter *l*, is doubtful. We know that it is not 10, or 18, or 90; and this limits the date within fifty years, between 321 and 371 Samvat, or A. D. 264 and 314. If the Saka era of 78 A. D. was used, the date will range between 399 and 441 A. D. I have used the earlier epochs instead of the Gupta era, because the latter would bring the date of the inscription down to the middle of the seventh century, at which period we know that the alphabets of India were the same as the modern Tibetan. The form of the characters shows that this inscription was not later than the time of the earlier Guptas. The date, therefore, whether reckoned in Samvat or in Saka, will range between 300 and 400 A. D.

26. A few feet to the east of the southern entrance there is still standing the lower portion of a magnificent lion pillar. Other portions of the shaft as well as the capital are lying on the ground to the south. By a careful measurement of the different pieces, I found that the height of the shaft must have been 31 feet 11 inches. Captain Fell calls it 32 feet.† The diameter at the base is 2 feet 10 inches; and at the neck it was only 2 feet 3 inches; the total

* See inscription No. 198, Plate XXI. of this volume, for a fac-simile of this date.

† Prinsep's Journal, iii. Plate XXXI.

diminution, therefore, is 7 inches, or nearly one-fifth of the lower diameter. At 10 feet the diameter is 2 feet 8 inches, and at 21 feet it was 2 feet 6½ inches. These measurements show that this pillar had a gentle swell in the middle of the shaft, and that the early Indian architects followed the same practice in this respect as the Greeks. The whole diminution being 7 inches, the proportional diminution (if the sides of the column were straight) would be 2·19 inches at 10 feet, and 4·60 inches at 21 feet. There is thus an increase in the thickness of the shaft of rather more than one inch at two-thirds of its height.

27. The capital of the column is 2 feet 10½ inches in height. It is somewhat like a bell in shape, but with a greater swell near the top, and is ornamented with narrow festoons. The bell was surmounted by a corded *torus* of 4 inches, above which was a plain circular band of 3¼ inches, surmounted by a very handsome circular abacus 6 inches in height. The abacus is ornamented with some very Grecian-looking foliage, and with four pairs of *chakwas*, or holy Brahmani ducks. These birds are always seen in pairs, and are celebrated amongst the Hindus for their conjugal affection. They are therefore represented billing, with outstretched necks, and heads lowered towards the ground.*

28. The total height of the capital is 3 feet 11¾ inches, or exactly one-eighth of the height of shaft.

* See the abacus of the Allahabad Pillar in Prinsep's Journal, iv. Plate IX., or Layard's Nineveh, ii. 295.

Its width is 3 feet, or just three-fourths of its height. If the dimensions of the capital were obtained from any multiple of the lower diameter, it is probable that the rule was to make the height of capital equal to 1½ diameter of the base. The south pillar is 2 feet 10 inches in diameter, but the northern pillar is only 2 feet 7 inches, and the mean of the two is 2 feet 8½ inches. This would give a capital of 4 feet and ¾ inch in height, which is within one inch of the measured height.

20. The capital is crowned by four lions standing back to back; each four feet in height. The heads are all broken; but the limbs, which are still perfect, are so boldly sculptured, and the muscles and claws are so accurately represented, that they might well be placed in comparison with many specimens of Grecian art. I attribute these pillars to the period of Asoka's reign, when Greek princes were ruling in Bactria and Kabul. We know that the "barbaric pearl and gold" of the Mogul emperors from Akbar to Aurangzeb attracted numbers of European jewellers and goldsmiths to the Indian Court: and we may therefore naturally infer that the architectural munificence of Asoka would have allured many Greek sculptors and architects from the neighbouring kingdoms of Bactria and Syria. But there is one reason which more than the others inclines me to attribute these lions to a Grecian artist, namely, the correct delineation of the feet, which have four large front claws, and one small hind claw. Now this lion

capital has been imitated by the sculptor of the pillars of the South Gateway, which we know was erected during the reign of Sri Sátakarni in the early half of the first century of the Christian era. On these pillars the lions are represented with *five large front claws,* and some straight channels up and down are perhaps intended for the muscles. The marked difference of style shows a considerable difference of age; and I attribute the pillars to the same early period as the railing. The native sculptor of Sátakarni's reign was no match for the Greek artist employed by Asoka.

30. To the north of the Tope there is a second isolated column of similar dimensions to the last. It stands on a square plinth 9 feet 3 inches in width at base, 8 feet wide at top, and 3 feet 6 inches in height. It is broken into three steps, as shown in the sketch in Plate X. The lower portion of the shaft is still standing; and the capital is now lying to the northward, at a distance of 32½ feet from the shaft. The other portions of the shaft are missing; but the socket in the lower end of the capital shows that the neck of the shaft was 2 feet 3¼ inches in diameter, or the same as that of the southern pillar. The base is only 2 feet 7 inches in diameter. As these dimensions are nearly the same as those of the other column, and as the measured distance of the prostrate capital from the base of the shaft is only seven inches more than the height of the remaining shaft, I have assumed that the two pillars were most probably of the same height.

31. The bell capital of the northern pillar is terminated by an octagonal abacus, 6 inches in height. Above this there is a massive pedestal 3 feet square, and 2 feet $2\frac{1}{2}$ inches in height, which is ornamented on all four sides with a representation of the Buddhist railing. The pillar is crowned by a human figure of rather more than life size. The arms are both missing from the shoulders, and the statue is broken off at midleg. The lower parts of the legs are wanting, but the feet are still adhering to the upper part of the large tenon which was morticed into the head of the pillar.

32. The figure is dressed in the Indian *dhoti* gathered around the loins, and drawn in folds across the thighs. The end of the *dhoti* cloth flutters behind the left thigh. The body and the legs are naked. There is a necklace round the neck, and a belt or girdle round the waist. The left hand probably rested on the left hip; but the position of the right hand I cannot even guess. The expression of the face is placid, but cheerful; the posture of the figure is easy, though standing with unbent knees, and altogether there is an air of calm dignity about the statue that places it amongst the finest specimens of Indian sculpture. It probably represents Asoka himself, for there is a figure of Sákya within the northern entrance.

33. The total height of this pillar was forty-five feet and a half, and that of the south pillar very nearly forty feet. They were formed of a light-

coloured compact sandstone and were very highly polished. This polish* still remains on the shafts, and on the smoother portions of the statues. The south pillar has an inscription in the oldest Indian Páli, but it is too much mutilated to be read with any certainty, excepting in the closing lines.†

34. There is every reason to believe that these noble columns would have been standing at this day, had it not been for the petty avarice of the neighbouring zamindars. The southern pillar has been broken off at 6½ feet from its base, and the rest of the shaft is now lying in two pieces on the ground *towards the south.* The capital of the northern pillar is lying to the *north* of its shaft. Thus both pillars have fallen *outwards* from the building. This could scarcely be the effect of an earthquake; but would naturally be the case if they had been pulled down for the purpose of making use of their material. Now there is a row of holes chiselled across the middle portion of the southern pillar, which prove that since its fall the people have attempted to cut it into lengths for their own use. Each of these pieces would have formed a sugar-mill, such as has been in use in India from time immemorial. But it may be asked, "Why did the cutter desist from his labour, and leave the wished-for stone at the top of the hill?"

* The same high polish is observable on the Allahabad and Delhi Pillars; and also on the Radhiya, Mathiya, and Bakra Pillars, as I am informed by Major Kittoe.

† See No. 177, Plate XIX.

The answer is simple and conclusive. During the operation of cutting, the stone split longitudinally from top to bottom, and was no longer of any use. The same cause preserved the upper portion of the southern pillar. I presume therefore that the shaft of the northern pillar did not split, and that it was long ago carried away and formed into sugar-mills. It is right, however, to add that I made inquiries for sugar-mills in the neighbourhood without success: although the ignorance of the people by no means proves their non-existence.

35. Close to the eastern gateway there is a third pillar with a shaft 13 feet high, and rather more than one foot in diameter. Its capital is bell-shaped, like those of the others; and it is crowned by a single seated lion.

36. To the north-east of the Tope also there are two small broken pillars, of which one bears an incomplete inscription in characters of the early Gupta period, about 400 A. D. This inscription is given in Plate XXI. No. 199. It reads, "* * *di Hariswámi-Gosha Sinha Baliputra* * *" that is, "HARISWÁMI GOSHA the son of SINHABALI."* This Hariswámi probably belonged to the same family as the Hariswámini before mentioned, who was the donor of lamps to the shrines of the four Buddhas.

37. At the north-west angle of the court, a flight of steps formerly led down the hill towards No. 2 Tope. Due north there is a ruined flight of steps

* This inscription had escaped the notice of previous visitors.

leading past No. 3 Tope into the road towards the village of Sánchi. At the head of these steps there are two colossal figures, probably of porters or gate-keepers. On the outside of the western wall, and about 20 feet below the level of the court, there is a long, dry tank cut out of the solid rock. Below this there are the ruins of a large oblong building, probably a Vihár, or monastery. Below this again are the circular bases of Topes Nos. 9 and 10, and the stone bowl which has already been described. From this point there is a ruined but well-defined flight of steps leading to No. 2 Tope.*

* See Plate IV. of this volume for all these ruins.

CHAPTER XV.

DESCRIPTION OF THE SÁNCHI BAS-RELIEFS.

THE bas-reliefs are carved upon the front and rear faces of the architraves, and upon the front and inner faces of the gateway pillars. The outer faces of the pillars are ornamented with flowers, garlands, and other devices, which need not be detailed. I will begin with the pillar of the eastern gate, and follow in my description the course of the sun round by the south, and west towards the north. The bas-reliefs on the pillars are divided into compartments, which I have numbered from top to bottom. The lowest compartments of the inner faces of all the pillars are occupied by large figures of porters or doorkeepers, some with spears, some with chaoris, &c.*

EASTERN GATEWAY.

RIGHT PILLAR—FRONT FACE.

I. *Palace Scene.—Audience Hall.*—Upper apartment of palace. Two royal personages seated with several attendants.

* A very correct view of the Eastern Gateway will be found in Fergusson's Illustrations of Ancient Indian Architecture: *Frontispiece.*

II. *Palace Scene.—Women dancing before the king.* Raja seated on a *morha*, or throne, in the palace-hall, holding the *vajra*, or thunderbolt, in his right hand, and in his left a gourd. Two attendants behind him hold the *chatta* and *chaori*, both being insignia of royalty. On his right is seated either the heir-apparent or the prime minister, attended by two *chaori* and *chatta* bearers. On the king's left are two *Nachnis*, or dancing women, who are dancing to the sound of two *sárangis* (or lutes) and two drums.

III. IV. and V. are the same repeated.

The whole of this front of the pillar represents a six-storied palace. Each story is supported on a front of four octagonal pillars, with bell-shaped capitals surmounted by recumbent winged horses.

Right Pillar—Inner Face.

I. *Adoration of tree.*—Royal figures paying their adorations to a tree.

II. *Dream of Maya.*—Maya, the mother of Buddha, represented asleep, and the *Chádanta* elephant touching her feet with his trunk. Below her the Prince *Siddhartha* is passing through the city gate of *Kapila* in a chariot drawn by two horses. He is preceded by musicians, and attended by elephant riders and horsemen. The rear of the procession is inside the city. In front are three figures with joined hands adoring a holy Bo-tree enclosed in a square Buddhist railing.

This second compartment is one of the most interesting bas-reliefs at Sánchi. The upper portion represents the dream of Maya the Queen of *Suddhodana,* Raja of Kapila. She dreamed that she was touched by a *Chádanta* elephant, which the wise men interpreted as a divine conception. It thus represents the incarnation of the last mortal Buddha, Sákya Sinha.

The lower portion represents the last act in the life of the Prince Siddhartha, before he took the vows of asceticism. It is in fact the last of the "four predictive signs."* On emerging from the city in his chariot, Sákya saw some healthy, well-clad persons wearing the peculiar robe of those dedicated to religion. These are the three ascetics paying their adoration to the Bo-tree.

EASTERN GATE.

LEFT PILLAR—FRONT FACE.

I. *Adoration of Symbol of Dharma.*—Temple containing the symbol or monogram of *Dharma* on an altar; over which some fabulous *Kinnaras* are waving garlands and making offerings. On each side of the temple are two royal or lay

* See the account of the four predictive signs in the second chapter of this work.

personages with hands joined in adoration (see Plate XXXII. for symbols of Dharma).

II. *Boat Scene.—Sákya's Nirvána.*—A boat is represented on the ocean; containing three persons; one rower, one steersman, and one passenger, all of whom are clad in the costume of the higher ranks of Buddhist ascetics. In the right and left upper corners there are trees; and scattered about in the waters there are lotus flowers, alligators, ducks, and shells. On the shore below are represented four figures also in a religious garb; one with dishevelled hair and uplifted arms; and the others, who wear caps, with hands clasped together in attitudes of devotion. In the right hand corner below is a tree with an altar.*

This scene I have already described in my account of Sákya's death. The passenger is, I think, Sákya Muni, who is represented, after the attainment of *Nirvána*, or freedom from transmigration, as being wafted over the waters which are said to surround this transitory world. The figures on the shore are a Bhikshu of the lower grade, bewailing the departure of Sákya with dishevelled hair and uplifted arms, which, from the accounts given in the Páli

* See Plate XI. of this volume. The manner in which the planks of the boat are secured together is the same as that which is now practised. I have reduced Major Durand's sketch to one-half size. Numerous shells, ducks, and lotus-flowers have been omitted.

annals, would seem to have been the customary manner of expressing grief at that period. The other figures are Bhikshus who had attained the higher grade of *Arahat*, and who comforted themselves with the reflection that "all transitory things are perishable." The difference of rank is known by the bare head of the mourner, and the capped heads of the others; a distinction which still prevails in Tibet, where the lower grades *Ge-thsul* and *Chhos-pa* invariably go bare-headed, whilst all the Lámas (or higher grades), including the Grand Láma himself, have their heads covered.

III. *Prince in chariot leaving Kapila.*—Gate and walls of city. Chariot with three persons leaving the city, followed by elephant riders and horsemen, who are represented inside the city. Beyond the walls there are an altar and two royal or lay personages standing before it with hands joined in adoration. The three figures in the chariot are the king, the driver, and the *chaori* holder.

This scene probably represents another of the "four predictive signs;" and the figures at the altar may be intended either for the sick or aged persons, whom Sákya met before he became an ascetic.

EASTERN GATE.

Left Pillar—Inner Face.

I. *Kitchen Scene.*—To the right is the city gate, and a man carrying a banghy, or small load, suspended by ropes from both ends of a pole. Beyond him are two women, naked to the waist; one stooping to fill her water jar from a tank or stream, and the other with a water jar under her left arm. On their right is a male personage, also naked to the waist, his loins and thighs covered in the folds of a dhoti, standing with hands joined in adoration before an altar. On the left of the compartment there is a very lively kitchen scene. A woman, naked to the waist, is husking corn in a large wooden mortar, with a two-handed pestle. A second woman is seated winnowing the corn from the chaff in a flat shovel-shaped basket. A third woman is standing at a four-legged table rolling out *chapattis*, or unleavened cakes; and a fourth woman is seated grinding spices or condiments on the *sil*, or "flat stone," with a *bánt* or round muller. Behind her, seated on the ground, is the Raja, or master of the household; and in the background are two houses with dome-shaped roofs. The lower portion of the compartment is filled with goats, sheep, and oxen.*

This scene is one of the most curious and interesting of all the Sánchi bas-reliefs. Women only are employed in all the domestic occupations: in drawing water, in husking and winnowing the corn, and in

* See Plate XV., fig. 2, of this volume, for the kitchen scene, which is copied from one of Lieutenant Maisey's beautiful sketches.

the cooking of food. The last fact is noticed by Quintus Curtius, who, speaking of the Indian king, says: "Women prepare his food."* The mortar and two-handed pestle are the same as those in use at the present day in India. The mortar (*okhli*) is exactly the same as the Greek ἴγδη, and the Roman *pila;* and the pestle (*musar*) is the same as the Greek κόπανον, and the Roman *pilum.* The primitive method of winnowing represented in the above scene is still used in India; and it recalls one of the blessings of the prophet promised to the children of Israel:† "The oxen likewise, and the young asses that ear the ground, shall eat clean provender which hath been *winnowed with the shovel and with the fan.*" Bishop Lowth reads, "winnowed with the *van* and the *sieve.*" But *shovel* is the nearest descriptive word in English for the present winnowing-basket, which does not seem to differ, even in the slightest, from the ancient one represented in the bas-relief.

II. *Worship of the Supreme Buddha as Flame.*—Temple with altar inside, and a small vessel filled with fire, behind which a five-headed *nága,* or snake, forms a canopy. Flames issue from two windows in the roof of the temple.‡ To the left,

* viii. 9.—Feminæ epulas parant.

† Isaiah xxx. 24.

‡ See Plate XXVIII., vol. xvi., Journal of the Asiatic Society of Bengal, for a sketch of the roof of this temple. The worship of fire was repudiated by the Buddhists; and one of the principal objects of the assembly of the Third Synod was the expulsion of worshippers of fire from the Vihárs.

three figures in the dress of *arhatas*, with caps on their heads; their right hands raised, and gourds or water-vessels in their left hands. To the right, five figures, in the same religious costume, with both hands joined in adoration. In the lower corner, to the right, a small hut roofed with leaves; before or in which a very holy *arhata* is seated on a mat, with only the *sanghâti*, or kilt, about his loins.* His *uttara-sanghâti*, or cape, is hanging up inside the house. Apparently he is in deep abstraction, for a cord is passed round his waist and knees as if to keep him from losing his position. In front stands another *arhata*, with hands joined in supplication to the holy ascetic. Behind the last ascetic there is a fire-vessel, and some instruments, apparently a spoon, a ladle, and a pair of pincers. In the foreground is a sheet of water filled with lotus flowers, wild ducks, and shells. One ascetic is bathing, a second is filling his water-vessel, and two others are coming down to the water with jars. The intermediate space is occupied by an elephant and several buffaloes.

At first sight this scene has every appearance of genuine fire-worship. But as Buddhism has nothing in common either with sun-worship or fire-worship, some other explanation must be sought for the scene of this bas-relief. According to the modern Bud-

* See Plate XV., fig. 1, of this work, for an ascetic and his hut.

dhists of Nepal, VAIROCHANA, or "Light," is supposed to occupy the centre of every *chaitya* dedicated to *Adi Buddha*. Amongst the numerous titles of Buddha contained in the Tibetan works, are "the universally radiant sun," and "the chief lamps of all the regions of space."* A common name also for Buddha was *Chakku*, or "the eye." In all these titles, "light" is considered as a mere attribute of the all-seeing Buddha. "Adi-Buddha was never seen," said Mr. Hodgson's old Bauddha friend: "he is *light*."† Now, as light could not be represented, the sculptor was obliged to seek some form which should be typical of it. In the present instance he has selected flame, and in another instance, as we shall see in the next bas-relief, he has taken a pair of eyes. Both are sources of light, and therefore types of the All-seeing. The *Sambhu Purána*, indeed, distinctly states that Buddha was manifested in the shape of flame‡ (*jyoti-rupya*, or "flame-formed"). From these statements it is clear that the fire itself was not worshipped by the Buddhists, but was looked upon simply as the visible type of the All-seeing. This explanation is fully confirmed by the occurrence of other symbols in temples of the same description, both at Sánchi and at Gya, and by the total absence of image-worship. Indeed at this time the Buddhists would appear to have repudiated image-worship, and

* Prinsep's Journal, i., 383. Wilson's Abstract.

† Hodgson, p. 67.

‡ Hodgson, p. 86, and p. 103 note.

to have paid all their adoration to symbols of Buddha and of Dharma, and to Topes and trees which had been dedicated to Buddha.

III. *Tope dedicated to the Supreme Buddha. Ascetic Life in the Woods.*—A Tope marked with horizontal layers of masonry, and decorated with a pair of eyes, one placed above the other. The Tope is surrounded by a square Buddhist railing.* Background of various trees, amongst which the plantain is easily distinguishable. To the left, a hermit naked to the waist is bringing in a pile of faggots on his shoulder; a second is carrying a *banghy*, or pole, with baskets slung at the ends by ropes. A third is seated on a mat, and is apparently feeding a fire kept in a small vessel. A fourth is seated in the same way, and is fanning a fire in a similar vessel. A fifth is fanning an empty-looking vessel, but which may be supposed to contain some hot embers that could be fanned into flame. To the right, two other ascetics are engaged in splitting a log of wood with large felling axes.

It appears to me that this scene is intended to represent the fewness of the wants of ascetic life. Each hermit is employed in looking after his own wants, which would seem to be limited to the collection of a small quantity of firewood. At first sight I thought that this scene represented the building of a wooden

* See Plate III., fig. 7, of this volume.

Tope; but the Tope is *finished*, and the whole of the figures are ascetics. It is possible that they may be preparing small huts for their own residence similar to that shown in the last bas-relief. The neighbourhood of the Tope makes this supposition highly probable, as it was the usual custom of the Buddhist hermits to congregate around their Topes. The *chaitya* in this scene is evidently dedicated to the Supreme Buddha, as I have explained in my account of the last bas-relief.

EASTERN GATE.

Architraves—Front.

I. *Worship of Topes.—Upper.*—Numerous figures paying their adoration to Topes.

II. *Procession of Buddha's Feet.—Middle.*—To the left a city gate into which a procession is entering. In the centre a sacred tree, and to the right a chariot behind which are the holy impressions of Buddha's feet.

III. *Worship of Tree.—Lower.*—Procession advancing to the worship of a tree in a small Temple.

Architraves—Rear.

I. *Worship of Trees.—Upper.*—Numerous figures paying their adoration to trees.

II. *Worship of Trees by Animals.—Middle.*—Various animals, such as Rams, Buffaloes, Lions,

Vultures, and others not identified, together with the Nága Raja, or King of the Snakes, are all paying their adoration to a tree.

III. *Worship of Tope by Elephants.—Lower.*— Several Elephants are perambulating a Tope with garlands.

This scene, I think, represents a tradition preserved by Fa Hian relative to the Tope at LAN-MO, or Rámagráma.* "In this sterile and solitary place there are no men to sweep and to water; but you may there see continually herds of elephants which take water in their trunks to water the ground, and which, collecting all sorts of flowers and perfumes, perform the service of the tower. There were TAO-SSE (Rationalists) from various countries who had come to perform their devotions at this tower. They met the elephants, and overcome with terror, concealed themselves among the trees, whence they witnessed the elephants performing the duty according to the law. The TAO-SSE were greatly affected to observe how, though there was no one to attend to the service of the tower, it was nevertheless kept watered and swept. The TAO-SSE thereupon abandoned their grand precepts, and returning became *Shámi.* Of themselves they plucked up the grass and the trees, levelled the ground, and kept the place neat and clean. They exerted themselves to convert the king, and induce him to found an establishment of eccle-

* *Fo-kwe-ki,* c. xxxiii. Laidlay's Translation.

siastics, as well as to erect a temple. There is at present a habitation of ecclesiastics. This happened not long ago, and tradition has transmitted it to the present time." The expression "not long ago" must mean three or four centuries, otherwise the story could scarcely be said to have been transmitted by tradition. At any rate the story illustrated the bas-relief; and proves that there was a belief prevalent at that period that elephants had *somewhere* paid their devotions to a Tope. See the description of the lower architrave, Western Gateway, front face.

SOUTH GATEWAY.

Right Pillar—Front Face.

I. *Triple Symbol of Dharma.*—A temple supported on pillars, and containing an altar on which are placed three symbols or monograms of Dharma.*

II. *Scene in Palace.*—King seated with his two wives. Four other females, two seated (wives of less rank), and two standing (attendants).

III. *Casket Scene in Palace.*—The king with his family and ministers seated in the foreground to the left. In the centre a relic-casket, with two attendants holding the *chatta* and *chaori* over it. To the left, a seated female beating a drum, and a female dancer naked to the waist with her arms stretched before her in a peculiar

* See Plate XXXII., fig. 22.

manner, still practised in India. In the back ground two male figures, and one female figure with a round cap similar to those worn by the Kashmiri women of the present day. To the right numerous figures, all standing. Two in the foreground with hands joined in adoration appear to be the Raja and his ministers. They are naked to the waist; but are literally covered with necklaces, armlets, and bracelets.*

I. *Worship of Topes.—Upper.*—Three Topes, the middle one bearing the inscription No. 190, with the name of Sri Sátakarni. On each of the bosses of this architrave, immediately over the pillars, are two men riding oxen. The oxen are regularly caparisoned for riding. The nose-string is passed through the nostrils, and twisted together to avoid the eyes; the ends are then passed outside the horns, where they are secured from slipping by a head-band. Of the figures on the right boss, one carries a lotus, and the other a relic-box. Those of the left boss both carry trays containing some indescribable object. Between this boss and the end volute a led horse is represented passing through a temple gateway of two architraves. The horse is attended by two figures, one carrying a *chaori*, and the other a vessel exactly resembling a tea-pot.

II. *Worship of Tope.—Middle.*—A Tope with in-

* See Plate XII. of this volume.

scription in two lines (No. 191). *Kinnaras* with garlands. King in a chariot with driver and *chaori*-bearer, attended by elephant riders.

III. *A siege and Relic Procession.* — *Lower.* — A part of this interesting scene has been made known by James Prinsep;* but the architrave is broken, and the portion to the right of the boss, which has not been published, seems to complete the story, although it forms a different compartment. The scene in the middle of the architrave represents a besieged city. The battlements, the city gate, and the upper stories of the houses, are filled with defenders, who are shooting arrows and hurling stones upon the assailants below. The attack is carried on with arrows only; but as several of the besiegers are covered with long shields, they were no doubt furnished with swords. One horseman and several elephant riders appear on the left, with two standard-bearers.

To the right of the boss, the king appears in his chariot, attending an elephant, which bears a relic-box on its head, covered by the honorary *chatta*.

The siege represented in this scene was probably undertaken for the purpose of gaining possession of some holy relic, which the king is carrying off to the right. The dresses of the soldiers are remarkable,

* Prinsep's Journal, vol. vi., Pl. XXIX.

and the mode of fastening the quiver to the back is very peculiar and picturesque. The quiver is fastened to the right shoulder, and the fastenings, which are apparently leather straps, are passed over both shoulders, crossed in front, and carried to the back, where they were probably passed through a ring in the end of the quiver, and then carried to the front and again crossed, the ends being secured by loops to the upper straps.* The only *apparent* clothing is a kilt; but there was no doubt a tight fitting jacket of some kind to cover the body. The whole costume has a striking resemblance to that of the Highlanders of Scotland.

The swords throughout the Sánchi sculptures are all short and broad. A specimen, hanging by one of the porter's sides, is given in Plate XXXIII., fig. 2. It agrees exactly with the description of Megasthenes:† "All wear swords of a *vast breadth,* though scarce exceeding *three cubits* in length. When they engage in close fight, they grasp these with both their hands that the blow may be stronger."

The whole account of Megasthenes, although three hundred years earlier in date than the Sánchi bas-reliefs, is still partially applicable, and may be quoted as much to show the changes which had taken place in that period as to illustrate the military equipments

* This description recalls the words of the Psalmist regarding the children of Ephraim, who, being *harnessed,* and *carrying bows,* turned themselves back in the day of battle.—Ps. lxxviii. 10.

† Arrian, Indica xvi.

of the sculptures. In the time of Megasthenes, "the infantry *usually* carried a bow of the same length with the bearer." This agrees with the bas-reliefs, which represent nearly all the foot soldiers as archers; but the less ancient bows are much shorter than the bearers, and do not appear to have been more than four feet in length. Most of the bows appear to be straight pieces of *bambu*, but a few have the double curve, with a straight hand-piece in the middle, similar to the modern ornamental bows of buffalo's horn. "Their arrows," says Megasthenes, "are little less than three cubits long, and fly with such force that neither shield nor breast-plate, nor any armour, is strong enough to withstand them."* The arrows in the bas-reliefs appear to be from 3 to 5 feet in length. "Some of them," he adds, "use darts instead of arrows." In one of the bas-reliefs a soldier covered by a shield is represented holding a dart horizontally ready to launch it forward. The same dart is placed in one of the porter's hands at the western gate. "Upon their left arms they wear something resembling *peltæ*, made of raw hides, rather narrower than their bodies, but nearly as long." The most usual shield represented in the bas-reliefs is long and narrow, and rounded at top. It covers the bearer from the head to the knee, and must therefore have been about 3½ feet in length and 1½ in breadth. In

* Arrian's Indica. Q. Curtius, however (viii. 9.), says "that their arrows were only two cubits in length, and were discharged with more exertion than effect, as their weight checked their velocity."

the time of Megasthenes, however, it was fully five feet in length. "The shields of the cavalry were smaller than those of the infantry." This is the case throughout the bas-reliefs, in which the horseman's shield is always about two feet in length. It is very peculiar in form, being shaped like a bell with a very wide mouth, and much rounded at bottom. The usual ornament of the shields both for horse and foot was a double cross, the St. George and the St. Andrew; but a cavalry shield on the western gate bears only a crescent and two stars.*

WESTERN GATEWAY.

Right Pillar—Front Face.

Trial of the Bow.—A river; archer on the left bank shooting at a rock on the right bank, from which water is gushing forth. A monkey is leaping across the river to a tree on the left bank. Two figures seated under a tree; one with a bare head and clad in a a *dhoti*, the other richly dressed. Below, the prince on horseback, attended by a *chatta*-bearer, a flute-player, a bowman, and others in procession.

This story is also mentioned by Fa Hian,† who places the scene of action beyond the walls of the city of Kapila. There the Prince Siddharta "drew

* See Plate XXXIII., figs. 3, 4, 5, of this work.

† *Fo-kwe-ki*, c. xxii.

a bow, and the arrow flying to the south-west struck the ground at the distance of thirty *li* (five miles), and caused a spring of water to gush forth. In after times the people built wells on this spot to supply travellers with drinking water." M. Remusat* has given a long account of this popular story from the Chinese works; and it is curious to compare this with the original story preserved in the Páli annals of Ceylon. These annals, which were carried to Ceylon by Mahendra, the son of Asoka, in B.C. 240, give the following account:—† "When Prince Siddharta had reached the age of sixteen, his father demanded the daughters of the neighbouring chiefs in marriage for his son; but they all refused, because the Prince, though handsome, had not been taught any martial accomplishment, and was, therefore, incapable of controlling women. The Prince inquired "What accomplishment is it necessary for me to exhibit?" His father replied, "To string the bow which requires a thousand persons to bind." "Bring the bow," said the prince. The bow was brought to him, and he, while still seated, "twisted the bowstring round his great toe, and drawing it with his toe, strung the bow; and taking the bow in his left hand, and drawing the string with his right, let it (the cord) fly. The whole town started, and to the inquiry, "What noise is this?" the answer was, "The clouds are rolling with thunder;" some others

* *Fo-kwe-ki*, c. xxii., note 7.

† Turnour in Prinsep's Journal, vii. 804.

observed, "Ye know nothing about it; it is not the rolling of thunder: it is the ringing of the bow which requires the strength of a thousand persons, which the great archer, the prince endowed with a halo around his person, has rung." The *Sakya* princes on hearing of this, from that circumstance alone, commencing to rejoice, were highly gratified.

The great mortal then inquired "What more should be done?" They replied, "It is requisite that an iron target eight inches thick should be pierced with an arrow." Having pierced it, he said, "What else?" "It is requisite that a plant of the *Arsaná* tree four inches thick should be pierced." Having transfixed that, "What else should be done?" "Then carts filled with sand and with straw." The great elect, then transpiercing the straw cart, drove the arrow one *usabhan* deep into the water, and eight *usabáni* into the earth. They then said, "It will be requisite to pierce a horse-hair, guided by the mark afforded by the suspended fruit of the *watingáno*" (which is attached to the hair.) Replying, "Hang it up at the distance of one *yójanan*," he shot his arrow in a direction which was as dark, under the obscurity of dense clouds, as if it were night, and pierced the horse-hair, which at the distance of one *yójanan*, was indicated only by the *watingáno*, which was suspended from it, and it entered the earth. If fully related, these were not all that the great mortal exhibited on that day to the world, in proof of his accomplishments in martial deeds. Thereupon the Sakya tribes sent their daughters superbly decorated. There were forty thousand dancing and singing girls. The princess (who was afterwards) the mother of Ráhulo, became the head queen."

In this story there is nothing about the gushing forth of the water, which must therefore be an addition of after times, between B. C. 240 and A. D. 30, when the Sánchi gateways were erected. The Chinese account also refers the shooting to the occasion of Prince Siddharta's marriage: but his brothers Thiao-tha (or *Devadatta*) and Nan-tho (or *Nanda*) are brought to compete with him in the trial of archery. "First an iron target was placed at the distance of 10 li, and so on to seven targets. The shafts of the most renowned archers went no further than the first target. Thiao-tha having drawn, shot beyond it and reached the second. Nan-tho surpassed this, and pierced through the third. The other archers being unable to shoot so far, the prince broke all the bows of those who had shot before him; not one was equal to his strength. The king then said to his attendants, 'My ancestors possessed a bow, which is now in the temple of the Gods; go, bring it.' They went to fetch the bow, which required two men to carry. No man in that assembly could lift it. When the prince shot with it, the twang of the string was heard forty li. The bent bow hurled the shaft so as to pass through the seven targets. He shot again, and the arrow having passed the targets, *pierced the earth, and caused a spring of water to gush forth.* At the third shot he pierced the seven targets, and reached the mountains of the iron girdle. The whole assembly wondered at this unheard-of prodigy. All who had come to partake in the sports were overcome, and returned confounded." The figure shooting must be Sákya himself: the two personages seated under the tree are perhaps his two brothers, Devadatta and Nanda. The figure on horseback is the Prince returning in the very manner related in the Chinese account. "The Prince having thus obtained complete victory, the bells were rung, the *drums beaten*, and amidst vocal and *instrumental music, he mounted his horse*, and returned to the Palace."

II. *Worship of Tree.* — A tree with bunches of berries (perhaps a Pipal tree), with a terrace round it. To right and left *Kinnaras* and figures riding winged lions. In front, twelve royal or lay personages with uplifted faces and joined hands raised in adoration to the tree.

III. *Worship of Tree.*—Tufted tree with *Kinnaras* as above; but the tree is a different species, perhaps a Mango. In front nine figures with hands simply joined in adoration.

The worship of trees did not escape the notice of Alexander's followers, for Quintus Curtius* says, "They" (the Indians) "contemplate as Deities what-

* Q. Curtius, viii. 9.

ever their ancestors worshipped, particularly trees, to wound which is a capital crime."

IV. *Lions.*—Three Lions.

WESTERN GATE.

Right Pillar—Inner Face.

I. *Gateway.—Worship of Tree.*—Gateway, with one architrave, slightly arched, and similar to those of the gateways themselves. Inside the gateway a tree before which male and female figures are paying adoration with uplifted hands. Horse, Ox, Elephant, and Lion.

II. *Worship of Tree surmounted by Chatta.*—Tree covered with garlands, and surmounted by *chatta.* Kinnaras with garlands—male figures paying adoration with uplifted hands.

WESTERN GATE.

Left Pillar—Front Face.

I. *Social Scene.*—Tree in middle. To left a royal couple seated on a couch, the male raising a cup to his lips, and the female holding in her hand a round looking-glass similar in shape to those found in the Etruscan tombs.† To right a second couple in social dalliance. In the middle

† See Plate XXXIII., fig. 28, for this looking-glass.

below the tree, a couple of servants standing on a staircase, the male apparently speaking, and the female holding her right hand over her mouth.

The male servant in this scene is evidently making some allusion to the amorous dalliance of the loving couples on each side; and the female is trying to hide or silence her laughter by closing her mouth with her hand: but her bursting cheeks too plainly show that the effort is in vain.

II. *Love Scene*—To left a loving couple seated, the female behind with her arms thrown around the male figure. To right a second couple seated face to face. Water below.

WESTERN GATE.

Left Pillar—Inner Face.

I. *Ascetic Life.* — *Archers.* — Hut with roof of leaves: in front a bearded ascetic (*Srámana*) seated in contemplation, with a band passed round his loins and knees. A second leaf-roofed hut with a female ascetic (*Srámaná*). Between the huts a vessel containing fire and a spoon; and in the back-ground a monkey. To the left of the huts are two royal personages, one with uplifted hands in adoration, and the other with the right hand raised, and with a gourd in the left hand. Beyond them are two male ascetics, and behind, one female ascetic. In front of the figures there are three antelopes, and there is one antelope before the fire. In the foreground, to the right, there is a tree, beneath which are two buffaloes on the edge of a piece of water, to which a boy dressed in a kilt is approaching, with a waterpot on his shoulder. On the boy's right a royal personage is paying reverence to him with uplifted hands; and to the left of the scene are two archers, one standing with a quiver on his shoulder and a bow in his left hand, the other also standing, bow in hand, having just shot an arrow into a long-haired figure, who is struggling in the water.

I am unable to offer any explanation of this curious scene, but it may possibly have reference to some event in the early life of Sákya.

II. *Festival of the Tree.*—Altar, with tree surmounted by *chatta*, over which *Kinnaras* are hovering. To the left two females, one carrying a *chaori*, and the other a water-vessel: to the right a *náchni*, or dancing woman, and two other females, one playing a flute, and the other a *sárangi*, or lute. In front of the altar a male figure is seated on the ground, lotus in hand, canopied by a five-headed *nága*. To his left are three females, each holding a cup; and to the right are two females, each carrying a long drum. Each of these females is canopied by a nága.

III. *State Barge.*—A large vessel floating in the midst of the ocean. The prow formed of a winged griffin; and the stern of a dolphin's tail, raised very high out of the water, with a garland hanging from it. In the middle a stately canopy supported on pillars, and ornamented both above and below with the Buddhist railing. Beneath the canopy there is an empty throne, or state *morha,* over which one attendant is holding the state *chatta* and another a *chaori.* A third figure is steering the boat. The water is filled with lotus flowers. Five figures are swimming about, supported either on planks or on inflated skins; and a sixth figure is stretching out both arms towards the steersman, apparently for assistance to get into the boat.

It is difficult to say what this scene represents. Captain Fell* described it as a shipwreck. "The vessel," he says, "is on an open sea in the midst of a tempest; near it are figures swimming, and endeavouring, by seizing piles, &c., to save themselves from sinking. One on the point of drowning is making an expiring effort to ascend the side. The features of all betray their melancholy situation." But this description is far from accurate, for the figures in the water have their backs turned to the vessel, and seem to be floating about quite at their ease. In fact, the whole scene looks more like a

* Prinsep's Journal, iii. 491.

bathing party than anything else. I presume, however, that it has a religious meaning, and that it is typical of life; for "our terrestrial globe rests upon the waters *like a boat*," according to the Buddhists. The empty throne may, perhaps, denote Sákya's attainment of Buddhahood, and his final emancipation from this life. But I do not see how this explanation will suit the swimming figures. If I could find any authority for it, I should prefer the following explanation. The waters represent the ocean of life in which mankind are for ever struggling, and the empty throne is that of a Buddha, the *Chakravarti*, or Supreme King, who, by the suppression of all mortal desires, and by the continued practice of abstract contemplation, has freed himself from the trammels of this mortal coil. The figure struggling to get into the boat is, perhaps, a *Bodhisatwa*, or one who has nearly attained Buddhahood.

WESTERN GATE.

ARCHITRAVES.—FRONT FACES.

I. *Procession escorting a Relic Casket.—Upper.*—Street of a city to the left; houses on each side filled with spectators, some leaning on their elbows, and others hanging their arms over the window-sill. In the street a few horsemen heading a procession. Behind them the city-gate, and walls surmounted with battlements. Immediately outside the gate are four persons bearing either trophies or some peculiar instruments of office. Then follow a led horse, passing a tree, a soldier, with bell-shaped shield, two fifers, three drummers, and two men blowing conches. Next comes the king on an elephant, carrying the holy relic-casket on his head, and supporting it with his right hand. Then follow two peculiarly dressed men on horseback, perhaps prisoners. They wear a kind of cap (now only known in Barmáwar, on the upper course of the Rávi), and boots or leggings. The procession is closed by two horsemen (one either the minister or a member of the royal family), and by an elephant with two riders.

This scene is best illustrated by the account of a relic procession recorded in the Mahawanso.* Dutthagámini, Rajah of Ceylon, having prepared a golden casket for the enshrinement of some relics brought by the holy monk Sónuttaro, marched in "procession" to the Tope, with the casket "on the crown of his head;" and having deposited the relics therein, placed them on the throne. Afterwards "the monarch, attended by *Dévas* and men, and bearing on his head the casket containing the relics, making presentations of offerings thereto, and surrounded by the *bhikshus*, marched in procession round the Tope, and then

* *Mahawanso*, p. 190.

ascending it on the eastern side he descended into the relic-chamber."

II. *Worship of Symbol of Buddha.—Middle.*—A wheel on an altar; winged Kinnaras hovering over it with garlands in their hands. Royal personages with uplifted hands joined in adoration. Elks and antelopes.

III. *Worship of Tree by Elephants.—Lower.*—Adoration of Banian-tree by elephants carrying garlands, flowers, *chatta*, and *chaori*. Two elephants crossing a stream towards a Tope.

The story represented in this scene is the same as that which has already been described on the rear face of the lower architrave of the Eastern Gateway.

WESTERN GATE.

Architrave—Rear Faces.

I. *Worship of Topes.—Upper.*—Adoration of Topes, by numerous figures.

II. *Triumphal Procession. — Middle.* — Procession entering a city gate. Trophy bearers and musicians leading foot soldiers with long shields; one horseman and three elephant riders. Chariot bearing the Raja and two attendants, followed by two horsemen and two elephant riders.

III. *Temple Worship.—Lower.*— Temple. To left

several figures with uplifted hands in adoration. To right, giants.

NORTHERN GATEWAY.

RIGHT PILLAR—FRONT FACE.

I. *Tree, with Staircase.*—A long staircase with Buddhist railing on each side. Tree above, and several royal personages with hands joined in adoration.

RIGHT PILLAR—INNER FACE.

I. *Worship of Tope.*—Tope enclosed by Buddhist railing, and with an entrance gateway, surmounted by two architraves, similar to those of the gateways of the Sánchi Tope itself.* A second Buddhist railing which is represented round the side of the Tope, may probably be intended for the railing of the terrace or upper surface of the plinth. The Tope is surmounted by three *chattas*, emblematic of Buddha. Three figures, with garlands in hand, are perambulating the Tope inside the enclosure. Outside, one figure is carrying a relic-casket, and a second bearing a standard surmounted by the symbol or monogram of Dharma. Kinnaras hover above the Tope with garlands. Two figures bear offerings in shields; two are blowing long horns; one is

* This gateway misled Captain Fell, who supposed it to be an entrance into the Tope itself.

playing a double flageolet; and four are beating long drums and kettle-drums.*

This scene represents the whole ceremony of the solemn adoration of Topes, as practised on stated occasions. The perambulation of the Tope, and the open display of the relic-casket, are accompanied with instrumental music and waving of garlands, which have all been fully described in the account of the building and dedication of a Tope, taken from the Mahawanso.

II. *Adoration of Trees.*—Three trees, that to the left with an altar. Two females and a child kneeling between the trees. To the front, two royal personages with hands joined in adoration, and two females with offerings. In the foreground two monkeys, one with a cup.

III. *Worship of Tree.*—To left, tree and altar. The King and Queen, with hands joined in adoration, standing before the tree. Two attendants with *chatta* and *chaori.* To the right an altar, and Kinnaras hovering above it with garlands.

NORTHERN GATE.

LEFT PILLAR—FRONT FACE.

I. *Worship of Tree.*—Tree surmounted by *chatta.* Four figures, in royal costume, seated, to the

* See Plate XIII. of this work.

front, with hands joined in adoration; and four others, in similar dress, carrying garlands. Ten figures standing with hands joined in adoration. Two figures with large drums above.

II. *Reverence paid to a Boy.*—Three temples and three trees. A boy seated with a plumed head-dress (or canopied by a three-headed *nága*). Four figures, two royal and two others, with hands joined in adoration.

This scene, perhaps, represents the story of Bimbisára, King of Magadha, paying reverence to the Sákya.

III. *Simple Adoration.*—Three male figures and one boy with hands joined in adoration.

IV. *Procession.* — Procession through a gateway. Two figures on horseback, preceded by musicians. Battlements of city. Spectators in the upper apartments of the houses.

This scene, perhaps, represents the return of Sákya to Kapila at the earnest request of his father.

V. *Domestic Scenes at Fountain.* — Wild rocks, and water gushing forth into a pool, which is overflowing. A female seated on the rock with her legs in the water. To the left, a loving couple seated, with their arms thrown around each other; the male with a cup in his hand. To the right, a royal personage playing the *sárangi*, or lute. In the foreground, two elephants in water. The king, seated on the left elephant, is assisting a female to get up behind. On the right elephant two females are seated behind the king.

This bas-relief appears to represent four different domestic scenes in the life of Sákya. In the first, he is seen seated in playful dalliance with his wife Yasodará. In the second, he is playing the *sárangi*, while she is bathing. In the third, he is assisting her to mount an elephant; and, in the fourth, they are seated together on the elephant.

NORTHERN GATE.

Left Pillar—Inner Face.

I. *Cave Temple.*—Entrance to a cave temple; numerous figures standing with hands joined in adoration. The king's face turned towards the temple.

II. *Procession.*—Figure in a two-horse chariot issuing from a city gate, preceded by musicians. Standard-bearer mounted on an elephant, and horsemen inside the city. Spectators in the upper apartments of the gateway and in the verandahs of the palace.

III. *Worship of Tree.*—Tree and altar. Four females, with long plaited hair, seated in adoration. Seven females standing with joined hands. One male figure paying adoration.

This scene represents the king and his family paying their private adorations to one of the sacred Bodhi trees.

CHAPTER XVI.

INSCRIPTIONS.—NO. I. TOPE.—SÁNCHI.

FROM NORTH TO EAST—INSIDE.

Plate XVI.

No. 1.—*Kekateyapurasa Dhama-Sivasa dánam.*

"Gift of DHARMA SIVA of *Kekateyapura.*"

This is No. 21 of James Prinsep's Sánchi inscriptions.* He reads *Kekateyakasa* as a part of the donor's name.

No. 2.—*Haná-bhichhuniyá dánam.*

"Gift of HANÁ, the mendicant nun."

No. 3.—*Vaja-Gutasa dánam.*

"Gift of VAJRA-GUPTA."

This is No. 25 of Prinsep, who reads *Vajágato-dánam,* "Gift of VRIJAGÀN;" because in Páli *án* becomes *áto* in the genitive; but he has omitted the vowel *u*, and the final *s* in *gutasa*, both of which are very distinct even in his own fac-simile.

* The Nos. of James Prinsep's inscriptions are taken from the Plates in his Journal—vol. vi., Plate XXVII., and vol. vii., Plate XXIII.; the lesser Nos. being in the former Plate, and the greater Nos. in the latter.

No. 4.—*Dhamagirikasa—mátu-dánam.*
"Gift of DHARMAGIRIKA's mother."

Prinsep, No. 5, reads *Dhamagálika*, but the vowels are very distinct in the inscription.

No. 5.—*Kekateyakasa Jamata Vijitasa dánam.*
"Gift of JANAMATA VRIJITA of *Kekateyaka.*"

No. 6.—*Kádasa-bhichhuno-dánam.*
"Gift of KÁNDA, the mendicant monk."

Prinsep, No. 15, translates *bhichhuno*, "poor man;" but the *Bhikshu* was a mendicant who had taken vows of poverty, and who begged his bread.

No. 7.—*Devo-bhág (iniya) Dhamanaka (ya) bhichhuniyo dánam.*
"Gift of Deva's sister, DHARMANAKÁ, the mendicant nun."

FROM EAST TO SOUTH—INSIDE.

No. 8.—*Vákaláye Deviye Ahi-Mitama (tu-dánam).*
"(Gift of) VÁKALÁ-DEVI, the mother of Ahi-Mitra."

Prinsep, No. 40, reads Akilaye Deviye ahi matu mara; but the vowel *i* in *Mita* is distinct even in his own fac-simile. The mother's name is nearly the same as that of No. 11.

No. 9.—*Phaguyavasa . . ikaya.*
"Of Phalguna the *Upásiká.*"

No. 10.—*Nagadinasa-bhichhuno-dánam.*
"Gift of NAGADINA, the mendicant monk."

No. 11.—*Ujeniya Vákiliyáná dánam.*
"Gift of VÁKILIYÁN of *Ujain.*"

See No. 76 for another gift of this person.

No. 12.—*Ujeniya Gopálasa-Visa(ka)masa-dánam.*
"Gift of GOPÁLA VISWAKARMA (the architect) of *Ujain.*"

No. 13.—*Ayapasanakasa—bhichhuno-dánam.*
"Gift of ARYA-PRASANAKA, the mendicant monk."

No. 14.—*Nadinagará Achalaya-bhikhuniya dánam.*
"Gift of ACHALÁ, the mendicant nun of *Nadinagara.*"

No. 15.—*Nadinagará Kabojasa-bhikhuno dánam.*
"Gift of KÁMBOJA, the mendicant monk of *Nadinagara.*"

FROM SOUTH TO WEST GATE—INSIDE.

No. 16.—*Siha-Rakhitasa-pajavatiya Sono Devaya dánam.*
"Gift of Sinha-Rakshita's sister-in-law, SONA-DEVA."

Pajavati is the Sanskrit *Prajávati*, a brother's wife. Prinsep, No. 8, reads this inscription quite differently :—

Siha-rakhitasa-paravatiyasa-rudováya dánam.
"Gift of *Sri* (or *Sinha*) *Rakhita*, the hill man, to Rudova?"

but the lady's name is again mentioned in the next inscription :—

No. 17.—*Sono-Devaya-parijaya Agidoviyadha-dánam.*
"Gift of Sona-Devá's servant, AGNI, the washerman" (?)

No. 18.—*Subhagáyasa-bhágini kaya-dánam.*
"Gift of SUBHAGÁYA's sister."

Prinsep, No. 7, reads *Sabhageyamasa-aginikeya dánam*, "Gift of Sabhageya, the fireman (or black-smith);" but I had the letters of all the inscriptions well cleaned before I copied them, and I have full confidence in my own transcript (See No. 36 for a gift of Subhaga himself):—

No. 19.—*Dhama-Rakhitasa—bhichhuno-dánam.*
"Gift of DHARMA RAKSHITA, the mendicant monk."

No. 20.—*A (ya) sa-kamakasa-dánam.*
"Gift of ARYA-KARMAKA."

No. 21.—*Pusagirino—bhichhuno-dánam.*
"Gift of PUSAGIRI, the mendicant monk."

No. 22.— . . . *pasa-kama Chaḍa bhichhuniya dánam.*
"Gift of . . . pakarma CHANDÁ, the mendicant Nun."

No. 23.—*Samanerasa Abeyakasa Sethino dánam.*
"Gift of the ascetic ABEYAKA, the Sreshti." (See No. 124.)

Sreshti means the master of a trade or guild; a "deacon" in Scotland. Prinsep, Nos. 4 and 11, makes *Samanera* a man's name; and reads "Gift of Samanera and of Abeyaka;" but the omission of the conjunction *cha*, which should follow each name (if this were the true reading) shows that *Samanera* is only the common title of श्रामणेर, *Srámanera*, an ascetic.

No. 24.—*Pati-bánasa bhichhuno Páḍayasa Atevásino dánam.*
"Gift of PRATIBÁN, the mendicant monk, pupil of *Pándaya*."

No. 25.—*Udubaragahariyasa Sa . . . Rakhitasa-dánam.*
"Gift of SANDHA RAKSHITA, of *Udubaragahariya.*"

This inscription has puzzled Prinsep from its rudeness.

No. 26.—*Udatikaye bhichhuni Vedisikayá dánam.*
"Gift of UDATIKÁ, the mendicant nun of *Vidisa.*"

FROM WEST TO NORTH GATE.—(INSIDE.)

No. 27.—*Yasopálasa-da (nam) bhadanaka.*
"Gift of YASOPÁLA, the fortunate?"

No. 28.—*Mahamaragimusapagirino-dánam.*
"Gift of SARPAGIRI, the . . .

No. 29.—*Pusasa-cha-Hatiyasa bhichhunodánam.*
"Gift of PUSA and of *Hatiya*, the mendicant monks."

No. 30.—*Dhama Rakhitaya Madhava-nikáye dánam.*
"Gift of DHARMA RAKSHITÁ, of the *Mádhava* community."

नकाय, *nikaya*, means an assembly, a congregation.

No. 31.—*Dhana-bhikhuno dánam.*
"Gift of DHANA, the mendicant monk."

No. 32.—*(Ga) ha-patino Budha Ghosa . . .*
"(Gift of) the householder, BUDHA GHOSHA."

No 24.—*Gotiputasa Bhadukasa bhichhuno dánam.*
"Gift of Goti's son, BHANDUKA, the mendicant monk."

See No. 110 for another son of Goti. See also the relic bones of Sánchi, Sonári, and Andher, for other sons of the same teacher.

No. 34.—*Vejajasa-gámasa-dánam.*
"Gift of VEJAJJAGRÁMA."

Prinsep, No. 10, suggests that the population of a village, called *Vrijagráma*, combined to make this offering; but the name is most probably that of a man.

No. 35.—*Araha-Gutasa Sásádakasa bhichhuno dánam.*
"Gift of ARHATA GUPTA, a mendicant monk of the *Sásárdaka* order."

Sásan is "devotion," and *arda* means "to beg;" *Sásárdaka*, therefore, means a religious mendicant, but as *Bhikshu* has the same signification, I have considered the former as the title of a particular class or order.

No. 36.—*Sabhagasa Koragharasa dánam.*
"Gift of SUBHAGA, of *Koraghara*.

(See No. 18 for a gift of Subhaga's sister.)

No. 37.—*Aya Rahilasa Sárhineyakasa-Mátu dánam.* .
"Gift of ARYA RAHILÁ, the mother of *Sarhineyaka*.

There is a grammatical mistake in the masculine termination of the female name, which should have been *Rahilaya*. The son's name may be read *Saphineyaka*.

FROM EAST GATE—OUTSIDE.

No. 38.—*Vadániye Upasikáyá dánam.*
"Gift of VADÁNÁ, the *Upásiká*."

Upásiká means literally a "worshipper," or rather a "female worshipper." M. Burnouf* renders this term by "devotee," which certainly appears to be the best equivalent for it. I consider the *Upásaka* and *Upásiká* as male and female devotees who had not taken the vows of celibacy and mendicancy professed by the *Bhikshu* and *Bhikshuni.*

No. 39.—*Kákanáye Bhagavatopamona-lathi;* or
Kákenoye Bhagavatopamáne-rathi,

as Prinsep, No. 18, reads it; but he gives no translation. I can only suggest *Bhagavata-upamanorathi,* which may be translated—

"Gift of Kákaná, an anxious longer for Bhagavat."

Manoratha is "wish, desire," and *upa* means "excess of anything." Bhagavata is the "Supreme Being," and is often applied to Buddha.

No. 40.—*Tubavani-gahapatinopatithiya-nasáya-visamana-datiya-dánam;* or
Gobavaná-gahapati-nopatidhiyanusaya vesa-man-dataya dánam,

according to Prinsep, No. 6, who thus translates

* Introduction à l'Histoire du Buddhisme Indien, p. 279—"La lecture attentive des textes, et quelques autorités non moins respectable à mes yeux que celles que je viens de citer, m'ont décidé en faveur du sens de *dévot* ou *fidèle.*" See also Wilson's Hindu Theatre, i. 123, where the heroine of the Mrichhakati is called *Buddhopásiká,* the "devoted-to-Buddha."

it: "Gift of the cowherd AGRAPATI, commonly called NOPATI, to the highly ornamented (Chaitya):" but Agrapati would be written Agapati, and not Agahapati. In fact, *gahapatino* is the Páli genitive of the Sanskrit *grihapati*, a "householder," and the inscription may be read thus:—

"Gift of VISARMANA-DATTI the . . . of PRATISTHIYA, a householder of *Tubavan*."

taking *patithiya* for *pratisthiya*. The next inscription, which is four times repeated, refers to the same person, and proves the correctness of my reading. It is Prinsep's No. 9.

No. 41.—*Tubavani-gahapatino-patithiyasa-dánam.*
"Gift of PRATISTHIYA, a householder of *Tubavan*."

No. 42.—*Namámakádisá rakhitasa dánam.*
"Gift of ISA-RAKSHITA, of *Narmamakádi*"?

No. 43.—*Nadavuno-cha Nadisirohisa-cha dánam.*
"Gift both of NANDABU and of NADISIROHI."

No. 44.—*Pothá Deváya dánam.*
"Gift of POTHÁ-DEVÁ."

No. 45.—*Kandarigámiyasa - Sethino - pajavatiya Nágáya-dánam.*
"Gift of NÁGÁ, the sister-in-law of the Sreshti of *Kandarigámiya*."

No. 46.—*Kandarigámiyasa - Sethino - pajavatiya - Dásáya-dánam.*
"Gift of DÁSÁ, the sister-in-law of the Sreshti of *Kandarigámiya*."

No. 47.—*Kandarigámá-varhasa dánam.*
"Gift of VARHA, of *Kandarigráma.*"

Kandarigráma, or *grámiya*, must have been a considerable place, or it would not have had a *Seshti*.

No. 48.—*Mulagirino dánam lekhakasa.*
"Gift of MULAGIRI, the scribe."

Prinsep, No. 30, reads *lakhakasa*, the "millionaire." But the inscription occurs twice, and is quite distinct.

No. 49.—*Ujeniyi* . . .

No. 50.—*Yakhadánasa-bhikhuno-dánam.*
"Gift of YAKSHADÁNA, the mendicant monk."

No. 51.—*Padonáya-Upasikákaya-dánam.*
"Gift of PADONÁ, the devotee."

No. 52.— . . . *raha-Savánodasa Isadatasa-dánam.*
"Gift of ISA-DATTA, the humble in all things"?

I have taken *savánoda* as a compound of *sarvva*, "all" and *anuddhat*, humility; but this rendering is a mere conjecture.

No. 53.—*Navágámikaná Upasikána-dánam.*
"Gift of NAVÁGÁMIKÁ, the devotee."

No. 54.—*Isi-Mitáyá Vahilasa dánam.*
"Gift of ISI-MITRÁ of *Vahila.* (Bhilsa?)"

This inscription is on the coping to the north-east.

No. 55.—*Ujeniya Rohuniya dánam.*
"Gift of ROHUNI of *Ujain.*"

No. 56.—*Ujeniya Dhamagirino-dánam.*
"Gift of DHARMAGIRI of *Ujain.*"

Prinsep, No. 29, reads *Dhamagilino*, but the meaning of the name remains unchanged, the two liquid letters *r* and *l* being constantly used the one for the other.

No. 57.—*Ujeniya Sonasa dánam.*
"Gift of SONA of *Ujain.*"

No. 58.—*Ujeniya Tapasayána Pusánajaya dánam.*
"Gift of the tapasyá (ascetic) *Pusánajá* of *Ujain.*"

Prinsep, No. 35, reads *punsanamjaya*, and translates "The victory gift of the people performing austerities at Ujain." But *tapasyá* is only a title, like that of *Bhikshu* or *Upásiká*; and it is not easy to imagine how the gift of a stone-slab could have anything to do with a victory.

No. 59.—*Ujeniya Tapasayana Isi Mitasá-dánam.*
"Gift of the ascetic ISI-MITRA of *Ujain.*"

Prinsep, No. 32, reads *Isi-mátasa*, and translates, "The gift of the body of rishis performing their austerities at Ujain."

No. 60.—*Ujeniya Mula-dataye dánam.*
"Gift of MULA-DATTÁ of *Ujain.*"

No. 61.—*Ujeniya Balakaya dánam.*
"Gift of BALAKÁ of *Ujain.*"

No. 62.—*Ujeniya Upedadatasa—pajavataya Maya-dataya dánam.*
"Gift of MAYADATTÁ, the sister-in-law of Upendradatta of *Ujain.*"

Prinsep, No. 34, reads *padavalayuchhaya*, and translates, "The gift of Upendradatta of Ujain, for a perpetual charity to the itinerants." But it is difficult to conceive how the gift of a stone to the Sánchi enclosure could form a charity to anybody. The correctness of my reading is proved by the two following inscriptions. Upendradatta's own gift is recorded in No. 90.

No. 63.—*Ujeniya Upedadatasa bhaginiya Himadataya dánam.*

"Gift of HIMADATTÁ, the sister of Upendradatta of *Ujain.*"

No. 64.—*Ujeniya Upedadatasa bhaginiya Budhaye-dánam.*

"Gift of BUDDHÁ, the sister of Upendradatta of *Ujain.*"

No. 65.—*Ujeniya Kadiye bhichhuniye dánam.*

"Gift of KADRU, the mendicant nun of *Ujain.*"

No. 66.—*Ujeniya Chheta-mátu dánam.*

"Gift of CHHETRA's mother of *Ujain.*"

Prinsep, No. 31, prefers *Kshatra's* mother; but the meaning is exactly the same.

No. 67.—*Ujeniya Tapasiyena Siha-dataya dánam.*

"Gift of the Ascetic SINHA-DATTÁ of *Ujain.*"

This is probably the same inscription as Prinsep's No. 37. If so the *p* of *Tapasiyena* has been omitted.

No. 68.—*Ujeniya Saphineyakina Isakasa dánam.*

"Gift of ISAKA, the Saphineyaki (?) of *Ujain.*"

Prinsep, No. 33, translates "The gift of the

morality students of Ujain to the rishis." By reading *savineyaka*, as Prinsep has done, the translation would rather be "learned in Vinaya," which was the name of the lowest class of Buddhist scriptures.

No. 69.—*Kuraghara Isi Mitaya dánam.*
"Gift of Isi Mitrá of *Kuraghara*."

No. 70.—*Ujeniya Vipulaya dánam.*
"Gift of Vipulá of *Ujain*."

No. 71.—*Kuraghara Naraya dánam.*
"Gift of Nárá of *Kuraghara*."

No. 72.—*Kuraghari Nágá Mitaya dánam.*
"Gift of Nágámitrá of *Kuraghari*."

No. 73.—*Bodhe Gothiye Dhama Varhananá dánam.*
"Gift of Bodhi-Gothi for the advancement of Dharma."

No. 74.—*Nagádinasa-bhichhuno dánam.*
"Gift of Nagadina, the mendicant monk."

No. 75.—*Phaguyavasa . rikáya.*
"(Gift of) Phalguna . . ." (See No. 9.)

No. 76.—*Ujeniya Vakiliyáná dánam.*
"Gift of Vakiliyan of *Ujain*."

Prinsep, No. 28, reads *Phakiliyánám*, and translates "Gift of subscribers of Ujain." See No. 11 for another of this person's gifts.

No. 77.—*Ujeniya Gohilasa Visasa-cha dánam.*
"Gift of Gohila and of Viswa of *Ujain*."

No. 78.—*Chirátiya bhichhuniyá dánam.*
"Gift of Chirati, the mendicant nun."

Prinsep, No. 14, translates *bhikshuni* as "poor woman."

No. 79.—*Sadhanasa bhichhuno dánam.*
"Gift of SADHANA, the mendicant monk."

No. 80.—*Aswa-Devaye Bahadata mátu dánam.*
"Gift of ASWA-DEVÁ, the mother of Bahadatta."

Prinsep, No. 41, reads "Aswa Devi."

No. 81.—*Utareyekasa Satigutasa dánam.*
"Gift of SATYA GUPTA of *Utareyaka.*"

Prinsep, No. 38, reads *Ogireyakasa*, the "*Agarwala*," or "son of *Agra*;" but his fac-simile begins with *u*, and not with *o*.

No. 82.—*Araha Gutaya dánam.*
"Gift of the Arhatá, GUPTA," or
"Gift of ARHATÁ GUPTÁ."

Prinsep, No. 13, *Arahagataya*, of *Arahagatá*. I am not sure that the lady had attained the rank of *arhat*; for it is quite possible that *araha* should form only part of her name, arhata Gupta, or "cherished by the *arhats*;" for a Bhikshuni, even of eighty years of age, was inferior to an *upasampada*, or newly ordained monk of twenty years.

No. 83.—*Aswa Devaya Samikasa Mátu dánam.*
"Gift of ASWA DEVÁ, the mother of Samika."

(See No. 80, and No. 119).

No. 84.—*Yasilaya Atevasini Sagha Rakkhitaya dánam.*
"Gift of SANGHA RAKSHITÁ, the pupil of Yasilá."

No. 85.—*Sethino-mátu Kaniya dánam.*
"Gift of KANIYA, the mother of the Sreshti."

Prinsep, No. 17, reads *mata*, and translates "the

Sethin's deceased daughter;" but the word *dánam* shows that the inscription records a "gift," and not an "obituary notice."

No. 86.—*Yasiláya dánam.*
"Gift of Yasilá."

See No. 84 for this lady's name. She is there recorded as the teacher of Sangha Rakshitá. Prinsep, No. 27, reads *Yasili.*

No. 87.—*Sethino-ghati-kamakárikáná dánam;* or,
Sethino-paṭi-kamakalikáná dánam,

of Prinsep, No 26, who translates "Gift of the serving women of the nobility." But the second word is *ghati,* a *ghát,* or landing-place; and as *makarin,* or *makarika,* means the ocean, I think that the translation should be—

"Gift of the Sreshti of the Sea-ghát."

that is, "of the harbour-master."

No. 88.—*Vasulaye dánam.*
"Gift of Vasulá."

Prinsep, Nos. 24 and 25, reads *Vasuliye,* but notices that the name, which occurs more than once, is also written *Vasulaye,* and states that these differences are caused by an attempt to render without compound letters the Sanskrit genitive *Vasulyah.*

No. 89.—*Dadatasa Páwárikasa dánam.*
" Gift of DANDATA of *Páwárika.*"

The town of *Páwá* was on the northern bank of the Ganges between Vaisáli and Kusinagara.

No. 90.—*Upedadatasa dánam.*
" Gift of UPENDRADATTA." (See Nos. 62, 63, 64.)

No. 91.—*Semakaye Dhitaye dánam.*
" Gift of SEMAKADHRITÁ."

No. 92.—*Vághumanyo Saghadanáya bhichhuniye dánam.*
" Gift of SANGHA-DANÁ, the mendicant Nun, of *Vághumanya*" ?

No. 93.—*Yakhiya bhichhuniye- Vedisa dánam.*
" Gift of YAKSHI, the mendicant nun of *Vidisa.*"

Prinsep, No. 42, translates " Gift of Yakhi, the priestess and traveller."

No. 94.—*Kudurasa Sethi Bha (dasa) dánam.*
" Gift of BHADRA, Sreshti of *Kundura.*"

No. 95.—*Kuraráye tapasiye matu dánam.*
" Gift of KURARÁ, the ascetic's mother."

No. 96.— . . . *pidatuya Sadina pajava(ti)ya dánam.*
" Gift of . . . *pidattá*, the sister-in-law of Sadi."

Prinsep, No. 45, reads *hidatáye sada dinadhe jiváya dánam*, and translates, " A gift for those living here (for distribution of food) at midday for ever." But the gift of a pillar or rail of the stone enclosure can have no connection with the provision of food.

No. 97.—*Chada Gutasa sá . . . kagomiya . . . mita dánam.*
"Gift of CHANDRA-GUPTA . . ."

No. 98.—*Dhara-kiná Sátilasa dánam.*
"Gift of SÁNTILA of *Dharaki* (? Dháranagara)."

No. 99.—*Kápasigama Arahasa dánam.*
"Gift of KÁPASIGRAMA, the arhat."

This may be read in another way as, "Gift of the arhat of *Kápasigráma* (cotton-town);" but the former seems the more simple reading, and is also in keeping with the other inscriptions, each of which records the gift of a particular individual. This inscription occurs twice.

No. 100.—*Ketakareyakasa Araha-dásasa dánam.*
"Gift of ARHATA-DÁSA, of *Ketakareya.*"

No. 101.—*Ketakareya Bhadakasa dánam.*
"Gift of BHADRAKA of *Ketakareya.*"

This inscription occurs three times.

No. 102.—*Apathakasa dánam.*
"Gift of APRASTHAKA."

No. 103.—*Bhoga-varhanakasa Ajiti-gutasa.*
"(Gift) of AJITA-GUPTA, the increaser of enjoyment."

No. 104.—*Rajáhikátá Arahadinasa dánam.*
"Gift of ARAHADINA of *Rajahikati.*"

No. 105.—*Bhoga-varhana Dhama Rakhitaya Siva Nadino matu.*
"Gift of SIVA-NANDI's mother, DHARMA RAKSHITÁ, the increaser of enjoyment."

This occurs twice. The use of the names of Siva

and Nandi at this early period is very remarkable. The Bhogavarhana of this inscription, as well as of No. 103, may perhaps be the name of a place.

No. 106.—*Saghaya dánam.*
"Gift of SANGHÁ."

No. 107.—*Navagámakasa Mikaye Ujenihárá danam.*
"Gift of MRIKSHÁ, of *Navagámaka* (New-town), in *Ujain.*"

No. 108.—*Sri Gutasa Vánijasa danam.*
"Gift of SRI-GUPTA, of *Vánija*;" or
"Gift of SRI-GUPTA, the grain merchant."

It is not impossible that *Vánijà* may mean only "nephew, or "sister's son;" the *bhánjá* of Urdu.

No. 109.—*Subáhitasa-pajavatiyá Majhimáyá dánam.*
"Gift of MADHYAMÁ, the sister-in-law of Subáhita."

No. 110.—*Subáhitasa Gotiputasa, Rajalipákarasa dánam.*
"Gift of SUBÁHITA, son of *Goti*, the royal scribe."

This is the most valuable of all the inscriptions on the Sánchi colonnade; as it belongs to the family of Goti, whose eldest son Gotiputra was the teacher of the celebrated Mogaliputra. This inscription therefore serves to fix the date of the Sánchi enclosure in the early part of Asoka's reign.

No. 111.—*Taradapadáná Upásikaya dánam.*
"Gift of TARANDAPADÁ, the devotee."

No. 112.—*Buráya musanagothiyajana Vedisányá.*
"Gift of BURÁ (?) . . . of *Vidisa.*"

No. 113.—*Dhama Rakhitaya bhichhuniye káchupathasa dánam.*

"Gift of DHARMA RAKSHITÁ, the mendicant nun, of *Kátyaprastha.*"

No. 114.—*Dhama Rakhitasa Káchhupathasa bhichhuno dánam.*

"Gift of DHARMA RAKSHITÁ, the mendicant monk, of *Kátyaprastha.*"

No. 115.—*Sandhánasa bhichhu dánam.*

"Gift of SANDHÁNA, the mendicant monk."

The possessive termination of bhichhu(no) is omitted in the original.

No. 116.—*Pusagirino Vagamakasa dánam.*

"Gift of PUSAGIRI, of *Vangamaka;*" or

"Gift of VANGAMAKA of *Pusagiri.*"

SOUTH GATE.—OUTSIDE.

No. 117.—*Bhichhakasa Padanayasa dánam.*

"Gift of the mendicant PADANAYA."

No. 118.—*Vághumato Kácháno-pitano dánam.*

"Gift of VAGHUMAN, the father of KÁTYA."

No. 119.—*Sámikasa-Vánikasa-*

No. 120.— *-putasa-cha-Siripalasa*

No. 121.— *dánam* ≡

"Three (≡) gifts of SÁMIKA, son of VÁNIKA, and of SRIPÁLA."

This inscription is carved on three railings of the colonnade, and, as the gift thus consisted of three rails, I presume that the three horizontal strokes which follow *dánam* are intended for that number. See Plate IX. of the Sánchi enclosure, where this curious inscription is shown in the actual position which it occupies on the three rails. For Sámika's mother see No. 83.

No. 122.—*Bhádata Vájukasa dánam.*
"Gift of BHÁDRATA VÁNJUKA."

No. 123.—*Visákhasa bhichhuno dánam.*
"Gift of VAISÁKHA, the mendicant monk."

Pl. XVIII. No. 124.—*Sámanerasa Abeyakasa Sethino dánam.*
"Gift of the ascetic ABEYAKA, the Sreshti."

See No. 23.

No. 125.—*Nadi-Gutasa dánam bhichhuno.*
"Gift of NANDI (or NADI) GUPTA, the mendicant monk."

Prinsep, No. 12, reads *Nadigata*, a "ferryman."

No. 126.—*Podaka dánadata Dha (mika) dánam.*
"The religious gift of PODRAKA DÁNADATTA."

No. 127.—*Arápánáto arahadi (nasa mátu dánam).*
"Gift of ARYAPÁNÁ (the mother of) ARHATADINA."

See No. 148 for another inscription of the same lady.

No. 128.—*Nyabalamidakajape-dánam.*
(?) . . . . .

No. 129.—*Madhuvana Dhama Gutasa bhichhuno dánam.*
"Gift of DHARMA GUPTA, the mendicant monk, of *Madhuvana*" (perhaps *Mahoba*).

No. 130.—*Nadasa Kurarayo.*
"(Gift of NANDA, of *Kurara* . . ."

No. 131.—*Mahagirino bhichhuno dánam.*
"Gift of MAHAGIRI, the mendicant monk."

No. 132.—*Madhurana Isidataya bhichuniye dânam.*

"Gift of ISIDATTÁ, the mendicant nun of *Madhurana.*"

No. 133.—*Isidataye bhikhiniye Kurariye dânam.*

"Gift of ISIDATTÁ, the mendicant nun of *Kurâriya.*"

No. 134.—*Dhama Pálasa . . . thukapadinasa dânam.*

"Gift of DHARMA PÁLA . . ."

No. 135.—*Upasijhasa Phagunasa bhatu bhichhuno.*

"(Gift) of UPASIDYA, the brother of Phalguna, the mendicant monk."

No. 136.—*Bhoga-varhanato Isi Rakhitaya.*

"(Gift) of ISI RAKSHITÁ, the increaser of enjoyment."

No. 137.—*Bhoga varhaná Dunyonáne.*

"(Gift) of DUNYONÁ, the increaser of enjoyment."

No. 138.—*Kurariyasa Vimalasa dânam.*

"Gift of VIMALA, of *Kurariya.*"

No. 139.—*Sámidatasa bhichhuno dânam.*

"Gift of SWÁMIDATTA, the mendicant monk."

No. 140.—*Devagirino Padenekayikasa.*

"(Gift) of DEVAGIRI, of *Pandenekayika.*" (?)

No. 141.—*Bhichhunosa Atevasa . . .*

"Gift of the mendicant's pupil . . ."

No. 142.—*Pasakasa bhichhuno dânam.*

"Gift of PARSWAKA, the mendicant monk."

No. 143.—*Chudasa-cha Dhama Rakhitasa bhichhuno dânam.*

"Gift of KSHUDRA and of DHARMA RAKSHITA, the mendicant monks."

No. 144.—*Ujeniye Agisamaye dânam.*

"Gift of AGNISARMÁ, of *Ujain.*"

No. 145.—*Patithánasa bhichhuno-dánam Aya . i . na Atevásino.*
"Gift of PRATISTHÁNA, the mendicant monk, pupil of Arya . . ."

No. 146.—*Budha Rakhitasa bhichhuno dánam Esavatasa.*
"Gift of BUDHA RAKSHITA, the mendicant monk . . ."

No. 147.—*Nadinagarikaya Isidináye bhichhuniye.*
"Gift of ISIDINÁ, the mendicant nun of *Nadinagarika.*"

No. 148.—*Arápáná Asadasamatu dánam.*
"Gift of ARYÁPÁNÁ, the mother of *Asada.*"

See No. 127 for another inscription of the same name.

No. 149.—*Ujeniye-tápasiyana Nasaya Mitaya.*
"(Gift) of NASA-MITRA, the (female) ascetic."

No. 150.—*Bharaḍiyasa Sapurisasa Yugapajakasa dánam.*
"Gift of BHARDIYA (son) of the emancipated YUGAPRAJNAKA." (Luminary of the age.)

The term *sapurisa* is the Páli form of the Sanskrit *sapurusha,* which is a compound of *sa,* with, and *purusha,* the divinity, or of the pronoun *sa,* which, when joined with *purusha,* means, "the man," or "that man," or simply "the mortal." The term is found on nearly all the relic-caskets, and must therefore apply to the dead. Accordingly I have every where rendered it by "emancipated," that is, from future transmigrations. This gives the meaning attached to the term by the Buddhists; but perhaps a more literal translation would be "absorbed," that is, into the divine essence. Each word gives the meaning in part only; for the term *sapurusha* implies one who has attained Buddhahood by "absorption" into the divine essence, and who is therefore "emancipated" from future transmigration. Perhaps the best rendering would be "the Buddha," that is, one who has attained Buddhahood: but as the sole aim of the Buddhist was to obtain *moksha*, that is, "liberation, or emancipation" from transmigration, I have preferred the well-known term "emancipated."

No. 151.—*Ayadhanakasa bhichhuno dánam.*
"Gift of ARYADHANAKA, the mendicant monk."

No. 152.—*Jonhakasa bhichhuno dánam.*
"Gift of JONHAKA, the mendicant monk."

No. 153.—*Jenakasa-bhichhuno dánam.*
"Gift of JENAKA, the mendicant monk."

No. 154.—*Dhama Rakhitáya Madhuranikaye dánam.*
"Gift of DHARMA RAKSHITÁ, of *Madhuranika.*"

No. 155.—*Mahamarati musipayarano-dánam.*

This inscription appears to be the same as No. 28; but I am unable to offer any translation.

No. 156.—*Yaso-Pálasa dánam bhasikadu.*
"Gift of YÁSO-PÁLA."

No. 157.—*Dhanagirino dánam.*
"Gift of DHANAGIRI."

No. 158.—*Pusasa-cha Hatiyasa bhichhuno dánam.*
"Gift of PUSA and of HATIYA, the mendicant monks."

FROM SOUTH GATE TO WEST GATE.

No. 159.—*Balikáya bhichhuniya madalá chhakatikaye dánam.*

"Gift of BALIKÁ, the mendicant nun of the temple of *Chhakrátika*."

No. 160.—*Dhamasthiriyá bhichhuniye madala chhikatikaye dánam.*

"Gift of DHARMA STHIRI, the mendicant nun of the temple of *Chhakrátika*."

No. 161.—*Avisinaye Sutatikiniyá madala Chhikatikaye dánam.*

"Gift of SUTRANTIKIRNI, the novice of the temple of *Chhakrátika*."

The term *Avisina* occurs in No. 190 as *Avesani*, which means an "entrance," from *vis* "to enter." *Avesana* and *Avesaná* may therefore be the titles of those who had entered into the religious life, but had not yet taken the vows. I have consequently, but not without hesitation, rendered the terms by "neophyte" and "novice." This inscription occurs twice. It may also be rendered "Gift of AVISINÁ, the *Sutrántiki* (or reader of the Sutras), in the temple of Chhrakrátika."

No. 162.—*Sagha Devasa Verohakatasa Vánidása dánam.*

"Gift of VÁNI DÁSA, the . . . of Sangha Deva."

No. 163.—*Bhadikiyasa Sanghilasa dánam.*

"Gift of BHADIKRIYA, of *Sanghila*;" or perhaps, "Gift of SANGHILA, of *Bhadikriya*."

No. 164.—*Arahata Palitasa . . .*

"Gift of the ARHATA PALITA . . ."

No. 165.—*Arahakasa Paripanakasa dánam.*
"Gift of the *Arhata* PARIPANAKA."

No. 166.—*Dhamagirika mátu dánam.*
"Gift of DHARMAGIRI's mother."

FROM WEST TO NORTH.—OUTSIDE.

No. 167.—*Udiya Nadinagariya dánam.*
"Gift of UDI, of *Nadinagari.*"

This occurs twice on portions of the fallen colonnade to N. W.

No. 168.—*Sadhathasa Va . . .*
"Gift of SADHANTHA . . ."

No. 169.—*Isi Dasiyena dánam: Garákaye bhichhuniye dánam.*
"Gift of GARÁKÁ, the mendicant nun, offered by ISI DÁSI."

No. 170.—*Nadinagara Dupasaha bhichhuniye dánam.*
"Gift of DRUPASAHA, the mendicant nun of *Nadinagara.*"

No. 171.—*Yakhadasiya dá(nam).*
"Gift of YAKSHA-DÁSI."

No. 172.—*Datakulavadasa dánam.*
"Gift of DATTA-KULAVADA."

ON SMALL PILLARS FALLEN FROM UPPER ENCLOSURE.

No. 173.—*Damakasa sotikasukasukapasa.*
"Gift of DÁMAKA . . ."

No. 174.—*Dhama-datasa dánam.*
"Gift of DHARMA-DATTA."

Plate, No. 175.—*Arahadásiya-bhichkhuniye dánam.*
"Gift of ARHATA-DÁSI, the mendicant nun."

No. 176.—*Sámidaráya dánam.*
"Gift of SWÁMIDARÁ."

INSCRIPTION ON SOUTH PILLAR.

Pl. XIX., No. 177. This inscription is carved upon a fragment of a broken isolated pillar near the south gateway. As it was a practice amongst the early Buddhists, before building a Tope, to erect a pillar on the spot, with an inscription recording their intentions, it seems possible that this broken column might bear a memorial inscription relating either to the erection of the Great Sánchi Tope, or to some additions or repairs. The latter is the more probable, as the pillar in the former case was generally if not always removed.

But the inscription is unfortunately so much obliterated that it baffled even the heaven-born sagacity of James Prinsep. Some few words he read; but apparently with hesitation, as he says,* "This inscription is in too mutilated a state to be restored entirely, but from the commencement of the third line, *bhakhatibhikhunábhi khamarase dátá*, it may be concluded that some provision was made by 'a charitable and religiously-disposed person for hungry priests,' and this is confirmed by the two nearly perfect lines at the foot,—

* Journal, vii. p. 505.

"*Sasijalá petaviye ichháhime(idi)si : sampesimate chilathitika siyáti.*

"'It is also my desire that camphorated (cool?) water should be given to drink; may this excellent purpose endure for ever.'"

I examined the inscription in several positions and in all lights: I took impressions on paper and made a copy by hand; but the surface of the stone has been so much injured that very few of the letters are readable excepting in the last two lines. There is, however, a sufficient blank surface on all four sides to make it certain that we have the whole of the inscription. It is therefore very much to be regretted that the general indistinctness of the letters should have rendered this inscription almost illegible. The opening is nearly obliterated; but, on a comparison of James Prinsep's copy with my own, I think it probable that the first word was Devánam; next comes a blank; and then *Maga*, or perhaps *Magadha;* and it is possible that the whole line might be read—

Devānam(piya) Magadhe raja.

"DEVÁNAMPRIYA, King of MAGHADHA."

The second line may be partially restored, thus:—

. *(a)bhi(vademá)nam Cheliyagiri* . .

"with salutation to the fraternity of CHAITYAGIRI."

At the end of the third line, the word Sangham "community" is distinctly legible; and I think that I can trace the name of Dhamagiri. The fourth line seems to have been correctly given by Prinsep :—

bhokhati-bhikhunábhikhamarisedáto.
"a gift of food to the much-emaciated Bhikshus."

I can make nothing of the fifth line and of one-half of the sixth, but the concluding portion of the inscription, which is nearly perfect, reads—

———————————— *Ichhahime Sán-*
-ti-Sangham samage milathitike siyáti.

"Is it my wish that the Sánti community may always be united."

The whole inscription, in Roman characters, may, with some conjectural restorations, be read as follows :—

1. *Devánam(piya) Magadhe (raja).*
2. . . *(a)bhi(vádemá)nam Chetiyagiri.* . .
3. . *tikhi-cha(Dha)magiri* . *ikeye sangham.*
4. *bhokhati bhikhunábhikhamavise dáto.*
5. *nidu* . *ti sanam* . . *chhava anná*
6. *Sasivi(ye) petariye. Ichhahime Sán-*
7. *-ti Sangham samage milathitike siyáti.*

The drift of this inscription, at least as I understand it, seems to be the following :—

"DEVÁNAMPRIYA, king of *Magadha*, offers his salutation to the community of *Chaityagiri* (and perhaps to that of *Dharmagiri* also) . . . with a gift of food for the *Bhikshus*, much-emaciated * (with their austerities?) . . . and prays that the SÁNTI community may always be united."

* By reading चाम, *ksháma*, "debilitated" for the Pali *khama.*

In my account of the great Sánchi Tope I have already identified the present name of *Sánchi* with the Sanskrit *Sánti*, which I presume was the name of the great Vihar on the *Chetiyagiri*, or "hill of *Chaityas*." If my reading of Dhamagiri be correct, we may identify the "hill of religion" in the long spur which stretches northward as far as Kánákhera. This hill is still covered with ruins, which no doubt once formed a part of the vast religious establishment of Sánchi-kánákhera.

LATER INSCRIPTIONS FROM THE GATEWAYS.

On the North Gateway.

Pl. XIX., No. 178.—*Dhamagirino bhikhuno dánam.*
"Gift of Dharmagiri, the mendicant monk."

No. 179.—*Isi-Pálitasa-cha Samanasa-cha dánam.*
"Gift both of Isi-Pálita and of Srámana."

Prinsep, No. 16, reads the same.

On the East Gateway.

No. 180.—*Arahadinasa bhikhuno Pokhareyakasa dánam.*
"Gift of Arhatadina, the mendicant monk of *Pokhareyaka.*"

Prinsep, No. 20, reads *Pakhareyakasa* doubtfully as the name of the donor, and takes no notice of *Arahadina.*

No. 181.—*Bhadata Nágilasa Savinamjnyátinam dánam thabho.*

"Pillar-gift of BHADRATA NÁGILA, the learned in all things." (?)

Prinsep, No. 47, reads *Danda-nagilalasa pavinanátinam* dánathambho; and translates, "This pillar is the gift of the illustrious family of DANDA NAGIRALA." But the fac-simile impression of this inscription, as well as a hand-copy now before me, agree in the reading which I have given above.

No. 182.—*Kirárasa Nágapiyasa Achhavado Sethisa dánam thabho.*

"Pillar-gift of NÁGAPRIYA, ACHHAVADA, the Sreshti (or master) of the weavers."

Prinsep, No. 3, reads *Karasa* and translates "Gift of ACHHAVADÁ SETHI, the beloved of KARASA NÁGA." See also No. 192 of the western gate. Prinsep evidently considered Sethi as the feminine form of Seth, a "banker." I have ventured to identify the *Kirár* of this inscription with the weaver caste, who bear the same name at the present day; but this is a mere conjecture.

No. 183. This inscription is too indistinct to allow even of a conjectural translation.

ON THE SOUTH GATEWAY.

No. 184.—*Budha Palitaya bhikhunaye dánam.*

"Gift of BUDHA PALITÁ, the mendicant nun."

Prinsep, No. 23, reads *Budha Palitasa bhikhuno dánam*, "the gift of BUDHA PÁLIT, the poor man."

No. 185.—*Pothakasa bhikhuno dánam.*
"Gift of POSTHAKA, the mendicant monk."

Prinsep, No. 23, reads *Panthaka*.

No. 186.—*Virasa bhikhuno dánam.*
"Gift of VIRA, the mendicant monk."

No. 187.—*Yakhaye bhikhuniyá vádiva.*
"Gift of YAKSHÁ, the mendicant nun

No. 188.—*Hanajaya dánam.*
"Gift of HANAJÁ."

No. 189.—*Vedisa Kehidántakarehirápakam mankata.*

This inscription is quite perfect: but as it seems to have formed only a part of a longer inscription, I cannot even make a guess as to its meaning. The donor was an inhabitant of *Vidisa*, and was perhaps named *Kehidánta*.

No. 190.—*Rajnye Siri Sátakanisa*
Avesanisa Vásithi-putasa
Anandasa dánam.
"Gift of ANANDA, son of the neophyte VASISHTHA, in the reign of SRI SÁTAKARNI."

This valuable inscription is carved on the bas-relief of a Tope, in the middle of the upper architrave of the south gateway. The King, Sri Sátakarni, was the third* of the Andhra dynasty of Magadha; and

* Wilson's Vishnu Purána, p. 472.

his reign extended from the year 19 to 37 A. D. The word, which I have translated neophyte, occurs also in No. 161; but in this instance it is possible that it may have another signification. *A'vesan* means simply "entrance," from *vis* to enter; but as there is a separate inscription on the middle architrave (see No. 191), and another on one of the pillars of the gateway (see No. 189), it is clear that the whole entrance could not have been the gift of Ananda. *A'vesani* must therefore have some other meaning which is not given in the dictionaries. Now as *ishá*, a ploughbeam, is derived from ईष, *isha*, to go, *ishani* may be taken for a beam of any kind; and thus we shall have *ava* + *ishani* = *aveshani*, or (as there is but one *s* in Pali) avesani, an entrance-beam, or gateway architrave. As *ava* means to "enter," this derivation is quite legitimate. But if this was the real meaning, it seems difficult to say why the term should have been separated from dánam; for in the pillar gifts the word thabho invariably precedes or follows *dánam*.

After a careful examination of all the inscriptions on the gateways of the Sánchi Tope, and a comparison of their alphabetical characters with those of other inscriptions of known dates, such as those of Asoka, B. C. 250; those of the Sah coins of Gujrat, A. D. 300; and those of the Guptas, A. D. 400 to 500; both Lieutenant Maisey and myself had concluded that the Sánchi gateways were erected about the beginning of the Christian era. It was with great satisfaction therefore that I afterwards discovered the name of Sri Sátakarni in a conspicuous situation over the southern gateway. This successful result of my long experience in Indian archæology has given me sufficient confidence to say that the age of any Indian inscription may be determined approximately by the forms of its alphabetical characters.

No. 191.—*Ayachudasa Dhamakathikasa*
Atevâsino Bala Mitasa dânam.
"Gift of BALA-MITRA, pupil of ARYA KSHUDRA,
the reciter of Dharma."

This inscription is taken from the bas-relief of a Tope on the middle architrave of the south gateway. Prinsep, No. 23, reads the "well-tonsured pupil," but *Antevásin*, अन्तवासिन, means simply a "pupil," being derived from अन्त, *anta*, near, and वस, *vasa*, to "abide"—that is one who lives near another; as a pupil near a master. Aya-chuda is the teacher's name: see inscription No. 193. Prinsep reads *kathaka* at the end of the first line; but my fac-simile impression gives kathikasa, the possessive case of कथिक, kathika, a "narrator, or story-teller," as Prinsep has translated it.

On the West Gate.

No. 192.—*Kiráraya Nágapiyasa Achhavada Sethi-putasa cha Sanghasa.*

"Gift of the son of Nágapriya Achhavada, the master of the weavers, and of Sangha."

See No. 182 for the term which I have translated "weavers." I rather suspect that it must be the name of a place, *Kirára.*

No. 193.—*Aya-chudasa Atevásino Bala Mitasa danam thabho.*

"Pillar-gift of Bala-Mitra, the pupil of Arya-Kshudra."

Prinsep, No. 22. In this inscription there seems to me to be no doubt that *Aya-chuda* or *Aryya-kshudra* is the teacher's name.

Nos. 194, 195, 196. These show that the inscriptions were carried on from one line to another. The word *dánam*, "gift," is carved at the end of the upper band of the column, and *thabho*, "pillar," begins the second line, which is carved on a central band. Here the sense is complete; and the *swastika*, 卍, separates this inscription from the following one; which, although it looks legible enough, has quite baffled all my attempts to read it.

It is worthy of remark that upwards of one-third of the gifts recorded in these inscriptions were made by the fair sex; who in all countries have been noted for their pious donations. The number is very remarkable, when we remember that in India women could not possess property; but were entirely dependent on their fathers, their husbands, their brothers, or their sons.

Another point which I have noticed is the extremely rare use of compound letters. Only three instances occur throughout all these inscriptions; and they are certainly exceptions to the common practice of Asoka's age, which adhered to the simplest Pali forms. The compound *sw* occurs twice in *aswa* (see Nos. 80 and 83), but the true Pali form of *Asa* occurs in the ink inscription found inside the lid of the steatite casket from No. 3 Tope at Andher, see Plate XXX. The compound *sth* is found only once in *Dhama sthiri* (see No. 160); but the regular Pali form of *th* occurs twice in patithiya for pratisthiya (see Nos. 40 and 41), and once in mila thiti for milasthiti in the inscription on the southern pillar. The compound *nh* occurs once in the name of *Jonhaka*, see No. 152.

CHAPTER XVII.

OPENING OF THE SÁNCHI TOPE, NO. 1.

1. The persons who tried to open the great Sánchi Tope in 1822 made a large breach on the south-west side, and carried the excavation to the foundation, but they failed in reaching the centre of the building. The Tope was thus partly ruined without any discovery having been made to repay its destruction. Lieutenant Maisey and myself determined to proceed in a different manner, by sinking a perpendicular shaft down the middle of the Tope, so as not to injure its external appearance. After a number of careful measurements, the centre was determined as nearly as possible, and a shaft or well, 5 feet in diameter, was sunk through the solid brickwork to a depth of 48 feet, or 6 feet below the level of the terrace, at the base of the Tope. But the only discovery which we made consisted of numbers of spiral shells (*Planorbis*), which had been gathered in the mud with which the bricks were cemented together. These will be valu-

able curiosities to the naturalist, as they *certainly* date as high as B.C. 300, and are probably not less than two thousand four hundred years old. The bricks are large—16 by 10 by 3 inches.

2. From the non-discovery of any relics or other objects, we are left to guess at the age and destination of the great Sánchi Tope, from less certain although very probable sources of information. From these I have deduced that the Tope itself was in existence not long after the period of the Second Synod in B.C. 443, that the massive stone railing was erected in the reign of Asoka, between 260 and 250 B.C., and that the gateways were added in the reign of Sri Sátakarni, between the years 19 and 37 A.D.

3. The age of the Tope itself depends on the identification of *Wessanagara* with *Chetiya*; a point which has been already discussed and settled. Wessanagara is still represented by the ruins of Besnagar, two miles to the north of Bhilsa; and *Chetiyagiri* (or Chaitya-hill) is undoubtedly the hill of Sánchi, on which the great Chaitya now stands. It was here that Asoka rested, on his way between Pátaliputra and Ujain. Buddhaghoso calls the place *Wessanagara*, and Mahanamo calls it *Chetiya* and *Chetiyagiri*. The Tope was therefore in existence in 270 B.C., during Asoka's government of Ujain; but as one of the eighteen heresies which prevailed after the meeting of the Second Synod was named the "*Chetiya Schism*," it is certain that the Sánchi Chaitya must date as high as the fourth century before our era,

and perhaps even a century earlier, or about B. C. 500.*

4. The date of the colonnade or railing might be determined approximately to belong to the age of Asoka, by the alphabetical characters of the inscriptions, which are exactly similar to those of the pillar edicts. But there is a still more certain proof of the correctness of this date in the short inscription, No. 110, which records the "gift of SUBÁHITA, son of *Goti* the royal scribe." This Goti was a descendant of *Kodini* (Sans. *Kohudinya*), one of the principal disciples of Buddha. As he was the teacher of VACHHI SUVIJAYATA, he must have taken the vows himself. His eldest son, *Gotiputra*, was one of the most famous Buddhist teachers of his day. We learn this fact from the relic inscriptions which record the names of two disciples of Gotiputra. Of these, the most celebrated is that of Mogaliputra, who conducted the proceedings of the Third Synod in B. C. 241. The other pupil was Váchhiputra.

5. A third son of Goti, named *Kákanava Prabhásan*, was the donor of Suvijayata's relics to the Sánçhi Tope, No. 2; and his own relics were found in the Andher Tope, No. 2. A fourth son, named *Bhanduka*, is mentioned in the colonnade inscription,

* I suppose that the interior brick Tope may be as old as 500 B. C., and that the stone casing was added by Asoka. This kind of addition was not unusual. See *Mahawanso*, p. 202, where Lajjitisso, king of Ceylon, encloses the Thuparamo with a case of stone.

No. 33. Thus three sons of Goti had taken the vows, whilst a fourth became the King's Scribe, or Secretary (*Raja-Lipákara*). As the eldest of these brothers was the teacher of Mogaliputra, he was probably somewhat older than his pupil, although not necessarily so. The younger brother may therefore be looked upon as the contemporary of Mogaliputra, which will fix his date from 260 B. C. to 230, during the most flourishing period of the Buddhist religion.

6. The age of the gateways has been ascertained from an inscription carved on a bas-relief representation of a Tope on the upper architrave of the southern entrance. This inscription (No. 190) records the "gift of an entrance architrave by ANANDA, the son of *Vasishtha*, in the reign of SRI SÁTAKARNI." This Prince was the third of the Andhra kings of Magadha; and his reign has been fixed, by the common consent of all archæologists, in the early part of the first century of our era. According to my chronology he reigned from 19 to 37 A. D.

7. The fact that the gateways are of later date than the colonnade or railing, is confirmed by the more recent character of the inscriptions, which approaches that of the Sáh coins of Gujrat. For the sake of comparison, I have collected all these gateway inscriptions in Plate XIX., beneath the more ancient record of the Southern Pillar. By this arrangement, a single glance is sufficient to show the great change which had taken place in the alphabetical characters in about two centuries and a half.

8. But there is still one more convincing proof that the gateways are of later date than the railing. In the plan of the Tope, in Plate VIII., the old railing on which the more ancient inscriptions are carved, is shaded lightly, and the additional railing and gateway pillars, on which the less ancient inscriptions are found, are made quite black. By this it will be seen that a half pillar of the more recent railing is made to abut against the third pillar of the older railing. Now, as most of the old pillars were inscribed, it seemed probable that one inscription at least would be found *hidden* by the half pillar of the less ancient railing. And such, indeed, is the fact at the northern entrance, where a long hidden inscription on the pillar of the old railing is now revealed by the separation of the two pillars of different ages.

9. The different dates of the Tope, of its colonnades and of its gateways, have been satisfactorily settled within certain limits; but the destination or object of the building is more difficult to be ascertained. From the non-discovery of relics, I infer that this great *chaitya* was dedicated to the Supreme Buddha. This conjecture is strengthened by the existence of statues of the four mortal Buddhas at the entrances. For it is the practice of the modern Buddhists of Népal, when they dedicate a *Chaitya* to Adi Buddha, to place four statues of the *Dhyáni Buddhas* at its base. *Vairochana* (or light), the first of the Pancha Dhyáni Buddhas, is supposed to occupy the centre of the building. It seems quite possible, however, that this

Tope contained some relics of Sákya; but if, as I believe, the relics of the holy teacher were always kept in some easily accessible place, for the purpose of being shown to the people on stated festivals, it seems probable that they would have been carried off by the monks, on the general break-up of the Buddhist monastic establishments throughout India.

CHAPTER XVIII.

NO. 2 TOPE.—SÁNCHI.

1. In 1819, when Captain Fell visited Sánchi, this Tope was "in perfect repair, not a stone having fallen;"* but in 1822 it was half destroyed by the same amateur antiquaries who ruined the larger Tope. It stands half way down the slope of the hill, about 400 yards from the great Tope, from which it bears 109¼° west. The hill has been carefully levelled, and the western side built up to form a court 100 feet square, in the midst of which stands the Tope surrounded by the usual Buddhist railing.

2. The Tope is a solid hemisphere (built of rough stones, without mortar) 39 feet in diameter, springing from a cylindrical plinth of the same diameter, and 3½ feet in height. The basement is 6 feet in height, with a projection of 5 feet 4 inches, which forms a terrace for the perambulation of worshippers. The terrace is reached on the eastern side by a double flight of steps (now in ruins) 5 feet 2

* Prinsep's Journal, iii. 494.

inches wide, which meet at a landing-place, 7 feet 6 inches square.

3. The hemisphere was flattened at top to form a terrace; which, when measured in its perfect state by Captain Fell, was 19 feet in diameter.* This was most probably enclosed by a coping, or cornice, similar to that which is represented around the terrace of No. 1 Tope at Andher. In the centre stood a square pedestal, surrounded by a square Buddhist railing of small dimensions, its whole height being only 4 feet. The fragments of this railing, which I measured, were:—pillars, 3 feet 1½ inch in height, with a section of 7¼ inches by 5¾ inches; rails, 10½ inches long by 8½ inches broad, at intervals of 2¾ inches. The pedestal was of course originally surmounted by a *chatta*, but of this no trace now remains.

4. The whole is surrounded by a Buddhist railing 7 feet 6 inches in height, with four entrances towards the four sides of the square court. The pillars are 5 feet 11½ inches in height, with a section of 15½ inches by 11½ inches. The rails are 18 inches broad, with a thickness of 5½ inches in the middle. The inter-columniation varies from 17 to 18 inches; and, as in the great Tope, seems to be equal to the depth of rail. The coping is 21 inches in height, and 14 inches thick, and is connected to the pillars in the same way as in the large Tope. This railing, like that of the great

* Prinsep's Journal, iii. 494.

Tope, is elliptical, the longer diameter from east to west being 74½ feet, and the shorter diameter from north to south only 69 feet. By this ellipticity of form, a clear breadth of more than 8 feet is preserved all round the base of the building.*

5. The pillars of the Buddhist railing which have already been described, are perfectly plain; but these are ornamented by medallions containing a variety of flowers, and numerous animals, both known and fabulous. The medallions are circular in the middle of the pillar, and semi-circular at its head and base. The semi-circular medallions are nearly all filled with flowers; but the full medallions have men and women, horses, bulls, lions and elephants, centaurs, winged horses, and winged bulls. Many of the flower ornaments are pretty, but the figures of men and animals are generally coarse and clumsy.

6. The pillars of the entrances are covered with bas-reliefs, all of the same inferior style of art, save a few remarkable exceptions at the eastern entrance, one of which is much superior, even to the best bas-reliefs of the great Tope. This represents a female standing in a doorway, with her right hand resting on her hip, and in her left hand a lotus flower. Her hair is parted on the right side. She is naked to the waist, from which a single piece of drapery is drawn over the left thigh. The graceful proportions and easy attitude of this figure place its sculptor almost in the same rank with the carver of the beautiful lions of the

* See Plate XX. for a plan and view of this monument.

south pillar. On another face of the same pillar there is a two-horse chariot containing two figures, and attended by an elephant carrying a standard-bearer. On a second pillar is represented a wheel, or symbol of Buddha, standing on an altar, and ornamented with garlands.* Two kneeling figures are bowing down to the steps of the altar.

7. On one of the pillars of the south entrance there is a representation of a Tope, enclosed with a Buddhist railing, and surmounted by a square pedestal, and by the usual chatta. On a second pillar is represented an isolated column surmounted by three lions bearing a wheel or symbol of Buddha.

8. On a pillar of the west entrance there is a bas-relief of a single column surmounted by three elephants carrying the same wheel emblem of Buddha. The base is enclosed by a square Buddhist railing; outside which two figures, a male and a female, are paying their adorations.†

9. On a pillar of the north entrance, the wheel or emblem of Buddha is represented resting on the peculiar monogram or symbol of Dharma.‡ On another pillar is shown an isolated column, surmounted by an elephant, and two lions, carrying the wheel emblem of Buddha.

10. The colonnade of this Tope, like that of the Great Chaitya, bears many inscriptions, of which

* See Plate XXXI., fig. 6, of this work.
† See Plate XXXI., fig. 1, of this volume.
‡ See Plate XXXII., fig. 1, of this volume.

none have yet been published. These inscriptions are chiefly valuable for the light that they throw on the changes which had gradually taken place in the language. The most remarkable of these is the substitution of *Bhikhu* for *Bhichhu*. With five exceptions, the latter is the only spelling used throughout the numerous inscriptions of *Asoka's age* on the colonnade of the Great Tope at Sánchi; while the former is the only spelling used in all the gateway inscriptions of the *age of Sátakarni*.

But on the colonnade of this Tope we have both spellings; *bhikhu* being used ten times, and *bhichhu* five times. From this fact we may conclude that the colonnade was certainly erected at some period between the ages of Asoka and Sri Sátakarni. This is borne out by the forms of the alphabetical characters, which, though generally like those of Asoka's time, yet present some differences which undoubtedly point to a later date. The principal change is seen in the manner of attaching the vowel *u* at the foot of the *kh*. In the Asoka inscriptions, this is done by the intervention of a dot, or point; but in those of the present Tope, the dot is replaced by a small circle.

CHAPTER XIX.

INSCRIPTIONS.—NO. 2 TOPE.—SÁNCHI.

Pl. XXI., No. 1.—*Nágilási dánam Ayasa-atevasino.*
"Gift of NÁGILÁSI, the pupil of ARYYA."

No. 2.—*Dhama Rakhitasa sejhasaka.*
"(Gift) of DHARMA RAKSHITA . . ."

No. 3.—*Pádukulákáyagámasa dánam.*
"Gift of ÁRYYAGRAMA, of the Pándu race."

The celebrated name of the Pandus is here met with, for the first time, on a genuine ancient monument. The use of the cerebral *d*, and the affix of the term *kula*, "race or tribe," prove that I am right in attributing this gift to one of the race of Pandu. See also No. 8, for another inscription of a Pandu.

No. 4.—*Budhilasa-bhogavarhanakasa dánam.*
"Gift of BUDHILA, the increaser of enjoyment."

No. 5.— . . *ma-devaya dánam Mitamajheya Antevásini(ya).*
"Gift of (DHAR)MA DEVÁ, the pupil of MITRA MADHYÁ."

No. 6.—*Isilasa bhikhuno dánam.*
"Gift of ISILA, the mendicant monk."

No. 7.—*Sagha Mitasa bhikhuno danam.*

"Gift of SANGHA MITRA, the mendicant monk."

No. 8.—*Budha Palitasa Sethino Padukuliniyase dánam.*

"Gift of BUDHA PÁLITA, the Sreshti (or master of a trade*) of the race of Pándu."

No. 9.— . . *yapaná* . . . *kasa dánam.*

"Gift of (AR)YYAPANA . . ."

No. 10.—*Budha Rakhitasa anammitakasa dánam.*

"Gift of RAKSHITA . . ."

No. 11.—*Vijhasa bhikhuno dánam.*

"Gift of VIDYA, the mendicant monk."

No. 12.—*Yakhilasa bhichhuno dánam.*

"Gift of YAKSHILA, the mendicant monk."

No. 13.—*Nágapáyasa·Achhava(da)sa Sethisa dánam.*

"Gift of NÁGAPAYA ACHHAVADA, the Sreshti."

See Nos. 182 and 192 of No. 1 Tope, which both give the name of *Nágapáya* (or *priya*) *Achhavada*, but the persons cannot be the same, as there is a difference in the dates of the inscriptions of the two Topes of about two centuries. The two donors must, however, have been of the same family.

No. 14.— . . *sápakiya Soraya dánam bhikhuniya.*

"Gift of (KÁ)SYAPAKI SORÁ, the mendicant nun."

No. 15.—*Válayá Korariye bhikhunaye dánam.*

"Gift of VALÁ KORÁRI (the weaver?), a mendicant nun."

No. 16.—*Dhama Sanaya Korariya dánambhi . . .*

"Gift of DHARMA SENA, Korâri, the mendicant nun."

* The meaning of this term has been given before; but it may be as well to repeat here, that Sreshti is the head of a guild, and is equivalent to the modern *Chaodri*.

No. 17.—*Naga Palitaya dánam thabho.*
"Pillar-gift of NAGA PALITÁ."

No. 18.—*Phagulúya bhikhuniya dánam.*
"Gift of PHAGULÁ, the mendicant nun."

No. 19.—*Balakasa Ayasa Arapa Gutasa sásá . (nan)-dakasa atevasino dánam.*
"Gift of BALAKA ARYYA, the pupil of ARAPA-GUPTA, the (delighter) in Scripture."

Balaka may mean simply a boy, and *Balaka Ayasa* will signify only the child ARYYA. My copy reads *Arapa*; but I believe the true name to be *Araha*.

No. 20.—*Yama Rakhitáya bhikhuniya dánam.*
"Gift of YAMA RAKSHITA, the mendicant nun."

No. 21.—*Mulúya dánam-thabho Yadaya Atevasiniya.*
"Pillar-gift of MULÁ, the pupil of YADÁ."

No. 22.—*Sagha Rakhitaya mata . . daka Isidásiya bhichhuniya dánam.*
"Gift of SANGHA RAKSHITÁ, the . . of ISIDÁSI, the mendicant nun."

No. 23.—*Yasa Budha Rakhitasa Pokhareyakasa dánam.*
"Gift of YASA BUDHA RAKSHITÁ, of *Pokhareyaka*."

No. 24.—*Vinákáye Vádyuvahanikáye dánam.*
"Gift of the lute-player, VADYUVAHANIKÁ."

This inscription is carved on the bas-relief of a wheel pillar of the western entrance. There has been an attempt to render some double letter, and I am not satisfied that I have read the middle part of the inscription correctly. If we might read वधु or वधू, vadhū, instead of *vadyu*, which seems perfectly allowable, the translation would be simply "Gift of VINÁKÁ, the daughter-in-law (son's wife) of VAHANIKÁ."

No. 25.—*Peḍaya bhikhuniya thabho dánam.*
"Pillar-gift of PENDA, the mendicant nun."

No. 26.—*Isadakaditisisasa dánam.*
"Gift of ISADAKADITYA (?) . (or Isadakanditi)."

No. 27.—*Isádekadiyá dánam.*
"Gift of ISADEKANDI."

No. 28.—*(I)sadúkadiya Patolaya dánam.*
"Gift of ISADAKANDI, of *Pratolá.*"

No. 29.—*Budha Pá(lita)sakodiya dánam.*
"Gift of BUDHA PALITA . . ."

This inscription is much mutilated; but I believe it to be the same as No. 8.

No. 30.—*Sagha Mitasa Sonadakasá dánam.*
"Gift of SANGHA MITRA, of *Sonadaka.*"

No. 31.—*Budha (Miti)sedakaḍiya dánam.*
"Gift of BUDHA MITRA . . ."

No. 32.—*Abha(ti)sá dánam adha-porikasa.*
"Half-gateway gift of ABHRATI (the brotherless)."

Adha-porikasa I have taken for *arddha-paurikasya,* "of half an entrance," which is not an unlikely gift to have been made to the Tope.

Plate, No. 33.—*Yasogirino dánam bhichhuno.*
"Gift of YASOGIRI, the mendicant monk."

No. 34.—*Arahakasa bhichhuno chanakaya dánam.*
"Gift of the holy bhikshu CHANAKYA."

This inscription will admit of several readings, such as—

"Gift of *Arhaka*, the mendicant monk of *Chanaká*."

"Gift of *Arhaka*, the mendicant monk, and of *Naká*."

No. 35.—*Bahulasa dánam.*

"Gift of BAHULA."

No. 36.—*Gadaya Nadinagarikaya.*

"Gift of GANDÁ, of *Nadinagariká*."

No. 37.—*Idagi(riya)sa dánam.*

"Gift of INDRAGIRIYA."

No. 38.—*Aya Nandakasa bhikhuno dánam.*

"Gift of ARYYA NANDAKA, the mendicant monk."

No. 39.—*Naga Rakhitasa bhichhuno Pokhareyakasa dánam.*

"Gift of NAGA RAKSHITA, the mendicant monk, of *Pokhareyaka*."

No. 40.—*Sagha Rakhitasa bhichhu danam koïsa.*

"Gift of SANGHA RAKSHITA, the mendicant monk."

No. 41.—*(Ya)khihanakasa Udabaraghariyasa dánam.*

"Gift of YAKSHIHANAKA, of *Udabaraghariya*."

No. 42.— . . . *Udabaraghariyasa.*

"(Gift) of . . . of *Udabaraghariya*."

No. 43.—*Sediya bhikhuniya thabho dánam.*

"Pillar-gift of SENDI, the mendicant nun."

CHAPTER XX.

OPENING OF NO. 2 TOPE.—SÁNCHI.

1. On looking at this Tope, which Captain Fell had seen perfect in 1819, I must confess that I felt a secret satisfaction that the labours of the bungling amateurs, who had half ruined it in 1822, had ended in nothing. But at the same time I had some misgivings, from the large size of the breach, whether their workmen had not reached the centre. After several careful measurements, however, both Lieutenant Maisey and myself felt satisfied that the actual centre had not quite been attained, although the excavators must have been within a single foot of it. After a few hours' labour in clearing away the loose stones from the middle of the breach, we began carefully to sink a shaft down the centre of the Tope. In three hours more the removal of a single stone from the western side of the shaft, disclosed a small chamber containing a stone box.

2. The chamber was made of six stones, four set on edge forming the sides, and two laid flat forming the top and bottom. The chamber was not in the

centre of the building, but two feet to the westward of it, the measurement from the south side being 18½ feet, or exactly half the diameter, while that from the eastern side was 20½ feet, or 2 feet more than the semi-diameter. The bottom of the chamber was exactly 7 feet above the terrace or upper surface of the basement, and 3½ feet above the centre of the hemisphere.

3. The relic-box, formed of white sandstone, is 11 inches long, 9½ inches broad, and the same in height, including the lid. It was standing with one of its long sides to the east, towards the Great Tope. On removing it from the chamber, we found the following inscriptions carved in three lines on its eastern face:—

Saviná Vinayakána Araṇ Kásapa
Gotaṃ Upádiya Aran cha Váchhi
Suvijayataṃ Vináyaka.

"Teacher of all branches of *Vinaya, the Arhat* KÁSYAPA GOTRA, *Upádiya* (or Abbot); and the *Arhat* VÁCHHI SUVIJAYATA, teacher of Vinaya."*

4. *Upádiya*, in Sanskrit *Upádháya*, was the Abbot or head of a Buddhist monastery, who had accomplished *Upádána*, or the complete restraint of all the organs of sense, and the consequent suppression of all earthly desires. *Vinaya* was the lowest of the three grades of advancement taught by the Buddhist religionists; and the fact that Kásyapa-Gotra was a teacher of Vinaya will account for his mission

* See Plate XX.

to the Hemawanta, where, as we learn from the Chinese travellers, the active mountaineers preferred the practical teachings of the *Vinaya* to the esoteric doctrines of the *Abhidharma*. The spelling of *Aran* for *Arhata* is peculiar, as this title is always written *Araha* in the inscriptions of the colonnade of the Great Tope.

5. On removing the lid of the stone box, we found inside four small caskets or boxes of mottled steatite, of which one is represented of half size in Plate XX. Each of these caskets contained small portions of burnt human bone, and each was inscribed with the names of the holy men whose ashes were enshrined therein. All these inscriptions will be found in Plate XX.

No. I.—STEATITE BOX.

Outside Lid.

Sapurisa(sa) Kásapa Gotasa Sava Hemavatácliariyasa.
" (Relics) of the emancipated Kasyapa Gotra, the missionary to the whole *Hemavanta*."

Inside Lid.

Sapurisa(sa) Majhimasa.
" (Relics) of the emancipated Madhyama."

Bottom.

Sapurisasa Háritíputasa.
" (Relics) of the emancipated Háritíputra."

No. II.—STEATITE BOX.

Outer Circle.

Sapurisasa Váchháya Suvijayatasa Gotantevásino.
"(Relics) of the emancipated Váchhá Suvijayata, the pupil of Gota."

Inner Circle.

Kákanava-púbhásasáhana dánam.
"The gift of Kákanava Prabhásana."

No. III.—STEATITE BOX.

Outside Lid.

Sapurisasa Maha Vanáyasa—Sapurisasa Ápagirasa.
"(Relics) of the emancipated Maha Vanáya, (and) of the emancipated Ápagira."

Inside Lid.

Sapurisasa Koḍiniputasa.
"(Relics) of the emancipated Kohudinya-putra."

No. IV.—STEATITE BOX.

Outside Lid.

Sapurisasa Kosikiputasa.
"(Relics) of the emancipated Kausikiputra."

INSIDE LID.

Supurisasa Gotiputasa.
" (Relics) of the emancipated GOTIPUTRA."

BOTTOM.

Supurisasa Mogaliputasa.
" (Relics) of the emancipated MAUDGALAPUTRA."

---

6. REMARKS.

No. I. Box.—The names of Kásyapa and Madhyama are recorded in the Mahawanso as two of the five missionaries who were despatched to the Hemawanta country, after the meeting of the Third Synod in 241 B.C. A second casket of Kásyapa's relics was discovered at Sonári, and from the inscription we learn that he was the son of Koti. Of Háritiputra nothing is known; but another portion of his relics was found enshrined alone in No. 3 Tope at Andher.

No. II. Box.—Vacchi-suvijayata must have been a man of some consequence, for his name is placed on the outside of the stone box, along with that of Kásyapa. Relics of his son, Vacchiputra, were found at Andher, along with those of Kákanava Prabhásan and Mogaliputra. He is thus doubly connected with Kákanava, who was the donor of his relics to the Sánchi Tope. Colonel Low gives a story from the Páli books of Burma, regarding a sea captain named *Káká-bhásá*, who traded to Takkasila in the reign of Asoka.* *Káká-bhásá* appears to be only a contracted form of *Kákanava Prabhásan.* The Captain was a servant of the King of *Rom*, whose subjects were famous for magic spells. Asoka, therefore, employed *Kákábhásá* to discover some hidden relics, and to superintend their enshrinement in a splendid Chaitya, which was duly accomplished with the recital of one hundred and eight Páli invocations. I presume that *Kákábhásá* was a native of Multan, or Sind, and that he traded to Takkasila for rock salt. *Kákanava Prábhásán* was the son of *Goti*, and a descendant of *Kodini* or *Kohudinya*, one of Buddha's eighty disciples. The name is a remarkable one, and as both parties were contemporaries of Asoka, it is at least quite possible that they were the same person.

No. III. Steatite Box.—Of *Maha Vanaya* and *Apagira* I know nothing; but *Kodini-putra* was probably a son or descendant of the celebrated *Kohudinya*, one of Buddha's eighty disciples.

No. IV. Steatite Box.—I know nothing of *Kosikiputra*; but Gotiputra, as we learn from one of the Andher inscriptions, was a descendant of Kodini or Kohudinya, who has just been mentioned. Mogali or Maudgala putra was the well-known head of the Buddhist Church, who superintended the proceedings

* Journal of the Bengal Asiatic Society, xvii. 91, 92.

of the Third Synod, during the reign of Asoka in B.C. 241. He died at eighty years of age, in B.C. 233.

7. The discovery in this Tope consisted of the relics of no less than ten of the leading men of the Buddhist Church, during the reign of Asoka. One of them conducted the proceedings of the Third Synod, in 241 B.C., and two others were deputed to the Hemawanta country as missionaries, after the meeting of the Synod. From this we may conclude that the date of the Tope cannot be earlier than about 220 B.C., by which time the last of Asoka's contemporaries would have passed away. The railing is most probably of the same period, for the use of the term *Bhikhu* instead of *Bhichhu* (of which latter there are only five instances amongst the numerous inscriptions on the colonnade of the great Tope), might readily be supposed to have extended in fifty years to that proportion in which we find it used in the inscriptions of No. 2 Tope at Sánchi. The general forms of the alphabetical characters agree too closely with those of Asoka's own age, to permit the assignment of a later date than 200 B.C., for the erection of this Tope.

8. The Tope itself would seem at first to have been intended only for the relics of Kásyapa Gotra, and of Vácchi Suvijayata, whose names alone are found on the outside of the stone box. But I suppose that during the several years of its erection the Sánchi community gradually became possessed of the relics

of other distinguished men who had worked long and well for the extension and glory of the Buddhist religion, during the long and prosperous reign of Asoka.

9. A comparison of all these different inscriptions establishes the intimate connection which existed between many of the principal leaders of the Buddhist faith during the reign of Asoka. The family of Kodini, in two generations alone, would appear to have furnished no less than six leading members of the Buddhist priesthood. His son Majhima was the missionary sent to the Hemawanta country in 241 B.C.; and his grandson, Gotiputra, was so eminent a member of the Bauddha community as to have merited the title of *dáyádo*, or, "brother" of the faith; which proves that he must have dedicated some of his own children to the service of his religion. This family, also, would appear to have been equally celebrated as successful propounders of Buddhism, for Goti is recorded to have been the teacher of Váchhi Suvijayata, and his son Gotiputra, to have been the teacher of the famous Mogaliputra, who was the head of the Buddhist Church at the Assembly of the Third Synod in B.C. 241. The connection between the different members of this family and their pupils is shown in the following table:—

KODINI
had three sons,

- KODINI-PUTRA, Relics at *Sánchi*.
- GOTI, had 4 sons and 1 pupil.
  - GOTI-PUTRA, Missionary to *Dárdábhisara*, Relics at *Sánchi* & *Sonári*, had 2 pupils.
  - KÁKANAVA PRABHÁSAN, Relics at *Andher*, Presented Relics of *Váchhi* to *Sánchi*.
  - BHANDUKA, a *Bhikshu* or Mendicant Monk. See *Sánchi* Inscriptions, No. 33.
  - SUBÁHITA, the royal scribe. See *Sánchi* Inscriptions, No. 110.
- MAJHIMA, Missionary to the *Hemawanta*, Relics at *Sánchi* and *Sonari*.

GOTI'S pupil was VACHHI-SUVIJAYATA, Relics at *Sánchi*, had 1 son.

GOTI-PUTRA had 2 pupils.

- MOGALI-PUTRA, Head of the Buddhist Church in B.C. 241. Relics at *Sánchi* and *Andher*.
- VÁCHHI-PUTRA, Relics at *Andher*.

10. This genealogy, obtained from the inscriptions of the Bhilsa Topes, shows what we might reasonably expect to get from the numerous Topes which still exist in the ancient Kapila and Magadha, the scene of Sákya Sinha's birth, teaching, and death. A few more genealogies, similar to the above, would probably give us a complete succession from the time of Sákya Sinha down to the age of Asoka, and so establish the accuracy of the date now assigned to the great founder of the Buddhist religion. As we have already discovered relics of his contemporaries, Sáriputra and Mogalána, who date from the middle of

the 6th century B.C., and of Mogaliputra and others who assisted at the Third Synod in B.C. 241, there is every reasonable expectation that a complete examination of the still existing monuments would yield us the names of many of the principal leaders of Buddhism during the 4th, 5th, and 6th centuries before Christ. We should thus, perhaps, obtain one or more complete genealogical successions during the most eventful period of Indian history.

CHAPTER XXI.

NO. 3 TOPE.—SÁNCHI.

1. At first sight this Tope presented a mere mass of ruins;* but a closer inspection showed the lower courses of the hemisphere and the terrace of the basement tolerably perfect, although hidden amongst a heap of fallen stones. The diameter of the hemisphere is 40 feet; the breadth of the terrace, which was formed of single slabs, and is still quite perfect on the western side, is 6 feet, and its height above the original level of the soil is 7¼ feet; but only 6 feet above the floor of the entrance door-way which is still standing to the south. The dome was crowned by a pedestal 4½ feet square, which supported a *chatta* about 3½ feet in diameter. A square slab, which once formed part of the pedestal, is now lying to the south of the Tope, and a fragment of the *chatta* to the north-east.

2. The Tope was surrounded by a Buddhist railing, of which the only remains are a few of the curved

* See Plate XXII.

coping stones, and some fragments of two pillars. The coping stones are 9 inches high and 7½ inches thick. The pillars have the same section; and we may therefore conclude that the railing was somewhat less than five feet in height. The railing of No. 1 Tope at Sonári, of which the pillars are 9½ inches by 8 inches, is only 4 feet 8 inches in height. The enclosure most probably had four gateways; one to the south is still standing, and I thought that I could trace the remains of a second on the east.

3. The pillars of the southern entrance are 14 inches square, with an interval of 5 feet 4 inches. The clear breadth between the railing and the base of the Tope must have been about 12½ feet; one side of each of the pillars, to which the railing was attached, is left plain; and as the arrangement is the same as that of the entrances of the Great Tope, it seems certain that the gateways of this Tope must have been of a later date than the railing. The bas-reliefs of the pillars and architraves are so strikingly similar in subject and in style to those of the Great Tope, that there can be little doubt that both are the work of the same period. There are the same representations of Topes and Trees, the same lion pillar surmounted by a wheel, and the same figures clad in the same dresses.

4. The Tope stood in the midst of a square enclosure, and was surrounded by a very thick wall, the foundations of which still remain on three sides. The

enclosure was 90 feet square, and the walls were built due north and south, and east and west.

5. A shaft was sunk in the centre of this Tope, and after a few hours' labour we came to a large slab upwards of 5 feet in length, lying in a direction from north to south. On raising this slab we saw two large stone boxes each bearing a short inscription on its lid. That to the south bore *Sáriputasa*, "(relics) of SÁRIPUTRA"; that to the north bore *Mahá Mogalánasa*, "(relics) of MAHÁ MOGALÁNA." Each box was a cube of 1½ foot, with a lid 6 inches thick. The position of the relics was on the same level as the terrace outside.

6. In Sáriputra's box we found a large steatite casket, upwards of 6 inches broad and 3 inches in height, covered by a very thin saucer of black earthenware 9½ inches in diameter with a depth of 2 inches. The saucer was broken, and the upper surface had peeled off, but the colour of the inside was still lustrous. Close to the steatite casket were two pieces of sandal-wood, one 4½ inches in length, and the other 2½ inches. The only other thing in this box was a live spider.

7. The relic-casket is of white steatite. It has been turned on a lathe; and its surface is now hard and polished. In Plate XXII. I have given a half-size sketch of this antique casket, which contained only one small fragment of bone, scarcely an inch in length, and seven beads of different kinds. These are no doubt the "seven precious things" which

were usually deposited with the holiest relics; as with the skull of Buddha* at Hilo near Jalálábád. There were two distinct sets of the seven precious things, the one containing the precious metals as well as precious stones, the other precious stones only.

8. According to the Chinese the first series consisted of—

Chinese.	Sanscrit.	
1. Su-fa-lo	*Suvarna*	Gold.
2. A-lu-pa	*Rupya*	Silver.
3. Lieu-li	*Vaidurya*	Lapis lazuli.
4. Se-pho-ti-kia	*Sphatika*	Rock-crystal.
5. Meu-pho-lo-kie-la-pho	....	(A pale blue stone—amethyst). (?)
6. Mo-lo-kia-li	....	(Variegated agate).
7. Po-ma-lo-kia	*Padmarága*	Ruby.

9. The second series consisted of—

Chinese.	Sanscrit.	
1. Po-lo-so	*Prabála*	Coral.
2. A-chy-ma-kie-pho	*Asmagarbha*(?)	Amber.
3. Ma-ni	*Mani*	Pearl.
4. Chin-shu-kia	....	(A red stone—garnet). (?)
5. Shy-kia-pi-ling-kia	....	(The most excellent of precious stones).
6. Mo-lo-kia-pho	*Marakata*	Emerald.
7. Pa-che-lo	*Vajra*	Diamond.

10. The seven precious things found with Sáriputra's relics differ somewhat from both of these series; but the correspondence is still very striking.

* *Fo-kwe-ki*, c. xiii.

1st, a flat piece of *pearl*; 2nd, 3rd, two small seed *pearls*; 4th, a *garnet* bead; 5th, a star-shaped bead of *lapis-lazuli*; 6th, a *crystal* bead; 7th, an oblong bead of pale *amethyst*. The same custom still prevails amongst the Buddhists of Ladák, who usually place with the ashes of a chief, or the dead body of a Lama, bits of gold, silver, copper, and iron; pearls, garnets, and turquoises; grains of wheat, barley, and rice; specimens of red and white sandal-wood; and of the holy *Shúkpá*, or pencil cedar (Juniperus excelsa).

11. In the northern stone box we found another steatite casket, somewhat smaller than that of Sáriputra. It is apparently of a softer substance; for the surface when first seen was white and powdery like chalk; but this has now nearly disappeared, and the colour is almost the same as that of Sáriputra's casket. Inside we found only two minute fragments of bone, of which the larger was rather less than half an inch in length.

12. On the inner surface of the lid of each casket there is a single ink letter, half an inch in height. In Sáriputra's casket the letter is *sá*, and in that of Maha Mogalana's it is *ma*; these being the initial letters of their respective names.

13. The relative position of these relics has its significance: for in their religious ceremonies the ancient Indians always sat facing the east, which therefore they named the front, *para*; while the south and north were respectively the "right,"

dakshina, and the "left," *váma*. The west was called *apara*, "behind." Now Sáriputra and Maha Mogalana were the principal followers of Buddha, and were usually styled his right and left hand disciples. Their ashes thus preserved after death the same positions to the right and left of Buddha which they had themselves occupied in life.

14. Sáriputra was the son of the Brahman Tishya, and of the beautiful-eyed Sári or Sáriká, who received her name from the resemblance of her eyes to those of a Sáras or Cyrus bird. Sáriputra, or son of Sári, is his most common name; but he is also known by the patronymic of Upatishya. The Tibetans call him Shá-ri-hi-bu, or Sári's son. Tishya was the most learned of all the Brahmans at the court of Rája-griha. Sáriká herself was a proficient in the four Vedas, and had overcome her brother in disputation. But her son excelled them both; and was much celebrated for his wisdom. His talents, which were attributed to his moral and religious merit in former births,* were so great, that Sakya himself proclaimed† that the "profoundly wise Sáriputra was competent to spread abroad the wisdom of Buddha;" and his fellow-disciple Káchháyano declared that "excepting the Saviour of the world, there are no others in existence whose wisdom is equal to one sixteenth part of the profundity of Sáriputra."

* Csoma de Koros in Asiatic Society's Researches, vol. xx., p. 52.

† Turnour, Introduction to Mahawanso, p. xxvii.

15. According to the Japanese chronology, this wisest of the disciples of Buddha embraced a monastic life, four years after Sákya's attainment of Buddhahood, that is in 584 B. C. He, and his fellow-student Maudgalyáyana, had attended all the philosophical schools of the day without obtaining conviction, until they heard the preaching of Buddha, when they gave up all and followed him.

16. In a Mongolian work translated from the Sanskrit, and entitled *Uligerün dalaï* (the Sea of Parables), we read,* "When SÁRIPUTRA learnt that Buddha was bent on entering *nirvána*, he experienced profound sorrow, and said to himself, 'It is soon indeed, and contrary to all expectation, that the Tathágata hath resolved upon entering nirvána; who after him will be the protector and shield of souls and of beings enveloped in darkness?' He then said to Buddha, 'It is impossible for me to witness the nirvána of Buddha.' Thrice he repeated these words, when Buddha replied, 'If thou believe thy time come, then do thy will, like all the *Khutukhtu* (in Sanskrit, *Nirmmánkáya, incarnations*), who enter the Nirvána of tranquillity.' Sáriputra, having heard these words of Buddha, arranged his dress; and, having a hundred times walked round Buddha, he repeated a great number of verses in praise of him. He then embraced the feet of the latter, placed them thrice upon his head, and joining the palms of his hands, said, 'I have been found worthy to ap-

* *Fo-kwe-ki*, c. xxviii., note 7, Laidlay's translation.

proach the gloriously accomplished Buddha.' He then worshipped Buddha, and proceeded with his servant, the monk *Yonti*, to Rájagriha, his native town. When arrived there, he said to Yonti, 'Go into the town, into the suburbs, and to the palace of the king, and to the houses of the high functionaries, and of such as give alms, and thus say to them: "The *Kutukhtu* SÁRIPUTRA hath resolved upon entering *nirvána*—come and prostrate yourselves before him."' The monk *Yonti* executed the orders of his master, went to the places indicated, and thus delivered his message: 'The *Kutukhtu* SÁRIPUTRA hath arrived here; if you would visit him, come without delay.' When the king *Ajátasatra*, the dispenser of alms, the great dignitaries, the officers of the army, and the heads of families, heard this announcement, they were all filled with sorrow, and with heavy hearts said, 'Ah! what will become of us when the second head of the law, the leader of so many beings, the *Kutukhtu* SARIPUTRA shall have entered *nirvána*.' Hurriedly they proceeded towards him, bowing down and saying, '*Kutukhtu!* if thou becomest *nirvána* who shall be our protector, and that of so many other beings?' Sáriputra then addressed them the following words: 'Since all is perishable, the end of all is death. As ye, too, belong to this world of torment, ye, too, will not remain long; death will come and terminate your career. But as you all, in consequence of meritorious works in a former existence, have had the happiness of being born in the world with Buddha, and that too in the human form, do you add other accumulative merits, and accomplish such works as shall save you from Sansára.' When SÁRIPUTRA had finished preaching thus to the bystanders the inexhaustible law, and had comforted their spirits with salutary medicaments, they bowed down before the *Kutukhtu*, and each returned to his home. After midnight, SÁRIPUTRA sat in a perfectly erect position; gathered all the faculties of his soul; directed these upon one point, and entered the first *Dhyána*. Thence he entered the second; thence the third; and from the third the fourth. From the fourth he passed into the *Samádhi of the births of boundless celestial space*; then into the *Samádhi of the births of complete nihility*. From this *Samádhi* he entered that of '*neither thinking, nor not thinking*;' then into that of *limitation*; and lastly into *Nirvána*.

17. "When Khourmousda, the king of the Gods, learnt of the *Nirvána* of SÁRIPUTRA, he came with several hundreds of thousands in his suite, bearing flowers, perfumes, and other objects meet for sacrifice. They diffused themselves through the whole space of heaven; their tears fell like rain; they scattered their flowers so as to cover the earth, saying, 'Oh! he whose wisdom was as the depth of the sea, who had passed through all the gates of knowledge, whose musical speech flowed sweetly as a running stream, who was perfect in the fulfilment of every duty, in self contemplation, in all wisdom—the sublime chief of

the doctrine, the excellent *Khutukhtu* SÁRIPUTRA—hath too hastily entered nirvána. Who shall succeed the gloriously accomplished Buddha and Tathágata to spread abroad the law?' All the inhabitants of the town and neighbourhood, as soon as they were apprised of the *nirvána* of SÁRIPUTRA, came, bearing much oil, perfumes, flowers, and other things appropriate for sacrifice. They wept loudly with accents of woe and sorrow, placing upon the ground the objects fit for the sacrifices. Khourmousda, the prince of the Gods, then commanded Vishwamitra to prepare a car of various precious materials for the body of SÁRIPUTRA. When the car was finished, the corpse of SÁRIPUTRA was placed thereon in a sitting position, and taken forth to a beautiful plain, all the while the Nágas, the Yakshas, the king, the commanders of the army, the officers, and the whole people, uttering cries of sorrow. There they raised a pile of *chandana* (sandal) wood. After moistening it with oil and butter, they placed upon it the body of Sáriputra, and applied fire. Then all bowed down, and each went to his home. When the fire was completely extinguished, the priest Yonti collected from the ashes the *sárira* of his master, and conveyed them, as well as his pot and ecclesiastical dress, to Buddha. He placed these things at the feet of Buddha, announcing, at the same time, the death of his master. When Ananda learnt this from the lips of Yonti, he was much grieved, and said to Buddha, 'Oh, Buddha! the first of our band has entered *nirvána*; to whom now shall we unbosom ourselves, and whom shall we regard as our protecting sun?' Buddha replied, 'Ananda! although SÁRIPUTRA hath entered *nirvána*, neither the charge of your duties, nor *samádhi*, nor understanding, nor plenary redemption, nor the prajna of plenary redemption, nor the nature of occult properties, hath become so; moreover, many generations ago Sáriputra once became nirvána, because he could not endure to see me enter upon nirvána.'"

18. As the funeral pile was formed of *chandana*, or sandal, it seems highly probable that the two pieces of this fragrant wood, which we found along with SÁRIPUTRA'S relics, must have been taken from the pile. We know that a Tope was built over the charcoal with which Buddha's body was burned, and that the Moriyans of Pipphaliwano celebrated a festival* in honour of their much-prized acquisition. From this account there would seem to be nothing improbable in supposing that fragments of sandalwood from the funeral pyre of Sáriputra should have been held in almost equal estimation.

19. MOGALÁNA, or MAHA MOGALÁNA as he was usually called to distinguish him from others of the same name, was the son of the Brahman Mudgala. His proper name was KÁLIKA or KOLITA, but he was generally called by his patronymic MAUDGALYÁYANA, or MOGALÁNA. Csoma de Koros† calls

* Turnour, in Prinsep's Journal, vii. 1013.

† Asiatic Researches of Bengal, xx. 49.

him Mongalyána, that is one of Mongol extraction; but his true Sanskrit name is Maudgalyáyana.

20. The relics of these two famous disciples of Buddha would appear to have been almost as widely scattered as those of Buddha himself: for we found another portion of their relics enshrined together in No. 2 Tope at Satdhára. We learn also from Fa Hian that at Mathura* there were Topes both of She-li-foe (or Sáriputra) and of Mou-lian (or Mogalána), while we know that the former died at Rajagriha, where a Tope was erected over his ashes which was still standing in 400 A. D.

21. It is not possible to fix the date of this Tope, more nearly than between 550 and 250 B. C. Sáriputra died a few years before† Sákya's attainment of nirvána, in 543 B. C. It is therefore just possible that the Tope may have been built as early as 550 B. C.; and if there was any proof that Buddhism had extended so far at this early period, I should have no hesitation in ascribing the Tope to the middle of the sixth century before our era. In the Tibetan *Dulva*,‡ it is recorded that Kátyáyana, and five hundred other monks, were despatched by Sákya to convert the King of Ujain to Buddhism. This would seem to show that the religion of Sákya had been established as far as Ujain, even during his lifetime; and that the omission of Ujain amongst the names of the

* *Fo-kwe-ki*, c. xvi.

† *Fo-kwe-ki*, c. xxviii.

‡ Asiatic Researches of Bengal, xx. 89, Csoma de Koros.

celebrated cities which had witnessed various acts in the life of Buddha, is to be accounted for by the fact that the people of Ujain were converted by Katyáyana the disciple of Buddha, and were never visited by the Great Teacher himself. At the time of the Second Synod, in B. C. 443, the fraternity of Avanti (or Ujain) furnished no less than eighty orthodox Bhikshus to assist the holy Yaso in suppressing the schisms of the community of Vaisáli. As conversion must have preceded the establishment of fraternities and monasteries, the propagation of Buddhism throughout Ujain may be dated with certainty in 500 B. C., and with probability even as high as 550 B. C., during the lifetime of Sákya.

22. On the other hand, it seems to me more likely that the relics of Sáriputra were all deposited in the Tope at Rajagriha; and that they remained there undisturbed until the time of Asoka; who, when he distributed the relics of Buddha over India, would most probably have done the same with the relics of Sariputra and of Máha Mogalána. I have already stated that the still existing gateway of this Tope is of the same date as those of the Great Tope, that is, the early part of the first century of our era. The railing I attribute to the age of Asoka, at which period I suppose it probable that this Tope was built, although it is quite possible that it may date as early as the middle of the sixth century before our era. The great Topes at Sánchi and at Satdhára were built principally of brick: and these I presume to be

the oldest of the Bhilsa Topes, most of the others, which are of stone, were certainly of the age of Asoka.

OTHER TOPES AT SÁNCHI.

23. The solid mounds of masonry marked Nos. 4, 5, 6, and 7 in Plate IV., were all opened without any results. They were built of large stones set in mud. In No. 4, the solid rock was reached at 8½ feet; and in No. 7, the earth was reached at 13 feet; Nos. 8 9, and 10, are merely circular foundations.

CHAPTER XXII.

SONÁRI TOPES.

1. The little village of Sonári is situated on a low spur of a sandstone hill, between the Betwa and Besăli Rivers, six miles to the south-west of Sánchi, and about twenty-one miles to the north-east of Bhupál. The name is only the spoken form of *Suvarnári*, or the "golden wheel," which is a symbol of Buddha as the Mahá Chakravartti Raja. The traditions of the Buddhists say that when the age of man attains four thousand years, there appears a *King of the Golden Wheel** "who is born in a royal family, and obtains supreme dignity on succeeding his father and being baptized in the water of the four oceans. For fifteen days he bathes in perfumed water, and fasts; then ascends an elevated tower, surrounded by his ministers and courtiers. Suddenly there appears a *golden wheel* in the east, shedding a brilliant light, and advancing to the place where the King is standing. If the King would proceed towards the East, the

* *Fo-kwe-ki*, c. xviii., note 12.

wheel turns in that direction, and the King, accompanied by his troops, follows. Before the wheel are four genii, who serve as guides. Wherever it stops, there does the King in like manner. The same thing takes place in the direction of the south, the west, and the north—wherever the wheel leads, the King follows; and where it halts, he does the same. In the four continents he directs the people to follow the ten right ways, that is to say, not to kill, not to steal, not to commit adultery, not to lie, not to be double tongued, not to calumniate, not to speak with elaborate refinement, not to abandon one's-self to lusts, not to entertain anger and hatred, and not to have immodest looks. He is called *the King of the Golden Wheel*, or *the Holy King turning the wheel*; and he possesses the seven precious things, of which the first is 'the treasure of the Golden Wheel.'" This wheel has a thousand rays. The monarch who possesses it is called "the Holy King who causes the wheel to turn," because from the moment of his possessing it, the wheel turns and traverses the universe, according to the thoughts of the King. Other wheels of silver, copper, and iron, are also mentioned; but they are all nearly the same symbols of Buddha.

2. From this explanation of the name, it seems probable that Sonári once possessed a golden wheel, which must have been elevated on a pillar, as shown in so many of the Sánchi bas-reliefs. A pillar of this kind is described by Fa Hian, as still standing at

Shewei or Srávasti in Oudh, when he visited the place in 400 A. D.

"There are," says he, "two pavilions and two stone pillars; on the pillar to the left, is executed the figure of a wheel—on that to the right is placed the figure of an ox." There is, however, no trace of a pillar now at Sonári; but the polished cylindrical shafts of these columns could be so readily converted into sugar-mills, that their entire disappearance offers no proof of their non-existence.

3. The Sonári Topes are situated on the top of the hill, about one mile to the south of the village.* To the north, east, and south of the Topes, the hill extends for some distance almost level, but to the westward it is broken into narrow ravines, which give rise to clear springs that once furnished the fraternity of Sonári with drinking water. The hill is covered with trees and low thorny jungul; and the place is now as wild and desolate as it was once cheerful and flourishing when the hymn of praise was chanted by several thousand voices.

4. The Great Tope at Sonári is situated in the midst of a square court, 240 feet each side. In the south-west corner there is a solid square mass of masonry, from 12 to 15 feet in height, and 36 feet on each side. In the north-east corner there is a flight of steps, 4½ feet wide, leading to the top. The object of this building and of similar structures at Satdhára puzzled me very much, until I had seen the ruins at

* See Plate V.

Bhojpur, amongst which there is a very large building of the same description, but in a more perfect state. As this was undoubtedly a temple, I presume that the Sonári structure was only the basement or terrace of a Buddhist temple.

5. The Tope itself* is a solid hemisphere, 48 feet in diameter, of dry stones, without either cement or mud. This is raised above the terrace on a cylindrical plinth 4 feet in height. The terrace itself is 5½ feet broad by 6½ feet in height. The Tope is nearly perfect, not more than 6 feet of its entire height having been lost. It was once surmounted by a square Buddhist railing, of which only a few fragments now remain. The pillars were rather less than 3 feet in height, with a section of 6½ inches face, by 6 inches side. There were three rails, each 8 inches deep by 3½ inches thick. The railing was all formed of white sand-stone, from the Udayagiri hill, while the Tope itself was built of the claret-coloured sandstone of the Sonári hill. (See figs. 2 and 3, Plate XXIII.)

6. The base of the Tope was surrounded by a Buddhist railing, 4 feet 8 inches in height, of which nothing now remains but a few broken pillars, and two or three small fragments of coping. The pillars were 3 feet 8½ inches in height, with a section of 9½ inches face by 8 inches side. There were three railings, each 15 inches long, 11 inches broad, and 3¼ inches thick. The coping was different from that

* See Plate XXIII.

of the Sánchi railings. It was $11\frac{1}{2}$ inches in height, and the upper half had a projection of 2 inches on the outer face. The pillars were ornamented on the outer faces with medallions of full and half lotus flowers, as shown in the fragment, Plate IX. This railing was erected in the same manner as those at Sánchi, by the gifts of many different individuals. Two of these simple records still remain (see Plate XXIII, figs. 8 and 9).

Fig. 8.—*Aya-pasanakasa Atevas(ino) Dhama Gutasa Navaka-mánasa dánam.*

"Gift of DHARMA GUPTA, the new man (*i. e.*, the regenerated) the pupil of ARYYA PRASANNAKA."

Fig. 9.—*(A)yapasanakasa Atevasino Sagha Rakhitasa aánam.*

"Gift of SANGHA RAKSHITA, the pupil of ARYYA PRASANNAKA."

7. In No. 13 of the inscriptions from the great Tope at Sánchi, we have a record of a gift made by ARYYA PRASANNAKA himself, who is there called a *Bhikshu*, or mendicant monk. As the name does not appear again amongst nearly three hundred inscriptions, it seems highly probable that the *Bhikshu* of the one record and the teacher of the others are the same person. This would fix the date of the Tope in the latter end of Asoka's reign, coëval with that of the neighbouring Tope, No. 2, which will presently be described.

8. A shaft was sunk down the centre of this Tope, and at a depth of little more than 5 feet a large slab was reached, which on being raised disclosed the relic-chamber strewn with fragments of stone boxes. The

fragments were carefully collected and afterwards put together, but no trace of bone or of other relic was discovered. The largest of the relic-boxes is a cylinder 4 inches in height and upwards of 8 inches in breadth, covered by a domed lid of the same fine sandstone having a rise of more than 2 inches. Inside this was a smaller stone box of the same description; but only $5\frac{1}{4}$ inches in diameter and $3\frac{3}{4}$ inches in total height. Inside this, again, there was a third stone box or casket only $1\frac{3}{4}$ inch in diameter, and of a different shape, being nearly spherical with a pinnacled top. Lastly, inside this there was a small crystal casket only seven-eighths of an inch in diameter. This little casket must once have enshrined some minute portion of bone, or perhaps a single tooth of the holy Buddha; but, after the most careful search of the chamber, no trace of any relic was discovered. As the relic-chamber was near the summit of the Tope, the probability is that the villagers had opened it long before, and that when the relic-boxes were broken the minute fragment of bone was dropped into the chamber, and after the lapse of years had become mingled with its kindred dust.

CHAPTER XXIII.

NO. 2 TOPE.—SONÁRI.

1. THE second of the Sonári Topes* is situated north by west from the Great Tope at a distance of three hundred and fifteen feet. The bearing, 103 deg. W., is so very nearly the same as that between Nos. I. and II. Topes at Sánchi, that I cannot help suspecting that there must have been some peculiar significance in this particular angle. The Sánchi angle is 109 deg., and the mean between the two is 106 deg. At Sánchi the line is prolonged to the eastward to a lofty temple. At Sonári also it is extended in the same direction to No. 3 Tope which bears 102 E. from the Great Tope.

2. No. 2 Tope is situated in an enclosure 165 feet square. It is a solid hemisphere of dry stone, 27½ feet in diameter, raised on a cylindrical plinth 4½ feet in height. The terrace is 5 feet 8 inches broad, and 12 feet in height. This is gained by a double flight of steps each 20 feet long, which meet at a landing 6½ feet long by 6 feet broad. No trace of railings or

* See Plate XXIV.

pinnacles could be discovered; but the Tope is otherwise tolerably perfect, not more than $5\frac{1}{4}$ feet having been lost.

3. A shaft was sunk down the centre of the Tope, which at 7 feet reached the slab forming the lid of the relic-chamber. The chamber itself was $1\frac{1}{2}$ foot in depth, and its bottom, where the relics were deposited, was on the same level as the base of the hemisphere.

4. In the chamber was found a large steatite vase profusely but coarsely ornamented with elephants and horses, and indescribable winged animals of rude execution. The vase was covered by a plain lid, secured by lac. Inside this vase were found five relic-caskets, each containing portions of human bone, with an inscription recording the name of the person whose relics were enshrined therein.

5. No. 1 Relic-casket is a round flat box of crystal, 2 inches in diameter, and six-tenths of an inch in height. As the crystal was too hard a substance to be inscribed, the name and title of the holy man were carved on a small piece of stone three quarters of an inch long and only half an inch broad. The inscription, which is engraved on both sides, is one of the most interesting of these discoveries:—

Sapurisasa Goti-	*-sa Dadabhisá-*
-putasa Sava Hemavata	*-ra dáyádasa.*

"(Relics) of the emancipated GOTIPUTRA, the brother of religion amongst the *Dardabhisáras* of the *Hemavanta.*"

As a full explanation of this legend has been given in my account of the different religious missions despatched by Asoka to different countries bordering upon India, nothing more need be added in this place. (See Plate XXIV.)

6. No. 2 Relic-casket is of a dark mottled steatite, nearly hemispherical in shape, with a flat bottom and pinnacled top, similar to the smallest of the stone caskets found in No. 1 Tope. The inscription is engraved on the outside of the lid.

Sapurisasa Majhimasa Kodini-putasa.
"(Relics) of the emancipated MAJHIMA, the son of *Kodini*."

Majhima is the Sanskrit *Madhyama;* and *Kodini* is perhaps the vernacular form of *Kohudinya*, which is the name of one of the eighty principal disciples of Buddha. In No. 2 Tope at Sánchi the relics of a second, or of the same Majhima were found, but in the inscription the patronymic is omitted. As the relics of *Kásyapa-gotra* were found in both Topes, it seems probable that the two Majhimas were the same person, who was placed at the head of the Hemawanta Mission after the meeting of the Third Synod in B.C. 241. His father *Kodini* was probably a descendant of the great *Kohudinya* the companion of Buddha.

7. No. 3 Relic-casket is similar in shape and size to No. 2, and is of the same dark-coloured and mottled steatite. The inscription, engraved around the outside of the lid, is

Sapurisasa Kotiputasa Kásapa Gotasa Sava Hemavatácha-riyasa.
"(Relics) of the emancipated son of Koti, KÁSYAPA-GOTRA, the missionary to the whole *Hemawanta*."

The relics of Kásyapa were also found in No. 2 Tope at Sánchi with the same inscription recording his mission to the *Hemawanta*, but omitting the patronymic.

8. No. 4 Relic-casket is similar to Nos. 2 and 3. The inscription engraved on the top of the lid is—

Sapurisasa Kosikiputasa.
"(Relics) of the emancipated KOSIKIPUTRA."

Another portion of Kosiki's relics was found in No. 2 Tope at Sánchi.

9. No 5 Relic-casket is of black steatite, and is shaped somewhat like a pear. The outside is ornamented by a succession of triangles, alternately plain and crossed. The inscription occupies the plain triangles on the lower half of the casket.

Sapurisa(sa) Álabagirasa.
"(Relics) of the emancipated ÁLABAGIRA."

Allakappo or *Aláwi* was one of the eight cities which obtained a portion of Buddha's relics, and perhaps the name of *Álabagira* may have been derived from the city. Relics of Apagira were found in No. 2 Tope at Sánchi; and I suspect that the two names are the same; the letter 𑀮 *l*, having been inadvertently omitted in the Sánchi inscription.

10. The erection of this Tope, which contained the relics of no less than four of the Buddhist teachers whose ashes had already been discovered in No. 2 Tope at Sánchi, must evidently be referred to the

same period, towards the end of the third century before our era, by which time all the eminent missionaries employed by Asoka for the propagation of his religion must have closed their earthly career.

OTHER TOPES AT SONÁRI.

11. The remaining Topes at Sonári are all of small dimensions.* The most perfect were Nos. 3, 5, and 8; but even these had been opened before, and on the removal of a little rubbish in No. 3, the broken chamber was discovered quite empty. Nos. 4, 6, and 7, were mere circular foundations. No. 3 has a diameter of 15½ feet, with a present height of 6 feet. The bottom of the chamber is 3 feet above the ground. No. 5 is a nearly perfect little Tope. It is 14 feet 4 inches in diameter at base with a height of 9 feet. The upper diameter is 10 feet 4 inches. The terrace is 2½ feet in breadth, and 1½ foot in height. Its whole height could not have been more than 12½ feet. No. 8 is very much ruined. It has a diameter of 12½ feet, with a terrace 3 feet broad and 3 feet high.

* See Plate V.

CHAPTER XXIV.

TOPES OF SATDHÁRA.

1. The group of Topes known as the Satdhára Topes are situated on the left bank of the Besali River just below the junction of the Ghora-pachár River.* Sat-dhára means literally the "hundred streams," and the place most probably received its name from the number of streams which meet at this point. The hill on which the Topes stand here forms a perpendicular cliff, beneath which flows the Besali River through a deep rocky glen. The view up the river is one of the most beautiful I have seen in India. Above are the Topes, those mysterious piles which have baffled the great destroyer Time for upwards of two thousand years. Beneath are the clear emerald waters of the Besali; on one side darkly shadowed by the overhanging trees and frowning cliffs; on the other side sparkling bright in the noon-day sun. The selection of this lovely spot shows that the Buddhist Bhikshu was not without a lively appreciation of the

* See Plates I. and V.

beauties of that nature which he worshipped under the name of *Dharma*.

2. The Topes are situated about two miles to the W.S.W. of the small village of Firozpur, and about three miles from the village of Sonári. The largest of the Topes is now a vast ruinous mound of brick-work that has once been faced with stone like the great Tope at Sánchi, which it almost rivals in size.* The base of the dome is 101 feet in diameter; but its present height is only 30 feet. The terrace is 9 feet wide with a height of 12 feet above the ground. The total height therefore is 42 feet as it now stands; but as the hemisphere was an essential part of every Tope, the height could not have been less than the radius, or 50½ feet; and was most probably somewhat more. The Tope was crowned by a Buddhist railing, of which several pillars still remain lying together upon the terrace. Some pillars of the square pedestal also remain; and there can be no doubt that this Tope was once completed with the *chatta* pinnacle, which has already been described in the account of the Sánchi Topes.

3. The circular railing which surrounded the top consisted of pillars 2 feet 4½ inches in height with a section of 9 inches face, and 7 inches side. There were only two rails, each 10 inches deep, and 3½ inches thick. The whole was surmounted by an architrave or coping, 10½ inches high and 9 inches thick. The square railing of the pedestal had pillars of the

* See Plate XXV., fig. 3.

same section; but as there were three rails the pillars were 3 feet 5 inches in height. They were ornamented with the usual medallions of full and half lotus flowers.

4. A perpendicular shaft was sunk to a depth of 10 feet, but without any discovery. As the great brick Tope at Sánchi had not yielded any relics, and as we were pressed for time, we gave up the farther opening of this Tope. My own opinion regarding these large Topes is that the relics were always placed near the top so as to be readily accessible for the purpose of showing them to the people on stated festivals. Now as the great Satdhára Tope has certainly lost at least ten feet of its height, and probably more, it seemed to me very unlikely that any relics would be found in it: but, had time permitted, I should have carried down the shaft to the level of the ground.

5. Around this Tope there are three of those remarkable solid masses of building, of which one has already been described in my account of the Great Tope at Sonari. The first, which is half engaged in the northern wall of the court-yard, is 55 feet long from east to west, and 48 feet broad, with an average height of from 16 to 18 feet. The second, which is immediately outside the western wall of the court-yard, is 80 feet long from north to south, and nearly 60 feet broad. The third is in a more perfect state. It stands due west from the second, and on the very edge of the cliff overhanging the river; the wall on

this side being built up to a considerable height. This building is about 98 feet long and 55 feet broad, with an average height of 16 feet above the ground. It is pierced on the eastern side with a doorway leading into an open passage, from which a flight of steps, 4½ feet wide, ascends towards the north to the top of the platform. All of these buildings were most probably temples, of which nothing but the raised basements now remain. The people know them by the common name of *Siddh-ka-makán*, or "saints' houses." As the term *Siddha*, the "perfected," or "finished," was a common title of the Bodhisatwas, it is probable that these places are only the remains of their residences.

NO. 2 TOPE.—SATDHÁRA.

6. This ruined Tope stands at a distance of 230 feet to the N.N.W. of the great Tope. It is 24 feet in diameter, but only 8 feet in height, and has a trace of a small raised terrace.* A shaft was sunk in it to a depth of 6 feet, when some stones falling in, two small steatite caskets were seen lying at the bottom. The stones were loose; there was no trace of any chamber; and the caskets were both much discoloured on the upper surface. It is evident therefore that the Tope had been opened before by the villagers; who, finding nothing but a few calcined bones, had replaced

* See Plate XXV., fig. 2.

the relic-caskets, and filled up the holes again with loose stones.

7. These caskets are of a pale mottled steatite, each three inches in diameter, and two inches in height. They are inscribed inside the lids, the one with *Sári-putasa* "(Relics) of SÁRIPUTRA," and the other with *Maha-Mogalánasa* "(Relics) of MAHA MOGALÁNA." See Plate XXV., figs. 4, 5. The history of these two holy men, the right and left hand disciples of Buddha, has already been given in my account of the opening of No. 3 Tope at Sánchi. The only real difference between the alphabetical characters of the Sánchi and Satdhára inscriptions, is in the position of the vowel *o*, which, in the Sánchi legend, is attached to the top of the *m*, whereas in the Satdhára legend it is attached to the middle of the letter. This variety may have been only a mere matter of taste with the engraver; but as it is also possible that it may be the result of a difference of date, it is worthy of remark.

NO 7 TOPE.—SATDHÁRA.

8. This Tope is similar in all respects to that which has just been described, but somewhat more perfect.* The diameter of the hemisphere is 24 feet; the terrace is 2 feet broad; and the whole height at present is 9 feet. A shaft was sunk down to the centre to a depth of 4 feet, when a large irregular-shaped slab, 8 inches thick, was reached. On this

* See Plate XXV., fig. 1.

being raised we saw a chamber, 1 foot 8 inches long from north to south, by 1 foot 3 inches broad, and 1 foot 6½ inches in depth. The bottom of the chamber was therefore only 1 foot 3½ inches above the terrace. In the chamber there were two red earthenware pots, or covers, shaped like beehives. See Plate XXV., figs. 8 and 9. On raising the larger cover, which was 11½ inches in height, we saw a cylindrical red earthenware box, 7½ inches in diameter, closed by a domed lid. There was no inscription of any kind. The mouth of this vase is broken in two places; and I believe that it was an alms-dish of the holy man whose relics were here enshrined.

9. On raising the smaller cover, which was 9¾ inches in height, we found a similar red earthenware box, containing two small caskets, one of steatite and the other of red earthenware, and both without inscriptions. Of these relics, therefore, nothing more can be said, than that they are probably the remains of some of the principal teachers of the Satdhára fraternity.

---

10. The remaining Topes at Satdhára are now little more than mere circles of stone, from 12 to 20 feet in diameter. Two of them are hollow in the centre, and contain trees; and it is therefore possible that these circular walls may once have been only the enclosures around different holy trees. It is remark-

able, however, that at Satdhára we found one solitary trace of the real builders of these Topes, in the name of *Buddha Bitha*, or "Buddha's Topes," which is the name still current amongst the people for these massive and mysterious piles.

CHAPTER XXV.

TOPES AT BHOJPUR:

1. THE Buddhist remains at this place were first visited by my brother, who gave a brief notice of them under the name of "the Pipaliya-Bijoli Topes."* The former name is so common in this part of the country, that it is the usual practice to add the name of Bijoli to distinguish it from the other Pipaliyas. In the same way Sánchi is invariably called Sánchi-Kánakhera, to distinguish it from two other places of the same name. As Bhojpur has long been a deserted village, my brother probably never heard of its name. The ruined houses of Bhojpur, however, still remain on the hill between the Topes, and I have adopted this name in preference to the others, as it may possibly have had some connection with the monastic establishment in the midst of which it is situated.

2. The Topes of Bhojpur† stand on the southern end of a low range of hills, 6 miles to the S.S.E. of Bhilsa, and 7 miles to the E.S.E. of Sánchi. To

* Journal Asiatic Society of Bengal, xvi. 752.

† See Plates VI. and XXVI.

the S.S.W. stands the celebrated Fort of Raysen, which offered so gallant a resistance to the treacherous Shir Sháh. On the west the great Sánchi Tope, and on the east the Andher Topes are all distinctly visible.

3. The Topes are situated on the south-east corner of the hill, on four successive stages, rising one above the other, and separated by rocky ledges, which here and there have been formed into rude steps. The principal Topes stand on the uppermost stage, and are very nearly in a straight line from north to south. On the same stage, to the east, are the ruined houses of Bhojpur, and to the west are the remains of a large square solid building, 96 feet long by 84 feet broad. The ruins of a second building known by two names, either as *Siddh-ka-makán*, the "Saint's house;" or, as *Mádhu-Deo-ka-mandar*, the "Temple of Mádhava Deva," that is, Krishna, are 113 feet long from east to west, and 82 feet broad, and upwards of 20 feet* in height. The walls slope considerably, and are supported by square towers of small projection at the corners. The entrance is in the north-east corner, from which a flight of steps leads to the top of the terrace, which is covered with grass. At the western end there is a small ruined temple,† of which the

* Seventeen feet high on north and east sides, and twenty-eight feet high on the other sides. The walls have a slope of one inch for every cubit of height.

† Amongst Sir Charles D'Oyly's lithographed sketches on the new road from Calcutta to Gya, there is one of an old temple at Budh-Gya or (Bodhi Gya), which stands upon a solid terrace, the same as this at Bhojpur.

doorway and a few pillars are still standing. The enshrined figure of Buddha is squatted in the usual manner, with the soles of the feet turned up, the right hand lying over the knee, and the left placed in the lap. To the right and left of the head there are representations of Topes and other ornaments. Below, there is the following inscription in characters of the seventh or eighth century, similar to that which I extracted from the Sárnáth Tope near Benares.

Yé Dharmmá hetu prabhava, hetun teshán Tathágato
Hyavadat teshán cha yo nirodha, evam vádi Mahasramánas.

"Of all things springing from cause, that cause hath the TATHÁGATA explained. The cause of their extinction the great ascetic hath also declared."

Dharma is personified Nature, or all existing things. *Tathágata* and *Maha Srámana* are names of Buddha. Besides this figure of Buddha, there are some small broken images, of which one is recognizable as Surya, or the Sun, with his seven-horsed chariot represented on the pedestal.

UPPERMOST STAGE OF TOPES.

No. 1 TOPE, A.—BHOJPUR.

4. There is a considerable breach on the south side of this Tope; but the hemisphere of dry stones is otherwise nearly perfect, excepting the upper surface, which is wanting in all the Topes. The diameter of the hemisphere is 66 feet 2 inches, and the

height of the cylindrical plinth above the terrace is 4 feet. The terrace itself is 11½ feet in breadth and 5 feet in height. The height above the terrace is 24 feet 8 inches.* A shaft was sunk to a depth of 13 feet without any discovery being made; and as we were pressed for time, we were reluctantly obliged to leave the excavation unfinished. I feel confident, however, that the complete excavation of this Tope will lead to some important discovery, perhaps more interesting than any that has yet been made. The Tope is situated in an enclosure 252 feet long by 214 feet broad.

No. 2 Tope, B.—Bhojpur.

5. This is one of the most perfect of all the Topes around Bhilsa. The top is, of course, gone, but the double flight of steps to the west is still complete, and the traveller may mount the terrace and perambulate the Tope. It stands just 200 feet to the south of the great Tope, and is surrounded by an enclosure 240 feet long, and 210 feet broad. The base of the hemisphere is 39 feet in diameter, and its present height, including the cylindrical plinth of 4 feet, is 14½ feet. The terrace is 6 feet broad and 7 feet high. It is reached by a double flight of steps, 4½ feet in breadth, which meet at a landing, 7 feet square, on the outside of the terrace. The whole is built of dry stones, without any mortar or mud.

* See Plate XXVI.

6. A shaft was sunk down the middle, which, at the end of two hours' labour, had reached the relic-chamber, at a height of $9\frac{3}{4}$ feet above the terrace. The chamber was a square of $1\frac{1}{2}$ foot, with a depth of $1\frac{1}{4}$ foot. Inside we found a hemispherical cover of red earthenware, 9 inches in height, and 1 foot 4 inches in diameter, beneath which was a red earthenware box, $8\frac{1}{4}$ inches in its greatest diameter, and 6 inches in height. The lid had been thickly coated with whitewash, on which the traces of ink letters were yet visible; but so much of the whitewash had peeled off in the lapse of ages, that not even a single letter was legible. This is the more to be regretted, as the relic-casket found inside is the most curious and costly of all our discoveries. The lid of the box was white-washed inside, and the white colour is as fresh as if it had been recently done. On seeing this I could not help wishing that the inscription had been placed inside the lid.

7. The relic-casket is a small crystal Tope, with its terrace, plinth, hemispherical dome, square pedestal, and double chatta pinnacle, all complete. It is shown in half size (in Plate XXVI.) placed inside the earthenware box in which it was found. The top is pierced with a small perpendicular shaft, to which the pinnacle forms a stopper. The bottom of the shaft is the relic-chamber, in which we found some minute pieces of bone. In the red earthenware box there were several small pieces of bone, and a series of the seven precious things usually placed along with

the relics of an eminent person. These consisted of 4 thin, round bits of gold, weighing altogether only a few grains, 1 bead of garnet, or Badakshání ruby, 1 crystal bead, 2 beads of pale greenish crystal, and some minute fragments of pearl. For another series of the seven precious things, see my account of the opening of No. 3 Tope at Sánchi, in which the precious metal is omitted.

No. 3 Tope, C.—Bhojpur.

8. This was a ruinous-looking mound, 14 feet in height, but with a slight trace of circular form on one side. The shaft was sunk down the centre to a depth of eight feet, but without any discovery. From the best measurements that I could make, the diameter appeared to be about 40 feet, or one foot more than that of No. 2 Tope. Now, the relics of that Tope were found at a height of more than 15 feet above the ground, and as the remains of this Tope were only 14 feet high, we concluded that the relics had long ago been removed along with the upper half of the Tope. One curious fact which we observed was that the Tope had been built in four distinct quadrants of masonry, meeting at a point, by which means the centre of the structure was accurately preserved.

No. 4 Tope, D.—Bhojpur.

9. This Tope stands in an enclosure of 130 feet square, and 750 feet due south from No. 2. The base of the hemisphere is 31 feet 2 inches in diameter. It is raised on a cylindrical plinth 3 feet in height above the terrace, which is itself 3½ feet in breadth, and 4½ feet in height. The present height of the Tope is 16 feet. A shaft was sunk down the centre, which reached the relic-chamber at a depth of 5½ feet. The chamber itself was 2 feet 5 inches deep; the level of the bottom being 4 feet 4 inches above the terrace. In the chamber we found a black earthenware box (see Plate XXVI., fig. 6), containing an earthenware bowl covered by a lid of the same material, on which is the word 𑀫𑀼𑀁 *Mun*, "the holy"—a title generally applied to Buddha himself. Inside the bowl was a small crystal casket, with a perfectly flat lid. This casket is remarkable for the thinness of its sides, which in such a hard material must have been most difficult of execution. This casket contained nothing but a little brownish-red powder, which I believe to be only a portion of the dust which had found its way into all the relic-chambers in the lapse of ages. I presume, therefore, that this Tope had been opened by the villagers.

10. To the east of this Tope, at a distance of 60 feet, there is the circular foundation of another Tope, 18 feet in diameter, with a terrace 3 feet in breadth,

and beyond this, again, there is another of the same dimensions.

SECOND STAGE OF TOPES.

No. 7 Tope, a.—Bhojpur.

11. This Tope is situated on the eastern edge of the second stage, at a distance of 850 feet from the Great Tope, on the uppermost platform. The diameter of the hemisphere is 32 feet 4 inches, and its present height is 11 feet above the cylindrical plinth, which is only 1 foot 8 inches in height. The terrace is very small for a Tope of this size,* its breadth being only 1 foot 8 inches, and its height 1½ foot. The whole height of the Tope is therefore little more than 14 feet.

12. A shaft was sunk as usual, down the centre; but at a depth of less than 3 feet the edge of the relic-chamber was discovered on the south side of the excavation. On measurement, the centre of the relic-chamber was found to be 3 feet to the south of the centre of the Tope. In cases of this kind, I always suspect that a second chamber has formerly existed, such as we found in Tope No. 17, k, at Bhojpur (See Plate XXX., fig. 5), and that it was destroyed when opened by the villagers. A presumptive proof of this supposition was found in the disposition and contents of the relic-chamber. One of the side stones

* See Plate XXVII., figs. 1 and 2.

was displaced, and its end thrust some three inches into the chamber. The lid of the red earthenware box was separated from the bottom, and each half contained an earthenware vase, both without lids, and one with a broken neck. The whole chamber was full of leaves and earth, and small stones, amongst which rubbish we found the lids of the two vases. Now, the relic-chamber, which was 9 feet 8 inches above the terrace, was only 15 feet square and 8 inches deep. It could scarcely, therefore, have been intended to hold both of the vases which were found in it. One of these vases was, no doubt, originally placed in the red earthenware box; and it is possible that the other vase may have been placed in the corner of the chamber; but it seems to me more probable that it should have been placed in another chamber.

13. Both of these earthenware vases are inscribed; and as these are the only inscriptions that were found at Bhojpur their occurrence is remarkable. The red earthenware box is shown in Plate XXVII., fig. 3, on a scale of one-eighth of the original size. The larger vase is given in fig. 4 of the same Plate. It is $4\frac{1}{4}$ inches in height and $6\frac{1}{4}$ inches in breadth—the width of the neck, which is broken, being 3 inches. The upper surface is ornamented with a succession of dotted figures, and on the body of the bowl is the legend *Patito*, "the degraded." This simple inscription is a curious and unexpected illustration of the most common punishment for breaches of discipline in the

ancient Buddhist Church. The punishment of "degradation" was awarded for indecent conversation, or for immoral behaviour, or for causing dissensions amongst the fraternity.* The Patito (Sanskrit Patitya) must therefore have been guilty of one of these three sins. The ceremony† of degradation consisted in turning the offender's alms-dish upside down, in which position it was left until reconciliation had taken place, when the alms-dish was again set upright. In the present case we may suppose that the offending monk had died during his degradation, and that his alms-dish had been thus inscribed at his own request as a mark of his penitence and humility.

14. The smaller vase is of red earthenware, 4½ inches in height and nearly 5 inches in width. On the upper surface of the bowl is the legend *Upahitakasa*, "Relics of UPAHITAKA," which was no doubt the name of one of the leading monks of the Bhojpur fraternity.

15. It is scarcely possible to determine the age of this Tope except conjecturally. The forms of the alphabetical characters in the two inscriptions show that its date cannot be much later than the end of the third century before our era; while the lowness of the plinth on which the dome stands shows that it was most probably erected in the beginning of Asoka's

* Csoma de Koros—Analysis of the Dulva; in Asiatic Researches of Bengal, xx. 82.

† Ditto, ditto, p. 87.

reign. The date may therefore be stated approximately as the latter half of the third century before the Christian era.

No. 8 Tope, b.—Bhojpur.

16. This is the largest Tope on the second stage of the hill, the base of the dome being 38¼ feet in diameter. It stands to the south-west of the last Tope at a distance of 260 feet in the direction of No. 4 Tope.* The plinth is raised 3 feet above the terrace, which is 5 feet 4 inches in breadth, and 6½ feet in height, with a slope of 6 inches. As the height of the mound is now only 19½ feet, or only two-thirds of the original height of the Tope, it is not to be wondered at that the shaft which we sank down to the level of the terrace should have yielded no relics.

No. 9 Tope, c.—Bhojpur.

17. At 160 feet to the S.S.E. of the Tope, there is another of less size but equally ruinous. The base of the dome is 29 feet in diameter, and the height of the cylindrical plinth is 1½ foot. The terrace is 2½ feet broad, and 5¼ feet in height, with a slight slope outwards. The whole height is now only a little more than 14 feet. The usual shaft was sunk to a depth of nearly seven feet to the relic-chamber, in which

* Fig. 6, Plate XXVII.

was a large box of red earthenware, Inside this was a double steatite vase* of a mottled purple colour, containing an abundance of human bones amongst which the following are recognizable :—

Portion of *temporal* bone.

Portion of *parietal* bone. The internal surface still retains the branching lines called *sulci meningei.* These portions of the skull are very much solidified, which proves that they belonged to an old person.

Three *incisors,* or front teeth.

One *molar,* or back tooth, not fully developed, and therefore the backmost, or wisdom tooth.

Portions of *ulna,* forming the lower end of long arm bone.

Portions of *tibia?*

Portions of *femur,* or thigh bone, with the *linea aspera* still strongly marked.

Portions of *phalanges unguium,* or finger bones.

No. 10 Tope, d.—Bhojpur.

18. This ruinous Tope had a diameter of 19 feet, with a terrace 2 feet 8 inches broad and 3 feet in height. The whole height was only 7½ feet. On removing a few stones we found a chamber, 1 foot square and 1 foot deep, filled with leaves and rubbish, and containing one complete earthenware box, and a part of a second. In the box there were a few small pieces of bone mixed with leaves and gravel. This

* See Plate XXVII., fig. 8. The lid of the large box is itself formed into a small box.

Tope had therefore certainly been opened before by the villagers.

No. 11. Tope, e.—Bhojpur.

19. A tree was growing in the middle of this ruined Tope which is only 15½ feet in diameter, with a terrace 3½ feet broad, and 5 feet high. On the west a double flight of steps 3½ feet broad meet at a landing 6½ feet long by 4¾ feet broad. The removal of a few stones showed a chamber 18 inches square, and 13 inches deep, the bottom being on a level with the terrace. In the chamber we found a round earthen jar full of bits of bone, leaves, and rubbish. Like the last Tope, this had evidently been opened before.

---

20. The remaining Topes on the second stage of the hill may be described in a few words.

No. 12 Tope, f, and No. 13, g, have each a diameter of 17 feet. No. 14, h, has a diameter of 17¾, and No. 15, i, of 18½ feet, the present height being only 4 feet. No. 16, j, has a diameter of 23½ feet, with a terrace 3 feet broad.

No. 17, k, has a diameter of 10½ feet, and a height of 6 feet. On removing a few stones we found two relic-chambers at a height of 5 feet above the ground. The chambers stood respectively to the N.E. and

S.W. of each other, although the direction of their sides corresponded with the north, south, east, and west. See Plate XXX., fig. 5. One chamber was 9 inches square, and the other only 7 inches square. Inside we found the remains of earthenware pots and bits of bone mixed with leaves and rubbish. This Tope had also been opened by the villagers.

No. 18, l, has a diameter of 10½ feet, and No. 19, m, of 13 feet; No. 20, n, is a mere circular foundation; No. 21, o, has a diameter of 18½ feet; and No. 22, p, of 9½ feet, with a terrace of 1 foot 1 inches.

THIRD STAGE OF TOPES.—BHOJPUR.

21. The third stage or platform of the hill is very narrow, and has only a few Topes, all of which are of small size.

No. 23, q, has a diameter of 19 feet, and a terrace of 1½ foot. A chamber was found in this Tope at a height of only 3 feet above the ground. It was 1½ foot long, 1¼ foot broad, and 9 inches deep; and it contained three earthenware jars filled with earth and leaves.

No. 24, r, is 6 feet in diameter, and is the smallest at Bhojpur; No. 25, s, is 9 feet in diameter, with a terrace of only 6 inches; No. 26, t, is 8 feet in diameter with a terrace of 14 inches; No. 27, u, is 7½ feet in diameter; No. 28, v, is 10 feet; and No. 29, w, is 7 feet.

LOWERMOST STAGE OF TOPES.—BHOJPUR.

22. There are only eight Topes now remaining on this platform of the hill all lying in a direction from north to south, and parallel to the other series.

No. 30 Tope, α, is $8\frac{1}{2}$ feet in diameter and 2 feet high, with a terrace of 1 foot 6 inches; No. 31, β, is $10\frac{1}{2}$ feet in diameter; No. 32, γ, is 9 feet; No. 33, δ, is 13 feet; No. 34, ϵ, is 10 feet; and No. 35, ζ, is $17\frac{1}{2}$ feet in diameter. All these Topes are standing close together at the northern end of the platform. At 600 feet to the south are the remains of No. 36 Tope, η, and again at 600 feet to the south of this is No. 37 Tope, θ, which is now a mere mound of stones with a diameter of between 30 and 40 feet. A shaft was sunk down the centre of this Tope to the solid rock without any discovery.

23. A more careful examination of all the little heaps of stones lying about these different stages of the hill would no doubt discover some ten or even twenty more of these small Topes; but as they have all long ago been rifled by the villagers the labour would be completely thrown away. The old village of Bhojpur was no doubt entirely built of stones taken from these little Topes, and from the surrounding walls of the great Topes. This will fully account for the few discoveries of interest amongst so many Topes; as not more than five, or perhaps six, of the largest had escaped the hands of the spoilers.

CHAPTER XXVI.

ANDHER TOPES.

1. THE little village of Andher is situated at the foot of a hill 10½ miles to the south-west of Bhilsa, and 5 miles to the west of Bhojpur. The Topes are perched on the northern declivity of the hill just two miles from Andher, and on the very edge of the cliff, about 500 feet above the plain. The position is a very fine one, from which the eye wanders over the whole of the Bhilsa district to the north, till checked by the blue hills beyond Gyáraspur, a distance of twenty-five miles. The Great Tope at Sánchi, the Loháugi rock at Bhilsa, and the holy hill of Udayagiri, are the most conspicuous objects in the landscape. Nearer, and almost beneath one's feet, are the numerous Topes of Bhojpur.*

NO 1 TOPE.—ANDHER.

2. This is one of the few Topes which has a Buddhist railing still standing.† Its preservation

* See Plates I. and V.

† See Plate XXVIII., figs. 1 and 2.

is no doubt due to the secluded and inaccessible position of the Topes, which are not large enough to *attract* the eye, although they can be distinctly seen when pointed out. The base of the dome, which is 35 feet 2 inches in diameter, rests on a cylindrical plinth only 4 feet in height. The terrace, 5¼ feet wide and 5 feet high, has a stone coping, along its outer edge, 15 inches in height, and 13 inches in thickness. This is the only instance of terrace-coping that now exists. From the style of the bas-reliefs of Topes on the Sánchi gateways, we had expected to have found some terraces surrounded by Buddhist railings, but we were disappointed, for not one of the numerous Topes excepting this has the slightest trace of a ledge of any kind. The rounded and massive coping forms an appropriate finish to the massive basement. On the west there is a double flight of steps, 4 feet 4 inches in width, which meet at a landing-place 7 feet 2 inches in length and 5½ feet in breadth. Several of the steps are perfect, 13½ inches broad and 10 inches high; and, as the gateway is still standing, we have here one of the most complete existing specimens of the second-rate Tope.

3. The base is enclosed by a Buddhist railing 7 feet in height, with an entrance on the west formed in the same manner as those of the Sánchi Topes. The pillars are 5 feet 8¾ inches in height, with a section of 14½ inches face and 10½ inches side. There are three railings each 18 inches broad, and 6¼ inches thick. The coping is the same as that of the terrace.

The pillars are ornamented with full and half medallions formed of lotus and other flowers. The quadruple emblem of Dharma, which is seen on so many of the old coins, here occupies a medallion.* On one of the pillars there is a short inscription in the usual style:—

Dhama Sivasa Mátu dánam.
"Gift of DHARMA-SIVA's mother."

The characters, which are very neatly cut and well formed, are apparently as old as those of the great Sánchi Tope which dates in the reign of Asoka. The pillars of the entrance are carved on both sides, and the two outer ones on three sides. The principal subjects are: a wheel-pillar with a capital formed of two lions and an elephant, a holy tree surmounted by a chatta, and a Tope. There is also another scene in which several figures are seated in a circle, each on a small square couch. This may perhaps represent the meeting of one of the Buddhist Synods. The Tope is surrounded by the remains of a walled enclosure, and to the south there is one of those massive foundations which have already been described. It is nearly 70 feet long, and between 30 and 40 feet broad, but not more than 6 feet high at present.

4. A shaft was sunk down to the centre of the hemisphere, where we found a chamber 10 inches square, and 18 inches in height on one side, by 10 inches on the opposite side. Within was a round

* See Plate XXXII., fig. 4, of this work.

stone box, $5\frac{1}{8}$ inches in height, $6\frac{5}{8}$ inches broad at bottom, and only $5\frac{1}{2}$ inches at top. The chamber, which is $3\frac{1}{2}$ inches deep and 4 inches wide, contained nothing save a small quantity of black ashes and something like calcined nut-shells. The lid of the box is $2\frac{1}{2}$ inches in height, domed, and slightly hollowed beneath. See Plate XXVIII., fig. 6. Three feet beneath this deposit, and on a level with the terrace, we found a second chamber, somewhat slightly formed, containing a hemispherical red earthenware vessel 10 inches in diameter turned with the mouth downwards. Beneath this was a second vessel of red earthenware, $8\frac{1}{2}$ inches in diameter, containing a black earthenware bowl 7 inches in diameter and $3\frac{1}{4}$ inches in height. Lastly, inside the bowl there was a black earthenware vase 5 inches in diameter and $4\frac{1}{8}$ inches in height, with a small lid of the same material.* This vase was empty. See Plate XXVIII., fig. 7.

NO. 2 TOPE.—ANDHER.

5. One hundred and twenty feet to the south-east of the last, there is a second Tope of much smaller dimensions, but in a much more perfect state than these buildings are usually met with. The base of the dome, which is 18 feet 10 inches in diameter, rests on a cylindrical plinth 4 feet in height above the terrace, which is 4 feet 4 inches broad and 6 feet

* The glaze of these black vessels is beautifully smooth, and of a bright metallic lustre.

high. It is reached by a double flight of steps, 4 feet 8 inches broad, each step being 6 inches high and 14 inches in width. The whole height of the Tope as it now stands, is only 14 feet 7 inches.*

6. A shaft was sunk down the centre of the Tope to the depth of 3½ feet, when we found the chamber 1½ foot broad and 1 foot deep. The sides of this chamber were not in the meridian as usual, but bore 57½ deg. and 147½ deg. E. and W. respectively. Inside we found a large box of red earthenware, 9½ inches in diameter and 7½ inches in height,† containing a small flat casket of red earthenware and a tall steatite casket, both inscribed. Beside the earthenware box, and mixed with the leaves and rubbish which half filled the chamber, we found a large steatite vase with the neck partly broken, but luckily with the inscription complete. This chamber had evidently been opened before by the villagers.

7. The flat earthenware casket is 3 inches in diameter, and nearly 1½ inch in height.‡ The inscription on the outside of the lid is partially obliterated, but by supplying a few letters, the sense is easily completed.

Sapurisasa Váchhiputasa Gotiputa Atevásino.
"(Relics) of the emancipated VÁCHHI-PUTRA (son of Vachhi), the pupil of GOTI-PUTRA."

The relics of VÁCHHI himself were found in No. 2 Tope at Sánchi.

* See Plate XXIX., figs. 1 and 2.

† Plate XXIX., fig. 4.

‡ Plate XXIX., fig. 5.

8. The tall steatite casket is $3\frac{1}{4}$ inches in diameter at bottom, and $2\frac{1}{2}$ inches at top, with a height of $5\frac{1}{2}$ inches. It is ornamented on the outside by bands of moulding, between which the whole surface is divided into triangles, alternately plain and barred.* The inscription on the top of the lid is—

Sapurisasa Gotiputasa Kákanava Pabhásanasa Kodinyegotasa.
"(Relics) of the emancipated son of GOTI, KÁKANAVA PRABHASANA, of the race of KODINI (or Kohudinya.)"

In my account of the discoveries made in No. 2 Tope at Sánchi, I have already stated all that I can suggest regarding *Kakanava Prabhâsan*, who was the donor of Váchhi Suvijayata's relics to the Sánchi fraternity.

9. The large steatite vase† is made of two pieces, which were fastened together with lac. Its ornaments are similar to those of the great vase found in No. 2 Tope at Sonári; but the Andher vase has a narrow neck and no lid, and was once furnished with a spout, for which the hole still remains. No trace of this spout could be found in the relic-chamber, but I presume that it was similar to those which are represented in the Sánchi bas-reliefs. See Plate XXXIII, figs. 20 and 21. On the upper rim of the neck there is the following inscription:—

Sapurisasa Mogaliputasa Gotiputa Atevásino.
"(Relics) of the emancipated MOGALIPUTRA, the pupil of GOTIPUTRA."

10. Every thing that I can collect regarding this

* Plate XXIX., fig. 3. † Plate XXIX., fig. 8.

celebrated personage has already been mentioned. As the pupil of Gotiputra, he was of course a contemporary of Goti's other son, Kákana Prabhásan; and it is therefore very natural that we should find their relics enshrined together. This Tope must of course be of the same age as No. 2 at Sánchi, or rather a few years later, as Kákanava Prabhásan was still alive when the latter was erected. The date may therefore be fixed with some certainty in 200 B. C., when the religious enthusiasm excited by the zeal and example of Asoka was still fervent.

NO. 3 TOPE.—ANDHER.

11. This little Tope, which was the last that we had the pleasure of examining, was likewise one of the most complete in its preservation, and one of the most interesting in its contents. It stands to the north-west of the other two, at a distance of rather more than 200 feet. The base of the dome is only 15 feet in diameter, and the whole height of the Tope is just 12 feet.* The base stands on a cylindrical plinth $3\frac{1}{2}$ feet above the terrace, which is 4 feet in width and the same in height. On the east there is a landing place, 6 feet by 4 feet, which is reached by a double flight of steps, 3 feet 2 inches in width.

12. A shaft was sunk as usual down the centre of the Tope, and the relic-chamber was reached at a height of 1 foot 8 inches above the terrace. The

* See Plate XXX., figs. 1 and 2.

chamber was 14 inches long by 13½ inches broad, and the same in height. The side stones were placed so as to overlap at one end, thus forming a Swástika or mystic cross of the relic-chamber. See Plate XXX., figs. 3 and 4. Inside there was a large box of thin red earthenware, 7½ inches high and 7 inches broad, containing a tall steatite casket,* similar to that of Kákanava, which was found in the Tope just described. This casket, however, is quite plain on the outside, with the exception of the ornamental bands. It is quite full of fragments of burnt bone. On the outside is carved the following inscription :—

Sapurisasa Háritíputasa.
"(Relics) of the emancipated HARITIPUTRA (son of Háriti)."

Inside the lid is the following inscription, written in ink :—

Asa Devasa dánam.
"Gift of ASWA-DEVA."

13. The relics of Háriti-putra were therefore presented to the Andher fraternity by Aswa Deva. As another portion of his relics was found in No. 2 Tope at Sánchi, enshrined in the same casket with those of Majhima and Kásapa Gota, the two missionaries to the Hemawanta, there can be little doubt that he was a contemporary of those once celebrated men; and that he was one of the principal Buddhist teachers of the age of Asoka. The date of the Tope may there-

* See Plate XXX., fig. 6.

fore be fixed with some certainty in the end of the third century before the Christian era, which will make the ink writing of the relic-casket about two centuries and a half older than that of the Papyri of Herculaneum and Pompeii.

CHAPTER XXVII.

SYMBOLS OF BUDDHA, DHARMA, AND SANGHA.

1. In my account of the sculptured ornaments of the different Topes, frequent mention is made of the symbols of *Buddha* and *Dharma*, which occur either singly or united amongst the bas-reliefs at Sánchi, and on many of the most ancient coins of India. The summits of the Sánchi gateways are crowned with these symbols. They occur as objects of worship amongst the bas-reliefs, supported either on pillars or on altars. They form ornaments for the arms and standards of the soldiers; and they are frequently placed both at the beginning and end of inscriptions.

2. The Triad of the Buddhists, which has already been explained, consisted of Buddha, Dharma, and Sangha. *Buddha* was Spirit, or Divine Intelligence; *Dharma* was Matter, or Concrete Nature; and *Sangha*, the "union" of the two, was the universe. This was the esoteric or metaphysical explanation of the terms; but according to the exoteric doctrine, Buddha was Sákya Sinha, the mortal author of the Buddhist

faith: Dharma was the religion, or the "Law,"* and Sangha was the "congregation" of the faithful. By the orthodox believers, Buddha was held to be the chief person of the Triad, and the Supreme First Cause and Creator of all things; but the Materialists exalted *Dharma* to the chief place, and taught that Buddha, or Spirit, was only an emanation from *Prajná*, or Nature, which was the Divine Source of all.

3. The symbol of Buddha was, I believe, the wheel; which in its revolution was emblematic of the passage of the soul through the circle of the various forms of existence. Hence, the wheel, or whole circle, was typicial of any one who, after obtaining *nirvána*, or emancipation from this mortal coil, had *completed* the *circle* of his existence, and was no longer subject to transmigration. Such a person was BUDDHA, the founder of the Buddhist religion, who was commonly called the *Mahá Chakravartti Raja*,† or Supreme Lord of the Universe; or, more literally, the Great King who hath turned the wheel (of transmigration). In the institutes of Manu,‡ transmigration is compared to the wheel of a car; and again, in the Vishnu Purána,§ "the mark of Vishnu's dis-

* The Buddhist reverence for *Dharma*, or the Law, will remind the English reader of the law in the Old Testament.

† See Fo-kwe-ki, c. xx., n. 10; and also Prinsep's Journal, vol. vii., p. 106, where Turnour states that as Buddha's attributes were those of a Chakravartti Raja, so was he called by that title.

‡ Chap. xii., sl. 124.

§ Wilson's Translation, p. 101.

cus" is said to be "visible on the hand of one who is born to be a universal emperor" (*Chakravartti*).

4. The wheel is the central emblem on the summit of each of the Sánchi gateways. This would seem to have been its usual position, and it was, no doubt, significant of the supremacy of Buddha. In the Mahawanso, Raja Sirinago of Ceylon is stated to have inserted gems in the centre of each of the four emblems of the "Sun" on the Mahá Stupo, or Great Tope.* This, perhaps, points to the absorption of the ancient sun-worship into Buddhism; for the wheel was one of the most common and obvious emblems of the sun.

5. In Plate XXXI., I have collected together several illustrations of the wheel-symbol of Buddha from the Sánchi bas-reliefs, and from coins.

Fig. 1. Bas-relief on a pillar of the western entrance of No. 2 Tope at Sánchi. A man and woman are represented perambulating the pillar. The illustration shows the importance attached to this symbol by the Buddhists of Asoka's age. The same wheel-pillar occurs again at the northern entrance.

Fig. 2. Central emblem on the summit of each of the four Sánchi gateways.†

* Mahawanso, p. 229.

† See Plate XXXI., fig. 7, for the celebrated wheel and club of *Surya*, from Udayagiri. This was the god whom the Greeks of Alexander's army mistook for Hercules; but one of them has preserved the true name in Σοροαδέιος, or *Surya Deva*, the "Sun-God."

Figs. 3, 4. Reverses of coins found at Ujain—quadruple emblems of the sun.

Fig. 5. Bas-relief on a pillar of the south gate of No. 2 Tope, and also on a pillar of the south gate of No. 3 Tope, both at Sánchi.

Fig. 6. Bas-relief on a pillar at the eastern entrance of No. 2 Tope, Sánchi. A figure is kneeling at its foot.

Figs. 8, 9. On the earliest silver and copper coins found in all parts of India, from Nepál to Ceylon, and from Kandahar to the Delta of the Ganges.

Fig. 10. Ancient Hindu coin of brass, literally covered with Buddhist symbols. On the obverse is a bull; to the left, a peculiar symbol, which is found on other Buddhist coins, and on the necklace of Buddhist symbols on one of the Sánchi gateways. Above is the quadruple emblem of *Dharma*. On the reverse (in the middle), is a tree surrounded by a Buddhist railing; below is a *chaitya*, or, more probably, Mount Sumeru; to the right, a *swástika*, or mystic cross; and to the left, the symbol of *Sangha*, being the united emblems of Buddha and Dharma. The latter is placed uppermost, which I presume is intended to show the superiority of *Dharma*, or Concrete Nature, over *Buddha*, or Spirit.

Fig. 11. Coins, both of silver and copper, found chiefly between the Indus and the Jumna. On the obverse is a deer, with branching horns, and before it a human figure with the arm raised. Behind the deer an emblem of the sun. Inscription in old Indian Páli.

Rajnya Kunandasa Amogha-bhatisa Maharajasa.
"(Coin) of the royal KUNANDA, the brother of AMOGHA, the King."

On the reverse is a *chaitya*, or Mount Sumeru, surrounded by the monogram or symbol of *Dharma;* to the right, a tree in a Buddhist enclosure, and to the left, a *swástika*, and the unknown triangular symbol. Inscription in Ariano Páli the same as on the obverse.

6. The quadruple symbol of Buddha, which is found on the Ujain coins, and the quadruple symbol of Dharma which occurs on coin No. 10, and on one of the pillars at Andher, most probably have reference to the other four mortal Buddhas, *Krakuchanda, Kanaka, Kásyapa*, and *Sákya Muni*. The four entrances at Sánchi, and at the Great Tope in Ceylon, with their crowning symbols of Buddha, may, I think, be also referred to the same.

7. *Dharma*, or Concrete Nature, was, I believe, neatly symbolized by a monogram which united the radical letters of the various elements of matter. According to the *Pujá-kand*,* "all things with their *veja-mantras* (radicals), came from *Swabháva* (the self-existent), in this order :—

From the *vija* of the letter	Y,	air.
From that of the letter	R,	fire.
From that of the letter	V,	water.
From that of the letter	L,	earth.
From that of the letter	S,	Mount Sumeru.

* One of the Sanskrit Buddhist works of Nepal, quoted by Hodgson, p. 105.

Now it is curious that the old Páli equivalents of these letters form, when combined together, a monogram of exactly the same shape as the symbol which I have attributed to Dharma. In Plate XXXII., fig. 3, I have given this monogram, with the single letters which compose it placed in a line below. In all the monograms, both of the bas-reliefs and of the coins, the symbol is crossed by a horizontal line in the middle, which I take to represent the lower stroke of the Páli letter , n, the radical of "void space, or vacuity." This, therefore, must be the fifth element, the *ákás* of the Hindus, and the αιθηρ of the Greeks. The symbol is thus strictly composed of the five radical letters of the five elements, y, air; r, fire; v, water; l, earth; and n, ether; which when combined contain the letter s, for Mount Sumeru, as well as the letter ŏ, m, or *manas*, or mind.* In Plate XXXII., I have given all the different specimens of this symbol that I can collect from various sources.

Fig. 3 is the simple monogram, composed of the five radical letters of the elements.

Fig. 4 is a quadruple specimen of this symbol, from a bas-relief medallion on one of the pillars at Andher. The same is found on No. 10 coin of Plate XXXI.

Fig. 8 shows the elemental symbol crowning the staff of a flag or military ensign.

* A strong proof of the correctness of this explanation is found in the , *swástika*, or mystic cross, which appears to be only a monogram or literal symbol of the old letters , *su*, and , *ti*, or *suti*, which is the Pali form of the Sanskrit *swasti*.

Fig. 9 is one of the ornaments from a necklace in the Sánchi bas-reliefs.

Fig. 10 is the same monogram, but very highly ornamented. Two of these symbols are placed on the summits of the Sánchi gateways, one on each side of the wheel-symbol of Buddha.

Fig. 13 is a copper coin from the ruins of the ancient city of Ayodhya, or Ajudhya, in Oudh. The inscription in Old Páli is *Vijaya Mitasa*, "(coin) of VIJAYA MITRA." In the centre is the monogrammatic symbol. Vijaya Mitra was most probably one of the ancient kings of Oudh, although his name is not to be found in the fabulous lists of any of the Puránas.

Fig. 14 is the reverse of a copper coin, procured from several old cities around Ujain. In the centre is the quadruple symbol of Dharma already described.

Fig. 15 is from one of the Sánchi bas-reliefs, on a sword scabbard.

Fig. 16 is from the coins of the Indo-Scythian Kadphises.

Fig. 17 is from the coins of Kunanda, the brother of Amogha.

Fig. 18 is from the coins of *Sasa*, of the family of Gondophares.

Fig. 19 is from the Sánchi colonnade inscriptions.

Fig. 20 is from the Sánchi colonnade inscriptions.

Fig. 21, from the Sánchi bas-reliefs, shows the symbol placed on an altar.

Fig. 22, also from the Sánchi bas-reliefs of the South Gateway, gives a triple representation of the symbol of Dharma, which is most probably intended for the Buddhist triad of *Buddha*, *Dharma*, and *Sangha*.

8. The third member of the triad is represented in Plate XXXII., fig. 1, from a bas-relief of No. 2 Tope at Sánchi. In this the wheel, or emblem of Buddha, is placed above the monogram or symbol of Dharma, perhaps to indicate the superiority of Spirit over Matter. On the obverse of coin No. 10, Plate XXXI., the symbol is represented in the contrary manner, with the monogram of Dharma above, and the wheel of Buddha below. This, I presume, denotes the belief of the striker of the coin in the superiority of *Dharma*, or elemental Nature, over *Buddha*, or Spirit.

9. Two different spellings have been given for the name of *sangha*. Schlegel writes it सङ्ग *sangga;* and Professor H. H. Wilson, सङ्घ *sanggha*. The latter appears to be the more correct reading, as the Bhilsa Tope inscriptions invariably spell it *sangha*, with the *gh*.

10. The triple emblem, represented in fig. 22, Plate XXXII., is one of the most valuable of the Sánchi sculptures, as it shows in the clearest and most unequivocal manner the absolute identity of the holy Brahmanical Jagannáth with the ancient Buddhist Triad. The *similarity* between the Buddhist procession of images described by Fa Hian and that o.

the modern *Rathyâtrá* of *Jagannáth* was first pointed out by the Rev. Dr. Stevenson.* Colonel Sykes discovered that both processions took place at the same time of the year.† Mr. Laidlay, after noticing both of these facts, adds his opinion that "the modern procession of Jagannáth originated in the Buddhist practice described by Fa Hian." He founds his opinion on the fact, that "in the ordinary native pictures of the *avatáras* of Vishnu, the ninth, or *Bauddha Avatáro*, is represented by a figure of *Jagannáth*, or the *Rath Játtrá*." ‡ To these facts I can now add that of the absolute *identity in form* of the modern *Jagannátha* and his brother *Balaráma*, and sister *Subhadrá*, with the Buddhist monogram or symbol of Dharma. This identity is rendered much more striking and convincing by the occurrence of the symbol of Dharma in a triple form amongst the Sánchi bas-reliefs. In Plate XXXII., fig. 23, I have given a sketch of Jagannátha and his brother and sister side by side, with the triple symbol of Dharma from Sánchi.§

11. But there are still two points of coincidence which, in my opinion, tend to complete the proof of

* Journal of the Royal Asiatic Society, vol. vii., p. 8.

† Journal of the Royal Asiatic Society, vol. vi., p. 420, n.

‡ See his translation of the Fo-kwe-ki, pp. 21—261.

§ Another drawing of Jagannath, and his brother and sister, may be found in vol. vi., p. 450, of the Journal of the Royal Asiatic Society. In this the identity of figure is even more striking.

the Buddhist origin of Jagannátha. These are, "the suspension of caste during the festival," and "the belief that the image contains the relics or bones of Krishna." The first is one of the fundamental principles of the Buddhist faith, that was promulgated by the great teacher Sákya Muni, and is so utterly repugnant to the deeply inwoven spirit of caste which pervades Brahmanism, that we may safely refer it to a Buddhist origin. The other is also not at all Brahmanical, while, as we have seen throughout this work, it is eminently characteristic of Buddhism.

12. When restored to its original monogrammatic form, the figure of Jagannáth, or the Lord of the Universe, becomes clear and intelligible, but its present uncouth shape has taxed even the ingenious mendacity of a Brahman to account for. According to the learned, a king named *Indradyumna* besought the divine artist Viswakarma to make a figure of Jagannáth to contain the relics of Krishna. The artist promised on condition that he should not be disturbed. But the king's impatience interrupted the work in the midst, and the enraged artist immediately gave up his labour, and left the figure of Jagannáth without arms. A trace of the Buddhist origin of the name may perhaps be found in the fact that one of the cave temples of Ellora is still called Jagannáth.

13. There is another modern Triad which I believe to be also of Buddhist origin, namely, *Vithoba* and his two wives *Rukmini* (or Rakhami) and *Satyavama*.

Their statues are represented standing with the arms a-kimbo. The Hindus generally do not recognise them as orthodox;* but their worshippers have attempted to identify *Vithoba* and his wives with *Krishna* and his wives, who are also named *Rukmini* and *Satyavama*. Dr. Stevenson was the first to point out that "the festivals of Vithoba correspond in a remarkable manner with the seasons of the Buddhists." The two principal festivals of Vithoba occur, "the one just four days before the commencement, and the other just four before the completion of the Buddhist Wasso, or season of sacred rest, which continues from the full moon of *Asarh* to that of *Kártik*.† The full moon of Asárh is the *pancha-dasam-sudi*, or 15th of the bright half, or waxing moon; and the full moon of *Kártik* is the 15th *sudi* of that month. Four days earlier would be the 11th of the bright half, or *ekádasi sudi*."

14. I have been thus particular in specifying the date of Vithoba's festivals, because the latter one at least appears to me to have some connection with the *mela*, or "fair," which is held at the old ruined city of Besnagar, near Bhilsa, in the same month of Kártik. According to one statement this takes place on *Kártik sudi* 9; but another authority makes

* Journal of the Royal Asiatic Society, vii. 5. I believe that the worship of Krishna is only a corrupt mixture of Buddhism and Christianity, and was a sort of compromise intended for the subversion of both religions in India.

† From the middle of July to the middle of November.

it *Kartik badi*, 11. The true date* is, however, *Kártika sudi ekádasi*, on the 11th of the bright half of Kártik; that is, just four days before the full moon of that month. According to tradition this fair was established by Raja Rukmángada, from whom it was named the *Rukhmángada ekádasi*.†

15. According to the *Bhagta-mála*, the Rukhmángada Ekadasi was instituted in commemoration of an *Apsara* (or heavenly nymph) having pricked her foot with the thorn of a Bhangan plant in Rukhmángada's garden.

16. According to the *Rukmángada cheritra*, Rukmángada was the son of Rohitaswa, and the grandson of Harischandra. He had a son named Dharmangada by his wife, whom he neglected for the beautiful Apsara *Viswâ Mohoni*, and his after life was embittered until he made propitiation by the establishment of the festival called the *Rukmángada ekadasi*.‡

17. Rukmin or Rukam was the name of a prince who was slain by Balaráma, the brother of Krishna. An existing tradition says that one of the Rajas of Bhilsa had a white horse, which, for security, was stabled on the top of the precipitous rock of Lohángi,

* The first date was obtained by my brother; the latter by Lieutenant Maisey, as communicated by Captain Ellis. The beginning of the Buddhist *Wasso* is still celebrated at Bhilsa by the illumination of the *Ziárat*, or shrine of *Lohángi Pir* or the "Saint of Lohángi," on the full moon of Asarh.

† My authority refers to the Matsya Purána for this account.

‡ For these two references I am indebted to the kindness of Captain Ellis.

to the eastward of Bhilsa. But the Raja was overcome by the Pândus, who carried off the white horse for the performance of the *aswamedha*, or horse-sacrifice. This prince was most probably the Rukam, or Rukma of the *Prem Ságar*, and the brother of Rukmani, who became one of the eight wives of Krishna. *Rukma*, in Sanskrit, means "iron," and therefore *Rukmángada* is only a synonyme of *Lohángada*, or *Lohángi*, the name of the famous Bhilsa rock.* It is true that Krishna was a Yádava and not a Pándava; but as I have always found that the latter name is used in a general manner throughout India to denote any hero of ancient times, the tradition of the Pandu conqueror may be applied to Krishna and his brother Balaráma.

18. According to the Prem Ságur, Rukma was the son of *Bhikmak*, the Raja of Vidarbha, or Berar. His sister Rukmini is often called Vidarbhajá, or "born in Vidarbha." The name of Vi-darbha implied a country in which the holy *Kusa* grass is not found; and it is generally applied to the modern Berar Proper. But if I am correct in my identification of Raja Rukma of Vidarbha with Rukmángada of Besnagar, there can be no doubt that Vidarbha must, in ancient times, have included the whole of Bhopal and Bhilsa to the north of the Narbada.

19. In my account of Asoka's reign, I have already shown that Besnagar was a large city in 270 B. C., and that it was also called Chaityagiri, or the "hill of

* It is also called *Loháchal*, or "Iron-hill."

chaityas," because the Tope-covered hill was in its immediate neighbourhood. According to tradition, Besnagar was founded by Rukmángada, in the Dwâpur-yug* (the third age, or age of copper), one million and three hundred thousand years ago. It stands at the *Triveni*, or triple junction of the rivers Betwa, Bes (or Besali), and Ganga, of which the last is believed to flow underground.

20. The less ancient city of *Bhilsa*, or *Bhadravati*, is said to have been the capital of *Yavanaswa* Chandravansi.† The same story which I have related above is told about him and the Aswamedha, or white horse with a black ear, which was carried off by a Pandu prince. The existence of the Pandus in this part of the country is proved by the inscriptions of No. 2 Tope at Sánchi, which certainly dates as high as 200 B.C. The trough from which the horse used to drink is still pointed out; but this is only a bell capital of a gigantic Buddhist pillar, of which nothing more now remains. The capital is 3 feet high, and 3½ feet broad; and as the Sánchi capitals are only 3 feet, the Lohángi pillar must have been nearly 50 feet high. The capital is now standing upside down, and has been hollowed out to a depth of 15 inches, with a diameter of 21 inches, so as to form a large bowl.

21. A glance at the map (Plate I.) will show the re-

* Captain Ellis's information says the *Satya-yug*; that is, the first, or golden age.

† Called Alamgirpur by the Mahomedans.

lative positions of all the Tope stations with respect to Besnagara and Bhilsa. The ancient city of Besnagara extended from the junction of the Betwa and Bes rivers, as far south as the Udayagiri hill, and the Lohángi rock of Bhilsa, from which point the Chetiyagiri (or Tope range of hills), stretching from Satdhára and Sonári, by Sánchi Káná-khera to Bhojpur and Andher, was only three miles distant. The presence of these large monastic establishments must, for a time at least, have brought both wealth and prosperity to the country; and the remains of three embankments thrown across the valleys between Sánchi and Satdhára, show that the Buddhist monks were as famous for practical agricultural, as for philosophical learning.

22. Let the imagination wander back for two thousand years, and the mind's eye will behold the Chaityagiri, or Tope range of hills, "glittering with the yellow robes" of the monks. Along the road side, and in sequestered spots, will be seen numerous trees, beneath which half-naked ascetics sit silent and still, brooding upon futurity. The classical reader will recal the *Tabasi Magorum* (or ascetic Magians), and the *Tabaso gens* (or ascetic nation), both of whom Ptolemy places to the eastward of Ujain, and who could therefore only be the *Tapasyas*, or "ascetics" of the Chaityagiri hills.

Thrice blest the man who with himself can hold
Communion deep; and, in his spirit, range
To lands far distant, into times of old,
And view successive ages as they change:
Strange countries, and inhabitants as strange—
By Tiber, where the Kesars held their sway,
Attic Ilissus, Nile, and sacred Gange;
Kingdoms and empires long since passed away,
And kings and conquerors, the mighty of their day.

Thus, Fancy-led, the aspiring Soul can spring
Her daring flight beyond the bounds of space,
And soar through heaven on unwearied wing,
Leaving slow Time behind her in the race
To crawl this world's monotonous foot-pace;
Call up the mighty of another age,
The men most celebrated in their day,
The young and beautiful, the old and sage,
And all who 've famous been in this life's pilgrimage.

Or, with prophetic eye and buoyant hope,
See into dim futurity; and pierce,
With quick-ey'd Fancy, the mind's telescope,
The lengthening vista of succeeding years,
Before which all Time-past as nought appears,
And Time-to-come, in beautiful array,
Smiling with hope amid her rainbow tears,
Trips gaily on, and points the unknown way,
Bright as the evening sky, and clear as the noonday.

And blest that spiritual happiness which sees
Perfect design in Nature's wanderings—
A beauty in her strangest images,
And in her quaintest forms; that power which flings
Its own bright joyance round the meanest things,

And, like the sun, makes gladness general;
That elasticity of thought which springs
Highest and quickest from the greatest fall;
That buoyancy of mind which rises above all.

And blest, oh! more than blest, those thoughts which spring
From the rich memory of historic lore,
The lonely heart with gladness deluging,
As moonlight floods the heavens; those thoughts of yore,
Which haply thousands may have dreamed before,
Yet we no poorer are; our fancies rove
Through distant times, and kingdoms now no more;
And the bold spirit broods on things above,
And human hopes and fears of ancient hate and love.

Like as an eagle on the wild winds playeth,
Or as a nightingale dwells on her song;
Like as a river in a vale delayeth,
Or as a breeze near rose-fields tarrieth long;
As young steeds loiter the green meads among;
As bees and butterflies, from morn till even,
Amongst the sweetest flowers their sports prolong;
The aspiring soul, in thoughts celestial weaven,
Dallies in bygone dreams, the dim foretaste of heaven.

How changed the busy scene of former days,
When twice five thousand monks obey'd the call
To general thanksgiving and to praise;
When the stone cloisters echoed, and the hall
Resounded with the solemn festival;
And gay processions filled each gorgeous gate.
No more do pilgrims round the solid wall
Of yon mysterious pile perambulate:
No more to Budh do kings their kingdoms dedicate.

Nought but the Topes themselves remain to mock
  Time's ceaseless efforts; yet they proudly stand
Silent and lasting up their parent rock,
  And still as cities under magic's wand;
  Till curious Saxons, from a distant land,
Unlock'd the treasures of two thousand years;
  And the lone scene is peopled;—here a band
Of music wakes the echoes; there the cheers
Of multitudes, alive with human hopes and fears.

THE END.

Plate II.

Druidical and Buddhist Monuments.

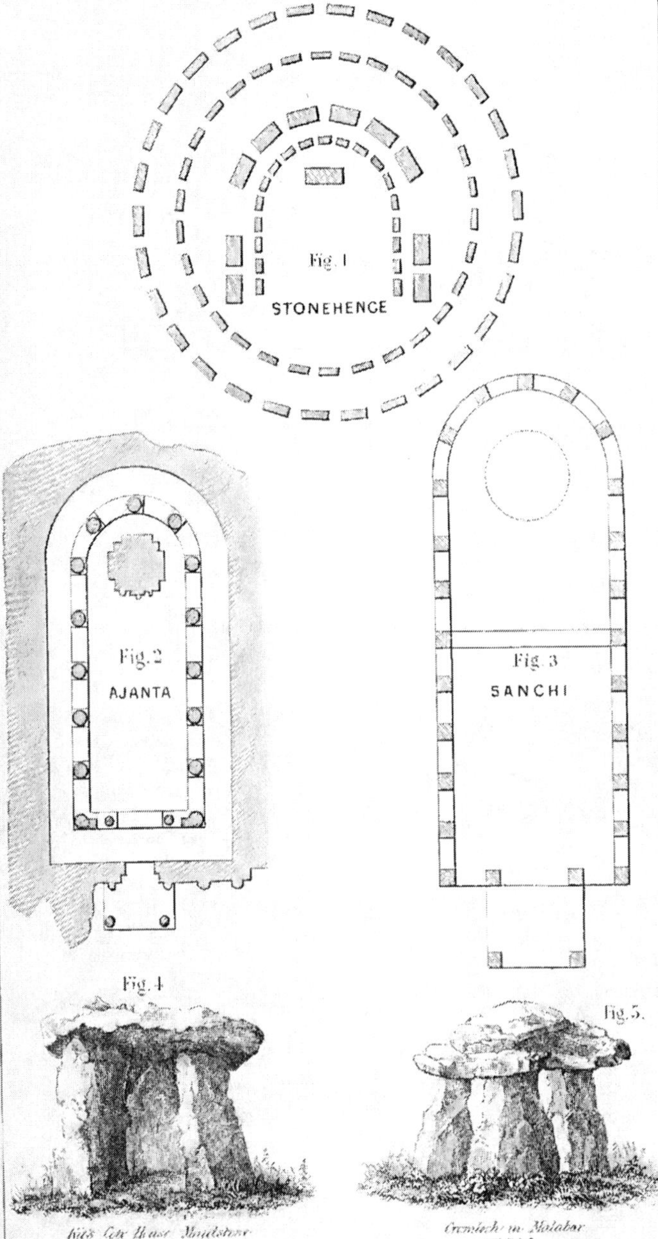

Kit's Cote House Maidstone
ENGLAND.

Cromlech in Malabar
INDIA.

Published by Smith Elder & Co. London

Plate III

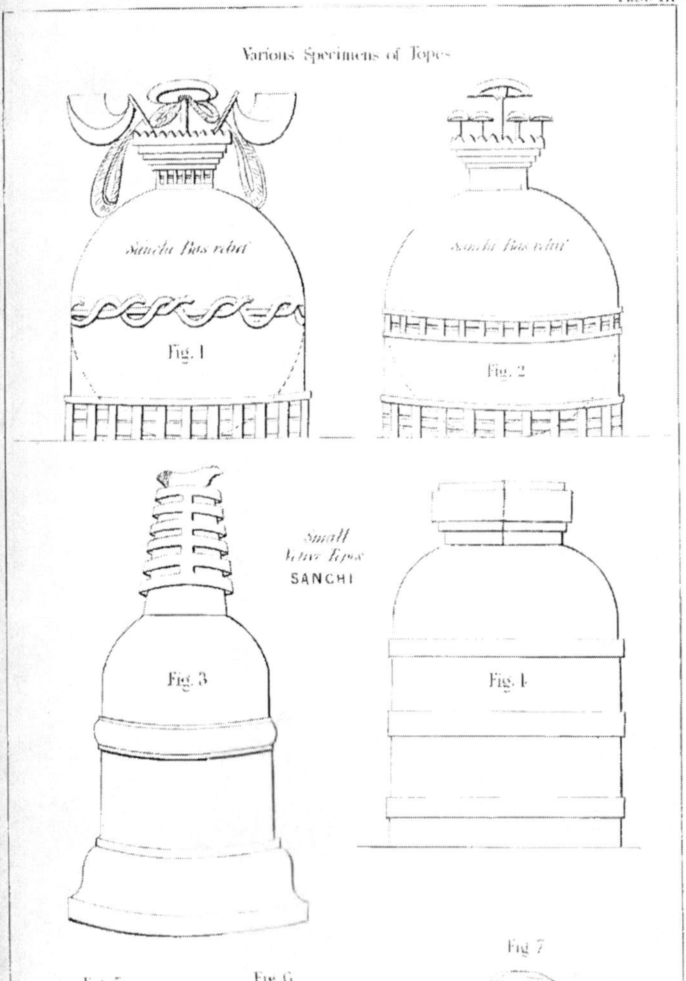
Various Specimens of Topes
Sanchi Bas relief
Fig. 1
Sanchi Bas relief
Fig. 2
Small
Stone Topes
SANCHI
Fig. 3
Fig. 4
Fig. 5
Fig. 6
Fig. 7
SANCHI
Bas relief
Nepalese Chaitya
Tibetan Chedten

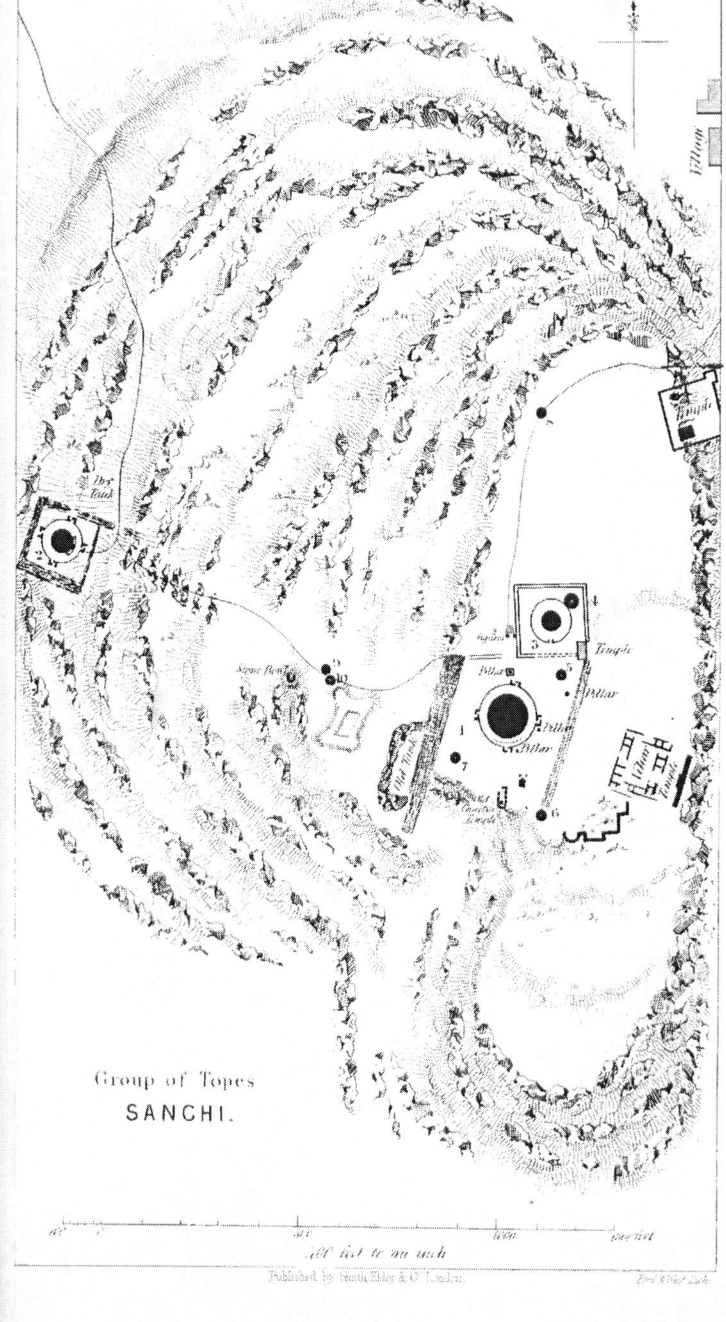

Published by Smith, Elder & Co. London.

Plate V.

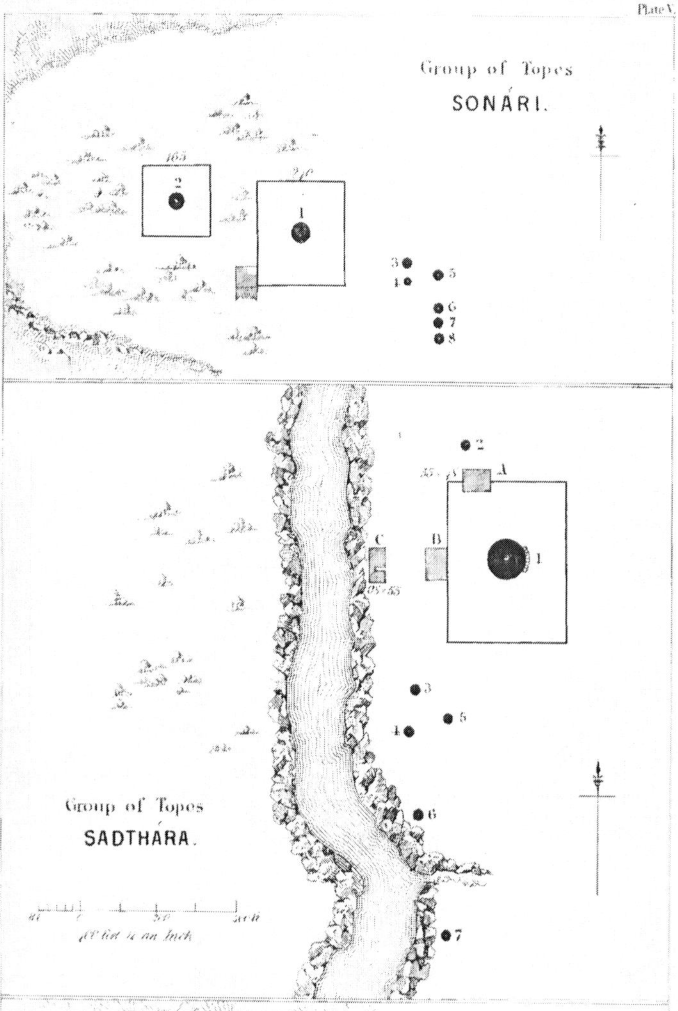

Published by Smith, Elder & Co. London

Plate VI.

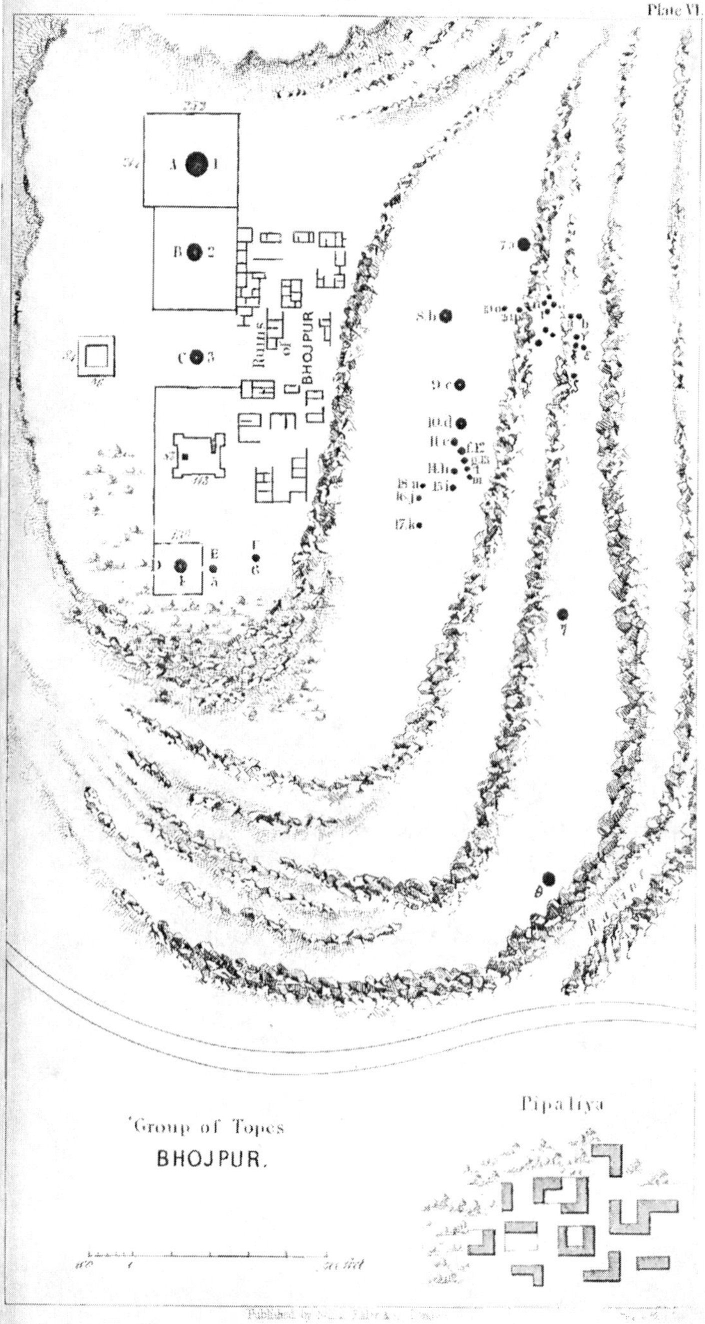

Group of Topes
BHOJPUR.

View of the Great SAN

Plate VII.

Ford & West, Lithog.

H TOPE, from E.N.E.

Plate VIII.

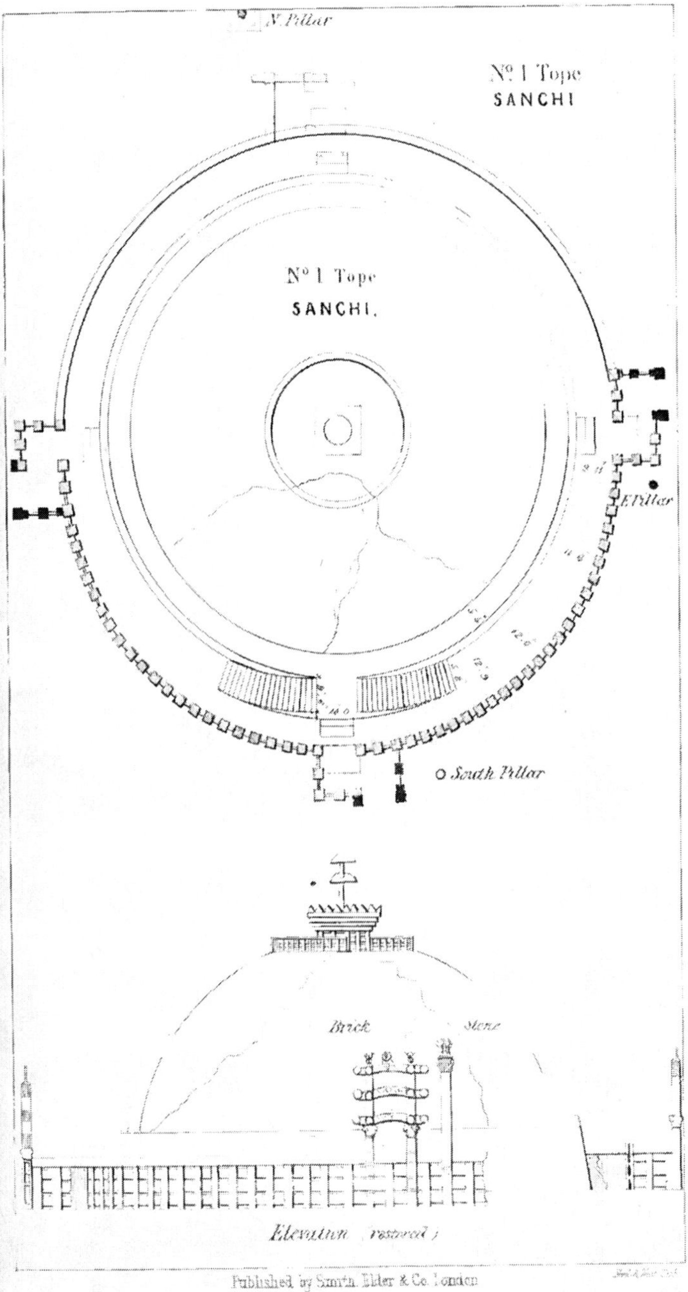

Published by Smith, Elder & Co. London

Plate IX.

COLONNADES.

Lower Enclosure SÁNCHI No. 1 *Tope*

Fig. 1.

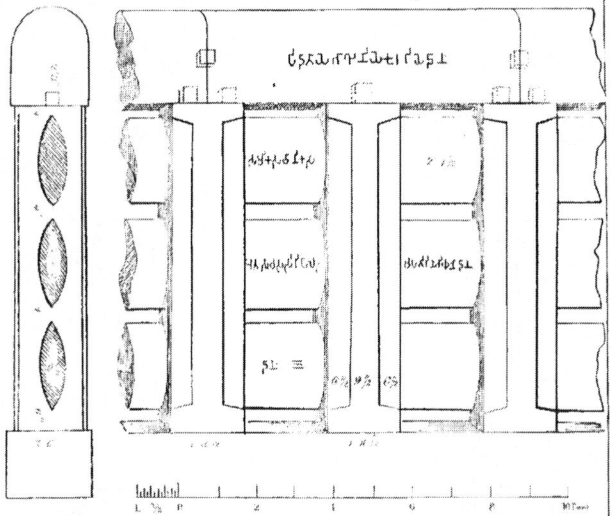

Fig. 2.

Broken Pillar at SONÁRI.

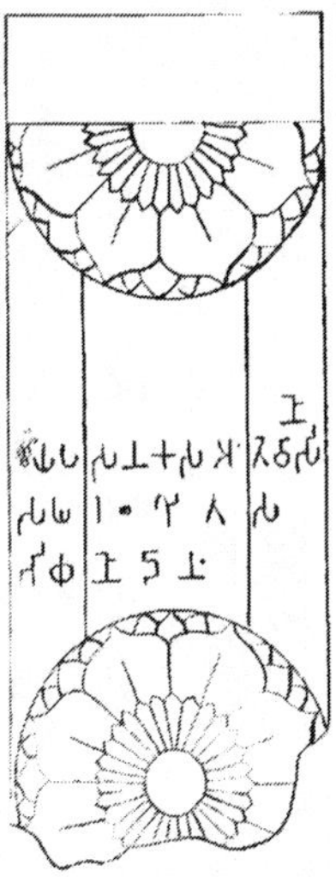

Fig. 3.

Broken Pillar,

S. Gate, Dipaldinna

AMARAVATI.

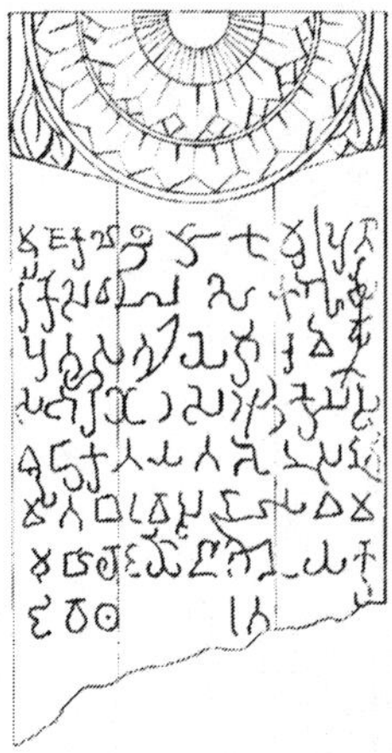

Published by Smith, Elder & Co. London

Plate X.

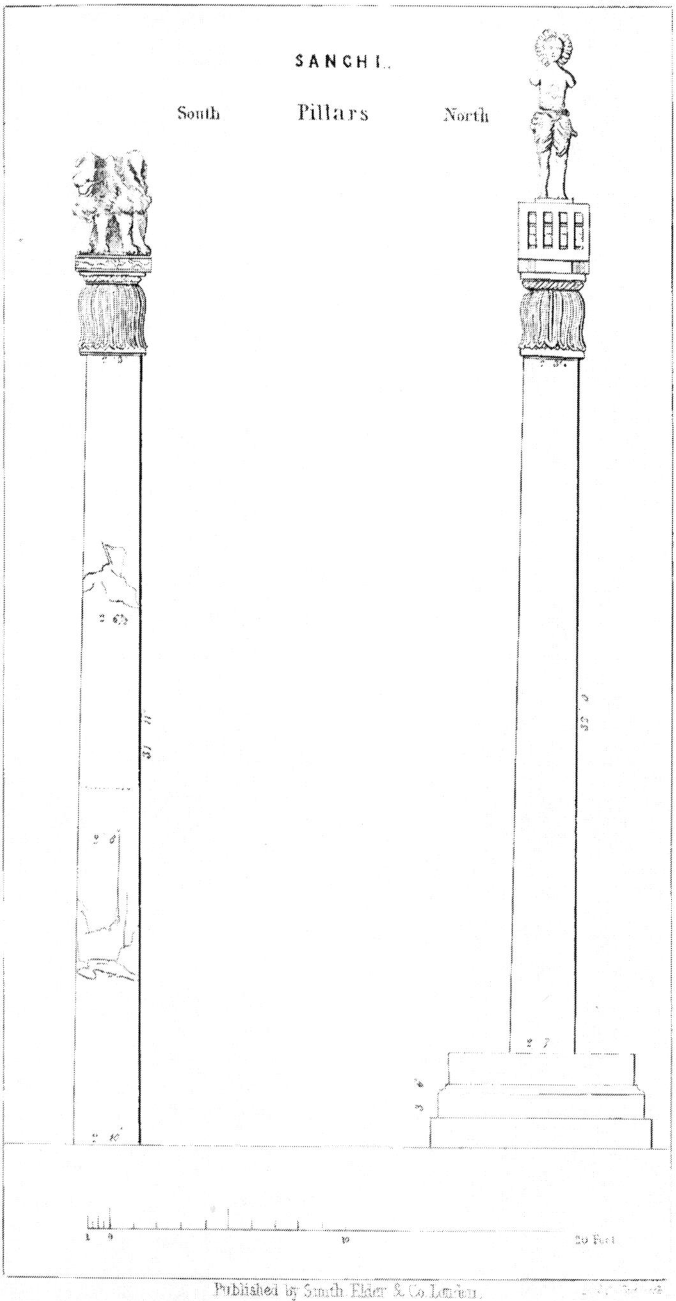

Published by Smith Elder & Co. London.

Plate XI

E. GATE.

Left Pillar, Front Face.

2nd Compartment

Published by Smith Elder & Co. London.

South Gate

Plate XIII.

SANCHI.

Tope Scene, from North Gateway.

Published by Smith, Elder & Co. London

Plate XIV

Female Dancer

Western Gate

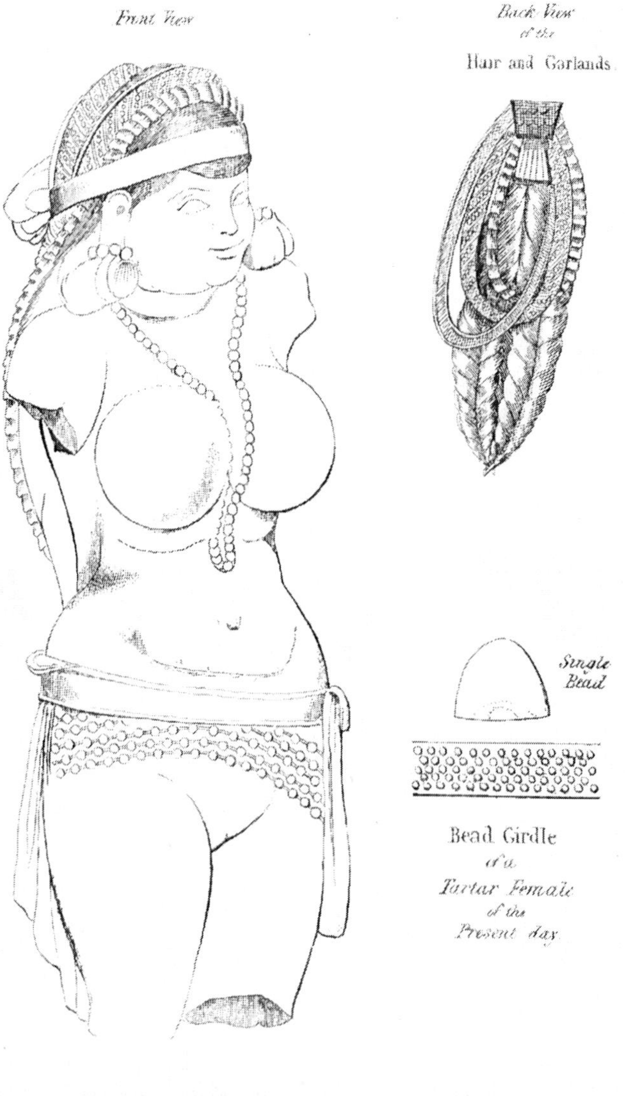

Published by Smith, Elder & Co London

Fig. 1.

Leaf roofed House
E. Gate Left Pillar Inner Face

Fig. 2

Kitchen Scene
E. Gate Left Pillar. Inner Face.

Fig. 3.

E. Gate

Published by Smith, Elder & Co. London

Inscriptions. No. 1. Tope. SANCHI.

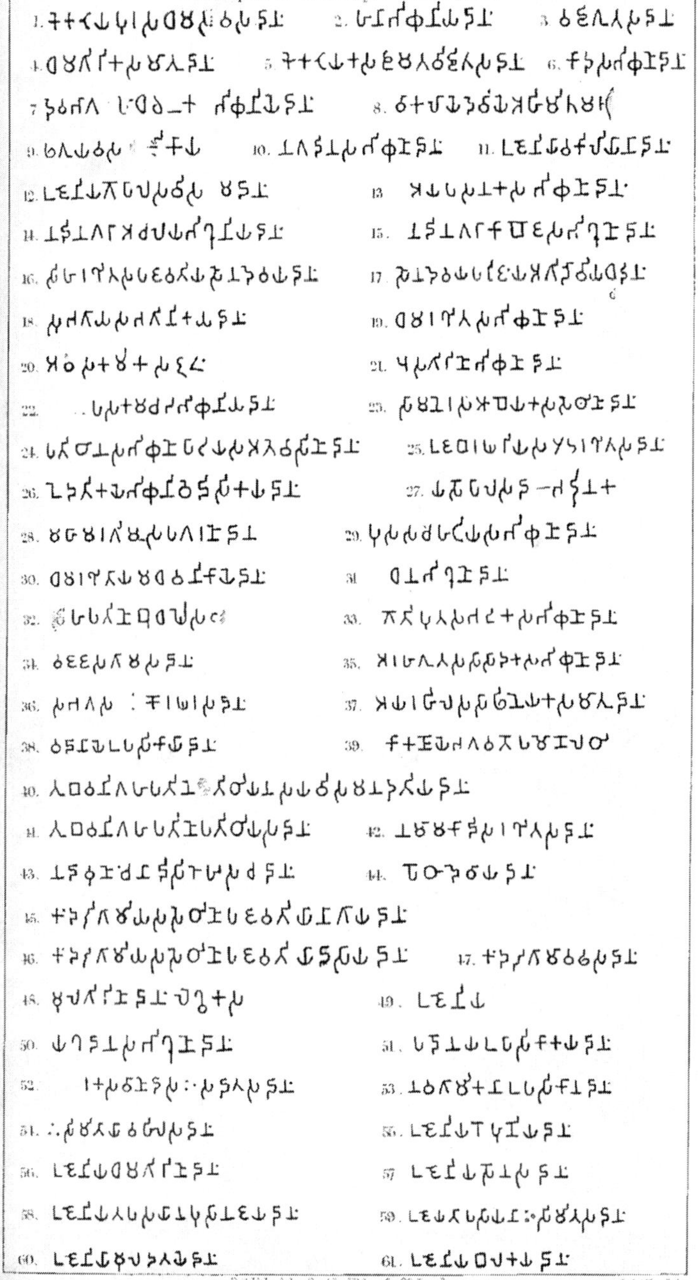

Published by Smith, Elder, & Co. London.

Plate XVII.

Inscriptions. No. 1. Tope. SANCHI.

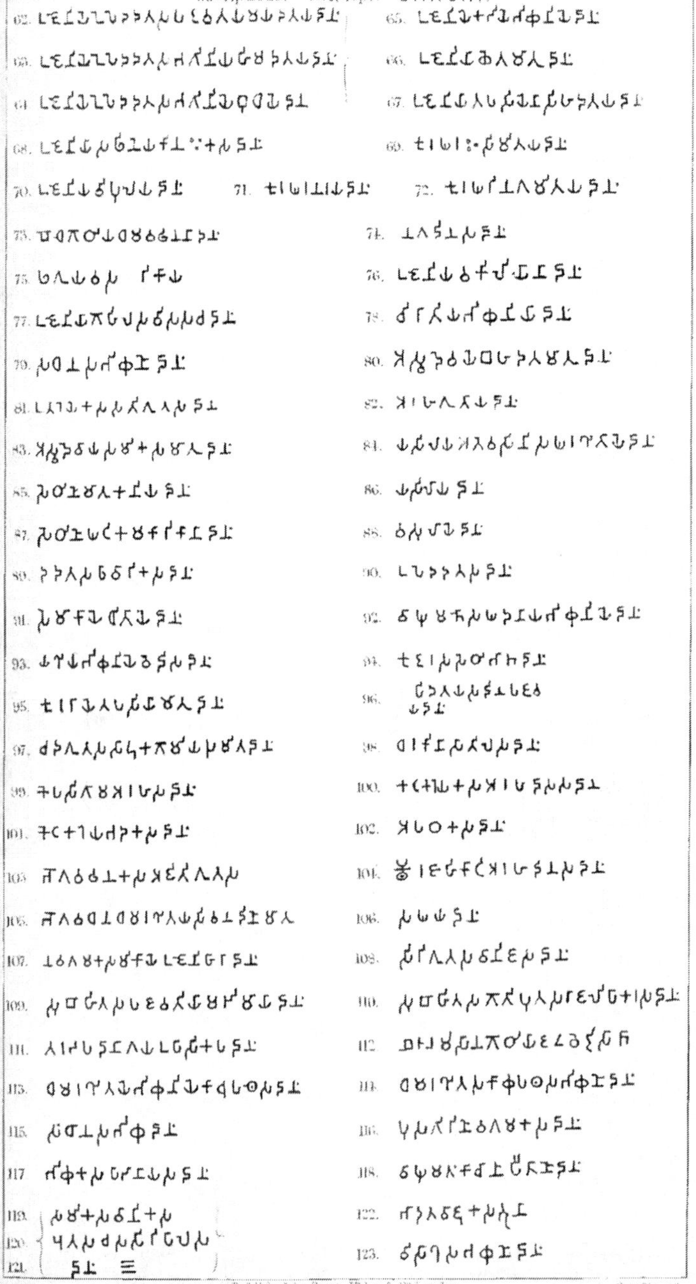

Published by Smith, Elder & Co. London.

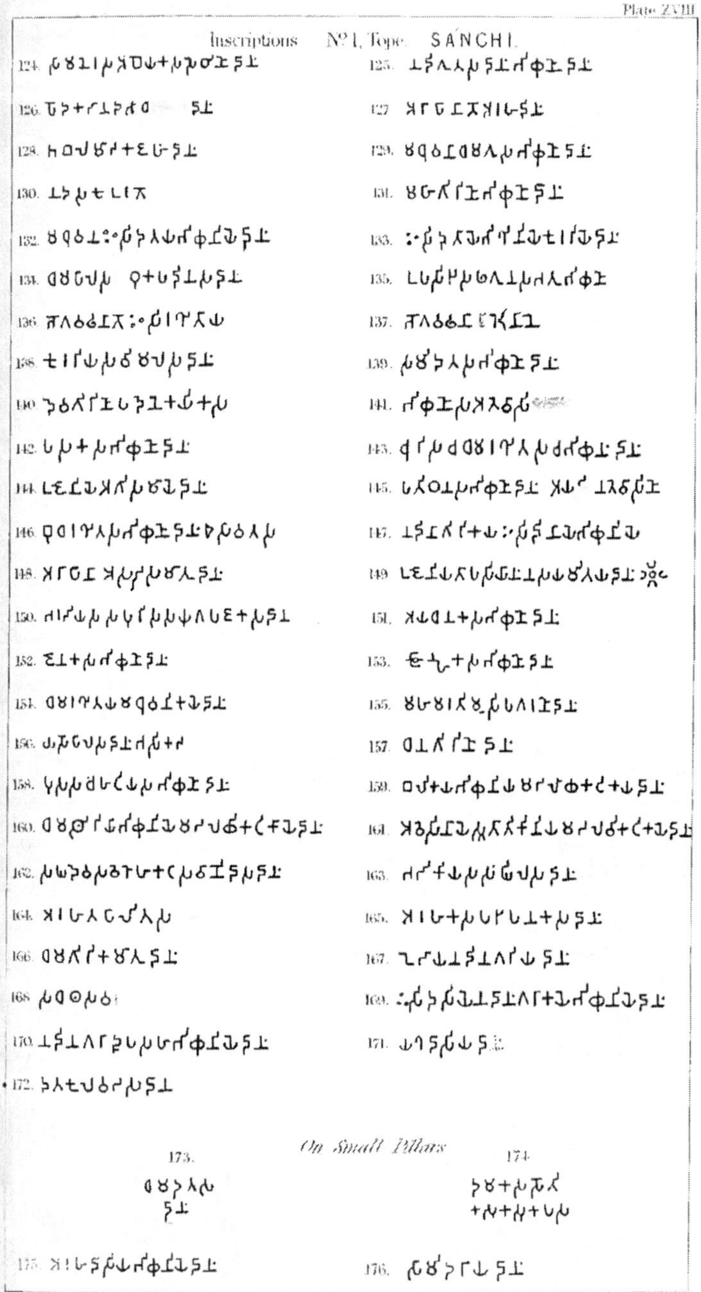

Published by Smith, Elder & Co. London.

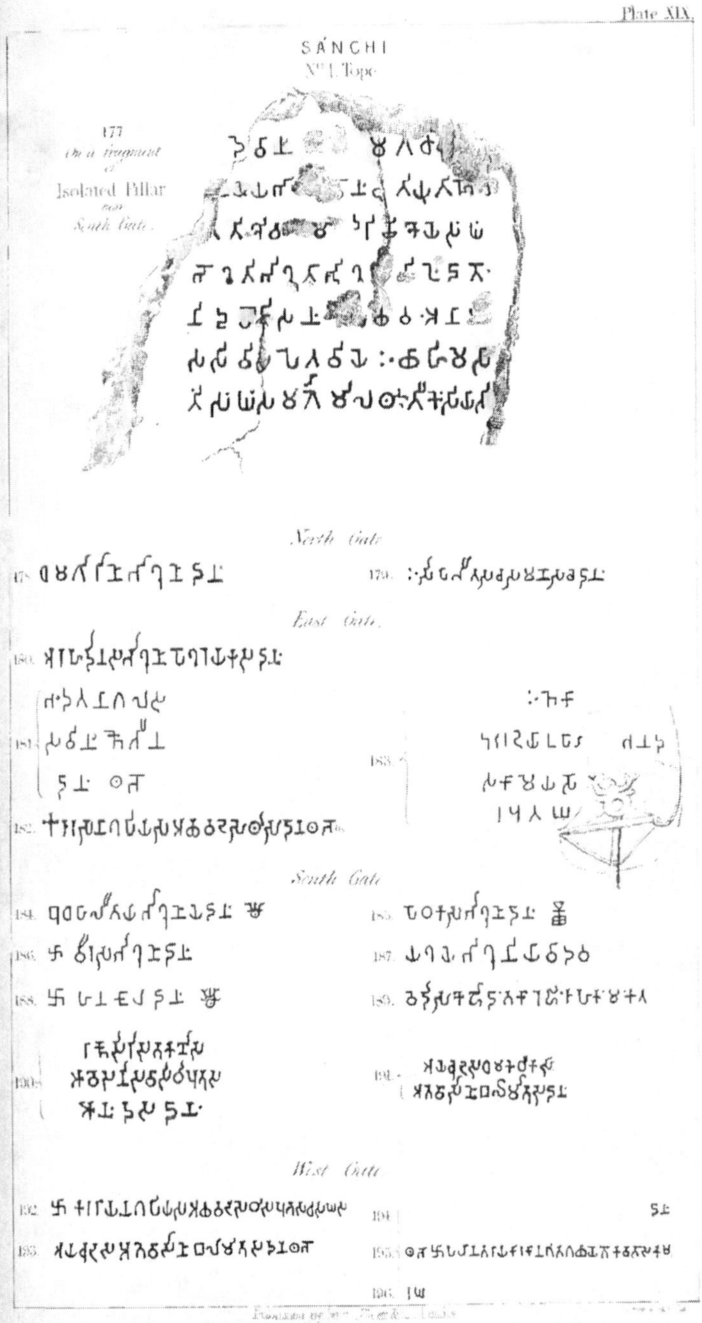
Plate XIX.
SÁNCHI
No. 1. Tope
177
On a fragment of Isolated Pillar near South Gate.
North Gate
179.
East Gate.
180.
181.
182.
183.
South Gate.
184.
185.
186.
187.
188.
189.
190.
191.
West Gate.
192.
193.
194.
195.
196.

Plate XX

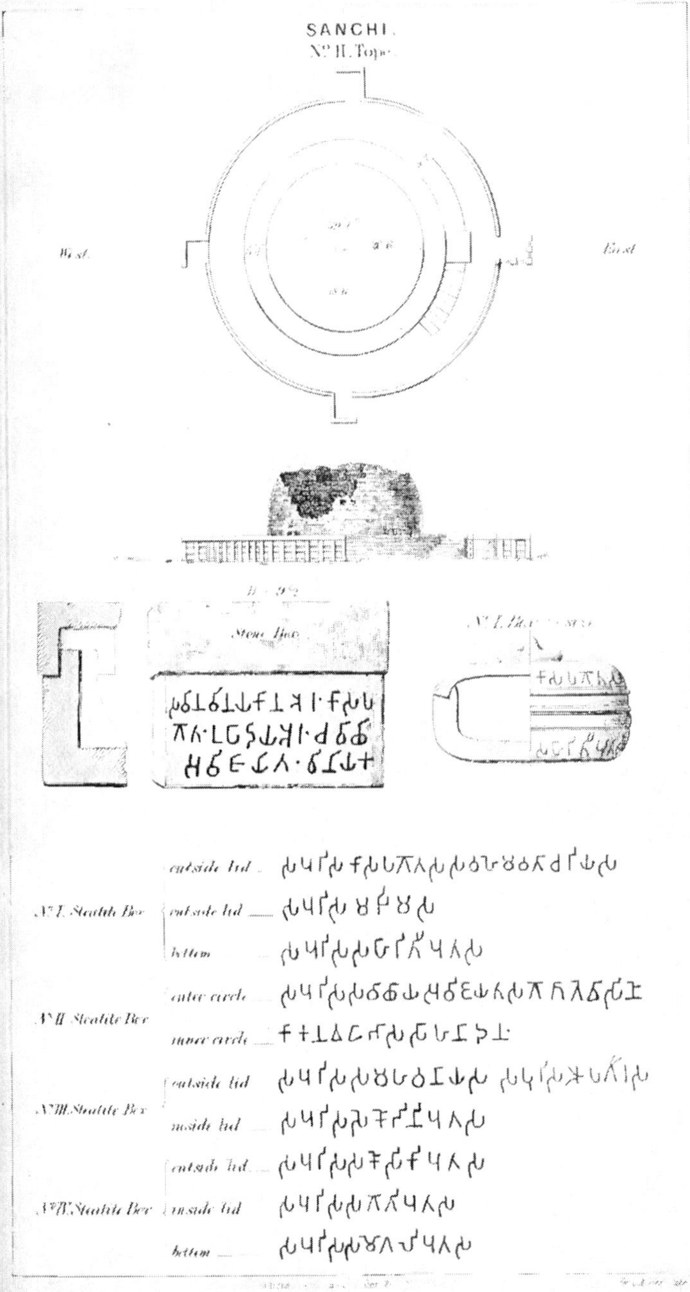
SANCHI.
No. II. Tope.
West
East
Stone Box
No. I. Box
No. I. Steatite Box
outside lid
inside lid
bottom
No. II Steatite Box
outer circle
inner circle
No. III. Steatite Box
outside lid
inside lid
No. IV. Steatite Box
outside lid
inside lid
bottom

Plate XXI.

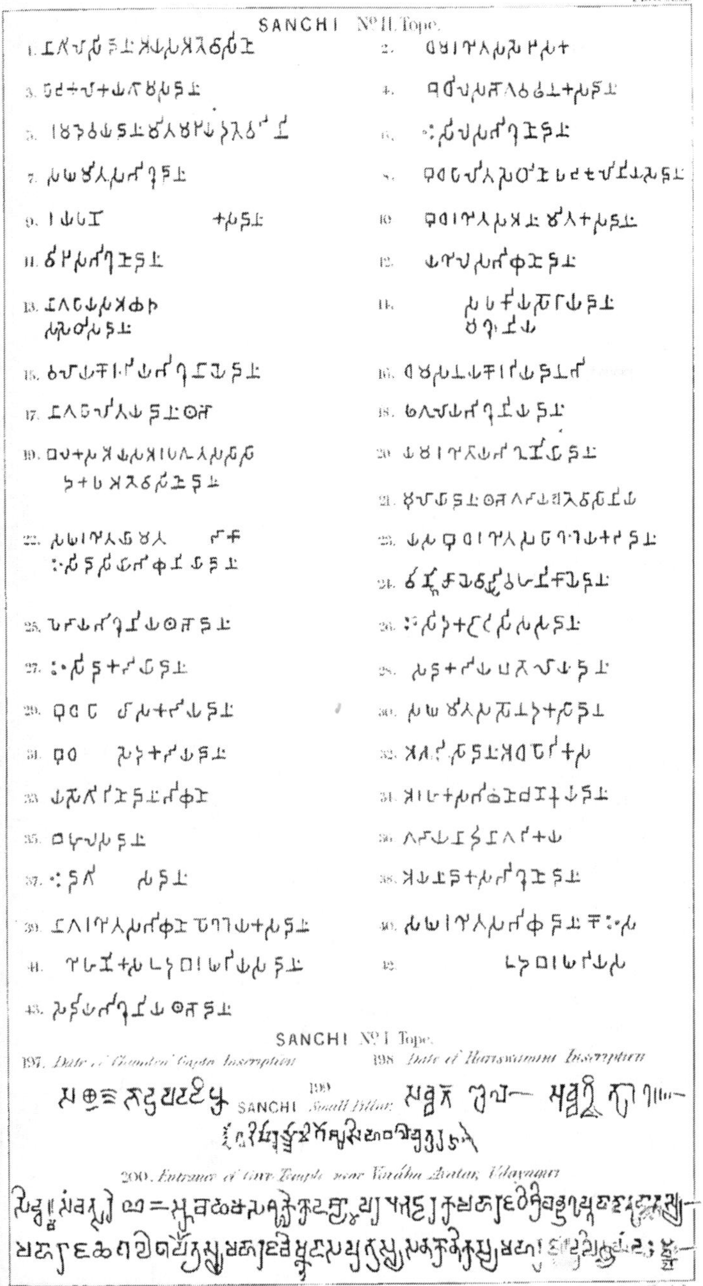

Published by Smith, Elder & Co. London.

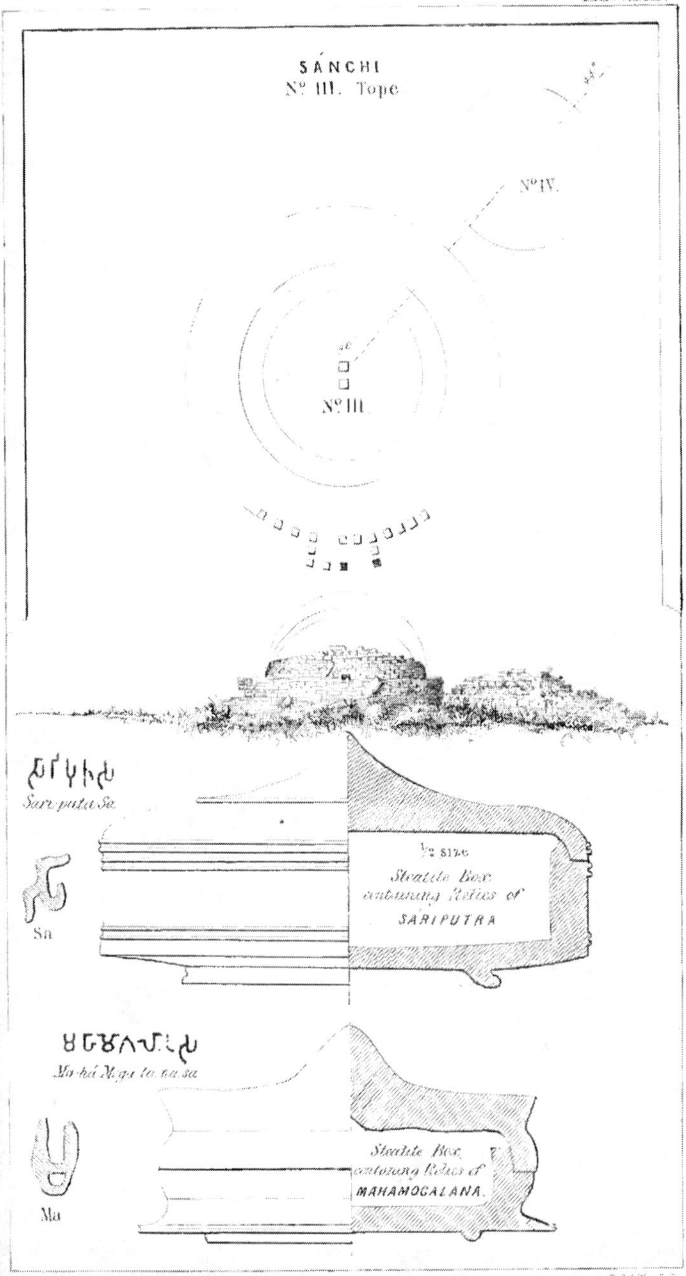

Published by Smith, Elder & Co. London.

Plate XXIII.

SONARI

No. 1. Tope

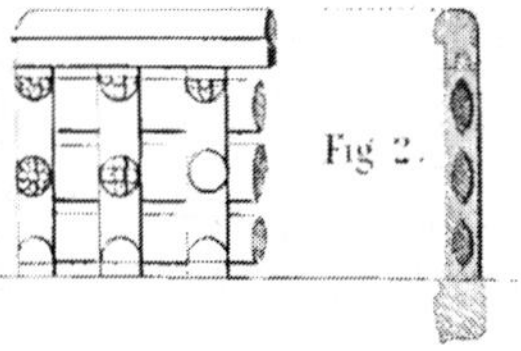

Fig. 2.

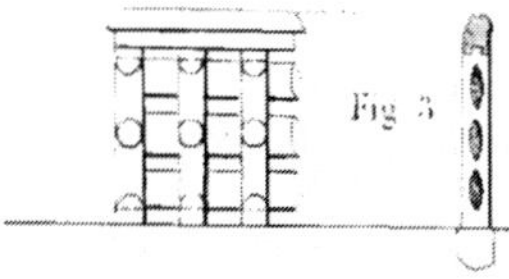

Fig. 3.

Relic Boxes found in No. 1 Tope

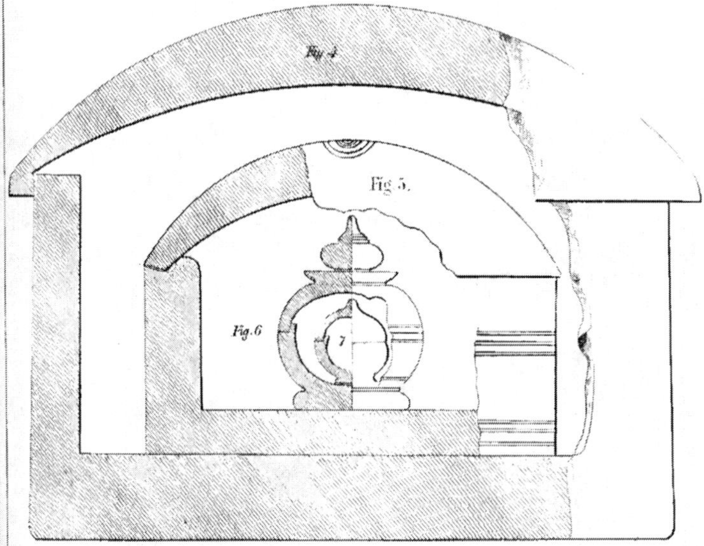

Inscriptions on broken Pillars of Enclosure

Fig. 8

Fig. 9

Plate XXIV.

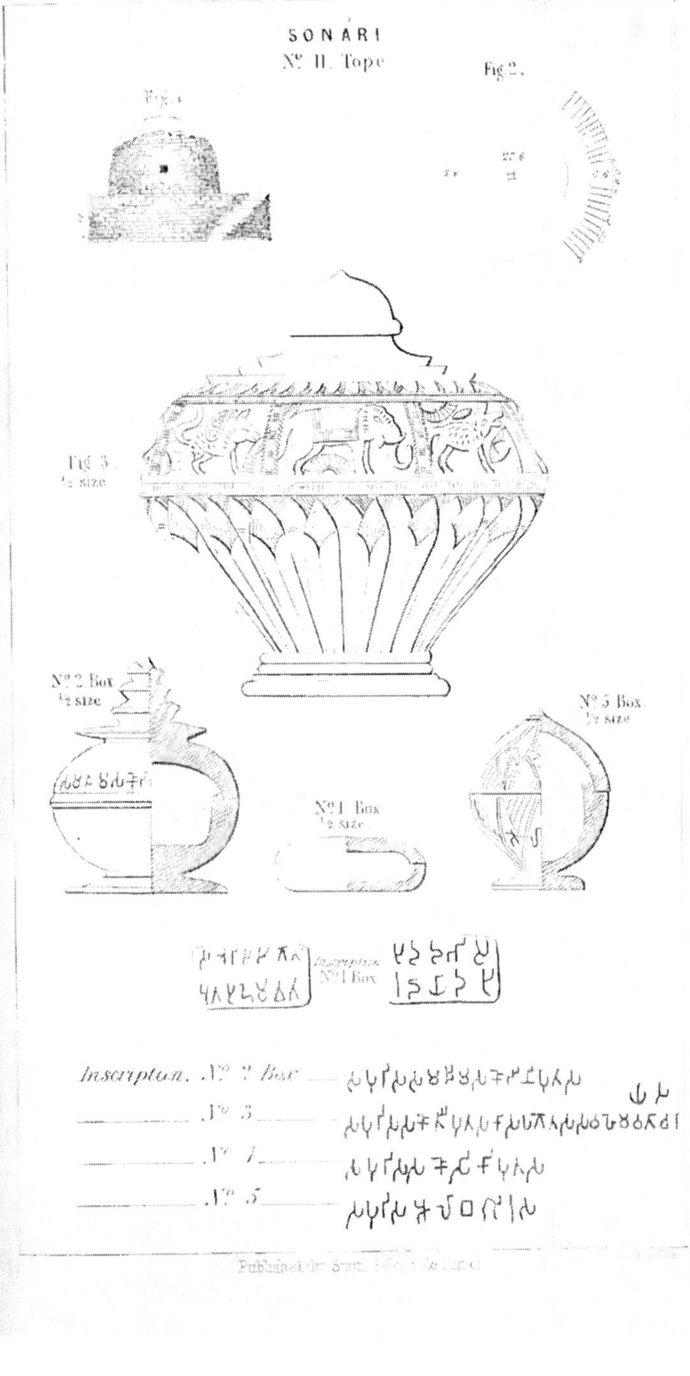
SONÁRI
No. II. Tope
Fig. 2.
Fig. 3.
½ size
No. 2 Box
½ size
No. 5 Box.
½ size
No. 1 Box
½ size
Inscription
No. 1 Box
Inscription. No. 2 Box
No. 3
No. 4
No. 5

Plate XXV

Published by Smith Elder & Co London

Plate XXVI.

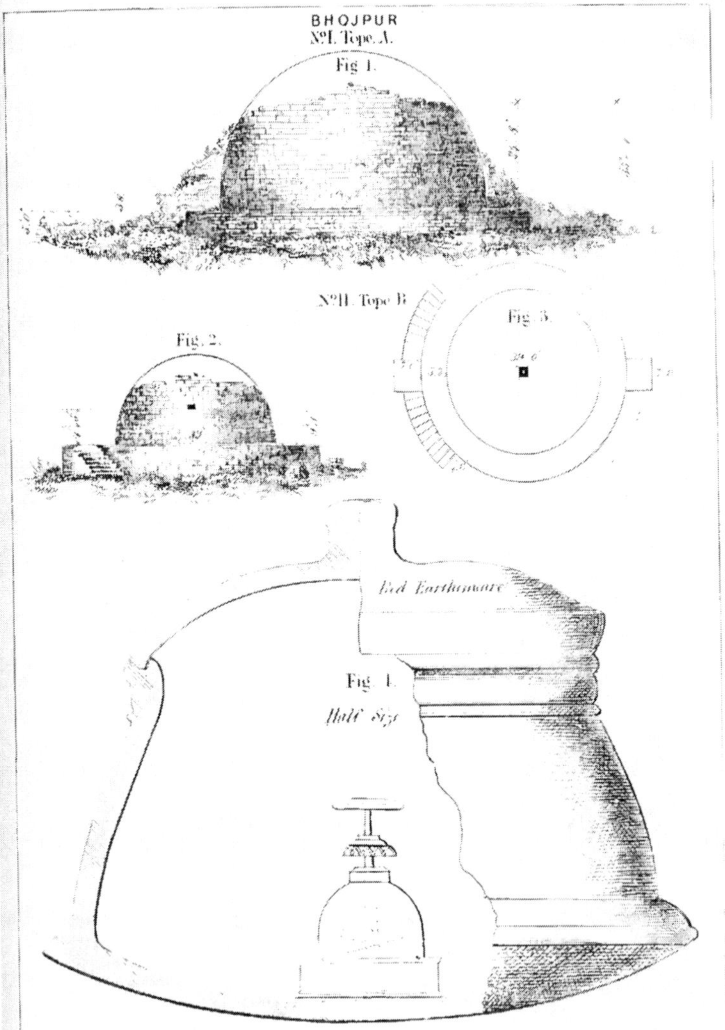
BHOJPUR
No. I. Tope. A.
Fig 1.
No. II. Tope B.
Fig. 2.
Fig. 3.
Red Earthenware
Fig. 4.
Half Size
No. IV. Tope D.
Fig. 5
Fig. 6.
Black Earthenware
Fig. 7.

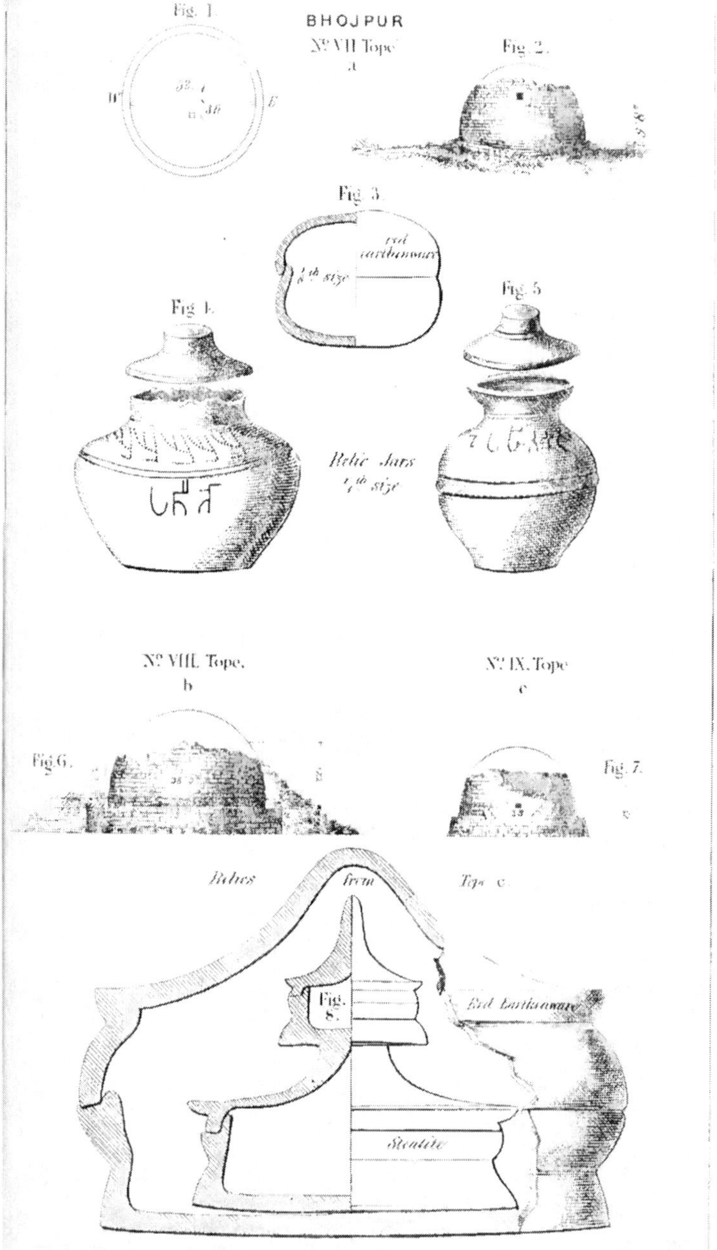

Published by Smith, Elder & Co. London

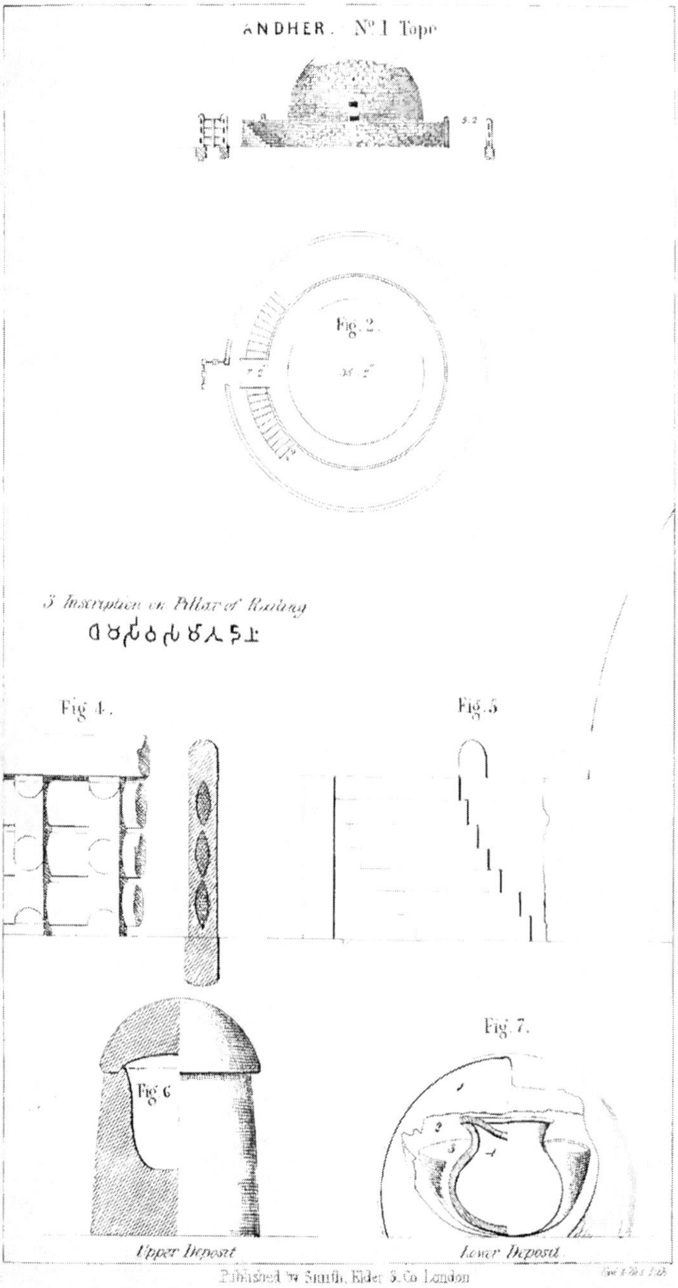

Published by Smith, Elder & Co. London

Plate XXIX.

ANDHER

No. II Tope

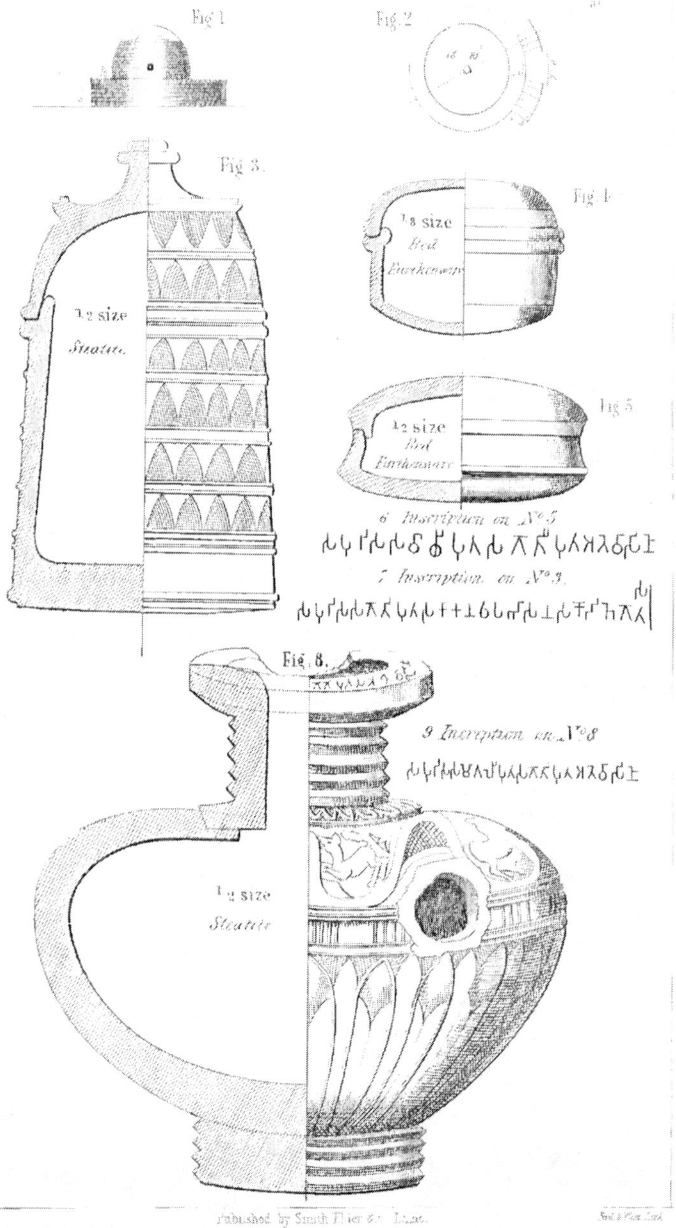

Published by Smith Elder & Co. London.

Plate XXX.

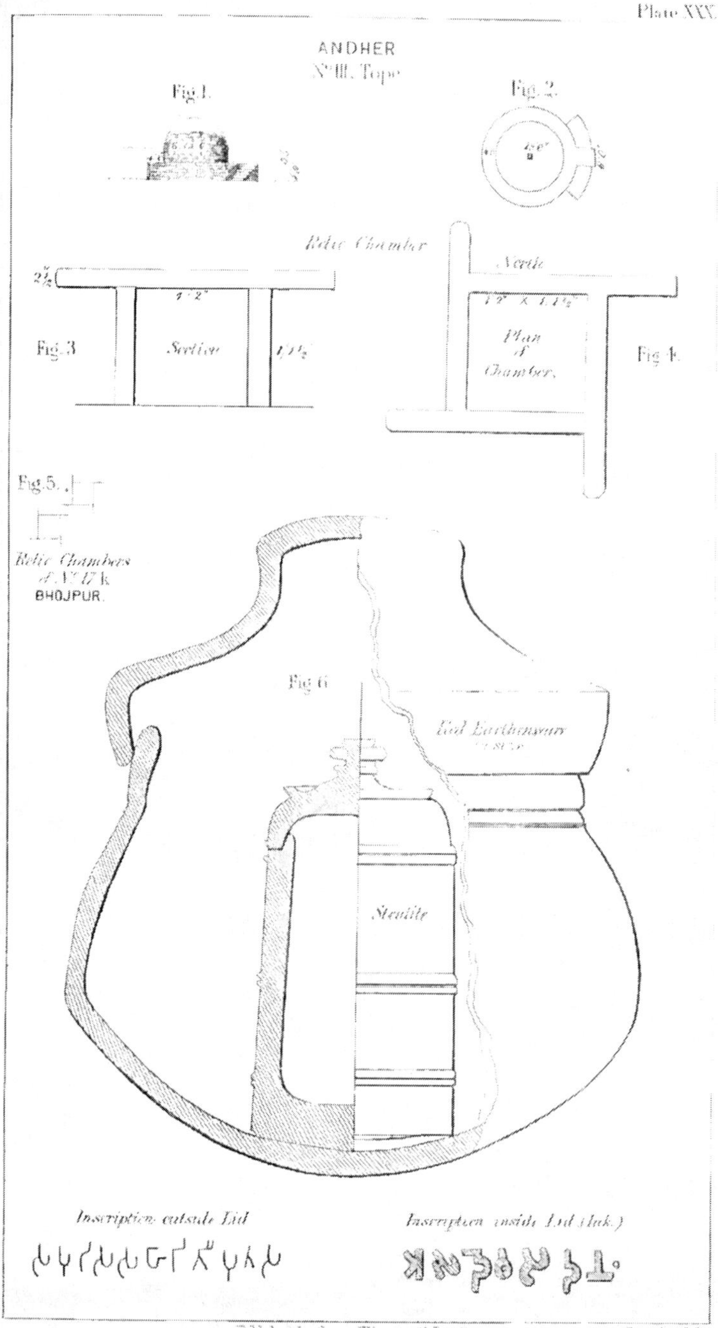

Published by Smith, Elder & Co London

Symbols of Budaha

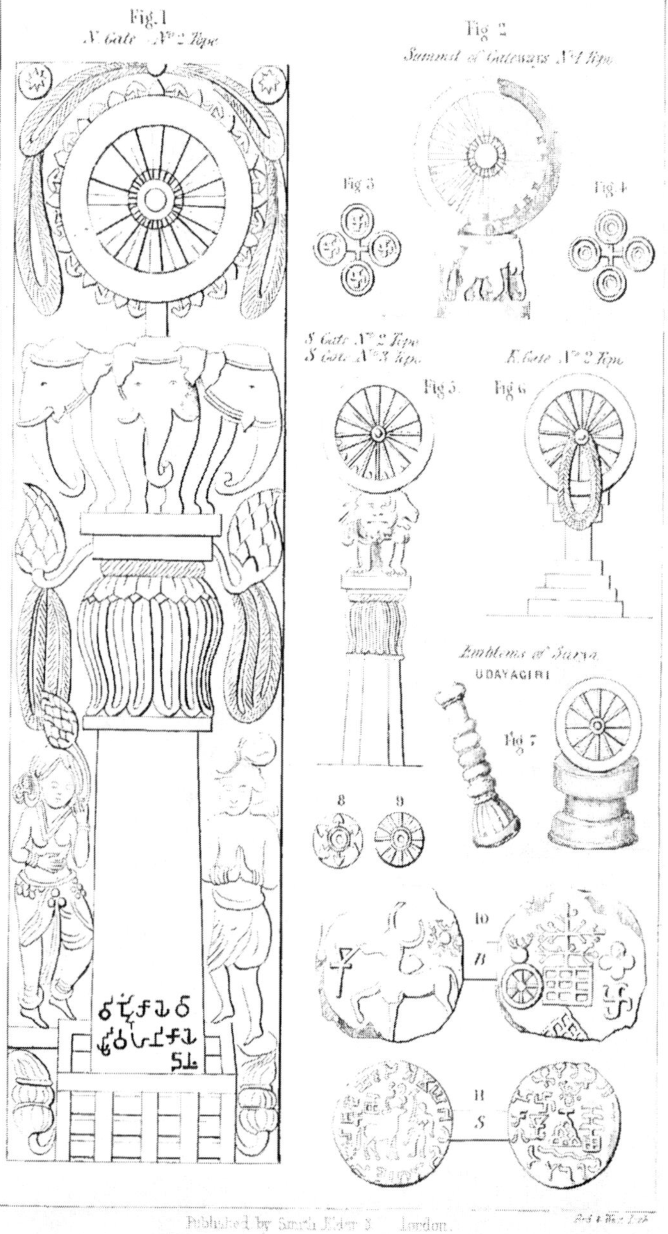

Published by Smith Elder & Co. London.
Day & Son Lith.

Symbols of Dharma.

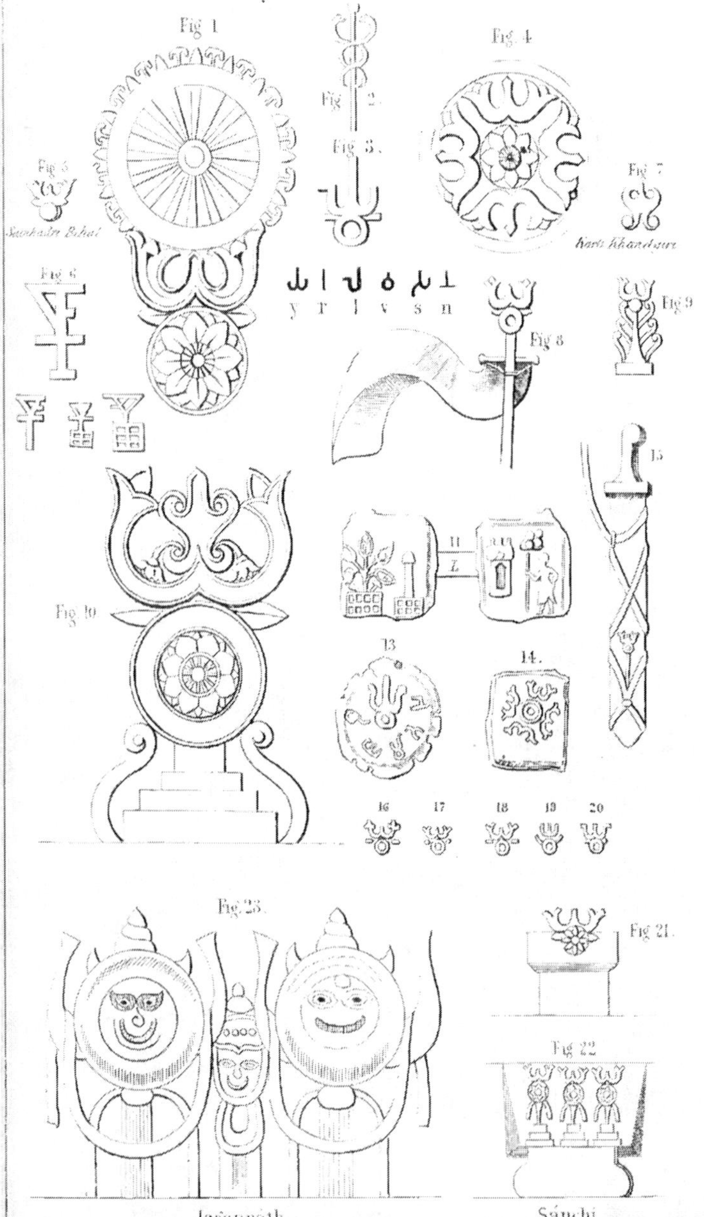

Jagannath. Sánchi

Published by Smith Elder & Co London.

Plate XXXIII.

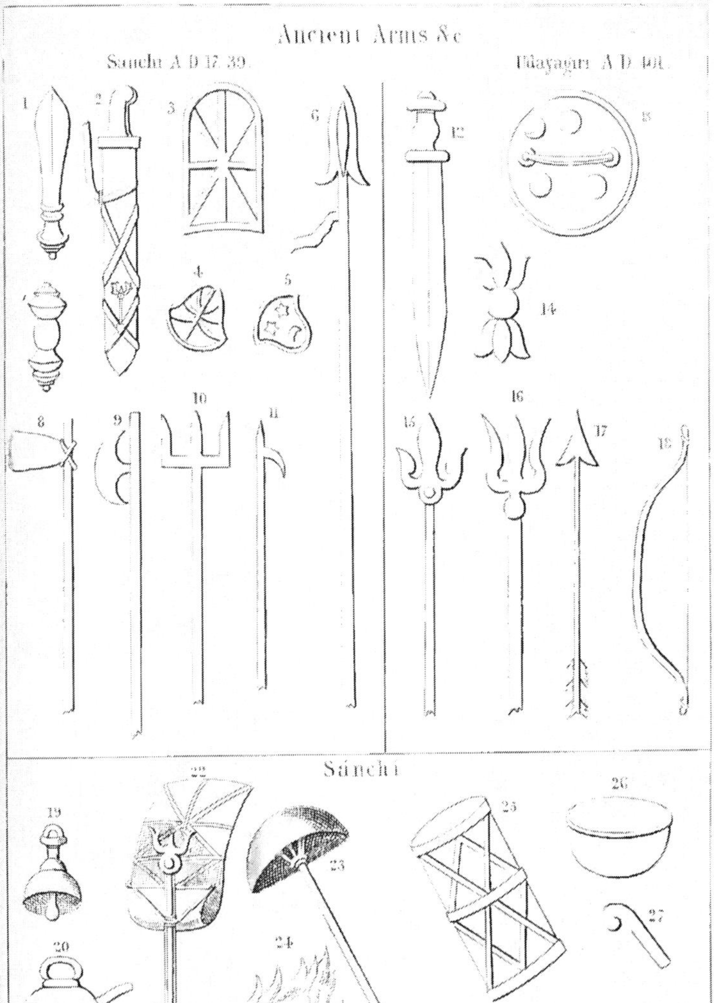

Published by Smith, Elder & Co. London

APPENDIX.

DESCRIPTION OF ANCIENT ARMS AND INSTRUMENTS IN PLATE XXXIII.

The figures in this Plate have been taken from the Sánchi bas-reliefs, which date between A. D. 17 and 39; and from the sculptures at Udayagiri, which were executed in A D. 401.

Fig. 1 is a dagger from *Sánchi*. I saw a similar weapon amongst the broken sculptures at Buri Chánderi, which has been in ruins for the last six hundred years.

Fig. 2.—Sword worn by a porter, or doorkeeper.—*Sánchi*.

Fig. 3.—Infantry shield.—*Sánchi*.

Fig. 4 and 5.—Cavalry shields.—*Sánchi*.

Fig. 6.—Pike, or javelin.—*Sánchi*.

Fig. 7.—The Indian *Vajra*, or thunderbolt; a symbol of universal dominion, usually placed in the hand of a king. Very common at *Sánchi*. Compare the form of the Vajra of four centuries later, in Fig. 14, from *Udayagiri*.

Fig. 8.—Falling axe.—*Sánchi*.

Fig. 9.—Battle axe.—*Sánchi*.

Fig. 10.—*Trisul*, or trident.—*Sánchi*.

Fig. 11.—*Ankhús*, or elephant goad.

Fig. 12.—Sword.—*Udayagiri*.

B B

Fig. 13.—Shield.—*Udayagiri.*

Fig. 14.—*Vajra,* or thunderbolt.—*Udayagiri.*

Fig. 15.—Trident in porter's hand.—*Udayagiri.*

Fig. 16.—Trident carried by the *Bhainsásur,* or buffalo-demon, at *Udayagiri.*

Figs. 17 and 18.—Bow and arrow.—*Udayagiri.*

Fig. 19.—Bell attached to elephant housings.—*Sánchi.*

Figs. 20 and 21.—Vessels carried in procession.—*Sánchi.* I believe they are the water-vessels (*uda-pátra*) of some holy personages. A vessel of similar shape is still used by the Grand Lama.

Fig. 22.—Standard from the *Sánchi* bas-reliefs. The staff is surmounted by the symbol of Dharma.

Fig. 23.—A *chatta,* or umbrella, with long handle.—*Sánchi.*

Fig. 24.—A *chaori,* or tail of the Yâk (Bos grunniens).—*Sánchi.*

Fig. 25.—A long drum.—*Sánchi.*

Figs. 26 and 27.—Kettle-drum and drum-stick.—*Sánchi.*

Fig. 28.—Looking-glass.—*Sánchi.*

Figs. 29 and 30.—*Morhas,* or ornamental seats, or thrones, without backs.—*Sánchi.*

WORKS OF MR. RUSKIN.

II.

Now in course of Publication, in Parts of Folio Imperial size, each containing Five Plates, and a short Explanatory Text, price 1l. 1s. each.

EXAMPLES OF THE ARCHITECTURE OF VENICE,

SELECTED AND DRAWN TO MEASUREMENT FROM THE EDIFICES.

PARTS ONE TO THREE ARE PUBLISHED.

Fifty India Proofs only are taken on Atlas Folio, price 2l. 2s. each Part.

III.

THE SEVEN LAMPS OF ARCHITECTURE.

WITH FOURTEEN ETCHINGS BY THE AUTHOR.

Imperial 8vo., 1l. 1s. cloth.

"By the 'Seven Lamps of Architecture,' we understand Mr. Ruskin to mean the seven fundamental and cardinal laws, the observance of and obedience to which are indispensible to the architect, who would deserve the name. The politician, the moralist, the divine, will find in it ample store of instructive matter, as well as the artist."—*Examiner.*

"From the series of works upon which Mr. Ruskin is engaged, we can scarcely hope too much for art. The brilliant manner by which the present and other works of Mr. Ruskin are adorned has placed them at once amongst the books that *must* be read. The views broached in this volume constitute the most significant piece of criticism which has appeared in the English language for very many years."—*North British Review.*

"Mr. Ruskin's mind is of that vigorous and searching nature which can be satisfied with nothing less than the elucidation of pure principles in art. He observes and investigates for himself, and expresses himself in a strain of eloquence which rivets the mind by its fulness of meaning, and fascinates the fancy by its singular appropriateness of language and richness of imagery."—*Britannia.*

"This eloquent and deeply-instructive volume is a book for amateurs to read; for it will make the thoughtless thoughtful, and open new fields of contemplation and sources of interest, and suggest and strengthen important principles to all."—*Ecclesiologist.*

"Mr. Ruskin's book bears so unmistakeably the marks of keen and accurate observation, of a true and subtle judgment and refined sense of beauty, joined with so much earnestness, so noble a sense of the purposes and business of art, and such a command of rich and glowing language, that it cannot but tell powerfully in producing a more religious view of the uses of architecture, and a deeper insight into its artistic principles."—*Guardian.*

"We hail Mr. Ruskin's book: we thank him for his industry; we admire his earnest eloquence; and on almost all *great* matters we defer to his judgment. He has, indeed, done high honour to the architect's calling."—Mr. WIGHTWICK, in *The Architect.*

"A lively, poetical, and thoughtful book; rich in refined criticism and glowing eloquence. Mr. Ruskin's poetry is always to the purpose of his doctrines, and always the vehicle of acute thought and profound feeling."—*Frazer's Magazine.*

WORKS OF MR. RUSKIN.

IV.

MODERN PAINTERS.

Imp. 8vo. Vol. I. Fifth Edition, 18s. *cloth.*
Vol. II. Third Edition, 10s. 6d. *cloth.*

"Mr. Ruskin's work will send the painter more than ever to the study of nature; will train men who have always been delighted spectators of nature, to be also attentive observers. Our critics will learn to admire, and mere admirers will learn how to criticise: thus a public will be educated."—*Blackwood's Magazine.*

"A generous and impassioned review of the works of living painters. A hearty and earnest work, full of deep thought, and developing great and striking truths in art."—*British Quarterly Review.*

"A very extraordinary and delightful book, full of truth and goodness, of power and beauty."—*North British Review.*

"One of the most remarkable works on art which has appeared in our time."—*Edinburgh Review.*

*** *The Third Volume is in preparation.*

V.

PRE-RAPHAELITISM.

8vo., 2s. *sewed.*

"We wish that this pamphlet might be largely read by our art-patrons, and studied by our art-critics. There is much to be collected from it which is very important to remember."—*Guardian.*

VI.

THE KING OF THE GOLDEN RIVER;

OR, THE BLACK BROTHERS.

With 22 Illustrations by RICHARD DOYLE.

2s. 6d.

"This little fairy tale is by a master hand. The story has a charming moral, and the writing is so excellent, that it would be hard to say which it will give most pleasure to, the very wise man or the very simple child."—*Examiner.*

VII.

NOTES ON THE CONSTRUCTION OF SHEEP-FOLDS.

8vo., 1s.

"A pamphlet on the doctrine and dicipline of the Church of Christ."—*Britannia.*

RECENT TRAVELS.

I.

A HISTORY OF THE INSURRECTION IN CHINA.

By Dr. YVAN, and M. CALLERY.

Third Edition, with a Supplementary Account of the most Recent Events.

Edited by JOHN OXENFORD.

Post 8vo., price 4s. 6d. cloth, with fac-simile of Chinese Map and Portrait of the Insurgent Chief.

"A curious book, published at an opportune moment, giving a lucid account of the origin and progress of the civil war now raging in China, bringing it down to the present day."—*Blackwood's Magazine.*

"The narrative is animated by traits of Chinese manners, opinions, and ideas, and by lively reminiscenses of the country and people.'—*Spectator.*

"A timely and interesting publication, full of most curious and valuable matter." —*Examiner.*

"The book can scarcely fail to find a curious and interested public."—*Athenæum.*

"The volume is instructive and attractive in a very high degree."—*Illustrated News.*

"The revolution in China is, in all respects, the greatest revolution the world has yet seen."—*Times.*

II.

MEMORANDUMS MADE IN IRELAND IN THE AUTUMN OF 1852.

By JOHN FORBES, M.D., Author of "The Physician's Holiday."

In Two Vols., Post 8vo., with Illustrations. Price 21s. cloth.

"The book is excellent, and, like all the writings of its author, points to a good purpose. Its tendency is to dispel prejudices against Ireland and the Irish. It contains sensible comments upon most topics in Irish affairs. It is honest, thoughtful, liberal, and kindly. By readers of all grades Dr. Forbes's volumes will be read with pleasure for the knowledge they give, and the cheerful way in which they give it."—*Examiner.*

"A complete handbook of the sister island. If there be any, who, knowing nothing of its social and political condition, meditate a tour in Ireland, the pleasure and profit to be derived from the journey will be much enhanced by a careful study of Dr. Forbes's very sensible observations."—*New Quarterly Review.*

"Dr. Forbes is evidently possessed of a candid mind, and though he has dealt with polemical matter, he does not write in a sectarian spirit."—*Athenæum.*

"A very complete description of the present condition of Ireland, written with the kindliest and fairest of pens."—*Economist.*

III.

AUCKLAND, NEW ZEALAND,

AND THE COUNTRY ADJACENT.

Post 8vo., with View and Colored Map. Price 6s., cloth.

RECENT TRAVELS.

III.

TWO THOUSAND MILES' RIDE THROUGH THE ARGENTINE PROVINCES:

WITH AN ACCOUNT OF

BUENOS AYRES, THE RIO DE LA PLATA, MONTE VIDEO, &c.

By WILLIAM MacCANN, Esq.

Two Vols., Post 8vo., with Illustrations. Price 24s. cloth.

"Mr. Mac Cann's volumes present an admirable account of life in the Argentine Provinces. The incidents of his adventures are replete with interest, practical value, and amusement."—*Literary Gazette.*

"This is neither a history, a commercial and political treatise, nor a book of travels, but a mixture of all three; containing good and instructive matter, much local knowledge of Buenos Ayres, and information concerning the Banda Oriental and Paraguay."—*Athenæum.*

"The unlaboured yet animated narrative of an observant and sensible man, containing much valuable information to commercial men."—*British Quarterly Review.*

IV.

THE SECOND BURMESE WAR.

A NARRATIVE OF THE OPERATIONS AT RANGOON.

By Lieut. WILLIAM F. B. LAURIE, Madras Artillery.

Post 8vo., with Maps, Plans, and Views. Price 10s. 6d. cloth.

"The events of the current campaign are here condensed into a well-replenished volume, written on the very theatre of war, and illustrated by skilfully-drawn plans of each important scene of action. A concise account of the Burmese Empire is furnished by the author, who combines with his talent for research a lively style of narrative."—*Globe.*

"The work before us is a military narrative, told in the cheerful tone of an officer who is proud of his profession, and anxious to do justice to his comrades: there is nothing about himself. It is illustrated by plans, views, and sections, and is calculated to remove many erroneous impressions as to the character of the Second Burmese War."—*Literary Gazette.*

"This volume exhibits war in its details, as seen by the subaltern, and in its larger aspects as picked up from the gossip and criticism of the camp. Mr. Laurie varies actual warfare by the antiquities of the country, and a description of the temples and tenets of Gaudama—a variety of Buddhism."—*Spectator.*

V.

TRAITS OF AMERICAN-INDIAN LIFE.

By a FUR-TRADER.

Post 8vo. Price 7s. cloth.

"The Fur-traders' little book, containing sketches of real life among the people of the Oregon Territory, is very welcome from his intimate knowledge of the Indian tribes."—*Examiner.*

"A genuine volume. The writer is an actor in the scenes he describes, and the hazards which our adventurous fur-traders undergo, and the savage life of the wilderness, are graphically delineated in these sketches."—*Morning Advertiser.*

"One of the most readable books of the day, and worthy of the best reception."—*Weekly Dispatch.*

WORKS OF MR. THACKERAY.

I.

LECTURES ON THE ENGLISH HUMOURISTS OF THE 18TH CENTURY.

By W. M. THACKERAY, Esq., Author of "Vanity Fair," "Esmond," &c.

SECOND EDITION, REVISED BY THE AUTHOR.

In One Volume, crown 8vo. Price 10s. 6d. cloth.

"To those who attended the lectures, the book will be a pleasant reminiscence, to others an exciting novelty. The style—clear, idiomatic, forcible, familiar, but never slovenly; the searching strokes of sarcasm or irony; the occasional flashes of generous scorn; the touches of pathos, pity, and tenderness; the morality tempered, but never weakened, by experience and sympathy; the felicitous phrases, the striking anecdotes, the passages of wise, practical reflection; all these lose much less than we could have expected from the absence of the voice, manner, and look of the lecturer."—*Spectator.*

"All who did not hear these lectures will wish to know what kind of talk they were, and how these English humourists and men of genius in past times were described or criticised by a humourist and man of genius in our own. * * * What fine things the lectures contain! What eloquent and subtle sayings, what wise and earnest writing! How delightful are their turns of humour; with what a touching effect, in the graver passages, the genuine feeling of the man comes out; and how vividly the thoughts are *painted*, as it were, in graphic and characteristic words."—*Examiner.*

"This is to us by far the most acceptable of Mr. Thackeray's writings. His graphic style, his philosophical spirit, his analytical powers, his large-heartedness, his shrewdness, and his gentleness, have all room to exhibit themselves. The lives of these famous writers are told in a few paragraphs, and illustrated by a selection of striking anecdotes."—*Economist.*

"These lectures are rich in all the qualities of the author's genius, and adapted to awaken and nourish a literary taste thoroughly English."—*British Quarterly Review.*

"Full of sound, healthy, manly, vigorous writing; sagacious in observation, independent and thoughtful; earnest in sentiment, in style pointed, clear, and straight-forward."—*Westminster Review.*

"A valuable addition to our permanent literature: eloquent when the author is serious; brilliant when he is gay; they are charming reading."—*Daily News.*

"One of the most amusing books that we have read for a long time, and one that we think will occupy a lasting place in English literature."—*Standard.*

A PORTRAIT OF W. M. THACKERAY, Esq.

Engraved by FRANCIS HOLL, from a Drawing by SAMUEL LAURENCE.

Engraver's Proofs on India Paper, £2 2s. Prints, £1 1s.

WORKS OF MR. THACKERAY.

II.

ESMOND.

By W. M. THACKERAY, Author of "Pendennis," "Vanity Fair."

SECOND EDITION.

In Three Volumes, Crown 8vo. Price 1l. 11s. 6d.

"A second edition of "Esmond" within a few weeks of the issue of the first, speaks significantly for Mr. Thackeray's growing popularity. * * * * Mr. Thackeray has selected for his hero a very noble type of the cavalier softening into the man of the eighteenth century, and for his heroine one of the sweetest women that ever breathed from canvass or from book, since Raffaelle painted and Shakspeare wrote. 'Esmond' will, we think, rank higher as a work of art than 'Vanity Fair' or 'Pendennis,' because the characters are of a higher type, and drawn with greater finish, and the book is more of a complete whole. The style is manly, clear, terse, and vigorous, reflecting every mood—pathetic, grave, or sarcastic —of the writer."—*Spectator.*

"Once more we feel that we have before us a masculine and thorough English writer, uniting the power of subtle analysis with a strong volition and a moving eloquence—an eloquence which has gained in richness and harmony. His pathos is now sweeter,—less jarred against by angry sarcasm, but perhaps scarcely so powerful. 'Esmond' must be read, not for its characters, but for its romantic though improbable plot, its spirited grouping, and many thrilling utterances of the anguish of the human heart. Having reached the middle of the first volume, 'forward' will be the wish of every reader of this highly-wrought work."—*Athenæum.*

"The interest of 'Esmond' is, in the main, purely human interest. The story is more than anything a family story. The effect is as if you had suddenly come into that old time as into a chamber; and the light you see things by is that of the warm domestic fire blazing there. By that light you see the faces of the painted old ladies, and the jolly men of letters, and the great lords, and the brave soldiers. The book is as interesting as any previous book of the author's, and more absolutely real than any historical novel since Scott's early ones."—*Daily News.*

"We have at once to express in the warmest terms of praise our appreciation of the skill and taste with which 'Esmond' is written. The story of the novel is ingenious and very elegantly constructed, and carried onward so as to gratify constant curiosity until the end. In short, the book thoroughly occupies our minds with a sense of strength on the part of the writer, of which the manifestation is always made gracefully."—*Examiner.*

"In quiet richness, 'Esmond' mainly resembles the old writers; as it does also in weight of thought, sincerity of purpose, and poetry of the heart and brain. It is wise and sweet in its recesses of thought and feeling; and is more hopeful, consolatory, and kindly than 'Vanity Fair.' Thinking and educated readers will discern in it an immense advance in literary power over Mr. Thackeray's previous writings." —*Frazer's Magazine.*

III.

THE KICKLEBURYS ON THE RHINE.

A new Picture-Book, drawn and written by Mr. M. A. TITMARSH.

SECOND EDITION.

With a Preface entitled "An Essay on Thunder and Small Beer."

5s. plain, 6s. coloured.

WORKS OF CURRER BELL.

I.

VILLETTE.

By CURRER BELL, Author of "Jane Eyre," "Shirley," &c.

In Three Volumes, Post 8vo. Price 1l. 11s. 6d.

"This book would have made Currer Bell famous had she not been already. It retrieves all the ground she lost in 'Shirley,' and it will engage a wider circle of readers than 'Jane Eyre,' for it has all the best qualities of that remarkable book. There is throughout a charm of freshness which is infinitely delightful: freshness in observation, freshness in feeling, freshness in expression. Brain and heart are both held in suspense by the fascinating power of the writer."—*Literary Gazette.*

"This novel amply sustains the fame of the author of 'Jane Eyre' and 'Shirley' as an original and powerful writer. 'Villette' is a most admirably written novel, everywhere original, everywhere shrewd, and at heart everywhere kindly."—*Examiner.*

"The tale is one of the affections, and remarkable as a picture of manners. A burning heart glows throughout it, and one brilliantly-distinct character keeps it alive."—*Athenæum.*

"'Villette' has that clearness and power which are the result of mastery over the thoughts and feelings to be expressed, over the persons and scenes to be described."—*Spectator.*

"The whole three volumes are crowded with beauties; with good things, for which we look to the clear sight, deep feeling, and singular though not extensive experience of life, which we associate with the name of Currer Bell."—*Daily News.*

"The author of 'Jane Eyre' and 'Shirley' has again produced a fiction of extraordinary literary power, and of singular fascination; it is one of the most absorbing of books, one of the most interesting of stories."—*Globe.*

"'Villette' is not only a very able but a very pleasant book."—*Morning Chronicle.*

II.

SHIRLEY: A TALE.

By CURRER BELL.

A new edition. Crown 8vo., 6s. cloth.

"The peculiar power which was so greatly admired in 'Jane Eyre' is not absent from this book. It possesses deep interest and anirresistible grasp of reality. There is a vividness and distinctness of conception in it quite marvellous. The power of graphic delineation and expression is intense. There are scenes which, for strength and delicacy of emotion, are not transcended in the range of English fiction."—*Examiner.*

"'Shirley' is an admirable book; genuine English in the independence and uprightness of the tone of thought, in the purity of heart and feeling which pervade it, in the masculine vigour of its conception of character, and in style and diction: it is a tale of passion and character, and a veritable triumph of pyschology."—*Morning Chronicle.*

"'Shirley' is very clever. The faculty of graphic description, strong imagination, fervid and masculine diction, analytic skill, all are visible. Gems of rare thought and glorious passion shine here and there throughout the volume."—*Times.*

WORKS OF CURRER BELL.

III.

JANE EYRE: AN AUTOBIOGRAPHY.

By CURRER BELL.

Fourth Edition. Crown 8vo., 6s. cloth.

"'Jane Eyre' is a remarkable production. Freshness and originality, truth and passion, singular felicity in the description of natural scenery, and in the analyzation of human thought, enable this tale to stand boldly out from the mass, and to assume its own place in the bright field of romantic literature. We could not but be struck with the raciness and ability of the work, by the independent sway of a thoroughly original and unworn pen, by the masculine current of noble thoughts, and the unflinching dissection of the dark yet truthful character."—*Times.*

IV.

WUTHERING HEIGHTS AND AGNES GREY.

By ELLIS and ACTON BELL.

WITH A SELECTION OF THEIR LITERARY REMAINS, AND A BIOGRAPHICAL NOTICE OF BOTH AUTHORS.

By CURRER BELL.

Crown 8vo., 6s. cloth.

"'Wuthering Heights' bears the stamp of a profoundly-individual, strong, and passionate mind. The memoir is one of the most touching chapters in literary biography."—*Nonconformist.*

V.

POEMS.

By CURRER, ELLIS, and ACTON BELL.

Fcap. 8vo., 4s. cloth.

"Remarkable as being the first efforts of undoubted genius to find some congenial form of expression. They are not common verses, but show many of the vigorous qualities in the prose works of the same writers: the love of nature which characterises Currer Bell's prose works pervades the whole of the present volume."—*Christian Remembrancer.*

NEW WORK BY THE AUTHOR OF "OLIVE," &c.

AVILLION, AND OTHER TALES.

Three Vols., Post 8vo. Price £1 11s. 6d., Cloth.

"'Avillion' is a beautiful and fanciful story; and the rest make agreeable reading. There is not one of them unquickened by true feeling, exquisite taste, and a pure and vivid imagination."—*Examiner.*

"These volumes form altogether as pleasant and fanciful a miscellany as has often been given to the public in these latter days."—*Athenæum.*

"In a nice knowledge of the refinements of the female heart, and in a happy power of depicting emotion, the authoress is excelled by very few story-tellers of the day."—*Globe.*

WORKS OF MR. GWYNNE.

I.

THE LIFE AND DEATH OF SILAS BARNSTARKE.

By TALBOT GWYNNE, Author of "The School for Fathers."

One Volume, Crown 8vo. Price 10*s.* 6*d.*

"In many ways this book is remarkable. Silas and his relations stand forth so distinctly and forcibly, and with so much simplicity, that we are far more inclined to feel of them as if they really lived, than of the writers of pretended diaries and autobiographies. The manners and ways of speech of the time are portrayed admirably." —*Guardian.*

"Mr. Gwynne has adopted the nervous and succinct style of our forefathers, while narrating the career of a lover of money. The reader will find little to impede his interest in following the career of this bad man to its bad end."—*Athenæum.*

"The gradual growth of the sin of covetousness, its temporary disturbance by the admixture of a softer passion, and the pangs of remorse, are portrayed with high dramatic effect, resembling in some scenes the gigantic majesty of ancient Tragedy." —*John Bull.*

"A story possessing an interest so tenacious that no one who commences it will easily leave the perusal unfinished."—*Standard.*

"A book of high aim, and unquestionable power."—*Examiner.*

II.

THE SCHOOL FOR DREAMERS.

By T. GWYNNE, Esq., Author of "The School for Fathers."

One Volume, Crown 8vo. Price 10*s.* 6*d.*

"The master-limner of the follies of mankind, the author of 'The School for Fathers,' has produced another tale to the full as attractive as the former, and abounding with traits of exquisite humour and sallies of sparkling wit.—*John Bull.*

"'The School for Dreamers' may be credited with life, humour, and vigour. There is a spirit of enjoyment in Mr. Gwynne's descriptions which indicates a genial temperament, as well as a shrewd eye."—*Athenæum.*

"A powerfully and skilfully written-book, intended to show the mischief and danger of following imagination instead of judgment in the practical business of life."—*Literary Gazette.*

"An admirable and caustic satire on 'equality and fraternity' theories."—*Britannia.*

III.

THE SCHOOL FOR FATHERS.

AN OLD ENGLISH STORY.

By T. GWYNNE.

Crown 8vo. Price 10*s.* 6*d.*

"The pleasantest tale we have read for many a day. It is a story of the *Tatler* and *Spectator* days, and is very fitly associated with that time of good English literature, by its manly feeling, direct, unaffected manner of writing, and nicely-managed, well-turned narrative. The descriptions are excellent; some of the country painting is as fresh as a landscape by Constable, or an idyl by Alfred Tennyson."—*Examiner.*

"'The School for Fathers' is at once highly amusing and deeply interesting—full of that genuine humour which is half pathos—and written with a freshness of feeling and raciness of style which entitle it to be called a tale in the *Vicar of Wakefield* school."—*Britannia.*

"Few are the tales so interesting to read, and so admirable in purpose and style, as 'The School for Fathers.'"—*Globe.*

Miss Kavanagh's Female Biographies.

I.

WOMEN OF CHRISTIANITY, EXEMPLARY FOR PIETY AND CHARITY.

By JULIA KAVANAGH.

Post 8vo., with Portrait. Price 12s. in embossed cloth, gilt edges.

"The authoress has supplied a great desideratum, both in female biography and morals. Her examples of female excellence are taken from the earliest ages of the church, and come down to recent times: she has a niche in her temple for every one who deserves a position there. The style is clear, the matter solid, and the conclusions just."—*Globe.*

"A more noble and dignified tribute to the virtues of her sex we can scarcely imagine than this work, which Miss Kavanagh has reared, like a monumental tablet, to the memory of the 'Women of Christianity.' To this grateful task the gifted authoress has brought talents of no ordinary range, and, more than all, a spirit of eminent piety, and admiration for the good and beautiful, and a heart entirely absorbed in the work she has so ably accomplished."—*Church of England Quarterly Review.*

"The women pourtrayed have been selected from every period of the Christian era; the same range of female biography is taken by no other volume; and an equal skill in the delineation of characters is rarely to be found. The author has accomplished her task with intelligence and feeling, and with general fairness and truth: she displays subtle penetration and broad sympathy, joining therewith purity and pious sentiment, intellectual refinement and large-heartedness, and writes with unusual elegance and felicity."—*Nonconformist.*

"Miss Kavanagh has wisely chosen that noble succession of saintly women who in all ages of Christianity are united by their devotion to the sick, the wretched, and the destitute."—*Guardian.*

II.

WOMAN IN FRANCE DURING THE 18TH CENTURY.

By JULIA KAVANAGH.

2 Vols., post 8vo., with eight Portraits. 12s. in embossed cloth.

"Miss Kavanagh has undertaken a delicate task, and she has performed it on the whole with discretion and judgment. Her volumes may lie on any drawing-room table without scandal, and may be read by all but her youngest countrywomen without risk."—*Quarterly Review.*

"Elegantly illustrated with a series of line engravings, this work has claims upon the boudoir-table, in right of its guise and garniture. But its letterpress is superior to the general staple of books of this class. Miss Kavanagh proves herself adroit in sketching, and solid in judging character. Which among us will be ever tired of reading about the women of France? especially when they are marshalled so agreeably and discreetly as in the pages before us."—*Athenæum.*

"There is a great deal of cleverness and good taste in this book. The subject is handled with much delicacy and tact, and takes a wide range of examples. Miss Kavanagh's volumes are to be commended as a compact view of a period of always reviving interest (now more than usually attractive), pleasingly executed. The book shows often an original tone of remark, and always a graceful and becoming one."—*Examiner.*

WORKS OF MR. LEIGH HUNT.

I.

THE AUTOBIOGRAPHY OF LEIGH HUNT;

WITH REMINISCENCES OF FRIENDS AND CONTEMPORARIES.

Three Volumes, post 8vo., with Portraits. 15*s. cloth.*

"These volumes contain a personal recollection of the literature and politics, as well as some of the most remarkable literary men and politicians of the last fifty years. The reminiscences are varied by sketches of manners during the same period, and by critical remarks on various topics. They are also extended by boyish recollection, family tradition, and contemporary reading; so that we have a sort of social picture of almost a century, with its fluctuations of public fortune, and its changes of fashions, manners, and opinions."—*Spectator.*

II.

THE TOWN:

ITS MEMORABLE CHARACTERS AND EVENTS.

Two Volumes, post 8vo., with Forty-Five Illustrations. 1*l.* 4*s. cloth.*

"We will allow no higher enjoyment for a rational Englishman than to stroll leisurely through this marvellous town arm-in-arm with Mr. Leigh Hunt. He gives us the outpourings of a mind enriched with the most agreeable knowledge."—*Times.*

III.

MEN, WOMEN, AND BOOKS.

Two Volumes, post 8vo., with Portrait. 10*s. cloth.*

"A book for a parlour-window, for a summer's eve, for a warm fireside, for a half-hour's leisure, for a whole day's luxury; in any and every possible shape a charming companion.—*Westminster Review.*

IV.

IMAGINATION AND FANCY. 5*s. cloth.*

"The very essence of the sunniest qualities of the English poets."—*Atlas.*

V.

WIT AND HUMOUR. 5*s. cloth.*

"A book at once exhilarating and suggestive."—*Athenæum.*

VI.

A JAR OF HONEY FROM MOUNT HYBLA. 5*s. cloth.*

"A book acceptable at all seasons."—*Athenæum.*

VII.

TABLE TALK. 3*s.* 6*d. cloth.*

"Precisely the book we would take as a companion on the green lane walk."—*Globe.*

MISCELLANEOUS.

POETICS: AN ESSAY ON POETRY.

By E. S. DALLAS, Esq.

In One Volume, crown 8vo. Price 9s. cloth.

"This book is one of the most remarkable emanations of the present time. It actually overflows with the nectar of thought. 'Poetics' should be read, for no reviewer can present a perfect idea of the richness of language and aphorism which run, like silver threads, through the soberer line of argument."—*Critic.*

"A remarkable work—the work of a scholar, a critic, a thinker. It contains many novel views and much excellent matter. The style is fresh, independent, sharp, clear, and often felicitous. Amidst the intricacies of his complex subject, Mr. Dallas moves with the calm precision of one who knows the labyrinth."—*Leader.*

"A mind at once acute and imaginative, a range of reading so wide as to seem marvellous, a power of classification which we have rarely seen equalled, are the characteristics shown on every page. The work is deserving of a most attentive perusal."—*Free Church Magazine.*

CONVERSATIONS OF GOETHE.

Translated from the German, by JOHN OXENFORD.

Two Volumes, post 8vo. 10s. cloth.

"These conversations present a distinct and truthful image of Goethe's mind during the last ten years of his life; and never was his judgment more clear and correct than in his closing years. The time spent on the perusal of this book will be usefully and agreeably employed. Mr. Oxenford's translation is as exact and faithful as it is elegant."—*Spectator.*

THE THEORY AND PRACTICE OF CASTE.

By B. A. IRVING, Esq.

One Volume, post 8vo. Price 5s. cloth.

"An elaborate performance, exhibiting a digested view of the old theory, and the actual operation of caste, from the best authorities; giving some hints that may be useful in our future dealings with the people of India."—*Spectator.*

"A volume worth consulting, especially for the indications it affords of the sources of our success in establishing a peaceful dominion in India amongst races of different religions."—*Globe.*

THE LAND TAX OF INDIA,

ACCORDING TO THE MOOHUMMUDAN LAW.

By NEIL B. E. BAILLIE, Esq.

AUTHOR OF THE "MOOHUMMUDAN LAW OF SALE," &c.

8vo., price 6s. cloth.

"Mr. Baillie, who has acquired a reputation for profound knowledge of the Mahommedan Law by former publication, has, in the volume before us, exhausted his subject. The reader may rely implicitly on the accuracy of Mr. Baillie's translations."—*Press.*

"A learned and valuable treatise."—*Literary Gazette.*

"A complete account of the Mahomedan Law of Land Tax."—*Economist.*

RELIGIOUS AND EDUCATIONAL.

THE NOVITIATE; OR, THE JESUIT IN TRAINING:
BEING A YEAR AMONG THE ENGLISH JESUITS.

By ANDREW STEINMETZ.

Third Edition, post 8vo., 5s. cloth.

"This is a remarkable book. It describes with a welcome minuteness, the daily, nightly, hourly occupations of the Jesuit Novitiates of Stonyhurst, their religious exercises and manners, in private and together; and depicts, with considerable acuteness and power, the conflicts of an intelligent, susceptible, honest-purposed spirit, while passing through such a process."—*British Quarterly Review.*

A CONVERTED ATHEIST'S TESTIMONY TO THE TRUTH OF CHRISTIANITY.
BEING THE AUTOBIOGRAPHY OF ALEXANDER HARRIS.

Fourth Edition, fcap. 8vo., 3s. cloth.

"A very interesting account of the experience of an intelligent and sincere mind on the subject of religion. We can honestly recommend the book to the notice of our readers."---*Eclectic Review.*

THE RECTORY OF VALEHEAD.

By the Rev. ROBERT WILSON EVANS.

Fourteenth Edition, 3s. cloth.

"Universally and cordially do we recommend this delightful volume. We believe no person could read this work and not be the better for its pious and touching lessons."---*Literary Gazette.*

ELEMENTARY WORKS ON SOCIAL SCIENCE.

Uniform in fcap, 8vo., half-bound.

I.—OUTLINES OF SOCIAL ECONOMY. 1s. 6d.
II.—PROGRESSIVE LESSONS IN SOCIAL SCIENCE. 1s. 6d.
III.—INTRODUCTION TO THE SOCIAL SCIENCES. 2s.
IV.—QUESTIONS AND ANSWERS ON THE ARRANGEMENTS AND RELATIONS OF SOCIAL LIFE. 2s. 6d.
V.—OUTLINES OF THE UNDERSTANDING. 2s.
VI.—WHAT AM I? WHERE AM I? WHAT OUGHT I TO DO? &c. 1s. sewed.

"The author of these various manuals of the social sciences has the art of stating clearly the abstruse points of political economy and metaphysics, and making them level to every understanding."—*Economist.*

PARENTS' CABINET OF AMUSEMENT AND INSTRUCTION.

Six Volumes, 2s. 6d. each.

Each volume is complete in itself, and may be had separately.

LITTLE STORIES FROM THE PARLOUR PRINTING PRESS.

BY THE AUTHOR OF THE "PARENTS' CABINET."

2s. cloth.

Published by

Facsimile Publisher
Ashok Vihar, Delhi-110052 (India)
Website: www.facsimilepublisher.com

Distributed by

Gyan Books Pvt. Ltd.
5, Ansari Road, Daryaganj, New Delhi-110002 (India)
E-mail: books@gyanbooks.com, Website: www.gyanbooks.com

2 222000 003838